HEINEMANN
AVCE

ADVANCED

Information and Communication Technology

Alastair de Watteville • Lester Gilbert

HEINEMANN
AVCE

ADVANCED

Information and Communication Technology

Alastair de Watteville • Lester Gilbert

FOR THE 2000 STANDARDS

Edexcel
Success through qualifications

Heinemann Educational Publishers,
Halley Court, Jordan Hill, Oxford OX2 8EJ
A division of Reed Educational & Professional Publishing Ltd

Heinemann is a registered trademark of Reed Educational & Professional Publishing Limited

OXFORD MELBOURNE AUCKLAND JOHANNESBURG BLANTYRE GABORONE
IBADAN PORTSMOUTH NH (USA) CHICAGO

First published 2000
2004 2003 2002 2001 2000
10 9 8 7 6 5 4 3 2 1

A catalogue record for this book is available from the British Library on request.

ISBN 0 435 45307 6

Cover designed by Sarah Garbett

Pages designed by Sarah Garbett

Typeset by TechType, Abingdon, Oxfordshire

Printed and bound in Great Britain by The Bath Press Ltd., Bath

Tel: 01865 888058 www.heinemann.co.uk

Contents

Acknowledgement

The authors, Lester Gilbert and Alastair de Watteville express their appreciation for the support that has been provided by Heinemann throughout the period of preparation of this book and the harmonious relationships with individuals in the firm that have been built up and maintained. They are particularly grateful to Richard James and the sales team who have been extremely industrious.

They would also like to thank Andrew Nash for his eye for detail and Mick Watson for his trouble-shooting skills.

Introduction

This book has been written to help you in obtaining the Advanced Vocational Certificate of Education (or VCE) qualification in Information and Communication Technology (or ICT). This may be with the 12 unit-award or 6-unit single award or 3-unit award. The formal names of the versions of this qualification are, respectively:

— Advanced VCE (Double Award)
— Advanced VCE
— Advanced Subsidiary VCE.

Our definition of ICT is:

> *The acquisition, analysis, manipulation, storage and distribution of information; and the design and provision of equipment and software for these purposes.*

Your qualification will be at the Advanced level in ICT, based on most of this definition. You will not be expected to know how to design or to provide individual items of equipment, although you will need to know about planning a whole ICT system, and about the selection and installation of hardware components and parts, and software products.

In order to meet the requirements of the qualification you will have to collect evidence to show that you have gained the understanding, knowledge and skills that are required. For the 12-unit award the work you need to do is arranged in twelve units. Six of these are known as **compulsory units**, all of which have to be taken by every student following your programme; and six are called **optional units**, and for these there is some choice, although you are likely to be steered towards particular units that fit in with the teaching plans of your school or college.

For the 6-unit award students must take Units 1, 2 and 3, which are all compulsory units, and any three other ICT Advanced VCE units. For the 3-unit award students must take Units 1, 2 and 3.

The 12-unit Advanced-level VCEs are usually run by schools and colleges as two-year courses. These courses will probably account for about two-thirds of the total time available to you.

Unlike GCSEs and A-Level courses, Advanced VCEs do not work towards big, all-important exams: rather, they are based on **coursework**, a scheme which allows you to build up evidence of your progress as you go along. There are, however, units for which assignments are set and assessed externally. Students registered with Edexcel will have two compulsory units and one optional unit assessed externally. Students registered with other Awarding Bodies will have three of the compulsory units, and none of the optional units assessed externally.

If you are successful in accumulating all the evidence you need, you will be given an E grade which indicates that you have *passed* the Advanced VCE. If you have done more than the prescribed minimum you could earn a grade from D up to A. The Advanced VCE specifications for your qualification lay down for each unit the requirements for some or all of the grades E to A.

You cannot *fail* an Advanced VCE. You can, however, fail to pass at a particular stage. You can go on trying after the end of your course, if you want to, to gather all the evidence you need for the qualification. There are, of course, disadvantages to extending your Advanced VCE in this way: the delay would mean that you had to register afresh at some centre to complete the work, and it would certainly delay moving into higher education. You should make absolutely sure that you complete the qualification within the timetabled period.

Awarding bodies expect most students following Advanced VCE programmes to wish to achieve some or all of the **key skills** units, even though they do not form part of the Advanced VCE. If you want to go into higher education your key skills units will count towards your UCAS points.

Accordingly, the **sample assignment** at the end of each unit in this book has been designed to provide opportunities for students to accumulate evidence for key skills as well as for the ICT Advanced VCE.

Assessment

Your work will usually be assessed, or marked, by the tutor who taught it, and who set you the tasks related to it. The assessment is directed at telling you and the teaching staff whether or not you have provided the evidence that the unit you are studying requires. If you have not provided all the evidence you will normally be asked to make good the gaps.

Two of the compulsory units, or three for some Awarding Bodies, are assessed externally. You will complete the assignments where you normally do your work, and hand them in by a prescribed date so that they can be assessed centrally, by your Awarding Body. Three of the optional units are also assessed externally: you have to choose one of them amongst the optional units you choose unless three of your compulsory units are to be assessed externally. You will be given plenty of warning of the assignments related to the units which are to be assessed externally.

Once you have assembled and submitted the evidence called for by a task you have been set, your assessor may give you an **indicative grade** in the range E to A for that work. The E grade means that you have only just managed to meet all the evidence requirements; the A grade means that you have done well in all the areas being assessed. The purpose of indicative grades is to let you know the standard of your work, and what your final grade might be if the quality of what you hand in stays the same for the rest of the course.

There will be someone called the **internal verifier** at your centre whose job it is to see that assessors are all working to the same standards and are assessing fairly.

Assignments

Much of the evidence you need to collect will arise from your response to tasks, or assignments, that are set. This response will mostly be on paper in a form which suits the demands of the assignments, though some evidence may arise and be recorded in other forms. Each assignment will have been designed to give you the opportunity to generate the evidence you need for one of the units that make up your Advanced VCE qualification: there may be more than one assignment for a unit.

You should always be sure to hand in your completed assignments by the submission dates you will have been given. Doing so shows that you can plan your time properly, and it also allows tutors to return assessed work to you as quickly as possible.

You may find that during your course you have created evidence covering a particular point more than once. No harm is done, and the extra evidence may give you a fuller understanding of some point.

Other sources of evidence

There are many ways in which you can accumulate evidence to supplement that coming from your assignments. For example:

- you can demonstrate some skill to your tutor

- you might be able to give a short talk describing work you have done

- you can explain in a discussion with your tutor some aspect of your work

- you can obtain, and write up, information gained on visits or from books

- you can gather facts and opinions from questionnaires you designed and used.

Your tutor will normally make a note of evidence you have provided in any of these ways.

Your portfolio

When you have collected pieces of evidence you will usually file them in a binder called a **portfolio**. All your evidence must be on paper. It can be assignment work, or scripts from tests you have done, or statements from members of the teaching staff, known as **witness statements**, certifying that you have achieved some specific task. Assignment output is generally put into your portfolio after it has been assessed.

Your portfolio becomes increasingly important as your course goes along. Your school or college will probably look after it safely for you, but whatever the arrangements you must make sure that it is kept securely somewhere. When you go to an interview for higher education or for a job you may want to take your portfolio with you.

Be painstaking about organising your portfolio tidily so that you can find any piece of evidence quickly. Whatever type of file you use to hold your papers you must not overfill it: it is very much better to start another binder before that happens.

Planning

You will want to be able to show that you can work independently to meet agreed deadlines. You can only do this if you plan your work for an assignment, setting out on some kind of grid the activities you will need to carry out, the order in which you intend to start them, the sources of information you expect to need, and the target dates for completing each activity.

You should also identify the places in your plan where you need to check that you are on schedule and, if your progress has slipped, where and how you can revise your plan, and what the effect of revisions will be. In your centre you may have to talk over with your tutor any postponement in your submission date that you want to make.

You should make a habit, for each unit, of reading carefully the parts of the specification which set out the requirements for each grade, and of making sure that you plan to do all the necessary activities.

More generally, you should plan in outline the work you will need to cover by the end of your course so that you can look ahead, identify the main milestones and check that nothing has been missed.

The case study

Throughout the book we use aspects of a business, Festivities Unlimited, to illustrate points within the specifications.

Festivities Unlimited, called 'FUN' for short, is a business based in Fulham, London (though it could equally have been put in Cardiff or Belfast or any other big city), which operates as a partnership. It provides staff, equipment, products and services for the entertainment of groups of people, typically staging birthday parties, wedding receptions and special events, and also offering facilities for corporate hospitality. Whatever products and services are provided for a particular client on a single occasion are known collectively as *an event*. For small events, FUN's own staff provide the products and services; for larger events FUN engages sub-contractors and freelance staff.

The enterprise was started six years ago by Fred Frollick, who now is semi-retired. He is part-time chairman and part-time managing director. FUN is managed by his son, Steve, 30, and his daughter, Sandra, 27. These three are the partners. They employ 13 staff. There are an office manager, a secretary, and two clerical assistants; a catering manager and two cooks; a transport manager and one driver; a stores manager and a stores assistant; and a marketing manager with a sales assistant. The organisational structure of the business is shown below.

In Chapter 2.1 we look at forms of organisational structures, and relate those forms of structure to the aims of the organisations in which they exist. FUN has a simple, conventional structure in which there is reasonable certainty about who is responsible for what, and to whom each individual reports.

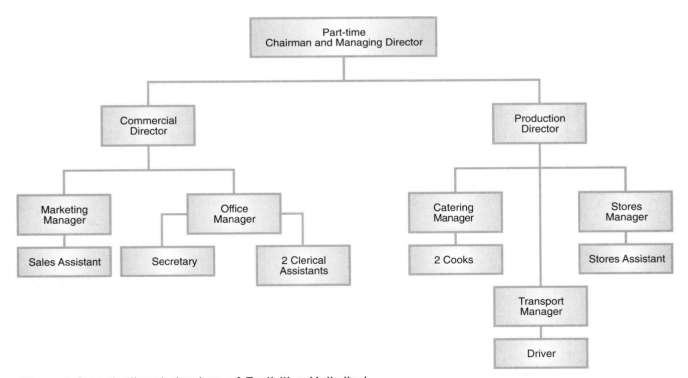

Figure I Organisational structure of Festivities Unlimited

Steve is the commercial director, responsible for marketing, sales, finance, human resources and administration. Sandra is the production director, responsible for research, preparation for events, conduct of events, stock control and transport.

The transport and stores departments operate from a row of five garages behind the main office building, a spacious semi-detached house that used to have three bedrooms. This building houses the directors, one each in an office that used to be a bedroom; the office staff work in what was the lounge; and the marketing staff are based in what was the dining room. The kitchen is an area for staff refreshment and relaxation. The utility room, basement, and attic provide storage areas. About 50 metres down the street the catering department is located in what used to be a small corner fish-and-chip shop, now refurbished to provide FUN with the facilities it needs for food preparation and cooking: there is plentiful capacity for refrigerated and frozen storage.

The business has grown each year, with annual sales now about £2 million. Current profit before tax, but after directors' salaries and all other costs, is about £120000. FUN tries to maintain a pattern of trading that contains a mixture of large and small events each week, with a spread of types of event, and client sites that are mostly no more than one hour away. This policy, as implemented at present, means that FUN is running about 400 events a year, mostly in the London area. There will usually be between six and ten events a week, with average billings for each event being around £5000. FUN will handle events serving up to about 500 people, down to those catering for as few as 10 people. About one-third of its events are repeated regularly and are often scheduled a year in advance.

FUN has a large list of freelance and sub-contracting staff who assist with large events and with special or unusual customer requirements. Other files of importance are the customer and prospective customer list, the invoice file, the supplier list, and the archives of trading and accounts history. The office manager is responsible for the accuracy and security of all these files.

Information technology currently plays only a small part in FUN's business. Steve and Sandra have a PC each, as do the office manager, the marketing manager, the sales assistant, and the secretary. These six machines are not networked, and are used only for word-processing and elementary spreadsheet work. The office has a fax machine and photocopier, and the secretary operates a small telephone switchboard. All directors, managers, and the sales assistant additionally each have a mobile phone.

Presenting information

Before discussing the presentation of information – that is, the ways in which one person conveys information to another – we must consider what *information* really is, why it is important to different individuals and organisations, and the steps that can be taken to safeguard it.

The unit is therefore divided into four chapters:

- Chapter 1.1 The value of information
- Chapter 1.2 Standard ways of working: security and safety
- Chapter 1.3 Styles of writing
- Chapter 1.4 Styles of presenting information

Chapter 1.1 establishes that information has value. That value can lie anywhere between 'we find it handy to have the information' and 'this information is vital: its loss or corruption might be life-threatening'. We also see that the age of items of information can sometimes affect their value.

The chapter introduces concepts of processing, storing, and transmitting information that provide a solid base of underpinning knowledge for the material covered in the rest of the book, helping you to understand the topics which are new to you. It also gives a degree of coherence to the book as a whole.

Chapter 1.2 looks at measures organisations can take to preserve the security and safety of their information. They will choose measures that match the severity of the risks and the value of the information. All steps to safeguard information cost money, so decisions on the choice of measures have to try to balance the cost against the risks.

It also covers good working practices you can follow as you work with computers. You should keep returning to Chapter 1.2 as you progress through your course.

Chapter 1.3 reviews the many purposes for which there is a need to impart information, and points out how in each case the style of writing affects the way in which a recipient reacts to it. Examples of a wide range of styles are given and discussed.

The chapter ends with thoughts on how to make your work as readable as possible, and on the importance of being accurate in what you write.

Chapter 1.4 emphasises that the style of presentation is crucial for giving your documents the appearance that will best meet your purposes. This focus on appearance includes a review of the role of various forms of graphic illustration.

Like the others that follow, the unit ends with a sample assignment which gives you opportunities to accumulate evidence for this Advanced VCE, and also for the key skills units that you may want to achieve.

Information can have many dimensions:

- it may be directed to a single person, or to more than one

- it may be official or social; simple or complicated; short or lengthy; urgent or routine

- it may be highly confidential or unrestricted

- it may be the response to a request or an instruction; or it may simply be unsolicited news or even tittle-tattle

- in the context of work it may be intended for someone senior to the sender, someone subordinate to the sender, or someone on the same level

- it may be going to someone within the same organisation or to someone outside; to someone nearby or to someone half way round the world.

All these aspects of transmitting any piece of information are likely to affect the best way for it to be expressed — the best style to be used in its presentation; and the importance that will be attached to its accuracy.

The information may be sent electronically, on paper or by word of mouth. It may have to reach its recipient by a specified date and time if it is to be of any use.

In considering this unit, we shall think in terms of *documents*, and not concern ourselves with oral communications even though these can on occasion, for instance in coping with emergencies, be crucially important: and we shall restrict ourselves to communications arising in the context of work.

Normally, whenever you send out a document you expect it to be read. If that were not so you would realise that you would be wasting your time and, perhaps, money, in sending it. By implication, in sending someone a document you are making a claim on the time of that person to read, to understand and, possibly, to respond to your document. As the sender you would be prudent to *sell* the reason why the recipient should invest time and thought in reading what you have sent. And you should make the task of reading as straightforward as possible.

Every document should be clear, attractive, and no longer than necessary: brevity, provided that it does not reduce clarity, is an important virtue. It saves both you, the originator, and the recipient, time. If you are intending to send a document to many people, you should give even more thought to how to make it inviting. We return to this issue in Chapter 1.3.

Every professional and technical field of work needs to rely on words and terms that may not be in general use, or that may have meanings that differ from those assumed in normal conversation. Doctors, lawyers, electricians, the armed services, and indeed any callings you think about, employ their own special words. The reasons are to save time and to express exactly what is meant.

Information and communication technology likewise has a need for its own distinctive words and terms. You should always use the correct technical language of the field in which you are working, because by doing so you give precision to your words: you must, however, be sure that the meaning you intend is the meaning assumed by the recipient. We return to this topic in Chapter 1.3.

The main theme of this unit is to help you to master, and to be able to demonstrate, sound ways of conveying ideas lucidly and persuasively. The ideas themselves may be technical: if they are, you need to be able to express them in words that are accurate but nonetheless clear to readers who are not familiar with specialist IT language. If you do not succeed, your document will contain jargon, which is always undesirable.

Chapter 1.1 The value of information

What exactly is information?

We probably all think we know what **information** is, but we would have trouble describing it. Dictionary definitions such as 'knowledge', '(desired) items of knowledge' and 'news' do not move us very far forward when we are thinking about information in relation to computers. The meaning depends on the context: a lawyer's view of the meaning would differ from the views of an economist or a mathematician.

In the world of information and communication technology (ICT) which we shall be inhabiting in this book we can settle for information being:

'Any potentially useful fact, quantity, or value that can be expressed uniquely with exactness.'

The *Oxford Dictionary of Computing* offers this interesting statement:

'Information is whatever is capable of causing a human mind to change its opinion about the current state of the real world.'

These two attempts at definition may appear to conflict, but actually they support each other.

Try it out	You can see that defining the word *information* is not easy. You might like to try and make up your own definition, bearing in mind that information can be in the form of images and sounds as well as words and all forms of machine-readable data.

Much writing on computer topics seeks to draw a rigid distinction between **data** and **information**. We do not do that, but prefer to use the words interchangeably, to suit the topic, with no attempt at discrimination. Normally it is obvious what is meant.

Most information can be considered as being numeric or alphabetic; or **alphanumeric** – a label embracing any items of information which can be represented by **characters**. These characters are letters, numbers, and the special characters used for punctuation, currency symbols, and the like. The exceptions, in which information cannot be represented this way, include some *industrial processes* from which the output may be streams of data that are unbroken, and not made up of characters; and *spoken communication*, such as that sent and received by telephone. We shall return to the subject of data communication later in this chapter.

Why is information important?

We make use of information to such a great extent in our everyday lives that we probably do not realise how much we are relying on it. This applies to trivial activities such as crossing the road, for which our brains need information about oncoming traffic, as well as for more substantial activities like planning a holiday, buying a second-hand car, looking for work, or finding a place at college. They all involve us in getting hold of the relevant information, and then figuring out how best to take advantage of it.

Although information is itself invisible and intangible, the information we may have to use repeatedly will have been recorded on paper or prepared for display on a computer screen; though we can also find spoken information, such as the weather forecast on radio, convenient at times.

Turning to the world of business we can soon see that obtaining and using information effectively is vital. Businesses make decisions, at all levels, more or less continually; and the quality of those decisions depends almost entirely on the quality of the information on which they are based. Businesses compete with one another, and thrive or wither, according to how sound their decisions have been.

Many of the decisions are taken automatically by computer so that they can be quick and reliable, and perhaps made available remotely, though of course the computer will have been instructed precisely how to take its decision in each situation it is likely to encounter.

Let us consider just three cases of the crucial importance of information to businesses where at least some of the decisions are taken automatically. In each case the quantity of information is very large, and it is wanted exactly when it is due.

- Air travel as we know it could not function at all without detailed information on reservations and ticketing, weather conditions, air traffic control limitations, fuel requirements, weight on take-off, and much more. International passenger and freight reservation systems alone are massive communications and processing networks.

  For each departing flight to be ready for its take-off slot all the required information has to be pulled together on time.

- The world of banking, and finance as a whole, runs on information. The operation of bank and building society accounts, foreign exchange, share and commodity dealing, retail credit arrangements, and many others, does not generally involve the handling of physical goods: its raw material is information.

- Hypermarkets, superstores, supermarkets, or whatever we call them, have massive stock control operations involving perhaps 30 000 product lines at each store, to be replenished in correct

Automatic decision-making

An example of automatic decision-making would be a credit approval system in which a computer could be programmed to decide immediately whether or not to authorise an increase in credit facility that had been requested. The Royal Bank of Scotland has introduced a system that does this job.

The bank has developed software to provide UK's first online loan approval service. It allows applicants to borrow money over the Internet without involving any bank staff. Equifax, the software concerned, uses an applicant's home address, electoral registration entry, and details of any county court judgements, in addition to standard information held within the bank, to reach its decision.

amounts at the right time. Every line must be priced, and the prices reviewed frequently to take account of action by competitors and levels of demand created by customers. Customer check-out and credit-worthiness verification, which relies heavily on up-to-date information, must run smoothly.

The information needs of these stores are vast, but they are likely to become much greater. As customers make more use of credit and loyalty cards opportunities are emerging for these retail chains to identify the buying patterns of individual shoppers and use the information for new marketing initiatives.

Imagine being welcomed at your favourite supermarket by a personal greeting something like:

We see that you used our Glasgow store last week, and we hope you enjoyed the experience.

We notice that you have been buying less dog food lately and trust that your pets are not poorly. You might like to know that this week there is a special offer on tins of 'Doggo'.

Leaving aside these large-scale and rather exotic applications, here are a few examples of down-to-earth decisions that have to be routinely taken by most businesses:

• **Buying**. How many items do we order, particularly when we are offered special terms for buying larger quantities? What lines are going to be popular next week or next season?

• **Selling**. How many sales staff would it be most cost-effective to employ? What

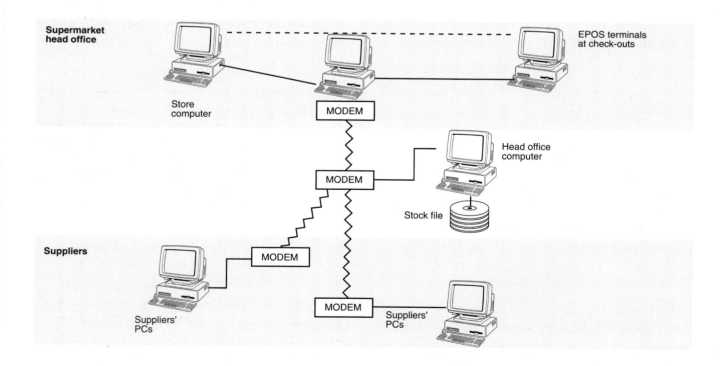

Figure 1.1 Order processing system for a supermarket

discounts should we offer to our customers to increase their purchase volumes?

- **Recruiting**. What other skills do we need to have in our workforce, and in what quantities? What commitments do we take on when we hire new staff?

- **Advertising**. What is the best level of expenditure on advertising? How shall we try to measure the effectiveness of any given advertising campaign?

These and dozens of other questions need information in order to be answered in a rational way in almost any kind of business; and the financial accounts which have to be kept also call for a flow of information.

Businesses thus need accessible information that is accurate, up-to-date, and sufficient – requirements that are sometimes known as having information or data that is of **good quality**. The central thrust of your course for the Advanced VCE qualification in ICT is to explore how information can be harnessed by ICT to provide users with systems that are effective in supporting their decision-making and which thus provide benefit for their activities as a whole.

ICT has two distinct qualities. Above, we have highlighted its **informing** capability; as important, but different, is its **automating** capability. Informing provides information to help individuals and businesses to make decisions: automating is concerned with replacing physical or mental processes by computer-based alternatives.

Although ICT has these two potential types of benefit for users to exploit, there is overlap. For instance, a **computer-aided design** (or **CAD**) system can at least partially automate the design activity,

---

Examples of informing and automating

Informing. A search by computer could provide a solicitor with details of a property that was being transferred to a new owner; or where litigation was being prepared it could provide pointers to legal precedents. The purpose of management information systems, which are discussed in Chapter 2.3, is purely to inform.

Automating. Processes such as paper-making or refining oil products, or mass-production manufacture, lend themselves to automation.

---

making it quicker and surer, and perhaps in some respects better. But to provide this service the CAD system also needs to be able to obtain information about materials, design standards and earlier designs: it needs to be informed.

Try it out	See if you can separate the informing from the automating aspects of applications you have met, perhaps the operation of cash dispensers or computer-controlled traffic lights.

The discussion above has inclined towards the application of ICT to the world of business, but services provided by, or on behalf of, central and local government need to harness ICT to increase their efficiency too. There are pressures on all public sector departments to design and offer improved services at costs which are as low as possible. Such organisations require information for much the same reasons as commercial organisations do.

Information, we have established, is important to enterprises of all kinds; but there can be too much of a good thing! The supply of information from computer systems in great quantities, very easily, has created a new hazard for individuals – **information overload** – which we shall think about in Chapter 2.3.

Storage of information

Information can exist and be held in two forms – *analogue* or *digital*. An **analogue** form of information storage allows a continuous and smooth variation in whatever means are used for holding the information: and for transmission, the signal carrying the information can vary in its amplitude and timing. Until recently all telephone lines carried voice traffic as analogue signals. The hands of a watch show the time in an analogue way: a **digital** watch shows it digitally – that is, as exact numbers.

In modern electronic computer systems the form of data storage is *digital*. Digital representation of information allows rapid processing that can be checked automatically for accuracy. Early computers were called specifically **digital computers** or **analogue computers** to differentiate between the two ways used at that time for holding their data. Now all general-purpose computers are digital computers.

The word 'digital' simply means 'based on numbers'. Internally, computers use a digital scheme in which the digits are all binary digits – that is, every item of information is, held magnetically or electronically in a way that can best be

regarded as consisting of a succession of 0s and 1s, and nothing else.

Thus a major item of systems software such as Windows, or a program product such as the database package Access, or the data processed by any software, are all held within the computer as binary digits, consisting of 0s and 1s. A single *bi*nary digi*t* is usually referred to in its contracted form as a **bit**. In business communication systems information is increasingly held and transmitted digitally, again in binary. The merits of binary representation are:

- items of information can be inexpensively checked for any corruption that might occur when they are moved; in some cases, errors that have been detected can be automatically corrected

- streams of data will be free from fading or other distortion: if transmission is checked, and can take place at all, the data will arrive exactly as sent

- data can be copied, to create duplicate data which can be shown to be an exact, true copy – this has notable advantages when the data is in the form of images or sounds

- and binary can be proved to be the most compact way of storing and transmitting a given amount of information.

References to data or information from now on assume that it is stored, processed and transmitted in binary form.

We noted, above, that for most business and administrative purposes data is held and moved as **characters**. We therefore need a standard scheme for representing characters in binary code.

Such a scheme, which is now universally used, is called the 'American Standard Code for Information Interchange' (or **ASCII**): it provides for each character within computer systems to be held and processed as a unique pattern of eight **bits**. The eight bits allocated to a character are known as a **byte** – a shorthand for 'by eight'. There are 256 possible ways of setting the eight bits in a byte, so there can be that number of different characters in ASCII.

> As an example of ASCII coding, the letter **A** is represented by the bit string '0 1 0 0 0 0 0 1'.

You frequently need to be able to refer to quantities of data. Whenever you want to say what the capacity of some data store is, or what the maximum rate of transmission in a data channel is, this need arises. The quantities of data stored in or by computers are measured in **bytes**. Thus, a **megabyte** (**MB**) is a million bytes. To be precise it is 2 raised to the twentieth power (2^{20}), or put another way that is 2^{10} (or 1024) squared, namely 1 048 576, bytes; but for most purposes the simplicity of thinking and saying a round 'million' outweighs the loss of precision. A **gigabyte** (**GB**) is a thousand megabytes.

> You might want to tell someone how many characters would occupy an A4 page: perhaps 50 lines of 12 words of six letters each would be a reasonable average giving 3600 characters, or bytes.
>
> A printed page in a book of about A5 size might have 4000 characters on a page. If the book has 250 pages it will contain about a million characters.

Articles on computing subjects are full of statements like: 'data is an organisation's most valued asset', and 'data is crucial for the survival of an organisation'. For many businesses these are accurate statements. The businesses want to preserve and protect very large amounts of data. As computer systems have assumed more and more tasks within organisations the demand for data storage capacity has risen continuously and steeply.

A big organisation, say an international oil company or a government department such as the National Health Service, needs storage of thousands or tens of thousands of gigabytes. Fortunately storage technology has moved to accommodate these needs. The cost of data storage has fallen, on average, by half every 18 months since its early days in the 1950s. The cumulative effect of this cost-reduction pattern is that to store a given unit of data in 1955 would have cost about 1 000 000 000 times as

? Did you know?

Huge and swelling demand for storage

Sales of hard disk capacity are going through the roof. The amount of data stored by computer users is said to double every year, and it is expected to continue doing so. Manufacturers of storage devices keep increasing the packing density on their disk products, and announcing new methods of data storage, yet they cannot keep pace.

One line of research, though, does look as if it might bring some relief to users: it is hologram storage, being pioneered by a company called Lucent. The technique can be used to store vast quantities of data as a three-dimensional hologram. The first devices brought to market by Lucent will be able to hold 125 GB on a removable 5.25-inch disk. Moreover, holography will allow shorter access times and faster data transfer rates than are available with current technology.

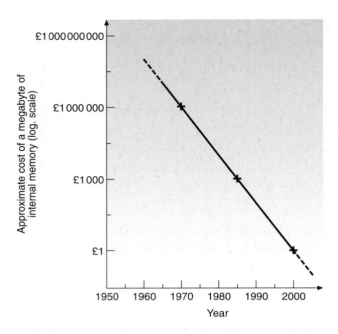

Figure 1.2 The cost of internal data storage from 1955 to 2000

much as in the year 2000. Prices continue to fall at this rate.

Figure 1.2 illustrates the general sharp, continuous fall in the cost of data stored internally in a computer. But it is no more than an indication of what has been happening, because storage technology has advanced, changing the precise way in which data has been held; and the high costs of storage in, say, the 1960s, meant that computers, to be affordable, contained only very small amounts of memory, packaged in tiny quantities that would not

Think it over

These figures alone make the successful lunar landing by the crew of Apollo 11 in 1969 a remarkable achievement.

The cost of storing binary data has now fallen so far that we may store far more data than we need, and find we are unable even to comprehend the significance of what we have stored.

make sense today. For example, there would have been no room for the software which makes the control of the computer possible.

There are many devices available to system designers in which data can be stored. Those you will meet are:

- read-only memory, or ROM
- random access memory, or RAM
- diskettes (or floppy disks) including 'Zip' disks
- hard disks
- magnetic tapes, including streamer tapes.

These devices have different characteristics. You will learn about them on your course. In particular, Chapter 4.1 gives detail on hardware. You will also meet the term **data warehouse** to refer to data derived from several sources which can be used in a coordinated way.

Organisations recognise that they may wish to attach greater value to some of their data than to the rest. Before we consider, in Chapter 1.2, how organisations place a value on the information they need to store, let us note two practices for safeguarding data followed by most computer centres and individual users:

- **Back-up.** As a noun this means a data store of some kind that can be used as a substitute for the original data should that become lost or corrupted. One speaks of 'taking' a back-up to describe the process of copying data on to a disk, diskette, or magnetic tape so that it can be recovered at short notice. 'Back up' is also a verb which means carrying out this process.

If you were working on an assignment and you had to leave it unfinished, intending to return to it later, you would

want to be sure that what you had done would be saved safely. You would be unwise to assume that no one would remove it from the hard disk you had been using. You would want to be as sure as possible that you would not have to do all the work again. You would back up carefully what you had done. Don't wait till disaster strikes!

- **Archive.** This can likewise be a noun or a verb. As a noun it refers to any repository of information that a user wishes to retain without the need to have immediate access. The verb means the act of transferring data to an archive system.

  Archiving strategy can be elaborate and complex if the demands of security warrant it.

Information on the move

For information to be useful it must not only be of good quality, but must also be available at the right place. And normally it is wanted at the right place almost immediately. These requirements have given rise to the whole world of data communications.

You should be conscious of the pace with which data communications have advanced. In 1980 the **Internet** had not been conceived, and **personal computers (PCs)** were seen only as vehicles for playing games or engaging the attention of computer fanatics.

Now the Internet is thoroughly established: and its resources of information are scanned by about half the population in UK; trading of many kinds takes place, reservations are made, advertising does its work, and e-mail traffic grows continuously. All these services, though sometimes awkward, are generally fast, accurate and almost free.

The Internet is becoming the vehicle for offering and supplying a growing range of services to individuals and businesses. The terms **e-commerce** and **e-business** and other *e*-words are joining the English language to name these fields of development. Collectively they can be called **e-services**.

Click for cucumbers in Singapore

Singapore One, the broadband computer network developed by Singapore's National Computer Board, allows and encourages e-commerce. A supermarket called Cold Storage has implemented a dial-and-deliver service over the Internet (www.coldstorage.com.sg) which immediately became popular with housewives. After two years there are 12 000 registered users, including businesses that use the service for corporate entertaining.

William Hill – The Bookie

William Hill have 1500 outlets in UK. In the 1990s they introduced telephone betting for debit card punters. The speed at which this service took off meant that computing and data communications systems had to be designed and implemented as quickly as possible.

The first lesson the ICT team learned was that if you have a telephone system that works well you must be absolutely sure you have something better before replacing it. They found their customers valued immediate response above any frills they might see on their online screens or hear over their phones. They also found that database management software that did exactly what they wanted for searching data in a flexible way was essential for the crisp responses they were intent on giving. William Hill attribute the success of the systems they now have installed as being largely due to their attracting in good time, and training, the staff with the ICT skills that would later be needed.

These Internet services are rapidly changing the way business is conducted between one organisation and another. The retail scene is also changing: the whole experience of shopping, and the structure of the retail trade, are expected to be markedly different within 10 or 15 years.

There seems no end to people's impatience: the prospect of being able to make late bookings through Lastminute.com, the availability of news updates on demand, the power to be able to send e-mail messages from wherever you are, and many, many other examples, provide new types of service providers with apparently endless fields of opportunity.

The activities of government and its agencies, and education, will be extensively altered by the Internet.

Although it is not subject to any overall managerial control, the Internet is proving

The National Geographic Society

In 1888 a group of 33 explorers, teachers, cartographers and financiers came together to create a society that would stimulate geographic investigation and, they hoped, would send out knowledge on a great scale. Within that same year they authorised their first publication – a slim scientific journal bound in brown paper called *National Geographic Magazine*.

From these origins the National Geographic Society (NGS) has grown into the largest non-profit scientific and educational institution in the world. Using Sun Microsystems technologies NGS has built a feature-rich site that includes interactive exploration, chats with photographers and writers, and links to its magazines and retail stores (www.nationalgeographic.com/).

to be astonishingly successful in meeting users' needs, and for that reason it goes on growing.

Apart from the Internet, which does not satisfy all the communications needs of the business community, there are other important channels available, including:

- **local area networks (LANs)**

- **wide area networks (WANs)**

- static and mobile **telephones**

- **facsimile (fax)**

- private, internal networks of various kinds, including **intranets** which mimic the Internet locally.

The transmission media for the transfer of data include:

- traditional wiring

- radio and microwave

- fibre optic cable

- satellite links.

In addition, infra-red and sonar beams can be used to notify systems of a change of status. For example, a beam broken by an intruder (who would not be able to see it) could activate a computer-based alarm system.

The reliability, capacity and speed of all communications systems are for ever being improved to meet the growing demands of users.

Information and communication technology (ICT)

The impressive advances of ICT in recent years makes these pronouncements by two illustrious people seem rather ill-judged:

> 'There will never be need of more than five computers in the world.'
>
> Thomas J Watson,
> Chairman of IBM, 1952

> 'Computers are useless. They can only give you answers.'
>
> Pablo Picasso, 1968

If we link the processing of data to the storage and communications capabilities that we touched on above we have assembled the ingredients we need for ICT – the technology that is so powerful and so versatile in meeting our needs. By **processing** we mean the acceptance by a computer of data, the manipulation of it in accordance with instructions within the computer, and the output of the resulting data.

Processing that fulfils the needs of users by providing cost-effective solutions will always be sought.

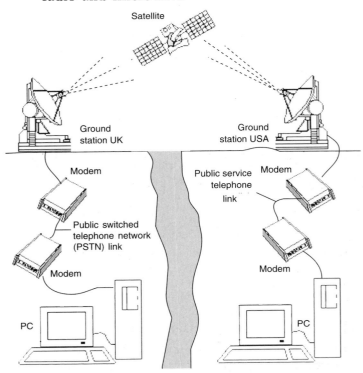

Figure 1.3 WAN using satellite links

These aspirations have been met, and go on being met, because of the unique attributes of ICT. Since the first commercial computers came onto the market in the late 1950s the cost of a unit of processing has been falling, because:

- the cost of equipment to carry out a given task is falling roughly in line with the decline of costs shown, in Figure 1.2 above, for internal storage

- the processing itself is getting faster

- the software carrying it out is becoming more capable and more comprehensive

- the computing equipment is getting smaller, more reliable and often more robust, with lower maintenance charges

- newer computers use less power and so they emit less heat.

No other industry or field of endeavour has ever previously been blessed with this dream combination of rapidly rising capability coupled to rapidly falling costs. It is unique, and it explains the uninterrupted, vigorous growth of ICT.

The cost-effectiveness of transferring any business application to computer is moving briskly in favour of the user: and, of course, many new applications that were never undertaken manually are running on ICT systems. No wonder that computers are harnessed to carry out or support almost every kind of endeavour.

Think it over

Just think what would have happened if the cost and fuel consumption of cars had improved at the same rate as the cost and performance of computing.

Chapter 1.2   Standard ways of working: security and safety

The aim of this chapter is to introduce the subjects of data security and safe working practices. We look at the reasons that individuals and organisations want to hold data, the threats to which the data is exposed, and the precautions that users can consider for safeguarding their data; and then we review standard working practices that raise personal productivity and reduce the risks to data.

The Advanced VCE specifications for all six compulsory units include passages on methodical and safe ways of working with computers. The discussion on working practices in this chapter therefore applies to all units of the book.

Reasons users want to hold data

All users of computer systems need to keep and protect the data they have in current use for carrying out their ICT procedures and development. Most also have to keep securely data that has been processed previously, for any of the following reasons:

- to allow recovery of their systems should the current data become damaged or lost or destroyed

- to allow, for example, the production of historical financial accounts or the analysis of business trends

- to meet the requirements of laws which provide for records to be kept safely for a specified number of years – the majority of businesses and government departments will have to preserve at least some of their data for this purpose

- other reasons, including the safekeeping of historical archives such as the papers of eminent people now dead, legal documents that may yet be wanted, protecting copyright, and satisfying personal and corporate desires to keep secure ageing information for any purpose.

Threats to data

We use the word *data* here to cover system software, application software and all other data of importance to computer processing. And by *threats* we mean any action, or neglect, that might place the data at risk. These are the most common threats to data:

- deliberate physical damage in which someone vandalises any part of a computer or communications system or data store

- accidental physical damage in which, for example, a diskette is taken through a magnetic field, or left in the sun, or used as a coffee mat; or a personal computer (PC) or laptop computer is struck or dropped, or suffers a head crash on its hard disk; or there is a fire or flood affecting a server or desktop computers or their external wiring

- accidental electronic damage, such as the deletion of everything on a PC's hard disk, caused by wrong keyboard operation

- industrial espionage in which information valuable to a competitor is copied and stolen, possibly leaving no trace of the theft

- theft of computer equipment which is holding data

- virus attacks which might alter or destroy data

- failure of the power supply while a system is in use, probably leading to loss of data.

? Did you know?

In the autumn of 1999 Dell's Limerick production plant had to be closed for two days when a computer virus was found in the factory. Dell run updated virus-checking software every day but it was still outwitted by the new virus. 12000 PCs had to be inspected for the virus.

This incident reflects the constant battle between the designers of viruses and the designers of anti-virus software, who must necessarily lag behind.

In addition to these threats there are other threats to the proper functioning of computer and communications systems. These include the mischievous swamping of e-mail services with large volumes of useless messages; or someone adopting a false identity without consent, known as 'spoofing', in order to obtain information improperly; or indulging in any form of illegal processing which needs to be investigated and stopped, thereby diverting resources from normal work.

Example of breaking into private network

Internet service providers have reported invasions of huge numbers of meaningless messages, and messages with vast attachments, sent with the intention of flooding the e-mail system and making it unusable.

There were reports that during the 1999 conflict in the Balkans some Serb supporters broke into NATO's e-mail service and inundated it with up to 2000 meaningless messages a day with a view to hampering the air operations over Kosovo.

The 'Love Bug' virus

On 4 May 2000, the most contagious virus up to that time ravaged the computer systems of governments, multi-national corporations, and thousands of computer networks, within a few hours.

The virus was transmitted by an e-mail attachment which simply said 'LOVE-LETTER-FOR-YOU.TXT'. By opening that attachment the user launched the virus which immediately copied itself to everybody in the user's e-mail address book and also into the computer's memory-ready to spring into action whenever the system was rebooted. In the e-mail messages put out by the virus were huge picture and video files able to gum up Internet communications.

Safeguarding systems and data

There are two principal approaches to protecting data — denying **access** to everyone not having the right to see or alter the data and keeping **copies** of all data.

Protecting the integrity and security of data sent over communications channels presents special difficulties.

Before any organisation can decide upon the precautions to take to protect its data it must carry out a **risk assessment**. This will rank the various categories of data by the importance they have for the organisation, estimating the cost of types of data becoming lost and thus placing a maximum figure on the acceptable cost of protecting it.

Each organisation will also want to assess the extent of the risks to the various types of data it has identified.

The next step is to develop and implement **standards** for the security of data, and provide training for the members of staff who are to be responsible for planning and installing and monitoring whatever security procedures are introduced. Guidance provided by British Standard 7799, 'The Code of Practice for Information Security Management', may be helpful.

The procedures adopted in all but the smallest ICT operations are likely to include the following:

- the appointment of a person to be responsible for security

- rules for the frequency of taking back-ups and for the places where backed-up files are to be stored and how they are to be labelled

- rules for archiving data and for protecting it — e.g. the most valuable archived data could be held in a fireproof safe at a remote location

- rules for the choice of **passwords**, for the occasions when they are to be used, and for managing the regular changing of passwords; the use of software which automatically reports all suspected violations of password protection, normally after three failed attempts to gain access

- rules for accepting input software that carries any risk of contamination by virus, and for the routine running of named virus-checking packages

- rules for allowing access to areas containing computing or communications equipment by anyone not on a list of approved individuals

- the installation of an **uninterruptable power supply (UPS)** to cut in immediately there is an electric power failure to provide a temporary replacement supply

- training in the **legal framework** of data security, covering particularly:

  o the Computer Misuse Act 1990, which makes hacking a criminal offence

  o the Data Protection Act 1984, updated by the Data Protection Act 1998, which restricts the data on living people that can legally be held on computer. Companies are now restricted from transferring personal data to countries outside the European Union unless subsequent protection can be guaranteed (the Data Protection Act 1998 is available on-line at **www.dataprotection.gov.co.uk**.)

○ the Copyright, Designs and Patents Act 1988, which gives **copyright** protection to software

○ **contracts**, or moral obligations, which may impose confidentiality on data such as personnel records; or which may transfer copyright, for example, from the writer of software to the employer of that person.

Personal action to protect data

You should learn, and always follow, good practice yourself, to protect data. Here are some important points for you to observe:

- **Confidentiality.** In both business life and social life you should not pass personal or private information to anyone else unless you are sure that it is proper to do so. At work that means taking care not to discuss business matters outside the organisation unless you are sure that the facts are in no way confidential.

  You need to be especially careful of medical, legal, and personnel records.

- **Copyright.** You need to be aware that copyright protection covers a wide range of material. For example, you are not allowed to copy, by scanning or photocopying, anything like pictures or research articles or even pages from a book without permission. If pictures, music, software or text are on the Internet or elsewhere in the public domain you are free to download them and use them: but if you are not sure that copying is permitted you must ask.

- **Identifying your own data.** You will find that you quickly build up large numbers of your own files, some of which will be different versions of the same file. You must get into the habit of naming your files systematically so that you can find what you want reliably, ideally at the first attempt. You do not want to have to look through many files to locate one that you want.

Protecting the security of transmitted data

Data to be passed over communication channels can be scrambled to render it unintelligible to anyone other than the intended recipient. This process is called **encryption**. Cryptography, the science of encryption, is highly technical: the principle is that sender and receiver hold agreed **keys** for encoding and decoding streams of data.

The importance of encryption lies in the confidence it gives users of public data communications links that information is proof against copying and misuse. Every time you use a credit card or a debit card there is potentially a threat to security. On-line services will only be trusted fully if users feel sure that they are safe in entering their card details.

There are constant attempts to break the main procedures for encryption by security specialists testing their strength, and also by those anxious to obtain personal financial data illegally. Encryption is therefore constantly evolving to provide users with ever greater levels of security for their data.

Computer networks are often isolated from one another so that if there is a break-in on one network adjacent ones should not be affected. If data does have to be passed between a pair of networks there should be some way of checking it as it does so. The electronic barrier between networks is known as a **firewall**.

The general rule for establishing good data security is to ensure that there are no easy routes for anyone to breach the security defences. Every aspect of the computing and communications systems must be safeguarded to an agreed level.

Did you know?

In addition to the use of passwords to protect systems, certain attributes of the human body are confidently thought to be unique and to offer possibilities for improved security.

Distinctive data from these features can be scanned, encoded, and processed in digital form. Authentication for access to a sensitive area could be denied to anyone whose code pattern failed to match the pattern held by the person in charge. Examples of the attributes being evaluated for this purpose include:

- fingerprints
- colour and pattern of the iris of a person's eye
- speech, particularly the way certain vowels and words are pronounced
- the structure of a person's face.

Standard ways of working

There is great merit in adopting standard ways of carrying out any activity that arises repeatedly. Examples can be found in all walks of life: the armed services learn deployment drills; designers of computer systems rely on development methodology; all of us work out patterns of doing tasks that arise frequently in ways that become routine.

This is important because it means that all the available mental effort can be directed to *what has to be done* rather than into *how to do it*. And if the standard ways followed are based on the best practice then that practice is effortlessly adopted for the range of activities concerned.

This principle can be applied to your use of a PC. You can follow regular procedures for backing up your data, at regular intervals; and, where you have control over these matters, you can also adopt working practices that are likely to make your work on the computer as effective as possible by giving attention to these aspects of your physical surroundings:

- use firm, comfortable seating, and correct desk height, to allow you to retain a good posture

- have your VDU screen at an angle that lets you see it clearly, free from glare or reflection; and your keyboard at a convenient distance and inclination

- avoid obstructions, like loose and trailing cables and nearby filing cabinets, that could cause accidents.

You can help yourself to avoid strain by refocusing your eyes from time to time on distant objects; and you should be sure to get up and move around after sensible intervals.

Try it out	Repetitive strain injury (RSI)
	RSI is a painful condition that can arise from prolonged use of a PC. The number of cases of RSI reported amongst staff at the Health and Safety Executive (HSE), which is itself the watchdog for office working conditions, rose by 30% to 132 in 1999. This presents HSE with a medical as well as a public relations problem.
	If you were in charge of clerical operations at HSE headquarters, what would you do to try and arrest the incidence of RSI? Make a list of the steps you would take. What should be the first priority?

The object of following procedures such as these is to contain the risk of exhaustion and injury so that you remain as productive as possible. Employers, of course, have an identical interest in trying to ensure that their staff look after their health and thus can be fully productive.

Finally, you should recognise that working at a PC is a lonely activity; you should make a point of exchanging words with other people now and again.

Chapter 1.3 Styles of writing

In this chapter and in Chapter 1.4 we consider information only in the form of documents.

This chapter is concerned with the choices you make in deciding on how to express yourself in writing, and especially on how you use the English language to obtain the effect you want. We look at writing style, and the importance of accuracy.

Style is an elusive concept. A student of English literature would probably be able to identify a paragraph or two written by, say, Sir Walter Scott or James Joyce, from studying the style of the writing. The prose style of established authors will usually have been developed gradually over several years.

Style in this sense is built on the skill, experience and personality of the writer. Some authors decide to try and develop a writing style modelled on the style of someone whose work they admire: but this is never wholly successful because a writer's style reflects, at least in part, the individuality of that person.

There are thus a great number of acceptable styles. Writers of fiction seek to develop a style that is suited to the telling of a tale: a style that captures and keeps the reader's attention, always holding out the lure of even greater interest or excitement on the next page.

That is completely different from a style that is good for use at work, which is what we are discussing here. You will be setting out to write what needs to be written as efficiently as you can: you want to contribute to the efficiency of your organisation by creating good documents for a given amount of effort.

Here are a few words from writers who should know what style is:

'Have something to say, and say it as clearly as you can. That is the only secret of style.'
Matthew Arnold (1822–1888)

'Style is the dress of thought; a neat dress, but not gaudy.'
The Rev Samuel Wesley (1666–1735)

'Proper words in proper places, make the true definition of a style.'
Jonathan Swift (1667–1745)

The last paragraphs of this chapter look at ways of helping you make your documents as readable as possible; and they highlight the importance of being accurate in what you write.

You should recognise the limitations of the book. It cannot teach you all you may need to know about the use of English. What is important for you, though, is that for your future career you learn to communicate well and easily. Beyond what is included in this chapter there may be further help in acquiring the skills of writing and in communication generally available in your school or college: your tutor will be able to tell you what there is.

Sources of help

There are several sources in which you, as the writer of a document, might find help in putting down your thoughts. They include:

- A **dictionary**, which gives you the exact meaning of a word you are thinking of using as well as the correct spelling.

- A **thesaurus**, which is similar to a dictionary but which offers you alternatives to any word you choose.

- The **spell-checker** in the word-processing package you use. All a spell-checker can do is to draw attention to words that it cannot match in its own dictionary. In Word that means that the software puts a squiggly red line under what it thinks is a mistake. If you key *there* when you meant *their* the spell-checker will not flag an error.

  Some words – *colour*, and *tranquillity* for instance – are spelt differently in the United States, so beware if the spell-checker is American.

  If there are words, such as your name, that are not in the spell-checker's dictionary, you can add them into a **custom dictionary** so that they are in effect added to the spell-checker's dictionary and therefore do not get flagged when you key them in.

- The **grammar-checker** in your word processor. This is less popular than the spell-checker because you can often legitimately disagree with it; but nonetheless once in a while it can prove helpful in pointing to an improvement you could make.

  Some grammar-checkers give you comments on the lengths of your sentences, on the apparent complexity of your prose, and on down-to-earth matters like repeated words and lack of capital letters.

You can, of course, ignore what your grammar-checker tells you, and just press on.

Most word-processing, spreadsheet, and other office applications will have at least two features that help with the preparation of documents.

- First, the applications package usually comes bundled with a number of **sample documents**, **spreadsheets**, and presentations which can be adapted. For **example**, a word-processing application would probably have sample memos, invoices, and reports. A spreadsheet package could have sample spreadsheets for tracking time and expenses.

- Second, modern applications usually support a feature called a **template**. You can think of a template as a skeleton of an item to be prepared, with layout, font, and graphic elements already in place. The package would come with a number of templates already provided, although the template feature is designed for you to create and use your own templates. You would use a template for a frequently needed task for which the layout was standard, such as a monthly sales report or letter heading (Figure 1.4). A template is stored as a separate file which can be easily retrieved.

Microsoft applications packages include features called **wizards**. A wizard offers a series of dialogue boxes which help you create and complete a document, taking you through a kind of complex template step by step.

No one expects you to write like Shakespeare: but you do need to be able to achieve your desired result. The tools mentioned above can help you.

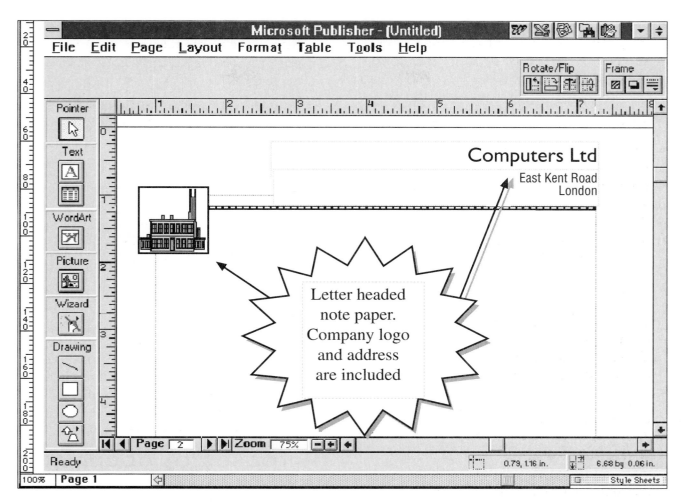

Figure 1.4 Part of a company letterhead design

Before you begin

When you first start thinking about a document you intend to write, it is vital that you are clear about its purpose. Unless the purpose is clear there is little hope of your interesting your readers; and what you write will almost certainly be woollier than it should be.

Before starting to write any document you must consider the interests of the intended readers. Readers are of many types but all have one characteristic in common: they have plenty of calls on their time apart from whatever time they would need for reading your document. You must therefore always strive to interest your readers, to be accurate in what you write, and to be as brief as possible consistent with the other two objectives. Otherwise you may simply alienate them.

Long documents

These points are especially important if you are setting out to produce a long document. You have to try in every way you can to capture and keep the attention of the reader. If you find at your future place of work that there is a standard layout for reports, there will probably be a word-processing template to help you with a new report you have to produce. Here are the most widely used approaches to creating a structure for reports:

- make sure the **title** of the document is right – that not only tells the reader what the document is, and is for; it also helps you stay on track while you are writing it

- identify the **author** or authors

- give the **date of issue** of the document – no one wants to waste time on something which is out-of-date

- divide the main body of the document into **chapters** that are self-contained, and give the chapters titles

- divide every chapter into **paragraphs**, each of which deals with a complete idea, and is not longer than the reader is likely to find comfortable

- include **diagrams** or other **illustrations** if you think that is the best way of conveying your meaning; and give them numbers so that you can refer to them in the text, and **captions** so that it is clear what each is

- put detail that is necessary, but which would interrupt the flow of the document, into **appendices**, and be sure to give the appendices names

- provide **page numbers**

- at the front provide a table of **contents** listing the chapter names and page numbers, and give the names of the appendices

- start the document itself with an **introduction**, an explanation of why it has been produced, who should read it, and why they should do so

- consider having a **bibliography** and an **index** at the back.

On your course you will probably be asked to write a report of three or more pages. Although this is hardly a 'long document', if you have not written many of this sort of report it may seem long and the points above will help you. Before you start you should think about its structure and layout – as usual, focusing on how to make your document attractive to the reader. There is more about report-writing later in this chapter.

Purposes of documents

Let us now look at various purposes for which you might have to create documents, and see how the purpose each time affects the style you will want to adopt.

Attracting attention

A handbill or poster advertising a public event is a typical example of a document whose main purpose is to attract attention. It should contain the least number of words that convey the essence of the message – an outline description of the event, and the date, time, place and price, and perhaps if the event takes place regularly some reference to its history. The words should be short, and the whole message prominent and easy to understand: it may have to do its job outdoors in a poor light in heavy rain.

Here is a classic notice which meets the criteria above, and is probably effective even if there are no corroborating smells!

Setting out facts clearly

If your document aims to present facts it can help the reader by offering those facts as a **list** or in a **table**, and by making sure that they are arranged in a sensible way. Put yourself in the position of the reader who is not familiar with the detail the document needs to convey. Think what form of words or diagram would display the facts as lucidly as possible.

Whatever else you do, do *not* allow yourself to fall into the trap of setting out to show the reader how clever you are. Just concentrate on making the facts as clear as you can.

Writing to impress

You should not set out to impress your readers: if the message in your document is itself impressive it will do the work for you.

Creating a questionnaire

Questionnaires are known to be hard to draft well. If you are designing a questionnaire you must think first about what it is for. For example, if you want to be able to derive statistics from completed questionnaires you must be sure that the replies will allow this.

The questions must be clear to the people being targeted. Before distributing a questionnaire you should always test it to check:

- that the people being targeted understand the questions, and

- that the form of response is what you expect and want.

You have to consider how questionnaires will be distributed and then collected; whether help will be provided in filling them in; whether the information supplied will be treated as confidential. The questionnaire must be friendly so that those approached do take the trouble to complete and return the form. You may decide to say 'Thank you for giving your time to completing this questionnaire' at the end of the questionnaire form.

The questions on your questionnaire can be **open**, as in 'What did you like best about the exhibition?' or **closed**, as in 'Would you recommend the exhibition to your friends?' Or closed with **multiple choice** responses, as in 'Which age band do you fall into (tick one): under 25, 25 to 40, 41 to 60, 61 and over?' You need to be careful to be sure that no age can fall into more than one age band.

You need to think, when you are designing a questionnaire, what form of question is most likely to provide you with the information you are hoping to get, and how the data will be analysed. At a higher level of subtlety you could consider what sort of questions are most likely to provide you with honest answers.

In designing your questionnaire remember that you may be able to use colour; and you can of course make use of any of the word-processing features, such as different fonts, shading, frames and boxes, that you know how to use. If you can obtain questionnaires that have been used previously you will find them helpful when you are deciding upon your own design.

Ordering or invoicing goods

We shall return to this topic in Chapter 2.3. In the meanwhile let us note that orders and invoices are documents which establish a contractual relationship between the parties involved. **Orders** state what is to be supplied, and **invoices** state how much is to be paid. Such documents must be unambiguous and wholly factual, setting out exactly what is expected, providing all the facts necessary for proper book-keeping by the vendor and the purchaser.

Figure 1.5 shows an example of a typical invoice. This one is from Festivities Unlimited (FUN) for the supply of party food items and catering books to one of the firm's clients. Note that books are zero-rated for VAT.

The following detail is on the invoice:

• seller's name, address, telephone and fax numbers, and e-mail address

• purchaser's addresses for the invoice and for the goods, which may or may not be at the same place

• date of invoice

• invoice number

• VAT registration number

• calculations, including discounts for early payment or for special promotions,

Festivities Unlimited

INVOICE

Invoice No. XXXXX   Date: DD MM YY
Order Reference:

(Invoice address)	(Delivery address)

Quantity	Description	Unit Price	Net cost	VAT Rate	VAT Amount
3 dozen	Pizza slices	0.40	14.40	17.5	2.52
100	Paper plates	0.21	21.00	17.5	3.67
2	Cookery books	6.99	13.98	0	0
VAT TOTAL	–	–	–	–	6.19
NET TOTAL	–	–	49.38	–	49.38
TOTAL TO PAY	–	–	–	–	55.57

Terms of Business: Payment within 30 days, please (No discount on this invoice.)

Please pay: Festivities Unlimited
221 B Wardo Road
Fulham, London SW6 XXX

Fax/Tel: 0207 XXX XXXX   E-mail: Fred@Funxx.co.uk
VAT Reg. No. XXX XXXX XX

Figure 1.5 A typical invoice

leading to the total VAT and the total to be paid

• how payment is to be made, and by what date.

You might want FUN to quote for running a child's birthday party in your own home. In that case you would let FUN have a statement of your requirement:

• date and time

• 15 children, aged 8 to 11

• pizza slices and jellies

• coke and squash

• balloons, six colours

• party bags

• magician, for 45 minutes.

You would need to say by when you would need to have the quote.

We discuss commercial documents in Chapter 2.3.

Summarising information

Information often has to be summarised – so that its main significance can be seen quickly, or so that it occupies only a little space on a page.

The most popular forms of summary involve some kind of graphics. These could be pie charts, bar charts, or conventional graphs; but they could also be tables. Examples of these ways of presenting summaries are shown below.

A **pie chart** is a clear and compact way of showing how the share, or proportion, of some quantity or opinion is distributed amongst the members of some group of people or things. Examples could include: the declared voting intentions of members of the electorate in some geographical area; or the proportions of each of the distinct colours that are used for new British-made cars in a given year.

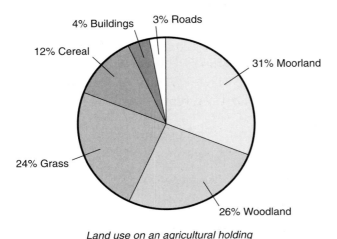

Land use on an agricultural holding

Figure 1.6 Example of a pie chart

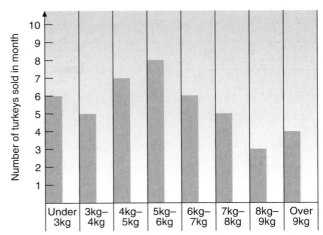

Sales of frozen turkeys at a village shop (December)

Figure 1.7 Example of a bar chart

A **bar chart** is a convenient way of displaying a development plan or schedule, or the frequency of occurrence of certain events. The term 'bar chart' covers two particular versions of this technique, both of which you will come across:

- A **histogram** is a diagram which represents frequencies of various ranges of values of a quantity: it can show frequency distribution. A histogram could be constructed to show, for example, the number of births, in 10-year bands, for a particular country.

- A **Gantt chart** is a grid showing equal intervals of time along the x-axis, with planned events listed down the y-axis; it is used extensively for scheduling the start dates and duration of the events to be monitored in ICT project planning and in programming building work.

A **graph** traces the relationship between two quantities that vary in a continuous way. A graph is distinct from a bar chart which represents situations that are measured at intervals.

One of the variables in a graph is often time. Thus, changes of air pressure or

SCHEDULE FOR:	GANTT CHART: CONSTRUCTION OF GARDEN SUMMER HOUSE	DATE	NO.

No.	ACTIVITY — WEEKS	1	2	3	4	5	6	7	8	9	10	11	12	13	14	15	16	17	18
01	DESIGN SUMMER HO.	▓	▓																
02	OBTAIN PLANNING PERMISSION			▓	▓	▓													
03	ORDER MATERIALS						▓												
04	CONSTRUCT APPROACH						▓	▓											
05	DIG FOUNDATIONS								▓	▓									
06	RECRUIT HELPER																		
07	RECEIVE MATERIALS																		
08	ERECT WALLS												▓						
09	FIT ROOF																		
10	INSTALL ELECTRICITY														▓				
11	FIT DOOR, WINDOWS															▓			
12	BRING IN FURNITURE																▓		
13																			
14																			
15																			
16																			
17																			
18																			
19																			
20																			

Figure 1.8 Example of a Gantt chart

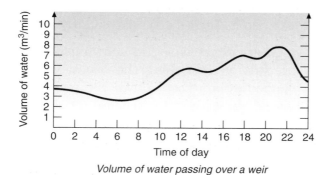

Volume of water passing over a weir

Figure 1.9 Example of a graph

quantity of rainfall, at one place, over some period, are suitable relationships to represent by graphs. Another is the record of temperature in a greenhouse over, say, a period of 24 hours.

You will sometimes want to use the data displayed in these ways in computing applications. The values taken to draw pie charts and bar charts can be used directly as data for processing. That is not the case with continuous graphs which provide an *analogue* trace, and such graphs cannot be used as input to processing by digital computer. However, numeric readings could be taken from a graph and handled digitally by computer software.

In addition to these techniques for displaying summarised information, you will often find that a **table** is what you really want.

Suppose you were going to buy a mobile telephone. You could list all the features, including the prices, of models you wanted to consider, and use the table to help your decision-making.

Similarly, if you wanted to decide how best to get to the south of Spain on a particular day you could build a table of the possibilities – fly scheduled, fly charter, train, drive, hitch-hike, or go by sea.

You can also use tables to compare the advantages and disadvantages of services which would be less tangible, such as deciding what kind of promotion would be most effective in selling some product – advertising a web site, advertising the product itself, using direct mail, and many other options.

Preparing a draft

If you are keying a rough **draft** for later improvement by yourself, the way you do it is largely a matter for yourself: speed is perhaps the main issue. You will be taking time and trouble over editing the draft, probably relying on spell-checker and grammar-checker software to help. You may find, though, that setting your text out in an open, uncluttered format is constructive.

On the other hand, if you are writing a draft for someone else you will have different goals. Here you are the source of ideas and of detailed knowledge, and you must not let careless expression distract the reader from what you say. You must help the reader to modify your draft as easily as possible by, for example, using double spacing, deep gaps between paragraphs, and generous margins. We return to these questions of layout in Chapter 1.4.

You also help your reader by restricting the length of each line to somewhere around 12 to 15 words. You might feel that a ragged right hand margin makes a document easier

to read because the spacing between the letters making up each line does not have to be stretched or closed up artificially.

Explaining technical details

The computer industry for many years had an appalling reputation for its **manuals** and **handbooks**. Many authors were more interested in the technology than in explaining it clearly to others less well-informed than themselves; and technical developments followed one another at such a rapid pace that there was a feeling that the products described could be obsolete before the job was finished – hardly an incentive for careful, thorough work!

These days there are plenty of excellent manuals, handbooks and sales brochures describing hardware and software. Look inside one or two and you will see:

- clarity of layout and structure
- the explanation of specialist terms before they are brought into use
- ample use of diagrams
- contents and index pages that are easy to grasp.

These attributes of technical writing are helpful to the reader.

When it is practicable to make use of **colour**, that too can add to clarity.

Remember, when writing, there are words that have precise meanings in the computer world that are different from the meanings in ordinary speech: they could mislead someone not familiar with their specialist meaning. Examples are:

mouse   *RAM*   *soft boot*
field   *WORM*

29

If you are not already aware of all these words do not worry: you will meet them soon. You should not be shy of explaining to your readers the meaning of any words you think may cause problems.

Writing a reminder

One of FUN's invoices has not been paid by the due date, and it is your job to send the client a reminder.

You could write:

Our Invoice no. 12345 of 1ˢᵗ September is two weeks overdue. We require payment within seven days or we shall withdraw your credit facilities and close your account.

Or you could write:

According to our records our Invoice no.12345 dated 1ˢᵗ September is still outstanding. If you agree, would you please be kind enough to settle the invoice now?

Remember, your purpose in writing is to secure payment on an outstanding bill, not to throw your weight about. Which form of words is more likely to succeed? There may be good reason for the delay in payment, or there may just be a muddle somewhere; but either way many businesses would be irritated by the first letter and not rush themselves to pay.

Preparing a report

Most people dislike writing reports, and reading them. Be careful to make them as appealing as you can. The pointers above to writing long documents generally apply to reports. A golden rule is to include only necessary material.

This is one possible structure for a report of more than, say, ten pages:

- outside **front cover** giving title, author and date

- page giving the name of the **authority** asking for the report, the list of **recipients**, the point of contact for **queries**, and any special knowledge or qualifications possessed by the **author**

- the **contents** page

- a brief **summary** of the **purpose** of the report, and the **main points** addressed in it and the main conclusions

- the **body** of the report

- **appendices**

- **references** or **bibliography**

- **index**.

The purpose of any report is usually to help someone reach a decision on some issue. In writing a report you should bear in mind as you go along what that purpose is and how you can support it.

For example, the manager of your department at your place of work has been told to look at the case for moving to a regime of 'hot-desking' in which there might be office desks for, say, only one-third of the staff who currently each have their own desk. The manager asks you to produce a report setting out the pros and cons.

The points you would have to cover in your report would include:

- reduced need for office space: reduced rent, heating bills and lighting bills

- increased working from home: lower personal travel costs; less pollution

- improved voice and data communications between staff become essential

- loss of community spirit; less frequent casual contacts; greater difficulty in holding team meetings

- reduced storage available to individuals within the office

- less space needed for car parking

- enhanced recruitment prospects thanks to attractive life-style followed by employees.

Documents for personal and social use

The purposes of producing documents, discussed above, have been in the context of the world of business. There are other kinds of document you may want to design and create from time to time, for example:

- Your own CV, or **curriculum vitae**, also known as a **resumé,** which will be important to you in applying for a place in higher education or in seeking an interview for a job. It will have to be amended frequently, because whenever you have done something that is relevant to your personal history you will probably want to add a description of it; and you may want to adjust the contents to match what you perceive the interests of the next reader to be.

- **Notices** of meetings, **agendas, minutes, accounts** and other papers to do with clubs or societies in which you are active. We cover the meaning and purpose of these types of document in Chapter 2.3.

- An **advertisement** to be placed in the local paper to help you sell something.

- **A request**, perhaps sent by e-mail, for details of a product offered for sale.

The guidelines you will want to follow in drafting any of these will be similar to those for the business scene, but, apart from the CV, you are of course free to be less formal in your style.

Try it out	As a group, collect a selection of documents intended for some sort of external use. Split them into categories such as advertising, informing, obtaining information. Examine the style and content, and decide who were to be the recipients. Then consider whether each document looked as if it would do the job it was supposed to do.
	Choose one good example and one poor example of these documents, and explain to the rest of the class the reasons for your choice.

There is no set way of writing a CV. There is though little scope for variation if the CV of a typical Advanced VCE student is to do its job of describing to a potential employer what that student can offer. Usually, the real purpose of sending out a CV is to be invited to an interview: it must therefore be laid out carefully, without errors, giving the information you believe to be relevant; and nothing else.

The structure and content might be along these lines:

CURRICULUM VITAE

Name: (names in full)

Address: (full home address)

Telephone Number: (full number, also e-mail address if you have one)

Date of Birth: (day, month, year)

Schools Attended: (list them in order)

Certificates: (list GCSE and other certificates with the grades obtained, and the year of each)

Holiday Jobs: (detail of employers, dates, type of work and level of responsibility)

Part-time Jobs: (details of term-time jobs, employers, dates, type of work and level of responsibility)

School Activities: (any clubs or societies you belonged to at school, with detail of how you participated – this would include sports, music and amateur dramatics, for example)

Other Interests: (say what you do, what you read, and in what ways you help others)

Skills: (driving, first aid, life-saving, astronomy or navigation, for example)

Ambitions: (what do you want to do? what steps are you taking to prepare yourself?)

Date: (end your CV with the date on which you drafted it)

Try it out | You plan to sell your ink-jet printer, which is limited to printing in black only, as you have just been given a colour printer. Draft a notice about the item for sale, to go in the window of your closest computer shop. The shop charges by the word for notices in its window. Also draft a sheet about the printer to sit on the counter in the shop.

Readability

In 1946 the author George Orwell proposed six rules for helping writers make their documents attractive to their readers. No one has yet improved on these rules. They are:

1 Never use a metaphor, simile or other figure of speech which you are used to seeing in print.

2 Never use a long word where a short word will do.

3 If it is possible to cut out a word, always cut it out.

4 Never use the passive voice where you can use the active.

5 Never use a foreign phrase, a scientific word or a jargon word if you can think of an everyday English equivalent.

6 Break any of these rules sooner than say anything outright barbarous.

We cannot expand on all these rules, and do not need to as they largely explain themselves. However you may find commentary on the first two rules interesting.

Rule 1 is supposed to encourage you, as a writer, to express exactly what you mean.

The figures of speech to which Orwell refers are usually clichés and as such are substitutes for thought. Examples are 'first and foremost,' 'sick as a parrot,' 'safe as houses' and 'kicked into touch'. You will be able to think of many more. How about this:

'As a matter of fact at this moment of time it is my considered opinion that all the world and his wife are in blissful ignorance of the cohorts of clichés that can be paraded alive and kicking and the picture of health in a single sentence.'

Rule 2 concerns the benefit of using short words in place of longer equivalent words. The Second Inaugural Address of the US President, Abraham Lincoln, has been widely considered to be a model of clarity, as well as of economy. It contained 701 words: 505 of them consisted of one syllable, and 122 were of two syllables.

Let us draw on Orwell again. He translated this passage from the Old Testament:

'I returned and saw under the sun, that the race is not to the swift, nor the battle to the strong, neither yet bread to the wise, nor yet riches to men of understanding, nor yet favour to men of skill; but time and chance happeneth to them all.'

into this modern, faceless, gobbledegook:

'Objective consideration of contemporary phenomena compels the conclusion that success or failure in competitive activities exhibits no tendency to be commensurate with innate capacity, but that a considerable element of the unpredictable must invariably be taken into account.'

You will often draft a document and later decide to amend it to introduce improvements. You may be asked to help a colleague by commenting on a draft document. Whenever you want to amend a hand-written or printed version of the document, and annotate it with instructions for making the amendments, you will want to be as clear as possible to avoid misunderstandings. The British Standard proofreaders' correction marks often form the basis for marking corrections and other changes.

The proofreaders' marks can be used in the body of the draft text or in one of the margins. Here are eight of the more commonly used marks:

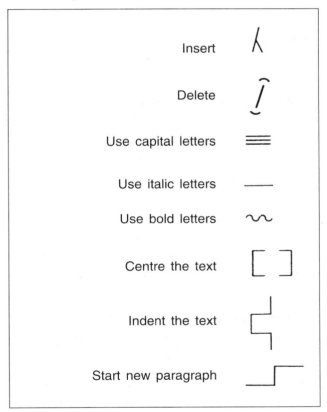

Figure 1.10 Proofreaders' marks

Whatever procedures you follow to prepare a document for issue you must always recognise that responsibility for every aspect of it rests with you as author.

Accuracy

Maintaining accuracy throughout any document you produce is important: it is also difficult, particularly with long documents.

Inaccuracy in any document, where it is noticed by the reader, is likely to lead to a loss of confidence in every aspect of the document. This means that the writer will have lost some of the impact of the message. If inaccuracy is serious, or if it occurs many times, it may prove so irritating that the reader abandons the struggle and gives up reading.

There are large numbers of kinds of inaccuracy. Here are some:

• *Mistakes in spelling*, including the spelling of people's names and the names of places. Particular words may not be in your computer's dictionary. Always check.

• *Errors of grammar*. This is a big subject; and the scope for making grammatical mistakes is enormous. Amongst the commonest mistakes are:

  ○ subject and verb not agreeing (e.g. 'A number of cars were on the road')

  ○ more than one main verb in a sentence. (The following example is taken directly from the official form used to compile the Register of Electors: 'This form is for the property below, if you intend to move before 10 October, please leave it for the incoming people.' There should have been a full-stop after 'below'.)

  ○ sentences that are so long that the reader becomes confused, and maybe even the writer has lost the train of thought.

• *Wrong use of words*. A best-selling author, in a recent book, referred to one of the characters 'kneeling on a cassock' in church (when he meant 'hassock'). It is sensible to use a dictionary if we have doubts about the meaning of a word.

• *Groups of words that are ambiguous*, or at least whose meaning may not be quite as clear to the reader as intended. The problems presented by the two examples below will be apparent, especially if you are in a pedantic frame of mind!

From a public park near Manchester:

```
UNDER 5s
CYCLING
ONLY
```

(Are the under-5s not allowed to walk or run?)

From outside a historic house open to the public:

```
LARGE FAMILY
CAR PARK
```

(What is large: the family, or the car, or the car park?)

• *Errors of fact*, including dates, times, distances, sizes and, of course, names of people and places.

As we have seen, software is widely available to help writers catch spelling mistakes and to raise doubts about possible lapses of grammar. Such software, though, would not help with the wording of the notices above, where the drafter has been so keen to save a word or two that the sense has become unclear.

In the next chapter, we consider how the clear accurate text of a document you have drafted can be presented in the most effective way.

Chapter 1.4 Styles of presenting information

In this chapter we consider the styles in which information can be presented to meet the needs of business.

In Unit 2 we shall study the information requirements of businesses, what information has to flow internally and externally, and the forms which it can take.

Scope for choosing styles

The main purpose of this chapter is to show the wide range of choices open to anyone setting out information in a document. We are concerned here with the **appearance** of a completed document, ready for despatch. We shall look in turn at each of the following aspects of appearance, noting that some of these aspects affect the convenience of handling and studying the document:

* page layout

* binding

* cover sheets

* textual styles

* paragraph formats

* graphics.

You should realise that this wealth of choices is unlikely to be open to you in any future place of work, because every organisation has its own **standards** for setting out correspondence, reports, accounts and, perhaps, for the design of screen layouts. These standards form part of the **house style** developed and reinforced and guarded by all organisations, to give each its distinctive identity.

If you look at any book or newspaper you will see that a house style is employed to suit the intended readership, and to provide consistency in each case. In magazines the style is less apparent, and may well vary from page to page: but if you examine successive issues of a particular magazine you will see that there is a pattern to the style and layout; and you can be sure that it was reached after much deliberation.

You will have opportunities for selecting your own style for the assignments you tackle on this Advanced VCE programme. You will find interest in discovering what scope there is for choosing the style of documents, and that the facilities described below can be activated through modern word-processing software. If you need to carry out page design that has special requirements, beyond those covered here, you may need to turn to **desktop publishing (DTP)** software.

Page layout

Paper size and shape. We might first note that the page of a document does not have to be A4, although that size (297 mm × 210 mm) is overwhelmingly the most popular throughout UK and the rest of Europe. There would have to be a fairly compelling reason for selecting something different, apart from envelopes for folded A4 sheets known as 'DL' size (around 225 mm × 112 mm), which are accepted by many computer printers.

The size of stationery commonly used for business correspondence in the United States is somewhat squarer than A4 and is called American Quarto. The '**Page Setup**' dialogue box in Microsoft Word offers several standard paper sizes.

Orientation. Next, the page does not need to have the long edge running up and down the body of the text, with the shorter edge running across it, although that is usual. This arrangement, which is known as **portrait** page orientation, is in contrast to **landscape** orientation in which the pages lie with the long edge parallel to the lines of text.

Many printers, which have to have their paper fed in with portrait orientation, are nonetheless able to print lines of characters laid out to be read in landscape orientation.

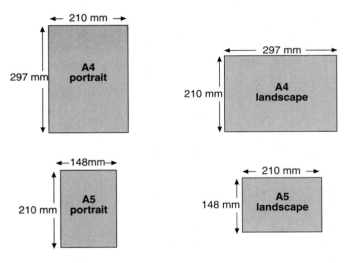

Figure 1.11 A4 and A5 sheets on portrait and landscape orientation

Margins. The margins at the sides and at top and bottom of the page can be set as desired, and all can be different. Wider side margins make for shorter lines of print, which may be easier to read; and a wide margin on the side of a page which is to be bound may prevent part of the text being hard, or even impossible, to read.

A page of text usually looks its best if the top and bottom margins are of equal depth, and the left and right margins are the same width as each other, but see what is said below about adjustments for the choice of binding. In general, and other things being equal, the wider the margins the greater the number of pages a given document will need.

You may wish to make margins narrower than usual in order to be able to display a table without breaking it, or to give space to fit the last line of a paragraph.

Pagination. This word simply means the numbering of pages. Any document of more than one page should have the pages numbered; and the numbering ought to be done by the word-processor, not the author or keyboard operator.

You can put the page numbers wherever you want, but most writers have them clear of the text, centred above the top line or below the lowest line.

Headers and footers. A header is a string of words that runs along the top of each page. It can, for example, carry the name of the document, the author's name, the date of drafting and, unless you have made other arrangements, the page number.

A footer is the same sort of thing, but at the bottom of each page. You do not necessarily want both headers and footers. Perhaps you do not want to have either, but if you do you can set them up in Word with the 'Header and Footer' command. Choose 'View'→'Header and Footer'.

Location of special details

On official business documents, and especially on letters going to other organisations, the presentation of detailed information must be given thought and must be consistent, because every such document has the power to reinforce or diminish the impact of the house style.

These are the main items to be considered and placed on the page:

- the addressee's name and address

- the names and addresses of any addressees to be sent copies

- the sender's logo, address, telephone number, fax number, VAT registration number, company registration number, e-mail address and web site address

- the date

- reference to previous correspondence

- the subject of the document

- the name and position of the person signing the document.

| **Try it out** | Find some letters from business firms, look through them to see how these items of information have been arranged. Consider the items collectively and gauge what impact they had on you. Could you have come up with a better layout? |
| | Draw up a checklist of what you should look for when assessing the layout of a document. |

Binding

The form of **binding** used for a document affects the ease with which the document can be read, the cost of producing copies of the document, the ease of storing copies, and how the pages are laid out. The four

most popular ways of binding business documents are:

- **Spring bound**, in which the pages are slotted to take the tines of a cylindrical spine made of plastic or metal. An advantage of spring binding is that in use the document can be opened out flat and the whole surface of a pair of facing pages can be seen without distortion. For this reason such documents are likely to last better than those bound in other ways, and the difficulty of manipulating the spine by hand makes the contents fairly secure.

- **Ring bound**, in which holes are punched in one edge of each page so that the pages can be held on metal rings. Standard ring binders have two rings or four or, occasionally, three: two are usually favoured because four-hole and three-hole punches are less common and more expensive than two-hole punches.

  Like spring bound documents, pairs of facing pages can be opened out flat; but the pages are less secure because the ease of opening the rings allows pages to fall out or be taken out; and the greater strain on the paper of the pages, because of the small number of anchorage points, means that there is more risk of pages becoming torn.

  Ring-bound documents are almost sure to occupy more shelf space than spring-bound documents because ring binders are made in only a small number of different sizes: in general, there will be spare, unused capacity in each binder.

- **Slide spine bound**. This is a technique of slipping a springy plastic, U-section spine over the edge of the document to hold the pages. A drawback of this method of binding is that the pages cannot be opened out flat, so the margins next to the spine – the right hand margin on a left hand page and *vice versa* – have to be wide enough in every case to allow the reader to see everything that matters. The area of a pair of facing pages that disappears into the binding is known as the **gutter**.

Pages of documents bound this way tend to fall out too easily. The offsetting advantages are low cost and relative ease of adding and removing pages.

- **Perfect binding** is the name given to the process of gluing pages of a document into a wrap-round cover, to give the feel and appearance of a book. This is an expensive process, as each page has to be notched before the glue is applied in order to hold the pages into the cover. Planning a perfect-bound book requires that allowance be made for the gutter. Removal of pages is not possible so this type of binding is reserved for bulky documents which may have to last a long time.

Cover sheets

Your tutor will probably ask you to fasten a **cover sheet** to the front of written work you submit. Cover sheets are useful in identifying the student and the piece of work, and also for recording the documents' progress through the assessment and verification processes.

A typical cover sheet will have places to put most or all of the following:

- student name
- student class or group
- the Advanced VCE qualification title
- the number of the compulsory unit
- the number of the assignment to which

the cover sheet relates, with issue date and the submission date that has been set

- the assessor's comments, including detail of any further work needed to satisfy the requirement, and date
- provisional, or indicative, grade given by the assessor, and date
- key skills criteria met, and date
- comments by the internal verifier, and date.

Textual styles

Here are some rather confusing definitions: a **typeface** is defined as a 'set of types in one design'; a **face** is the part of the type that takes the ink; and a **font** is a set of type of the same face and size. The definitions are confusing because they originate in old-fashioned typesetting methods.

The word-processing scene has altered the meanings, and simplified the usage, of these words, making **font** cover both the style of the face and the size chosen for it for a given job. Thus, for instance, the font 'Times New Roman 14' has come to mean a *point size of 14* in a face called *Times New Roman*. **A point** in 'point size' is one-72nd of an inch in height: '12 point' is therefore one-6th of an inch high.

The choice of font has a great bearing on the **feel** of a document. Newspapers devote much care to the font they select as standard.

Word-processors offer a large number of fonts from which to choose; and further, different font sets are available separately. Some of those provided by Microsoft Word are shown below:

This is Arial

This is Arial Narrow

This is Courier

This is Garamond

This is Times New Roman

THIS IS CASLON OLD STYLE

This is Univers

This is Impact

Tηισ ισ Σψμβολ (This is Symbol)

You will see that in this small selection of fonts there are differences in weight and feel. You will also note that, ignoring the two rather unusual fonts at the foot of the list, two of the fonts, Arial and Univers, do not have tails, known as **serifs,** on any of their letters. Such fonts are called **sans-serif** fonts. Motorway direction signs and railway station name signs use sans-serif fonts because the designers believe them to be clearer.

For continuous text most readers prefer a serif face, so for your assignments choose a serif typeface that is large and clear: 12-point is easier to read than 10-point.

Try it out	Explore the range of fonts provided by your word-processor and pick the ones you would choose for: (a) writing a letter to a prospective employer, who runs a bicycle repair business, for a part-time job, and (b) creating a poster for a Valentine's Night disco.

Apart from the particular font you choose, there are other facilities you can use to make your text clearer or more interesting or just more pleasing on the eye.

Emphasis

Words, phrases or sentences can be emphasised by:

Printing in bold
Printing in italic
Printing in bold and italic together
<u>Underlining</u>
<u>Underlining in bold</u>
<u>Underlining italic</u>
<u>Underlining in bold and italic together</u>.

You can also make your text bold by selecting a bold font.

Queen Victoria used underlining extensively in her letters, but you should be sparing with it or even decide against ever using it. This is because underlining can easily become self-defeating by inducing emphasis-weariness in the reader.

Superscript and subscript

Superscript text sits above the line, and is smaller, thus:

$$2^{10} = 1024$$

You access this in Word by pressing <Ctrl>+<Shift>+<=>

Subscript text sits below the line, and is smaller, thus:

$$H_2O = \text{water}$$

You access this in Word by pressing <Ctrl>+<=>

Headings and titles

In the first flush of excitement at getting word-processing software to do your bidding you will be tempted to experiment with a wide range of fonts for your headings and titles. The work will look far more professional if you exercise restraint!

Once the structure of your document is clear you can decide on how many layers of main headings, secondary headings, cross-headings and paragraph headings you need. You probably do not need more than four levels. Then you can decide on the font to be used, and the point size. Have a look at the way this book is laid out, and you will see that simplicity and consistency are the aims, as they should be in any document you produce.

There are software facilities in Microsoft Word that offer you built-in heading styles for your document's different levels. You can change the standard heading styles to suit your own needs. You may also feel that your headings should be in a different typeface from the body text.

Sometimes you will feel the need to number the individual items in some list, perhaps because you have to refer to particular items from elsewhere in the text. That is fine; but you should not number items just for the sake of it. You would do better to mark the start of each item with a **bullet point**. Choose '**Format**'→'**Bullets and Numbering**'.

Some organisations, especially some in government, number every paragraph. You should avoid this practice unless there is a clear need for it.

Animation

Current technology allows designers and programmers to provide animated displays on screen. Typically these are eye-catching, but they can be tiring and even annoying. A good rule is to avoid animation except where it is needed to illustrate, for example, a flow of materials or products on a conveyor system in a schematic layout of a factory.

Paragraph formats

In planning the layout of a document you need to remember the control you have over the shape of your paragraphs. This is entirely apart from how long you make each paragraph. Most students make their paragraphs too long, certainly at first. If in doubt about the length that gives greatest clarity to the thoughts you want to express, have a look at the lead story in a tabloid newspaper; but do not try to compete with its editor!

Having got the length right, these are the features you can fix for yourself:

- **Widows and orphans**. These arise on a printed page at a page break. A **widow** occurs when only the first line of a paragraph is printed at the bottom of a page, with the remainder of the text printed at the top of the next page. An **orphan** occurs when all but the last line of a paragraph is printed at the bottom of a page, and just the last line is printed at the top of the next page.

Most word-processors have a facility which, if selected, can prevent widows and orphans from arising. A widow is prevented by inserting extra space at the bottom of a page, so that the whole paragraph then starts on a new page. An orphan is prevented by breaking the paragraph across the two pages one or more lines earlier, so that at least two lines at the end of the paragraph are printed at the top of the following page.

Some word-processors have a facility which, if selected, will reduce the point size automatically so that widows and orphans are avoided. This must be used with care because a document with a range of point sizes can look very odd.

- **Justification**. You can have your work left-justified, or right-justified (but probably only rarely), or fully-justified. Earlier we pointed out that the legibility of your text is likely to be greater if it is not fully justified: the shorter the lines, the truer this will be.

> To show what we mean these three lines are left-justified, leaving a ragged edge on the right-hand end of the paragraph...

> whereas these lines are right-justified, allowing the left-hand edge to be ragged, or even very jagged, presenting the reader with a slightly uncomfortable format for reading normal text.

> And this is the effect of fully justifying the lines of the paragraph, one aspect of which is discussed immediately below. You can see the result of the full justification in the uneven spaces between the words in the different lines.

If you do want to justify your text fully you can consider using automatic **hyphenation** to reduce the crowding of characters where it occurs, though most people resist doing so as hyphenation itself slows down the reading process, especially if the software chooses odd places to split the words.

- **Paragraph spacing**. There are conventions for the space to be allowed between paragraphs, but you do not necessarily have to follow them. Modern practice is to leave one clear line of space between paragraphs; and, unlike many people's handwriting, it is unusual to indent the first line of a new paragraph.

- **Line spacing**. The spacing can be determined from the keyboard. You might want to give a more open appearance to your text for any one of several reasons. It can be convenient, for example, for editors who want to be free to amend your draft and have plenty of space for their annotations.

  For $1^1/_2$-line spacing use $<Ctrl>+<5>$
  For double-line spacing use $<Ctrl>+<2>$.

- **Tabulation**. The default settings of the **tab stops** in your word-processing software are probably at half-inch intervals, but you can reset them to suit your needs.

  Careful positioning of the tab stops when you have lists or columns to handle can add greatly to the attractiveness of your document.

  The ruler at the top of your screen tells you where tab stops are currently set. You can set extra tabs, and you can do more complicated things with tabs, by working with the 'Tabs' dialog box, reached by choosing '**Format**'→'**Tabs**'.

Try it out	You should now give your word-processing software some exercise! Select, or write, a block of text of about 100 words. See how it looks as you: - change the margins - change the font – typeface and point size - change the line spacing - change the justification. Try to make your text take up the form of an isosceles triangle.

Graphics

Under this heading we shall look at some of the features available to you for drawing attention to certain parts of your text, and for the inclusion of graphical images in your document.

> One handy way of making your heading or one of your paragraphs stand out is to put it in a box. There are many styles of border.

An alternative is to provide a shaded background for it. Again you could use this technique for making headings stand out.

In Word select '**Format**' → '**Borders and Shading**' for the options.

If you do not want to highlight a title or paragraph in either of these ways you can change the margin widths for the occasion, and restore them afterwards.

Let us now turn to the inclusion of graphical images in your document. You can use a variety of types of graphic to improve the presentation of your documents, including the following.

The use of graphic lines

These are usually called **rules.** They are normally horizontal lines, though occasionally vertical lines, which separate areas of the page or areas of text. It is common to have a page's header or footer separated from the body of the text by a rule.

The use of drawings, pictures and 'clip art'

Drawings and pictures often enhance a presentation or a document, following the dictum that a picture is worth a thousand words. Drawings are sometimes called **line art**, to emphasise the fact that they are mainly constructed from lines and geometrical shapes.

Pictures and photographic images generally use shades of grey and shades of colour to represent the objects they show. **Clip art** is a term given to digital images – drawings and pictures – supplied within a word-processing package: they are usually simple and cartoon-like.

You will find it useful to become familiar with **downloading** text and pictures of all kinds from the Internet.

Figure 1.12 Examples of clip art

Scanned images

A **scanner** is a device which converts 'normal' drawings and pictures on paper, or photographs, into digital images for inclusion in a document. Remember to check whether there are any **copyright restrictions** on scanning images that you did not personally create.

Unit 1 Assessment

This assignment is based on the Festivities Unlimited, or FUN, case study described in the general Introduction on pages xiii and xiv.

Scenario

The local paper covering the area where FUN has its offices, called *The Fulham Flier*, is shortly to carry a supplement about local businesses. The editor has invited FUN to supply material so that their business can be featured.

The partners of FUN are keen to derive as much benefit as possible from this opportunity to get publicity. They decide to produce a document which gives an overall account of their markets, products and services, and plans of the organisation, as briefing for the person assembling the supplement.

They also decide to try and find out what their clients like and dislike about their commercial operations, so that favourable statistics can be incorporated in the document to be prepared for the paper.

In addition FUN will be taking advertising space in the same issue of *The Fulham Flier* for prestige promotion and to announce a special offer.

The copy date for the issue that is to carry the local business supplement is in three weeks' time.

Your tasks

1 Your most urgent task is to design and produce a word-processed questionnaire that will aim at finding out what FUN's 50 most important clients think of the business. The questionnaire must have at least 12 questions, some of which are to be open questions. You need to have the responses in time to consolidate them for inclusion in the main document you will be creating.

You must imagine a plausible range of responses to your questionnaire, and display them graphically, using pie charts and bar charts appropriately.

2 Next, construct the main document for *The Fulham Flier*. Its length should be three or four A4 pages. It must cover, in whatever order you think best:

- FUN's trading history

- descriptions of services and products currently offered, with typical prices

- the business aims of FUN

- thumbnail word sketches of typical clients

- thumbnail word sketches of a selection of partners and employees

- the results of the recent survey into client perceptions of the business, suitably displayed

- FUN's logo, if you have one, and details of address, telephone number, fax number, e-mail number, and web site address.

In preparing this document you should choose styles of presentation that allow the journalist assigned to the job to understand as easily as possible what the highlights of FUN are. If you are able to draft the document in such a way that parts of it can be fitted into the supplement without much editing you will be likely to enjoy good coverage in the paper. Remember to use lines, borders, and shading where you feel doing so will help.

3 Finally, prepare the advertisement, which is to be A5 size, portrait orientation, when printed in the paper. It will be carried at the bottom right-hand corner of the front page. The advertisement has two purposes:

- to tell readers about FUN and its activities, in a general way, and

- to describe a special offer.

You must decide the scope and timing of the offer, and whether or not to take up space in the advertisement with a cut-out coupon.

Remember that you will be competing with other parts of the paper for the attention of readers. You need to think about layout, graphics, styles of writing and font, and what to say and what to leave out, in order to make the advertisement work for you as effectively as possible.

This unit is divided into the following chapters.

- Chapter 2.1 Characteristics of organisations

- Chapter 2.2 Internal functions and external relationships

- Chapter 2.3 The use of information in organisations

The unit ends with a sample assignment. Although this unit will be assessed externally you might like to work through the sample assignment in advance as practice. It can help you accumulate evidence for the key skills units that you may want to achieve.

Chapter 2.1 looks at the different kinds of organisations found in the UK, and identifies categories of organisation based on their main operational objectives, ownership, and size; and it relates types of management structure to the nature of the activities being carried out.

There are many forms of organisation. This Advanced VCE is concerned in the main with organisations for which ICT can make a useful impact: these are predominantly companies engaged in some kind of business. We therefore use the words 'company' and 'business' from this point onward, regardless of their exact legal form and their range of operations.

Chapter 2.2 looks at the internal functions existing in most companies, distinguishing between manufacturing and service businesses: and it reviews the external relationships companies may have to have in order to sustain their operations and to meet the demands of the law.

Chapter 2.3 considers how the assembly, processing and flow of information supports a company's internal and external functions. We look at the methods of handling information adopted by companies in different industries. We also look at management information systems.

There are no rules to say what the organisational structure of a company shall be. When a company is young its structure and its procedures are likely to reflect the personality and the wishes of the founder, and also the particular portfolio of experience, skills and ability that he or she brings to bear. That founder, or founders if there were more than one, will have had a vision of what the company should set out to do and of how it would try to do it. That is the way in which many, or perhaps most, new businesses start.

Companies that have been operating for a number of years may have lost the original entrepreneurial spark, for any one of many possible reasons. Managers on salary will probably have taken the place of the risk-taking individual who started the firm. The needs of customers and the effects of competitors will increasingly influence the products, procedures, and structure of any company.

If a company prospers it may repeatedly feel the need to change its shape, for example by establishing branches around the country; developing an export operation; or building trading relationships with businesses in related fields, as well as with its own suppliers and customers. If it grows into a substantial enterprise it will have to take note of the size and economic performance of the sector of the economy in which it is becoming more dominant and make adjustments to its structure if it sees fit to do so.

Strong companies stay strong by being responsive to external changes and by reacting quickly to them: their staff soon become accustomed to frequent reorganisations. There are thus ample reasons why company structures and procedures vary as greatly as they do.

Try it out	Look around the high street for businesses you respect, and see if you can learn anything about their trading history, organisational structure and, generally, how they carry on their activities. Use all this information to form a view on why they are successful.

Chapter 2.1 Characteristics of organisations

The purpose of this chapter is to start you thinking about the huge number of different ways in which organisations exist and operate. You will see at once that there is danger in generalising about any aspect of organisations.

Information and communication technology (ICT) plays an important part in the running of any organisation, but to be fully effective ICT systems must support the business aims of an organisation by being tailored to suit the organisational structure and business goals in each case.

An **organisation** can be defined as any individual or, more commonly, any group of individuals, working in a structured way to accomplish specified tasks or results. This is a very broad definition: you will see that it covers, at one extreme, a youngster who offers to valet cars part-time, and at the other extreme a multinational corporation producing a wide range of goods and services.

Let us look first at the main categories of organisation to be found. Then, concentrating just on commercial organisations, which make up the vast majority of all organisations, we shall consider:

- who their customers are

- who owns them

- what their modes of operation can be

- what forms their organisational structure can take

- how they are financed.

Main types of organisation

There are three sorts of organisation, namely commercial, public service and charitable.

Commercial organisation

A commercial organisation is one that has as its aim some form of trading intended to yield profit for the owners. We refer to a commercial organisation as a 'company' from now on, even though some commercial organisations exist in other forms.

A company derives its income from selling or hiring products or services to its customers. If it is to prosper its income must exceed its costs, and there must be surplus to pay for growth.

Companies operate in a **market** where there is competition between firms following the same line of business: the more successful ones generally flourish at the expense of the less successful. For example, travel agents in most cases offer similar services and so compete directly with one another. Those that do well will tend over a period to eliminate the others. The same is true of building societies, shoe shops, and any of a great variety of businesses.

Public service organisation

Public service organisations are bodies that operate under some kind of political control. They include national government departments, publicly owned agencies, local authorities, and international bodies such as the European Commission, the World Trade Organisation, and NATO. Most schools, nearly all colleges and universities, and most hospitals, are public service organisations: they are said to lie in the **public sector.**

Public sector organisations generally are not businesses, and do not seek to make profits, though some are required to raise money. In the UK, for example, the Inland Revenue is responsible for collecting personal and business tax, HM Customs & Excise for collecting value added tax (VAT) and various kinds of duty, and local authorities for collecting council tax and rents for local authority flats and houses. Post offices are businesses, and local authorities offer a few services which are expected to break even or, over the long term, to generate profit.

These public service organisations mostly operate only in the UK, and do so as monopolies: they therefore do not have to face competition.

Charitable organisations

Charitable organisations, of which there are thousands, are each dedicated to work for a specified charitable cause. They are not businesses, and they do not set out to make profits. The largest charities, such as Save the Children, The National Trust and Oxfam, are well known: you will probably be able to think of several more. Charities are regulated by law and have little freedom to vary the form of their operation.

Public service organisations and charities do not have to make profits, but they do still have to make the best use they can of their resources and to work as efficiently as possible. We often see and hear of schools and hospitals trying to reduce their costs by raising their efficiency: and charities make a

virtue of the small proportion of their income that they devote to internal administration. The greater the efficiency of their operations and administration, the more resources a public service organisation has, whether for NHS patient care or reducing class sizes in schools or helping the destitute or making an impact on thousands of other worthwhile public sector projects.

Try it out	Spend a few moments looking around at the organisations that you or your family use, and see whether you can identify their characteristics. You may be surprised at how wide the range is.

For the rest of this chapter we shall limit the discussion to companies.

Companies

Companies are often launched, or **incorporated** to use the proper word, by an individual we shall call the **founder.** The founder will have had a vision of the kind of business to be started; and the founder's instincts, experience and personality will determine the structure, the method of trading, and the initial location.

If the company prospers the founder is likely to leave after some years, the entrepreneurial flair and energy being replaced by the skills of salaried managers who will then be running the company. Procedures and structure become more formal and reflect less the strengths of the founder.

Should the company continue to grow it will increasingly have to take note of its share of the total UK market for its goods and services, the possibility of exporting, the advantages of diversifying into related fields, the question of building business links with other companies, or of acquiring some.

The Coca-Cola example below describes some of the growth achievements of that company, which has been outstandingly successful.

Customers

The first characteristic of a company we shall look at is its body of **customers**, because customers are the essence of the business carried on by any company.

Think it over

When you are frustrated by having to wait ages to board a plane or buy a stamp or pay for your purchases at a supermarket, it is hard to remember that earning and holding onto the loyalty of each customer is enormously important to every company.

Trading income comes from customers who buy or hire products or services. The population of customers built up by a company is called its **customer base.** The size and suitability of a company's customer base is always a key factor in determining the company's commercial health.

Case study: Coca-Cola

The supreme example of building up and supplying a customer base is Coca-Cola. The Coca-Cola products, taken together, make up the most successful offering in the history of commercial organisations.

The syrup for the original drink was first produced in the United States early in 1886 by a pharmacist, Dr John Styth Pemberton, who took samples to his local chemist shop where it sold at five cents a glass. One day he tried mixing the syrup with soda and found sales increased. Soon he started advertising the drink, and sales grew further.

In 1916 the company by then running the Coca-Cola business designed and started using the now distinctive contoured bottle, providing a further boost for sales, soon overtaking the demand for soda fountain drinks.

By 1929 there were 64 Coca-Cola bottling stations at work in 28 countries. The principle that the business rated above all others was the control it exercised over quality. No matter where a glass or beaker of Coca-Cola was bought, the taste would be the same.

Great store was placed on advertising, and sales continued to expand. Bottles of different sizes were introduced in 1955, but never content to trust to present sales the company introduced new soft drinks, including Fanta, Sprite, and TAB, its first low-calorie product.

In 1988 a worldwide survey declared that Coca-Cola was the best-known, and also the most admired, trademark in the world. A US national magazine stated that 'Coca-Cola is so powerful it's practically off the charts.' In a hundred years Coca-Cola had grown from an idea into a commercial empire with a place confirmed in history, selling almost half the soft drinks consumed in the world.

Customers are sometimes known by other names. Those buying services, as distinct from products, are usually called **clients**, though for some services they can be **patients.** Train operating companies like to refer to their passengers as **customers**, to emphasise their business-like approach to what they do. Hotels call their customers **guests.**

Customers consist of both individuals and other companies. For example, a car maker sells about two-thirds of its output to fleet buyers who are able to place large orders and negotiate advantageous discount and delivery terms. Makers of aero engines have only business customers, whereas a service business like hairdressing relies, except in a few cases, on individual customers.

Any business that uses distributors or wholesalers to feed the retailers who sell to the ultimate purchaser has those first links in the distribution chain as its principal customers. Examples are book publishers, suppliers of frozen foods, and manufacturers of clothing for whom their distributors are prime customers.

Several large companies have their own distribution organisations allowing them to exercise complete control over the delivery process and probably save costs: the names on the vehicles fulfilling this function tell us what sort of arrangement is in use. Some distribution companies own some of the retailers they supply; and some, like SPAR, offer the benefits of scale provided by bulk buying.

Ownership

Businesses have owners. There are three sorts of ownership, outside the public sector.

Sole traders. The young person mentioned above who valets cars as an independent part-time job is a sole trader; but so is any individual who elects to carry on business alone, possibly on a substantial scale and possibly engaging many assistants or contractors to help with the work. A sole trader is characterised by having to take responsibility for every aspect of the business, accepting the liabilities such as tax, and by meeting the costs of the business personally.

If you look around your own neighbourhood you will find many examples of sole traders, such as a greengrocer, a painter and decorator, a mobile hairdresser, a newsagent.

Partnerships. Some businesses, especially businesses carried on by professional people, usually operate as partnerships. Solicitors, accountants and stockbrokers often choose to work in this way; but so occasionally do industrial concerns. The individuals forming a partnership enter into a **partnership agreement** with each other. Such agreements have to cover the financial issues that arise when a new partner joins the partnership, when a partner retires, and when additional money is needed in the business.

The conduct of partnerships is governed by law, though from time to time there are changes in the law, for instance in relation to partnerships owning other businesses, taxation, and advertising.

Companies. Most companies are **limited companies**, meaning that unlike partnerships the risks (or liabilities) carried by the members of the company cannot exceed known amounts. **Members,** in this context, means the shareholders. This is in contrast to the unlimited liability carried by sole traders and the partners in a partnership.

Companies are regulated by law, by the Companies Acts. The terms of the legislation require companies to set out their aims; the law prescribes the rules about raising money, and share ownership; and requires that the directors are named. Companies are owned by the shareholders who can appoint directors and who, at least theoretically, enjoy many other powers.

The shareholders that own a company can include another company; or one company can be wholly-owned by another; or there can be a 'joint venture in which two companies together own a third. There are endless possibilities. The essential point is that the shareholders, whether they are individuals or other companies, have invested in a company in the expectation, or at least the hope, of getting a worthwhile return on that investment.

Large companies are likely to be **public limited companies (plcs)**. There are further laws within which they must operate. Large British companies usually choose to be quoted on the London Stock Exchange so that there is a convenient, that is *orderly*, market in their shares, and a mechanism for raising additional capital. They may also seek quotation on other stock exchanges such as the New York Stock Exchange or the exchanges at Tokyo or Frankfurt; or they may wish to be quoted on a specialist exchange such as Nasdaq.

Modes of operation

In this book, we are interested in the way in which ICT supports the various sorts of activity that companies carry out. ICT is expensive to provide: it has to make a contribution that is worth more than it costs. As the technology develops there are more and more ways for ICT to help businesses in distinctive cost-effective ways.

ICT systems become ever more crucial to the successful operation of organisations.

One accepted way of categorising businesses is according to which of these sectors their operations fall into: the primary, secondary, tertiary, or quaternary sector.

Primary sector. The primary sector consists of activities devoted to acquiring natural resources. It thus includes farming, forestry, mineral extraction, and commercial fishing.

Secondary sector. The secondary sector consists of activities which add value to natural resources or to products which have themselves been developed from natural resources. This definition covers all forms of manufacturing.

Tertiary sector. The tertiary sector consists of activities that are aimed at providing established services. It includes education, health care services, distribution and retailing, banking and other financial services, legal and other professional services, tourism, and transport services.

Quaternary sector. The quaternary sector consists of the operations of new

Did you know?

Patients' medical details may soon be held on smart-cards to be used with a mobile system for GP treatment in the home. Doctors will be able to access the encrypted information with a smart-card reader, and print it. Development of this facility in UK follows successful trials in France and Germany.

This proposal is itself under threat because one of the main expected uses of smart-cards has not materialised: the idea of a one-card society has been overtaken by the lightning-fast advance of e-commerce which may mean that the promoters of smart-card technology, and manufacturers of the associated devices for reading smart-cards, will abandon this endeavour.

information-based services, including the Internet, mobile phone networks, satellite communications systems, and space travel.

Organisations, even quite small ones, can operate in more than one of these sectors. For example, FUN has secondary sector activity in preparing food products, and tertiary sector activity in promoting and providing its catering and entertainment services.

In whichever of the four sectors the operations of a company lie there are ways, discussed below, for ICT to support them. First we point out that there are two important trends within these sectors which affect the impact ICT can make and that you should notice:

- The numbers of employees is shifting from the primary sector towards the other sectors. Sixty years ago there were a million coal miners working in deep pits in UK: now there are only a few. The offshore oil industry had a much larger workforce in its early days of intensive exploration than it has now. In 1850 agriculture accounted for half the population of UK: today it is less than 3%; and 55% work in offices. Deep-sea fishing operations have had to shrink severely in recent years.

  Growth in the other sectors is occurring continuously.

- In relation to the numbers employed, the scale and complexity of the ICT support is also less in the primary sector than in the other sectors, being greatest in the quaternary sector.

All companies operate commercially and therefore have certain needs in common, most or all of which can be met by the use of ICT. These include the running of their payroll and accounting systems, the administration of human resources, planning and budgeting, booking and enquiry systems, and other office work. These computer tasks are **administrative** applications, characterised by the management of files and databases, the routine processing of transactions such as purchase orders, the printing of documents such as invoices and standard letters; and the vital need to keep historical records.

In addition, many companies rely on ICT to handle industrial applications. These companies are to be found in all the four sectors described above. Here are some examples of industrial applications:

- In the primary sector: logging and interpretation of survey data for oil exploration, control of mining equipment, control of the environment in a commercial greenhouse.

- In the secondary sector: the operation of numerically controlled machines and conveyor systems in factories, automatic product research and testing equipment, and automatic selection and packaging equipment.

- In the tertiary sector: air traffic control and navigation systems, medical scanning and x-ray equipment, intruder alarm systems, a range of financial service systems which contain procedures that can intervene automatically in the processing.

- In the quaternary sector: the automatic management of mobile phone networks, and the control and monitoring of the many development processes taking place.

These industrial applications involve processes of measurement and control. They are explored comprehensively in Optional Unit 11 (Computers in Manufacturing) and Option Unit 21 (Data-logging, Computer Control and Robotics).

Try it out	Look around at the businesses in your home area and identify the sectors in which they are operating. For some of those businesses there will have to be activities taking place out of sight to allow them to operate successfully. See whether you can work out what these are.

Organisational structure

Every organisation needs to have a structure or there would be chaos!

Some functions are sure to be needed in every company: they are management control, purchasing, operations, marketing and selling, and administration. The emphasis placed on each will depend on the nature of the business. There may also be need for research and engineering. These functions are often carried out by **divisions** or **departments** in a company, each becoming the centre of expertise for one of the functions. In Chapter 2.2 we shall see how functions work together, and what relationships they need to maintain with outside organisations; and in Chapter 2.3 what communications need to pass between them, both inside the company and externally.

The word 'operations' used in the paragraph above needs to be interpreted rather broadly. It includes *production* as it would appear in a manufacturing context; but also in a service business like, say, banking it embraces the creation of the services offered to clients or customers.

The organisational structure of a company is necessarily complicated where the business operates in several countries, each with its own laws, currency, and language; and perhaps using partly-owned subsidiary companies. Putting this complexity to one side, let us consider the structure of a medium-sized manufacturing business in UK. It might look like Figure 2.1.

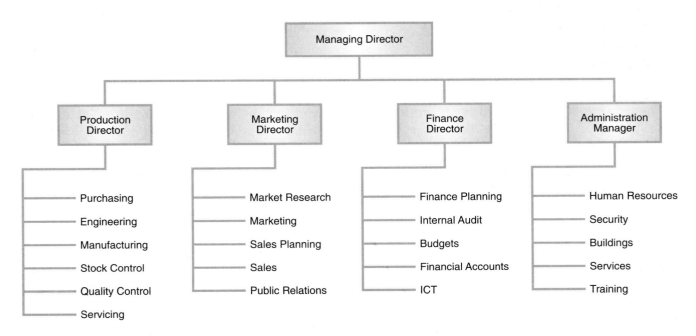

Figure 2.1 Organisational structure of a typical medium-sized manufacturing company

In the general Introduction there is the corresponding chart for the case study business, Festivities Unlimited. It is much simpler and therefore less vulnerable to misunderstanding; and in that firm everyone knows everyone.

For companies of all sizes the case for drawing up and distributing up-to-date organisation charts is strong. They should provide clear statements of relationships and responsibilities, helping companies avoid the troubles arising from lack of clarity. Everyone has to know who is responsible for what.

In Figure 2.1, you will see that the managing director has four staff reporting to him or her. There is a similar pattern of reporting at successive levels in the business. There are, however, no rules about the numbers reporting at each level.

Type of organisational structure	Advantages	Disadvantages
Hierarchical	Easier definition of roles and responsibilities	May hamper the assembly of special-purpose, *ad hoc*, teams
	Greater scope for developing expertise	Likely to encourage set ways of behaviour
	More frequent opportunities for promotion	May impede decision-making
Flat	May encourage personal development and display of initiative	Consequences of an individual leaving at short notice could be serious
	Possibly greater responsiveness to unforeseen events	Likely to impede the emergence of centres of competence

Figure 2.2 . A comparison of flat and hierarchical organisations

Comment

As an aside, we should mention that the title of managing director, long-established as meaning the director in charge of the day-to-day running of the company, is being supplanted more and more often by the title **chief executive officer** (CEO), which comes to us from the United States. The person in charge of ICT is, by the same token, becoming the **chief information officer** (CIO).

In a structure where there are few levels, the arrangement it is said to be a **flat organisation**; where there are many levels it is said to be **hierarchical**. Neither is right or wrong, but they do have different characteristics which affect the conduct of business and also the way in which ICT systems can best support the business.

Figure 2.2, shows how working relationships in a company will be affected by the type of structure. If it is too flat managers can be over-stretched and employees may not receive enough guidance. If it is too deep the corporate decision-making process may become ponderous, which could be a serious drawback in a fast-moving commercial environment.

One effect of the use of computers to distil and distribute information inside companies has been to reduce the work load of middle managers, and therefore to encourage a flattening of structures, thereby reducing costs.

Try it out	As a group, brainstorm and draw up a list of some kinds of business that might benefit from a flat organisational structure, and another list of some others that might do better with a strongly hierarchical structure.

An organisation chart such as the one in Figure 2.1 usually suggests that relationships and responsibilities are tidier than they really are. Employees are sometimes detached from their regular slot in the structure to perform a special task for a while; others receive guidance, or even direction on certain matters, from a manager who is not in the normal reporting line. Some companies try to cater for departures from the rigorously-defined relationships implied in the organisation chart by drawing up a scheme known as **matrix management** in which lines of responsibility are multiplied. The appointment of **co-ordinators** whose jobs straddle a number of divisions or departments, crossing the boundaries implied by the organisation chart, is popular but can add uncertainty or even confusion.

Promotions and departures make the chart inaccurate, so constant updating is needed.

How companies are financed

Companies need money to be able to operate. If they have factories, warehouses, a fleet of oil tankers or, indeed, any expensive items, they have to obtain the money to buy them or else enter into leasing or renting arrangements. Companies that provide a service such as ICT consultancy or advice probably need to make very little investment; but all companies have to have enough money to pay salaries, wages, rent, and electricity and other regular bills, as well as being able to buy whatever goods they need in order to be able to trade.

Sources of finance

There are two main types of finance: shareholders' funds and loan money. When shareholders buy newly issued **shares** from a company the purchase money goes to the company. Thereafter the value of the shares will fluctuate, but apart from any shares held by the company in its own name the company does not directly benefit from an increase in the share price. However, when the share price goes up the standing of the company rises.

If the shares are quoted on a stock exchange their value is open for all to see; but if they are not quoted the valuation of the shares has to be proposed by an accountant, and then perhaps negotiated.

The shareholders' funds and the loan money together make up the money available to a company, apart from what it earns by its trading. There is therefore always pressure to bring in payments from customers as quickly as possible to protect this money and to make repayment of loan money.

Shareholders' funds are the payments made to a company when it issues and then sells shares. If it wants to increase the amount of money from this source it can make a **rights issue** under which existing shareholders become entitled to bid, at a price below the currently quoted price, for additional shares from a new issue of shares. Recent rights issues made by quoted companies are reported in the national press every day.

The shares in major companies are largely held not by individual investors but by **institutions** including pension funds and unit trusts. This means that control of these companies rests with institutions, who, collectively, can decide matters of corporate policy.

Loan money can come from many sources. When a company first starts the directors may lend money to the business, often at a low rate of interest, occasionally by re-mortgaging their private houses; and a bank overdraft might be arranged. Banks and other commercial lenders always want to know how the loan is to be repaid.

There are **venture capital companies** that specialise in lending money to young companies, especially those in high technology markets. Venture capital companies are themselves businesses keen to flourish. They may sometimes take a shareholding in the company to which they are lending so that if the share price rises they make a capital gain.

Mature companies find borrowing easier than new ones, called **start-up** companies, and rates of interest lower. There are many sources of loan money available to them in the City of London and other major financial centres. Loans can be large, for example to finance the exploration for oil in a place where the sea is deep, cold, and often rough. The finance 'industry' is geared to provide whatever sums of money are needed, subject to appropriate safeguards.

Chapter 2.2 Internal functions and external relationships

In this chapter we look at the functions necessary within a company for it to operate efficiently and legally, and we also look at the more important external relationships maintained by companies. We shall base the topics discussed on a notional medium-sized manufacturing company, pointing out from time to time key differences with larger and smaller enterprises. We assume that the company is made up of departments looking after:

- operations

- marketing

- sales

- research and development

- finance

- administration, including the administration of human resources

- ICT

and that these seven departments are responsible directly to the managing director. The word *operations* covers the activities of manufacturing, or creating services, or in any way providing the company with whatever it offers to sell or rent.

In some companies the ICT department is placed inside the finance or the administration departments; but as the crucial and distinctive contribution that can be made by ICT becomes recognised, companies are more likely to want it to rank with these other departments. To make the issues clearer, we are treating it as if it were already positioned in that way.

The chapter is divided into three parts:

- ICT department functions

- functions of all departments in the company, and their interaction one with another

- functions of external bodies relevant to the company's business, and interactions between them and the company.

ICT department functions

Let us first note that the ICT department represents a substantial cost to its company: one that does not directly generate any income. This is important.

The benefit of having an ICT department lies entirely in the advantages gained for the company by the users of those ICT systems that have been supplied to them by the ICT department. ICT works across all departments and functions of an organisation in a way that no other part of the business does. By **users** we therefore mean all the other departments of the company, and, as individuals, its directors and managers.

It is the successful use of computer-based services that provides the company with its return on the investment it has made in ICT.

The ICT department staff probably think in terms of **systems,** the output of their development projects; whereas the users tend to think in terms of **services.** These are the services that users will employ both to increase the effectiveness of what they provide for their customers, and to improve their own internal operations. For this reason we shall normally use the word 'services' except where we need to focus on the technical nature of the systems that underlie the services.

The benefits that ICT services could provide to the users include:

- improved accuracy, internally and externally

- services to customers that are more comprehensive than before

- faster processing, leading to prompter responses to customers

- information for management, not previously available, or available too late to be useful; and tighter financial control

- new customer services, previously not possible

- new sources of information to allow improved product design and marketing

- reduced costs arising from the greater productivity of staff who are supported and assisted by appropriate computer services

- a more attractive, cleaner working environment in some cases, helping recruitment and the retention of staff.

Comment

There are two ways in which ICT can help departments get the benefits of computer working that they desire: ICT can build or buy in systems for departments to use; or the departments can build their own systems with training, troubleshooting and other help from ICT. Both routes have advantages. What happens in any one business depends on the policy on system development and on the skills in the departments.

The departments of the company will each have a different portfolio of benefits from the company's ICT operations. For example, computer-based stock control systems run by the operations department should reduce the quantity of stock, or **inventory**, without damaging the **level of service** given to customers. This means that less money is tied up in the company's inventory.

Better information for the marketing and sales departments allows marketing to become more effective, and selling to result in more sales.

We shall see below how the flow of information between departments is intended to realise these and many other benefits.

The combined effects of all the benefits for a company are usually impossible to quantify. What is certain is that taken together they improve the company's competitiveness. At the top level the company must believe that the *value* of the benefits exceeds the *costs*; if they did not they would close down the ICT department and buy from an external provider the services they wanted.

All user departments are sure to be calling out continuously for more and more ICT services to let them increase further their effectiveness.

The problem for management is to decide how much to invest in the ICT department. The aim of the company, and therefore of its directors and managers, is to make the value of the benefits exceed the costs by as much as possible. This, of course, is a problem that does not go away. It is one that has to be reviewed often, whenever services are affected by advances in technology and changes in the products and services the company decides to offer.

The directors run the company on behalf of the shareholders, or owners, who have invested in the company. We use the word **investors** to refer to one of the groups we shall be considering in the context of ICT, because the investors, working through the **board of directors,** decide on the importance and the role of the ICT department. We can now identify four groups that need to be studied:

- **Investors**. They have the key role explained above.

- **Users**. They know what services they want, both to serve customers more comprehensively and to extend their own internal efficiency.

- **Implementers**. They build or acquire the systems needed in order for users to mount and run the services that have been approved.

- **Providers**. They install and support those services, and the computer and communications systems on which they are based.

These four groups are identified with the four functions that determine what the ICT department does, and how it does it. Each one interacts with the other three. These interactions are represented by the diagram in Figure 2.3.

Perhaps we should again emphasise the wide range of differences that distinguish one company and its procedures from any another; however, what is said here is intended to apply to many or, perhaps, most medium-sized businesses.

In Figure 2.4 (on page 62) the diagram of the interactions between the functions shown in Figure 2.3 has been redrawn to place the investors at the centre, reflecting their pivotal role; and the main ingredients

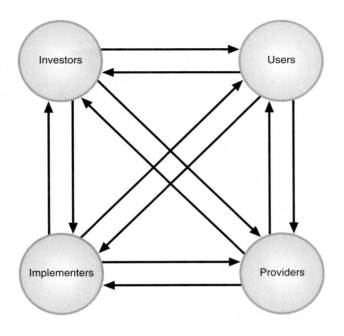

Figure 2.3   Interactions between the four ICT department functions

of the twelve interactions between the functions have been added. Chapter 2.3 will look at the information flow required for each of these interactions. Let us now look at the interactions.

Investors to users. Investors transmit to users their vision of the future of the business, their commercial goals, their plans for attaining those goals, their commitment to the support of users through the provision of ICT services, and a reminder of the business culture to be observed throughout the company.

Investors give users as much warning as they can of future changes of direction in the company's business.

Users to investors. Users report to the investors their evaluation of the benefits of using their ICT services, particularly those recently installed, pointing out whatever commercial risks to their services they see; and they make proposals for future services.

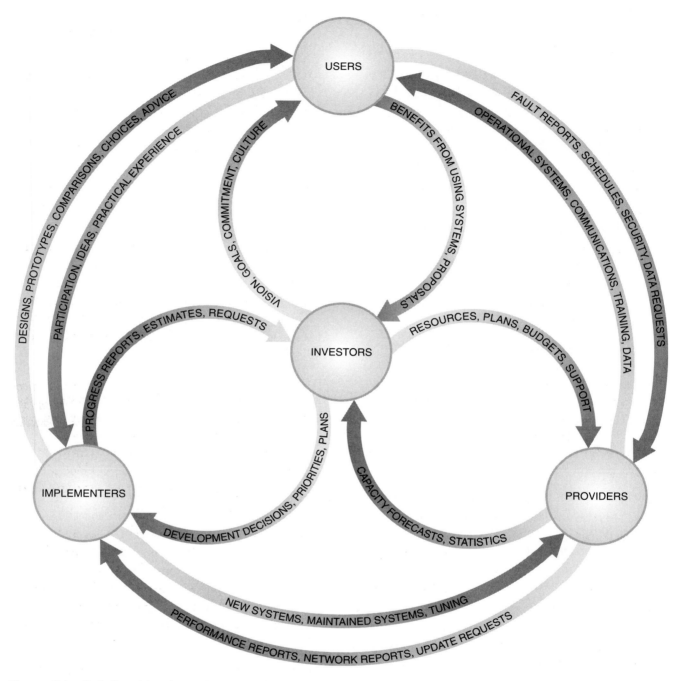

Figure 2.4   Relationships in and around the ICT department

Investors to implementers. Investors convey their decisions on what development projects the implementers are to undertake, what priorities they have set, and what plans have been made for bringing into use the new services the implementers build.

Implementers to investors. Implementers provide the investors with reports of progress on their development projects, estimates of dates of completion for each project; and any requests they need to make for additional resources for their current development programme, or additional projects on which to deploy resources not fully committed.

Investors to providers. Investors notify providers of the resources to be made available for supporting existing services, and also for new ones that have recently been built; the plans for installing new services; and the budgets and timetables within which they must be installed and run.

Providers to investors. Providers state what capacity they will need in order to carry out the tasks they have been set, within the time allowed; and they provide statistics on the uptake and reliability of installed services.

Users to implementers. Users must work closely with implementers, sending them ideas for future services that they would find useful, and lessons learned through experience of using recently delivered services. Implementers will find knowledge of these lessons helpful as they design new services.

Implementers to users. Implementers let users have the outline designs of proposed new services for comment; prototypes of partially developed services, again for comment; comparisons of different approaches to achieving some agreed service; choices for users to make, typically between getting a fuller new service that would take longer to deliver and cost more, or having a simpler, less expensive one, sooner; and advice on how to use new systems.

Implementers to providers. Implementers pass systems they have just developed to providers, not direct to users. Systems on which they have carried out maintenance or updating follow the same route, as do systems that have been tuned by

implementers to make a service already in operation perform faster or more conveniently.

Providers to implementers. Providers feed back to implementers reports from users on the performance of services that have been running live. These reports will be more technical, and therefore more helpful to implementers, than the reports sent to implementers by users, though users' reports do give implementers a feel for the importance to the company of particular services.

Providers supply reports on the performance of public and internal data networks, and they also pass to implementers details of difficulties that have arisen in training users in the use of new services, or with capacity or other resource problems found with new services.

Providers to users. Providers install new or upgraded computer and software systems for users; supply and connect new or upgraded communications systems; install new services ready for final acceptance testing; provide training in the use of new services of all kinds; and provide the channels for the flow of data the users will need.

They will also have responsibility for responding quickly to any call from users experiencing any kind of problem with their systems. The providers will diagnose the cause, and either repair the system or pass the problem to the relevant specialist for its solution.

Users to providers. Users send reports of operational difficulties they are having with their services to providers. They agree schedules with providers for the delivery of training and for the installation of new services. They raise and resolve security issues; and they make requests for whatever data they need from providers.

Functions of the departments

We have seen that the ICT department interacts with the other six departments. All departments will want to be in touch with all the others more or less continuously. There is therefore, at least in theory, a web of internal communications linking departments, and their functions, as shown in Figure 2.5.

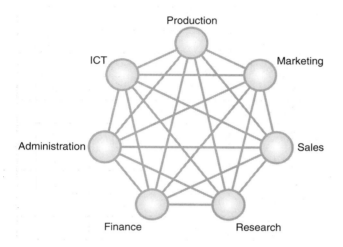

Figure 2.5   Theoretical, fully multiplexed pattern of information flow between functions

The diagram exaggerates the complexity, because in real life some of the links will have little information to pass. Top management identifies the roles of the various functions that are needed for the business to operate efficiently. Where there is strong central control exercised by management, the interactions may be represented more accurately as a spoked wheel, with the information flows into and out of the centre. In this model, drawn in Figure 2.6, the centre would act like a telephone exchange, directing items of information it received to the department or departments needing them.

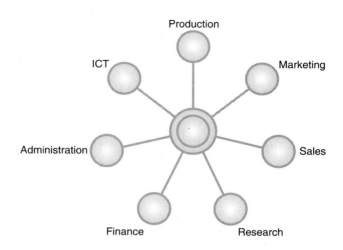

Figure 2.6   Centralised management of information flow between functions

As an example of the way the spoked wheel would work, suppose that the marketing department had seen an opportunity for the company to design, make, and sell a new kind of product; and wanted to tell finance (who would have to approve whatever expenditure would be needed to bring the prospective new product to the market), research (to give early warning of a possible design requirement), and production (so that they could start looking for sources of supply for the materials that would be needed).

The sales department is not involved at this stage, to avoid distracting the sales force from their job of selling current products.

The flow of information would be as shown in Figure 2.7.

Other examples of the information flows needed between functions, no matter whether the flows are centralised or direct, are:

Administration to finance. Reports of recruiting campaigns, giving finance the details of new staff including their names, departments, starting salaries and anything special about their terms of engagement.

Sales to production. Sales made, with full specifications of the optional features

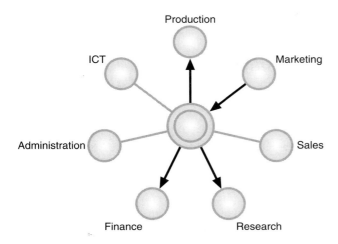

Figure 2.7 The distribution of marketing information

ordered, and delivery dates promised; with a request to production for confirmation of availability.

Sales to finance. Reports of sales made, delivery dates, and any discounts offered. (Finance will have to calculate, and pay, commission to the sales team.)

Sales to marketing. Information about competitive activity encountered; resistance to sale of particular products, or in certain markets; opportunities for product development that were seen.

Production to finance. Production has to give finance early notice of the cash it will need for buying the materials, parts and components it will have to have in order to fulfil its production schedules.

The interactions between functions are as important in service businesses as they are in manufacturing businesses. However, they may be more awkward in manufacturing because of the delays that are necessarily caused in the manufacturing process, which may consist of many stages, with the supply of all the required parts and components running smoothly.

External relationships

Companies do not operate in a vacuum: very much the opposite. Even fairly small companies have to have many external contacts giving rise to **external functions**. Figure 2.8 lists the key external bodies

Bodies of importance to companies	Small companies	Medium-sized companies	Large companies
Customers	✓	✓	✓
Competitors	✓	✓	✓
Suppliers	✓	✓	✓
Trading partners	–	–	✓
Shareholders	–	✓	✓
Lenders	✓	✓	✓
Inland Revenue	✓	✓	✓
Customs & Excise	✓	✓	✓
Accountants	✓	✓	✓
Insurers	✓	✓	✓
Advertising agencies	–	✓	✓
Market research agencies	–	–	✓
Recruitment agencies	–	✓	✓
Public relations agencies	–	–	✓
Internet service providers	✓	✓	✓
Voice/data service providers	✓	✓	✓
Computing & communications equipment providers	✓	✓	✓
Courier service providers	✓	–	–
Utilities	✓	✓	✓
Security advisers	–	–	✓
Economic advisers	–	–	✓
Political advisers	–	–	✓
Local authority departments	✓	✓	✓
Building contractors	–	✓	✓

Figure 2.8 Bodies likely to be important to companies of different sizes

likely to be important for small, medium-sized, and large companies.

Here are brief notes about why companies have to interact with these bodies, and how their relationships support the aims of companies. There are two lists: the first applies to all businesses, including FUN; the second applies only to large or medium-sized organisations.

Customers. Customers are the mainspring of any company. No customers: no business! Categories of customers are normally identified by marketing; but it is the sales force who actually convert prospective customers into real ones.

Customers can be end-users, retailers, or distributors; individuals or commercial firms; in the UK or overseas; new or established; large or small.

ICT can support the management of customers in several ways: keeping lists of prospective customers, producing analyses of market trends, operating the marketing and promotion budgets, and maintaining customer records, for example. FUN's marketplace is big enough, and their operations complex enough, for them to need some systematic way of keeping track of their customers and prospective customers.

Competitors. Competition provides much of the spice of business, giving customers choice and helping to prompt innovation. Competitors probably do not compete across the whole range of a company's products and services, but where they do compete the sales team try to defeat them and secure orders. Information about competitive products and selling techniques is important to a company in planning its sales strategy.

Competitors should always be treated fairly, partly because everyone should be treated fairly but also because one day there may be cause to work closely with them – or even to apply for a job with them. Competitive products should never be ridiculed in the presence of a customer.

Someone in a company will be responsible for collecting information about competitors. ICT can keep the details on a database, update the database frequently, and provide analyses of trends and noteworthy events. For example, a chain of UK booksellers would be extremely interested if a big US chain moved in to compete with them: they would want to see what impact the new business was having, perhaps analysed by categories of book sold, and by location.

Suppliers. Suppliers are chosen by a company. Normally there will be several from whom the choice can be made. Their size, range of products, reputation and location are important. Beyond that a company hopes for a steady, long-lasting relationship with its suppliers; though it must not be allowed to become too cosy.

If a supplier is small in comparison with the company it is supplying there is a danger that a large proportion of its output

Case history

When Marks & Spencer found themselves in financial difficulty in 1999 because of falling sales of clothing, they changed their policy of selling goods most of which had been made in Britain. They began to import more, replacing output from their previous suppliers, with an immediate and severe impact on UK jobs in the textile industry.

is going to that one customer, making the supplier vulnerable to serious damage should it lose that business at short notice. A supplier may have a conflict of loyalty if it is supplying not only the company but the company's competitors.

FUN's purchasing activities are not especially complicated but it might still want to compare the prices and performance of its suppliers.

Lenders. They too want to know how a company is faring. Interest rates and repayment schedules have to be agreed and regularly reviewed.

There is every likelihood that FUN had to borrow money in its early days, but perhaps only from the founder, Fred Frollick. Sooner or later matters must be formalised with the lender or lenders.

The Inland Revenue. It is responsible for collecting personal tax from employees and corporation tax from companies. It issues tax tables on disk or over the Internet to allow employers to deduct tax due automatically. Each company has to send tax deducted through the payroll to the Inland Revenue.

Even though it is a small business, FUN still has to work with the Inland Revenue.

HM Customs & Excise. It collects VAT from all registered companies, so those companies have to keep VAT records. Certain companies also have to account to Customs & Excise for the duty charged on road vehicle fuel, agricultural vehicle and machinery fuel, alcohol, tobacco, and other kinds of goods.

FUN is registered for VAT and so has to account to Customs & Excise for the VAT on its sales and purchases.

Accountants. Companies have to engage external qualified accountants to audit their financial accounts each year; and they are likely to have accountants, who may or may not be the same firm, to prepare figures for the Inland Revenue and for the annual accounts to be presented to shareholders.

The Inland Revenue and any commercial lender will want to see FUN's audited accounts prepared by an accountant each year.

Insurers. Companies have to carry insurance covering their employees, and they are almost sure to want to insure their business assets such as buildings, stock, and equipment. They may want to insure against several other risks, such as loss of profit, litigation arising from the sale of faulty goods, losses on foreign exchange, or losses due to professional failure.

Insurers may be asked to manage a company's pension scheme.

FUN will certainly have to take out insurance cover for employee liability, and for the firm's property and equipment. They may also feel it wise to have some protection from the risks of poisoning customers!

Internet service providers (ISPs). ISPs provide for Internet users the route they need for access to the World Wide Web and to e-mail services. They also act as Web hosts for small organisations. As companies move towards reliance on e-commerce and e-mail the importance of the chosen ISPs is clear. The service offered by an ISP must be fast enough for the user's needs, reliable, affordable, and of course, secure.

FUN definitely needs an ISP.

Voice/data service providers. Companies

have to evaluate the services available for mobile phones, fixed phones, fax, and for accepting digital data traffic. The best solution will depend on volumes, speeds, and distances. Companies must not allow themselves to be starved of crucial information because of speed or capacity restrictions.

These businesses can count on FUN as a customer as FUN develops new ways of selling and operating.

Computing and communications equipment providers. Companies have a continual battle to keep up with the state of the art in equipment performance, while not retiring a perfectly good item simply because something very much faster has been announced. Within the company there have to be people able to make impartial judgements on new equipment, test it thoroughly before placing any orders, and brief senior managers accordingly.

FUN will enter this market from time to time.

Courier services. Small companies, such as FUN, rely on courier services to deliver papers and goods to customers without loss of time. The advantage is that the company pays only for the services actually used, and does not have to carry any of the overhead costs of having its own vehicles and drivers.

Utilities. Every company has to buy from the utilities electricity, water, and possibly gas. Buyers of large quantities may be able to negotiate worthwhile discounts. The bills raised by utilities must be paid punctually if disconnection is to be avoided.

Local authority departments. Companies, including FUN, have to maintain contact with their local authorities in connection with assessment and payment of business rates, planning issues, and environmental

issues. This will be true of areas away from head office where a company sites a branch office or a warehouse.

Some companies find membership of the local chamber of commerce a useful link with the business community amongst whom they work.

The second list, which follows, describes in outline some of the outside bodies with which some businesses have to maintain a relationship.

Trading partners. Large companies are likely to have trading partners in the form of partly-owned subsidiary companies, especially overseas; joint venture projects; and possible targets for agreed mergers. One company may make an investment in another company. Increasingly companies work closely with agencies of central government.

Confederation of British Industry (CBI). This is an organisation which represents the interests of UK companies and publishes surveys of business confidence.

Shareholders. We saw in Chapter 2.1 that a company's shareholders, who may be corporate or individual, are the owners of the business. They have to be sent information about company financial performance, and they require an annual general meeting at which to consider resolutions about matters of corporate policy. They have to be paid a dividend on the shares they hold.

Advertising agencies. When making their plans for promoting products, and for promoting the business as a whole, an approach known as **prestige advertising** can be adopted. A company will use an advertising agency to design and produce advertisements for TV, magazines, posters, newspapers, and radio; perhaps on their web site; and possibly to create special-purpose publications such as the annual report and accounts.

Market research agencies. These firms specialise in finding facts and figures about the sizes and composition of given markets and competitive activity in them, and also about rates of change in the markets. They can undertake opinion surveys regarding the products of a company, and they can find out about opportunities for selling given products in countries abroad.

Building contractors. Any company will probably need to engage building contractors to repair faults in the structure of offices and factories, internal electricity and water services, and car parks, roads and paths. In addition they will be needed whenever there is to be new building.

Recruitment agencies. They will accept contracts to produce short-lists of applicants for particular jobs which a company wants to fill. They can help draft and place recruitment advertisements and they can give advice on current salary levels and fringe benefits.

Public relations agencies. They have the role of bringing into the public eye a company's products on which they have been briefed, and the highlights of the company itself. They do this by arranging press conferences, by issuing leaflets to carefully chosen recipients who they hope will be influential and able to help reinforce the presence of the company in the market, and by trying to get editorial coverage in the media.

Security advisers. Where a company has a serious security problem, perhaps handling sensitive government data, security advisers from the police and from the private sector can help to evaluate risks and suggest safeguards.

Economic advisers. Where the sales that a company can make are heavily influenced by the strength of the economy and, in overseas markets, the strength of sterling, large companies may seek economic advice to help them to optimise a difficult or uncertain situation.

Political advisers. In some valuable export markets there is a tendency for political instability. Large companies may want to take advice to supplement what they can learn from the Foreign and Commonwealth Office by consulting political advisers with deep knowledge of the areas in question.

These two lists are long but not necessarily complete. The external relationships of a company, even if they are required by law, are normally harmonious; but you should recognise that companies, apart from the smallest, have a substantial burden to carry in handling their external functions. As you would expect, computers are harnessed whenever possible to add efficiency and to reduce work.

Chapter 2.3   The use of information in organisations

In Chapter 2.2 we looked at the internal functions and external relationships for a typical medium-sized manufacturing company. Using this same example in this chapter we consider, for the same six user departments, namely operations, marketing, sales, research, finance, and administration:

- the computer-based systems each will need

- the tasks of the ICT department

- the way information flows between the departments to support the internal functions

- management information systems.

User department systems

The main systems that user departments are likely to want are listed below. In addition, every department may want to use computer-based systems for its own planning and budgeting. For each department, comments on one of the systems are included.

Operations

- stock control, sometimes called **inventory management**

- purchasing

- work scheduling

- job costing

- delivery.

Stock control systems can be complicated, giving attention to seasonal trends, the different speeds at which product lines move through the warehouse, economical order quantities, space occupied by the total stock, the total amount of money tied up in stock, and maintaining the target level of service to customers.

Figure 2.9 represents a simple stock control system.

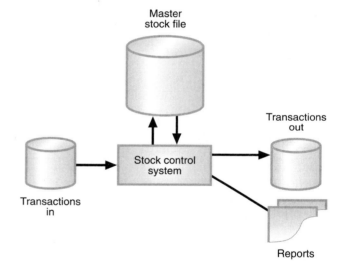

Figure 2.9   Simple stock control system

The master stock file holds the records of the stock held. It is updated from **transaction files** showing the items taken into the warehouse, and items issued from it.

Reports would go to the finance and sales departments. Physical stock in the warehouse must be compared frequently with the records held in the master stock file to check that they agree.

Case history: A big success over the Web

You may not associate the North York Moors with dot com lingerie, and nor, until very recently, did Mrs Sally Robinson.

She started a business selling outsize bras by mail order. The product is suitable for mail order selling as it is light, and can fit through customers' letter boxes; and in any case she had had trouble when shopping for herself. She based the enterprise in the unused barns on the farm her husband runs. At first sales achieved by the new company, Amplebosom, were modest and Sally did not see how to expand them, although she knew that across the country there is a considerable demand for bras sized between 36C and 60J.

Then she hit on the idea of using the Internet. She designed and set up a website and began trading from it two months later. Success was almost immediate. Within six months monthly turnover reached £20000. She now employs one assistant full-time and two part-time. The volume and value of sales are both still growing.

Marketing

- market trends
- analysis of competitive activity
- planning and analysis of promotion campaigns.

Systems for studying market trends need to record and present details of population growth, age distribution, and buying habits, as well as characteristics of the industrial markets, in all the areas important to the company. Price and performance trends are also covered.

Try it out	Suppose that the company makes bearings for all types of machinery. What would be the effect on its markets if a nearby car factory closed down? How could the company try to limit the damage to its business that would follow if it did nothing? How could its ICT systems help it to identify alternative outlets for its products?

Sales

- receiving and logging customer orders
- invoice production
- customer details
- recording all sales visits and other sales activity.

The ICT team will have an important role in designing, introducing, and developing e-commerce systems.

Try it out	Look on the Internet at some of the businesses selling their products and services over the Web. Amazon.com, and its UK off-shoot Amazon.co.uk, are amongst companies selling books; travel firms sell holidays and journey tickets; supermarkets sell goods in increasing volumes.
	In a group, make a list of the ways in which firms offering products for sale draw attention to their web sites.

The e-commerce sales, which are likely to build up slowly, will at first be augmented by earlier ordering methods under which customers place their orders by personal visit, telephone, fax, or purchase order sent through the post.

Did you know?

High hopes are held for the benefits that could flow locally and nationally from the adoption by business of e-commerce. New developments in e-commerce, sometimes called B2B, are announced almost daily. Clearly a revolution is taking place in the way every aspect of trading is conducted.

However, a survey has shown that many companies expect their *ICT teams* to develop the corporate e-commerce strategies, whereas in ICT the people expect *top management* to identify the commercial goals and then call upon ICT to help them in attaining these. The result for such companies could well be stagnation and lost opportunities.

Faultless Towers Hotel

99 Wimbledon Park Drive
London SW19 XXX

Fax/Tel: 0802 999 8888
E-mail: Basil@F-Towers.co.uk

PURCHASE ORDER

To: Festivities Unlimited
221 B Wardo Road
Fulham, London SW6 XXX

Date: DD MMM YY

Please supply:

Quantity	Description	Catalogue no.	Unit price
3 dozen	Pizza slices	FUN 2222	0.40
100	Paper plates	FUN 7777	0.21
2	Cookery books	FUN 8888	6.99

Proprietor: Basil Faultless
VAT reg. no.: ZZZ ZZZZ ZZ

Figure 2.10   Example of a purchase order

In Figure 2.10 is an example of a purchase order.

The customer details that the sales department would want to keep on file include: sales person responsible for the customer, customer name, address, telephone number, fax number, e-mail address, customer contact, buying history, and details of current sales status.

Research and design

- product design
- engineering design
- analysis of new developments.

In Chapter 1.1, on page 7, we touched on computer-aided design (CAD) software. One of the most valuable advantages that a CAD system usually provides is the possibility of reducing the overall time between the decision to make and sell some new product, and the first of the completed, tested products being wheeled out of the factory door.

Another virtue of CAD is that ideas for products can be evaluated, and rejected or accepted, very quickly.

CAD is an intensely technical application, in which advice from ICT is probably wanted on the choice of software and equipment.

Finance

- sales, purchase, and nominal ledgers
- credit control

- payroll
- payments in and out, including EFT
- budgets, projections, and accounts
- historical financial records.

Finance has to be able to give instant statements on the financial situation in the company to the directors, on request.

EFT stands for **electronic funds transfer**. It refers to any use of computers in making payments to organisations or individuals. It is a rapid way of transferring money, but raises doubts about security.

These administrative applications are largely similar between one organisation and another. There is nonetheless an important task for ICT to advise on the particular software products to be obtained.

Administration

- personnel records and pension scheme
- legal and statutory matters
- insurance
- external authorities and contractors
- board meetings and annual general meetings.

Personnel records must include, for each employee: name, home address and telephone number, National Insurance number, employee number and department, date of birth, sex, date of joining the company, job history before joining the company, job history since joining, training, qualifications and skills.

As for the finance department, the systems needed can be chosen from many that are used in other companies. The advice of ICT is likely to be both helpful to the users and

able to support the organisation's policy on standardisation.

The ICT department

In Chapter 2.2 we examined the roles of ICT, and how ICT interacts with the user departments. ICT is a service department, providing all kinds of support and advice, reports, plans, training, and data to the users. It contains people with skills and experience that are distinct from those in other departments, and it needs to think how users can best derive advantage from the work of these people.

A key role for the ICT team is to explain the advantages that may be available for managers and their departments of making greater use of computer-based systems. The team needs to explain the structure and characteristics of ICT projects; how the cost-effectiveness of potential new applications can be assessed; and, crucially, how to dispel any fear of computer working that may be holding some back.

Users will be keen to develop their own systems and databases for their own desktop and laptop computers, and make independent use of communications systems within their reach. An important task of ICT is to devise and manage centralised systems in the following areas:

- procurement of computer equipment, so that the variety is held in check; and technical support staff can be trained in the agreed makes and models
- procurement of computing and communications equipment, and specialised office equipment, so that the company can get the discounts earned by bulk purchase

- use of e-mail and other Internet access procedures, database administration and control over the data, and accessing standards

- systems development, testing and documentation standards.

There are important benefits for the company in standardising these matters; but those benefits have to be understood, and insisted upon by senior management if full advantage is to be realised.

The ICT operation is both the nerve centre of the current business activities, and the source of inspiration for new development in the application of computers. ICT should see as one of its tasks the briefing of directors and senior managers on exactly what the ICT team does, and on the great advantages that extending computer working into new areas might bring to the organisation. The ICT team must explain to these individuals the importance of integrating departmental systems, of using standard approaches to project evaluation and other aspects of computer operations whenever possible, and to investment in training.

Information flow

We now have a firm idea of the types of information that are needed by users and the ICT department for the company to run successfully. Let us look at the ways in which information can flow from those that have it to those who want it.

In Chapters 1.3 and 1.4 we explained how information should be presented for it to do its job with greatest certainty. Here we review the means by which the information can be directed to the intended recipients.

Letters

Letters are sent to bodies outside the company to inform, to reply to a request, or to make a request. Such letters should be written in a formal style: regardless of who drafts a letter, it is signed and sent on behalf of the company. Care must be taken with what is said.

Letters may be copied to people inside the company, so that they know what is being said; and often the internal distribution is not disclosed to the external addressee.

Letters are also sent to employees, with the appropriate security classification (such as **private and confidential**), on promotion, retirement, or other personal events.

Memoranda (memos)

The purpose of sending memos is now met in many companies by internal e-mail. Where memos are still in use they are sent only to people within the company. The writing style should be compact. As with letters, copies can be sent to other internal addressees. It is usually convenient to keep a memo short, putting in an appendix any detailed information.

E-mail

Subject to local rules laid down by the company, e-mail can be used both internally and externally. It is fast and inexpensive, and allows outgoing and incoming messages to be filed or deleted. The filing is mostly handled by the system and is therefore economical with clerical effort. As before, any message going outside the company is sent on behalf of the company, with appropriate care being taken over what is said. Internal e-mail may be carried by an intranet which would be a secure data network within the company running on the same lines as the Internet, and offering similar facilities. An **extranet** is an extension of an intranet to include access to a limited range of external people and businesses; and e-mail can be used over an extranet.

Local area networks (LANs)

LANs allow a group of computer users to share software, files, printers, and perhaps other resources. Except for certain small networks, each LAN is controlled by a computer known as a **server**. The server will contain procedures for denying access to the network to anyone without authority to use it; and it will probably provide data storage capacity for the LAN users.

Each department might have its own LAN. As LANs can be linked, and pass data from one to another, they provide one way in which departments can communicate with each other electronically. LANs can also give access to external networks including the Internet. In most LANs the computers are linked to one another by cables, but some LANs have wireless channels instead. Wireless links can carry data, voice, video, and graphics traffic.

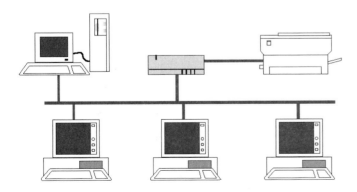

Figure 2.11 A local area network (LAN)

Wide area networks (WANs)

LANs are usually limited in their reach to about 1000 metres. WANs are unrestricted in this sense: they rely on external telecommunications carriers for transmitting their traffic. WANs can be private, within a single dispersed company, or may use public services.

Telephones and voice mail

The telephone is useful for conversations in which there is expected to be a degree of dialogue. A conversation can be recorded by either of the parties if the topic seems important, or if it contains details that might need subsequent review. An attraction of the telephone is that it conveys expression, in contrast to e-mail whose words are free of emphasis or feeling. **Viewphones** transmit facial as well as spoken expression.

Voice mail is a formalised scheme for inviting callers to leave messages which can be heard later. In that respect it resembles e-mail: the party called does not lose the communication by being away from the telephone when the message is being sent.

Did you know?

Wireless Application Protocol (WAP)

The latest wireless developments are allowing businesses to extend their use of mobile communications. Portable PCs connected to mobile digital phones, or specialised radio facilities, have their drawbacks. But WAP-capable phones can access both information and applications by radio; and software developers are rushing to add WAP support to applications and to build WAP interfaces for software products they use.

A big advantage of WAP phones is that you have the facilities you most need in a single hand-held device.

Some telephone connections allow data and voice to share the same circuits. Viewphones, which combine voice with pictures of the people having a telephone conversation, are technically possible and may become popular if they can be made affordable.

Meetings

Meetings can be fruitful opportunities for a number of people to acquire the same understanding of a new or changed situation – or they *can* be a total waste of time, possibly for a large number of people. For a meeting to be successful there are four requirements:

- a notice calling the meeting must be sent out in advance to the intended participants, and someone must check that they will all attend

- an **agenda**, setting out the topics for discussion, must be distributed before the meeting, together with papers to be studied in advance, allowing enough time for everyone to arrive at the meeting fully briefed

- someone must be appointed secretary for the meeting, to take down the **minutes** which will note, as a minimum, what actions have been agreed and who is to carry them out – the secretary has to type the minutes and get copies to everyone present while the discussions are still fresh in their minds

- there must be, as chairman of the meeting, someone able to work through the agenda, attract contributions from all those with anything valid to say, summarise the discussion and state the conclusions; and do all that quickly enough to hold the attention of the whole meeting.

Reports

Reports are a strong way of passing information because of their standardised structure and the possibility of their having a sufficiently long life to remain accessible whenever they are wanted. In Chapter 1.3 we dealt with the drafting and structure of reports (page 30).

Management information systems

As a rule managers do not handle materials or even money: they handle only information. To obtain the information they need for making and monitoring decisions they have to have access to a company's databases and to means of manipulating the data in them.

Management information systems (MIS) set out to offer these facilities, protecting managers from having to work directly with databases and processing programs in order to get the information they want.

They also protect managers from receiving information they do not really need. This information may be unnecessary, or it may be potentially useful information that ought to be summarised. Computer systems are capable of generating so much printed output so rapidly that there is a risk of managers, suffering from **information overload.** Unless there are ways of sieving and digesting information before it reaches managers, they will be in danger of wasting time, becoming frustrated and, possibly, ill.

There are two forms of MIS, known as **decision support systems (DSS)** and **executive information systems (EIS).** A DSS usually provides individual managers with tools for making stand-alone enquiries, analyses, and computer models. An EIS typically provides internal information from a company's databases and external information from on-line services.

The whole area of MIS is active and dynamic. Some companies establish EIS teams to extend the scope of their original EIS, which may have been started by an enthusiastic senior manager competent in ICT. The term **knowledge management** is used to describe the general development of EIS into what is expected to become one of the most vigorously expanding software application fields.

Unit 2 Assessment

This assignment can be used as practice for the externally set assignment.

This assignment is based on the Festivities Unlimited case study described in the general Introduction on pages xiii and xiv.

Scenario

Following a strong trading performance last year, FUN started to look at ways of expanding its business. It took the view that the existing style of business could only be grown by reaching out to clients beyond the range it set at present, leading to increased marketing and transport costs. It therefore looked at various diversification possibilities.

The company decided that rather than try to generate organic growth, based on the existing pattern of services, it would be wiser to seek a suitable organisation to buy. After a study of several potential acquisition targets it decided to bid for a chain of four medium-sized shops, all nearby, in the Hammersmith area.

These shops trade under the name Shop All Day, or SAD. All sell groceries and related items such as cooking pans, plates, tablecloths, and kitchen implements. They also sell newspapers. The SAD shops each turn over on average about £2500 a week, representing about £500 000 a year for the chain.

The chain is run by the SAD manager from a room next to one of the shops. Each shop has a supervisor and part-time staff. Sales are made over the counter, with a small number of modest contracts for the supply of groceries to other businesses. Purchasing of most lines is carried out through a wholesale supplier called YARD. There are

no ICT systems beyond a PC used for word-processing.

The commercial logic of the acquisition is seen by the partners of FUN to be that:

* the shops could provide outlets for surplus FUN catering products

* FUN's purchasing should benefit from the shared use of YARD

* opportunities for cross-promotion of the FUN and SAD products and services would help both sides of the combined business

* there should be improved operational efficiency and financial control through the design and installation of new ICT systems.

The bid put in by FUN has been successful. In two months the SAD shops will belong to FUN. The combined organisation will still be known as FUN. The SAD manager will report to the FUN commercial director, Steve, as the FUN marketing manager and catering manager do now.

Your tasks

There is no need to consider the bid price or the financial reconstruction that the success of the bid makes necessary.

1 Draw a diagram of the organisational structure of the newly expanded FUN.

2 Draw a diagram to show the internal functions of the organisation.

3 List the kinds of information that must flow between each pair of functions to sustain the normal functioning of the business. Indicate the volume, frequency, and urgency of each of these flows of information.

4 Think about the transmission and processing of these information flows.

There may be advantages in handling some or all of them within ICT systems, but these advantages have to be set against the complexity and cost of designing and implementing the systems.

Now rank the information flows for which there appears to be a positive net advantage from automating them. Put the one with the greatest net advantage first.

5   Starting from the top of your list, pick those entries that you think should be automated at once. Without trying to cost the conversion from manual working, write about 1000 words about how you think the automation project should be handled, mentioning responsibilities, equipment, software, documentation, and training.

Are there any new systems that could be installed before the amalgamation becomes effective in two months' time?

6   Finally, the directors of FUN are going to want information about the performance of the business as a whole. Make a list of the sorts of information that they would most like to have, and the frequency with which they would want them.

Making use of your earlier choice of applications to be handled automatically by ICT systems, write 500 words describing the scope of a management information system that could be provided that would be helpful to the directors.

Unit 3 Spreadsheet design

The next three chapters address the requirements of Unit 3 – that you:

- design spreadsheets to process data to produce required information

- prepare standard spreadsheets that others can use with their own data

- learn and apply good design and test principles.

You will create spreadsheets to meet specified requirements. Some of these specified requirements will need you to make use of complex spreadsheet facilities.

This unit builds on the themes explored in Unit 1, relating to AVCE Unit 1, 'Presenting information'. It also links with Unit 5, 'Systems analysis', and Unit 6 'Database design'.

Unit 3 will be assessed through your portfolio of evidence.

There are three chapters in this unit:

- Chapter 3.1   Using spreadsheet facilities

- Chapter 3.2   Spreadsheet specification and development

- Chapter 3.3   Spreadsheet documentation and testing.

You will meet new technical terms in each of these topics. Some of the words may be familiar but are likely to have specialised meanings in this area of study. You need to know how to use these terms correctly.

Microsoft Excel

Throughout this unit the examples and illustrations are based on Microsoft Excel. There are other spreadsheet packages, but Excel is the product most widely used by students. We have not allowed the differences that exist between the versions of Excel to affect the validity or usefulness of the text.

Terms used in this unit

The basis of spreadsheet operations is a grid of lines lying up and down the page, and lines running across it. The spaces between any adjacent pair of the up-and-down lines are called *columns*, and the spaces between any adjacent pair of crossways lines are called *rows*. The box formed where a column and a row meet is called a *cell*. Figure 3.1 shows an EXCEL spreadsheet as it first appears to the user before any work is done with it.

Each cell has a unique address formed by the identifiers of the column and row that meet at the cell. In Excel the columns are designated A, B, C . . . from the left, and the rows 1, 2, 3 . . . from the top. A cell could thus be identified as D8 or P17, for example.

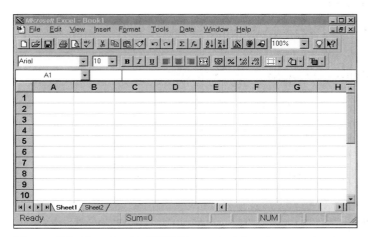

Figure 3.1 An empty EXCEL spreadsheet

The word *spreadsheet* strictly refers to the program that manipulates the tables consisting of the cells in use, and their display on a screen. The page of columns and rows is known as a *worksheet*; a number of worksheets form a *workbook*. Related data is usually best kept on separate worksheets within the same workbook. In EXCEL the default number of worksheets in a workbook is three, but the number to be used can be increased or decreased.

You may come across these words 'worksheets' and 'workbook', but the AVCE ICT specifications use the word 'spreadsheet' to cover the meanings of both worksheet and workbook, and in this book we shall do the same.

Spreadsheet software allows the contents of the cells making up a worksheet to provide information that can be useful in many ways. Typical examples of spreadsheet applications are the presentation of accounts, the display of projected figures, and solutions to 'what if?' queries. Output can be numeric, textual, or graphical.

Spreadsheets are useful at all levels in a business. For management they allow many possible future financial situations to be explored and compared. At an operational level they can present plans and outcomes quickly and clearly, offering different ways in which results can be displayed.

Spreadsheet tables can be too large to be displayed as a whole. The part that is seen on the screen at one time should be regarded as the view obtained by looking at the worksheet through a window, with the possibility of moving the worksheet at will to alter the view.

Use of the case study

The case study which runs through the whole book is described on pages xiii and xiv of the general Introduction. In this unit we follow the commercial director of Festivities Unlimited (FUN), who wants to have a spreadsheet which will help with the planning of events and which can later record details of how each event performed financially.

The spreadsheet must take input data relating to the expected income and cost of an event, and produce output data and graphs which show its expected financial attractiveness.

FUN begins the work of preparing for an event when the customer accepts the quotation. The quotation is based on an estimate of how profitable the event should be. We use the term *gross profit* for a particular event, meaning the excess of income over expenditure for that event. The production director will have generated the forecast of costs from a separate spreadsheet.

All the directors will want consolidated financial figures from another spreadsheet so that they can monitor corporate performance against budget, and make forecasts.

Group activity

In the first two chapters of this unit, Chapters 3.1 and 3.2, there is an activity that can be tackled by groups of students. Its aim is to offer a sequence of tasks based on the business needs of FUN that can be progressively moved forward as the knowledge of spreadsheet facilities and techniques is built up.

Chapter 3.1 Using spreadsheets

This chapter introduces those facilities of the Microsoft Excel spreadsheet software that you will find most useful, and discusses issues of the presentation of completed spreadsheets.

You may have worked with spreadsheets, but there are sure to be facts in this chapter that you have not met before. You should keep referring to this chapter in order to develop your work with spreadsheets as thoroughly as possible.

You will soon become wholly familiar with some of the facilities through repeated use. Your aim is to be able to use *all* of the facilities without help.

This chapter also gives you an opportunity to consider which facilities you would want to use in a new spreadsheet for FUN. In Chapter 3.2 you will be able to specify and develop the spreadsheet. The activity is first offered to you at the end of this chapter, but you might like to keep glancing at it as you work through the chapter so that you can begin thinking about how you will make use of Excel facilities in the FUN spreadsheet.

Spreadsheet facilities

These are the spreadsheet facilities, described below, that you can expect to know well:

- selecting and setting cell formats to match the data format
- selecting and using suitable cell presentation formats
- use and manipulation of spreadsheet data
- appropriate use of cell referencing facilities

- correct application and use of operators and formulas
- appropriate use of built-in spreadsheet functions.

There are other more advanced facilities that you will probably use less often. For these you may need to use either the on-line 'Help' assistance provided by Excel or the instruction manual. They include:

- *lists* and *tables* – sorting, lookup tables, subtotals and totals
- making use of *list boxes* and *drop-down boxes* to select data for entry
- styles – to create a customised *cell format*
- *named cells* and *ranges* – for use in formulas
- *auto-fill lists*, for lists of dates or days of the week
- *validation* – restricting data input to acceptable values
- *templates* – creating standard spreadsheet layouts for repeated use
- protecting cells – *hide* and *lock* cells
- *sort* – to sort single and multiple rows and columns of data
- use of control buttons to initiate *macros*
- use of *multiple sheets* with links between them
- use of *multiple views* or windows.

At the end of Chapter 3.2 we look at four of these advanced features which are the ones you will be most likely to want to use. We shall introduce the presentation features when we reach them, on page 100.

	A	B	C	D	E	F	G
1	**Festivities Unlimited**						
2	Event Gross Profit Calculator						
4	Customer	Mary Smith			Event name	21st birthday party	
5	Quote date	07/09			Event type	Birthday	
6	Calculation date	01/04			Event size	30	
7							
8		Catering	Transport	Staff	Extras	Total	
9	Quote	£2,000	£500	£1,000	£1,500	£5,000	
10	Est cost	£1,000	£300	£700	£1,200	£3,200	
11	Est gross profit	£1,000	£200	£300	£300	£1,800	
12	Est GP %	50.0%	40.0%	30.0%	20.0%	36.0%	
13	Actual cost	£1,150	£250	£800	£1,200	£3,400	
14	Actual GP	£850	£250	£200	£300	£1,600	
15	Actual GP %	42.5%	50.0%	20.0%	20.0%	32.0%	
16	GP variance	(£150)	£50	(£100)	£0	(£200)	
17	GP variance %	(15.0%)	25.0%	(33.3%)	0.0%	(11.1%)	
19	Notes	Data entry cells are shown in grey. Type the data in here.					
20		Click on the "Graph" tab to see the bar graph.					

Event Gross Profit / Graph /

Figure 3.2 The completed FUN spreadsheet: event gross profit

As a framework for the descriptions that follow, Figures 3.2 and 3.3 show spreadsheets containing details of an analysis made by our case study business, Festivities Unlimited. Do not, at this stage, worry about their contents, which will become clear in Chapter 3.2.

	A	B	C	D	E	F
1	Festivities Unlimited					
2	Event Gross Profit Calculator					
3						
4	Customer				Event name	
5	Quote date				Event type	
6	Calculation date				Event size	
7						
8		Catering	Transport	Staff	Extras	Total
9	Quote	2000	500	1000	1500	
10	Est cost	1000	300	700	1200	
11	Est gross profit					
12	Est GP %					
13	Actual cos	1150	250	800	1200	
14	Actual GP					
15	Actual GP %					
16	GP variance					
17	GP variance %					
18						
19						

Sheet1 /

Figure 3.3 The first draft of the FUN spreadsheet

Cell formats

You will always want to set the **cell formats** in your spreadsheets to match the data format.

Formats for numeric data

Numeric data items come in a number of different formats. Financial or currency numbers are preceded by the '£' sign, for example; percentages are indicated by a trailing '%'. Both kinds of numbers, as well as other kinds, may have the position of the decimal point specified. In Excel, these data formats are usually available as buttons on the tool bar.

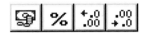

Figure 3.4 Basic number format buttons

To have the number in a cell shown as a percentage, for example, select the cell and then click on the '%' button on the toolbar. To have the number shown with a certain number of decimal places, click on either the '**increase decimal places**' or the '**decrease decimal places**' button as required.

Custom or special numeric formats

In Excel, more complex data formats are set by first highlighting the cells whose format is to be changed, and then selecting the '**Format**'→'**Cells...**' menu item. The cell formatting dialogue box in Figure 3.5 corresponds to cell B16 of the FUN Event Gross Profit spreadsheet in Figure 3.2.

In the finished FUN spreadsheet, Figure 3.2, the custom cell format has been specified as '£#,##0;(£#,##0)', which we assume is a requirement of the user specification, where losses – or negative values – are to be shown in parentheses.

In Excel, a full custom cell format has four parts, separated by semicolons. The first part concerns the format of positive

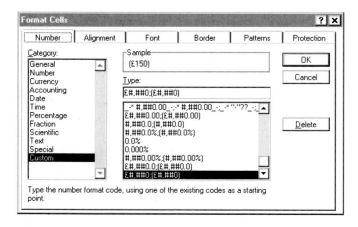

Figure 3.5 'Format Cells' dialogue

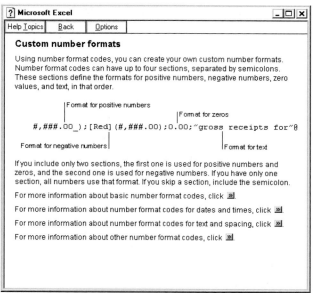

Figure 3.6 Custom cell format Help screen

numbers, and the second part concerns the format of negative numbers. Normally, a negative financial number would have a custom format something like '-£#,##0', indicating that the minus sign '-' is to be placed in front of the '£' sign. In order to have negative numbers shown in parentheses, delete the '-' sign, and place opening and closing parentheses around the format, as shown.

The third and fourth parts deal with the display of zero numbers and text, and need not concern us here. Details of custom cell formatting are available from the **Help menu**; Figure 3.6 shows part of this help.

Dates and times

Dates and times can be displayed by Excel in many ways. Select the cell you want to format; then from the '**Format**' menu choose '**Cells**' and click on the '**Date**' category. You will be offered a list of possible formats; you can select one, and edit it if you wish.

Column width

In almost all spreadsheets some variation in the widths of columns is required, both to accommodate the variety of data item sizes,

and to space out the spreadsheet contents so that they are neither too crowded nor too far apart.

The finished FUN spreadsheet, Figure 3.2, has column A expanded to be about twice its **default** width, while columns B–F have been expanded by 25% of default.

In Excel, the easy way to expand the width of a column is to place the mouse cursor on the border between two columns at the top of the worksheet. The cursor turns into a special pointer to indicate that the border can be moved. Drag the border to one side or the other, and release the mouse button. The column is now resized. The same technique works for a number of adjacent columns: highlight a set of columns, and drag any one border to resize the whole set to identical widths.

A more precise way of changing the column width is to highlight the column (click on the column heading letter) and open the '**Format**'→'**Column Width...**' dialogue box (Figure 3.7). Type in the desired column width, then click the '**OK**' button.

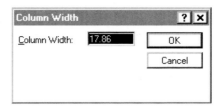

Figure 3.7 'Column Width' dialogue

When we reach the user requirement specification for the FUN spreadsheet, you will see that it calls for sufficient space to accommodate a customer name of up to 40 characters. In Chapter 3.3 we shall look at how to test the spreadsheet to satisfy ourselves that it meets the user requirements.

Cell presentation

In preparing a spreadsheet you have control over many aspects of presentation. Here we look at how you can set these presentation formats:

- horizontal alignment

- colour

- vertical alignment

- shading

- fonts

- borders.

Textual data items, and numeric items as well, can be presented in a number of different ways. The particular **font** can be set as, for example, 'Arial' or 'Times New Roman'; the **typestyle** can be set as bold or italic; and the **point size** can be chosen. The text can be black or, if the printer you will be using has colour, you can pick a colour to suit the task.

In Figure 3.2, the first cell of the FUN spreadsheet, which contains the text

Figure 3.8 Text presentation toolbar

'Festivities Unlimited', has been set in Arial font, 16 points, bold, and left aligned, as shown by the settings and entries for the text presentation toolbar items in Figure 3.8.

The business area headings in the spreadsheet (row 8 of Figure 3.2) have been set as right-aligned (to have them aligned with the numbers that appear below them) and bold. The left-hand-side row headings (column 1) have been set as bold as well, while the details about the customer, dates, and event (rows 4–6) have been set as italic.

It is always sensible to design a spreadsheet so that it looks inviting and is as easy as possible to read.

Row height

When a cell is set to display its contents in a larger point size, the height of the row increases automatically. Sometimes you may wish to change the row height yourself. In the FUN spreadsheet, rows 3 and 18 have been made narrower to improve the look of the display. As with adjustments to column width, there are two ways of instructing Excel to alter the depth of rows: either position the mouse cursor between two rows, and drag the row border up or down as required; or highlight the row and open the 'Format'→'Row'→'Height...' dialogue box. Then right-click on the selected '**Row Height**'.

Cell shading

The data entry cells in Figure 3.2 have been shaded by selecting them in turn, and clicking on the '**cell colour**' button (Figure

3.9). If the colour button does not show the desired colour at first, click on the drop-down arrow and select the desired colour.

Figure 3.9 'Cell colour' tool button

Borders

In Figure 3.2 the headings of the four columns of the FUN analysis and the 'Total' column (row 8) have been underlined with a single-line border using the 'Border' button on the toolbar. The borders could also have been specified by using the 'Format'→'Cells' menu, as in Figure 3.10.

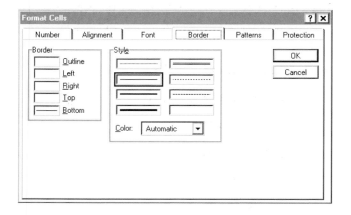

Figure 3.10 'Format Cells': 'Border' dialogue

Other presentation settings

Almost all of the format and presentation settings can be found from the 'Format' menu, though some of the presentation settings are found on the 'Tools'→ 'Options' menu. For example, the finished FUN spreadsheet has had the cell grid lines excluded, as well as the scroll bars, by setting the relevant boxes in the 'View' tab dialogue – see Figure 3.11.

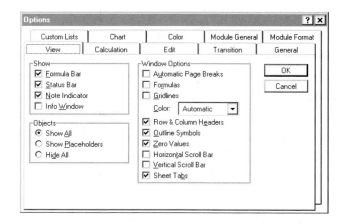

Figure 3.11 Spreadsheet 'View' dialogue from the 'Tools'→'Options' menu

The use and manipulation of spreadsheet data

You can use and manipulate your spreadsheet to:

- find data
- go to a specified cell
- search and replace data
- cut, copy, paste, move
- clear cell formats or contents
- use 'paste special'.

The 'Edit' menu in Excel has the usual features to allow you to cut, copy, and paste data; to find and replace data; and to go to a specific cell.

There are enhanced facilities to clear a cell or a range of cells. Apart from simply clicking on a cell and pressing the <Delete> or <Del> key, the 'Edit'→'Clear' menu item offers you the ability to clear the cell contents while leaving the cell formatting intact; or to clear the cell formatting while leaving the contents intact; or to clear both contents and formatting.

Paste special

The 'Edit'→'Paste Special' menu item also offers an enhanced paste facility. If previously a spreadsheet cell or range of cells has been cut or copied to the clipboard, the dialogue shown in Figure 3.12 allows you to paste selected parts of the copied cells, as well as allowing additional arithmetical calculations to be carried out during the paste operation.

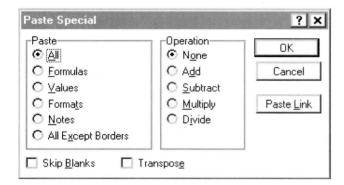

Figure 3.12 'Paste Special' dialogue for Excel clipboard data

If previously some other item has been cut or copied to the clipboard from a different application (such as Word), the 'Paste Special' dialogue allows the pasting of the clipboard contents in one of a number of different formats (Figure 3.13).

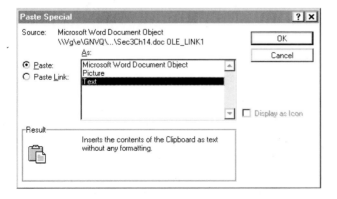

Figure 3.13 'Paste Special' dialogue for other clipboard data

Moving cells

Moving a cell or a block of cells from one place in the spreadsheet to another can be done in two steps using 'Edit', then 'Cut' and 'Paste'; but Excel provides a one-step 'drag and drop' facility using the mouse. Highlight the cell(s) that you want to move, position the mouse cursor on the border of your selection so that it changes from the normal 'fat plus sign' to an arrow, *drag* the selected cells over to their destination, and *drop* them by releasing the mouse button.

Cell referencing

The following paragraphs explain the different ways in which you can refer to spreadsheet cells. The names Excel gives to these are:

- relative cell referencing
- absolute cell referencing
- mixed cell referencing
- 3D referencing
- cell ranges
- R1C1 referencing.

The crucial point of a spreadsheet is that it can be set up to perform calculations. For the FUN event gross profit spreadsheet, for example, we need to calculate the event gross profit by subtracting the costs from the revenue. In order for the spreadsheet to carry out this calculation, the appropriate cells must be identified, and this is called **cell referencing**. A cell is referenced by its *column letter* and *row number*. The 'Est gross profit' for 'Catering' is cell B11. As can be seen in the screen fragment in Figure 3.14, while cell B11 *displays* the value '£1,000', it in fact *contains* the formula, '=B9-B10', which is how the value of '£1,000' came to be calculated. The formula says: 'subtract the contents of cell B10' (the estimated cost of catering, £1,000) 'from the contents of B9' (the quote accepted by the customer for catering, namely £2,000).

B11	▼	=B9-B10

	A	B	C
1	**Festivities Unlimited**		
2	Event Gross Profit Calculator		
4	Customer	Mary Smith	
5	Quote date	07/09	
6	Calculation date	01/04	
7			
8		Catering	Transpor
9	Quote	£2,000	£50(
10	Est cost	£1,000	£30(
11	Est gross profit	£1,000	£20(
12	Est GP %	50.0%	40.0%
13	Actual cost	£1,150	£25(

Figure 3.14 Cell references for 'Est gross profit' for 'Catering'

In any spreadsheet, there is a distinction between the *contents* of a cell and what is *displayed* at that cell. What you *see* in a cell – what is displayed – is the result of the Excel software applying the formula in the cell to the appropriate data.

Relative cell referencing

The same calculation needs to be done for the estimated gross profit for transport, staff, and the other business areas. Copying the formula from B11 into C11 gives the display shown in Figure 3.15.

Excel has automatically changed the formula from '=B9-B10' to '=C9-C10', which is what we want. The cell references that we have been using – B9 and B10 – are references which were *relative* to cell B11. When we want the same sort of calculation for cell C11, the references should 'naturally' become C9 and C10. Similarly,

C11	▼	=C9-C10

	A	B	C	D
1	**Festivities Unlimited**			
2	Event Gross Profit Calculator			
4	Customer	Mary Smith		
5	Quote date	07/09		
6	Calculation date	01/04		
7				
8		Catering	Transport	S
9	Quote	£2,000	£500	£1,
10	Est cost	£1,000	£300	£
11	Est gross profit	£1,000	£200	£:
12	Est GP %	50.0%	40.0%	30.
13	Actual cost	£1,150	£250	£

Figure 3.15 Cell references for 'Est gross profit' for 'Transport'

cells D11, E11, and F11 carry the estimated gross profit calculation formula with its cell references adjusted to be relative to and appropriate for the columns in which they appear.

You will have noticed that, in Excel, a **formula** – a command to Excel to make a calculation – starts with the equals sign, '='.

Absolute cell referencing

Sometimes the same sort of formula in different cells needs to refer to a *specific* cell for part of the calculation, such that this specific cell remains the same cell no matter where the formula appears. In this case, the specific cell must be referenced **absolutely**, and this is done by inserting a '$' sign in front of the column and row numbers, such as '$F$6'.

Suppose that an enhancement to the FUN spreadsheet was to have the costs and gross profit shown on a 'per guest' basis. The number of guests for the event is held in cell F6 as the event size. We want to divide each of the financial values in column F – F9, F10, F11, and so on – by the value of cell F6. Suppose we set up column H to take these 'per guest' values. If we entered the formula '=F9/F6' into cell H9, we would have the 'per guest' quote (£166.67) correctly calculated; but if we then copied H9 and pasted it into H10, H11, and so on, the values would be all wrong. The reason, of course, is that Excel would modify the formula and so that in H10 it became '=F10/F7', in H11 it became '=F11/F8', and so on. To stop this happening and force Excel not to change the reference to cell F6, the formula in H9 should be modified to be '=F9/$F$6'. Then, copying it and pasting it into H10, H11, etc. would correctly yield '=F10/$F$6', '=F11/$F$6', and so on.

Event name	21st birthday party
Event type	Birthday
Event size	30

Extras	Total	Per guest	
£1,500	£5,000	£166.67	=F9/$F$6
£1,200	£3,200	£106.67	=F10/$F$6
£300	£1,800	£60.00	=F11/$F$6
20.0%	36.0%		
£1,200	£3,400	£113.33	=F13/$F$6
£300	£1,600	£53.33	=F14/$F$6
20.0%	32.0%		
£0	(£200)	(£6.67)	=F15/$F$6
0.0%	(11.1%)		

Figure 3.16 Additional 'Per guest' calculation

Mixed cell referencing

It is sometimes useful to have part of a cell reference kept constant or absolute, and part of the reference left variable, or relative. This is best illustrated by way of an example. Suppose we construct a simple spreadsheet to calculate all the possible results of rolling two dice – that is, the total of the spots shown. It might look like Figure 3.17.

DieRoll.xls

	A	B	C	D	E	F	G	H	I
1					Die A				
2			1	2	3	4	5	6	
3		1	2	3	4	5	6	7	
4		2	3	4	5	6	7	8	
5	Die B	3	4	5	6	7	8	9	
6		4	5	6	7	8	9	10	
7		5	6	7	8	9	10	11	
8		6	7	8	9	10	11	12	
9									
10									

Die Roll

Figure 3.17 Dice roll spreadsheet

To start with you might think that the formula for cell C3 should be '=C2+B3', and indeed that would work for C3. If that were copied and pasted to the other cells of the spreadsheet, however, we would get the wrong answers, because the cell references to C2 and B3 in the formula would change in the wrong way.

The solution is to change the C3 formula to '=C$2+$B3'. The **mixed reference** 'C$2' ensures that when Excel pastes the formula from C3 to, say, the cell in the next column, D3, the reference changes to become 'D$2' – without the '$' sign in front of the column letter, the column letter would change. The other part of the formula in C3 has a mixed reference to '$B3'. When Excel pastes the formula from C3 to the cell in the next column, D3, the reference stays the same, '$B3' – '$' sign in front of the column letter prevents it from changing.

Similarly, consider what happens when the C3 formula '=C$2+$B3' is pasted from C3 to, say, the cell in the next row, C4. The 'C$2' reference remains as 'C$2' – the '$' sign in front of the row number prevents it from changing. The other part of the formula has the reference '$B3'. This cell reference changes to '$B4' – without the '$'

	A	B	C	D	E	F	G	H
					Die A			
1								
2			1	2	3	4	5	6
3		1	=C$2+$B3	=D$2+$B3	=E$2+$B3	=F$2+$B3	=G$2+$B3	=H$2+$B3
4		2	=C$2+$B4	=D$2+$B4	=E$2+$B4	=F$2+$B4	=G$2+$B4	=H$2+$B4
5	Die B	3	=C$2+$B5	=D$2+$B5	=E$2+$B5	=F$2+$B5	=G$2+$B5	=H$2+$B5
6		4	=C$2+$B6	=D$2+$B6	=E$2+$B6	=F$2+$B6	=G$2+$B6	=H$2+$B6
7		5	=C$2+$B7	=D$2+$B7	=E$2+$B7	=F$2+$B7	=G$2+$B7	=H$2+$B7
8		6	=C$2+$B8	=D$2+$B8	=E$2+$B8	=F$2+$B8	=G$2+$B8	=H$2+$B8
9								

Die Roll

Figure 3.18 Dice roll spreadsheet formulas

sign in front of the row number, it changes to suit its new row location. See Figure 3.18.

3D referencing

Most cell references in a spreadsheet are to cells in the currently displayed sheet. Sometimes, however, it is useful to have a worksheet refer to cells in a *different* worksheet. The FUN spreadsheet has two worksheets: these are called 'Event Gross Profit' and 'Graph', as shown on the sheet tabs at the bottom. The 'Graph' worksheet refers to cell A1 of the 'Event Gross Profit' worksheet by using 3D reference '='Event Gross Profit'!A1', as illustrated in Figure 3.19.

The '!' mark labels the cell reference(s), for example 'A1', as coming from a different worksheet, in this case 'Event Gross Profit'.

Cell ranges

In the 'Totals' column of the FUN spreadsheet we need to enter formulas which calculate the sum of the values in each of the rows holding financial values. For example, the spreadsheet requires the sum of the quote values for catering, transport, staff, and extras to be placed in cell F9. You could just type in this total, which you happen to know is £5 000, but that would defeat the whole purpose of using a spreadsheet. You want the spreadsheet to calculate the total for you, so that you can change the quotation as needed and have the spreadsheet **recalculate** and show you what happens to the gross profit.

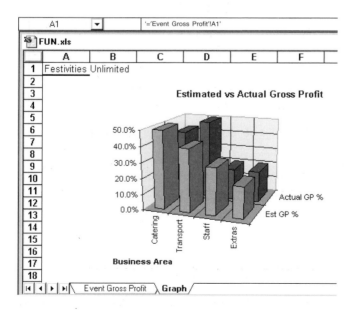

Figure 3.19 3D reference in cell A1 of the 'Graph' worksheet

We will use a **function**, SUM(), to calculate this total. This function, and others like it, are discussed in more detail below. For the time being, we will enter the formula '=SUM(B9:E9)' into cell F9.

Notice that the cells to be added together have been identified as a **range** of cells, 'B9:E9'. The colon ':' is Excel's way of saying 'All the cells starting at B9 and ending at E9'. Identifying a range of cells in this way has two important benefits.

The first is that a cell range is a convenient and quick shorthand which saves having to type in the individual cell references. You could have typed in the formula '=SUM(B9, C9, D9, E9)' instead, but this would quickly become tedious for, say, a row of twenty adjacent cells.

The second benefit of using a cell range is more subtle, and much more important. Suppose you had typed in the formula '=SUM(B9, C9, D9, E9)'. (Or, indeed, you might not have bothered with the SUM() function at all, but just typed in '=B9+C9+D9+E9'.) The spreadsheet would work perfectly until the time came to add a new, fifth column to the FUN gross profit calculator. Perhaps the 'Catering' column needs to be split so that its values are divided between 'Food' and 'Preparation', so you would place the cursor in the 'Transport' column (remember that columns and rows are inserted *before* or *above* the cursor position), column C, and insert a new column from the '**Insert**'→'**Columns**' menu item. If you now looked at the formula for the total of the quote values in cell G9, it would read '=SUM(B9, D9, E9, F9)', as shown in Figure 3.20 where the new column has been inserted into the spreadsheet.

If previously you had typed in '=B9+C9+D9+E9' to total the 'Quote' row

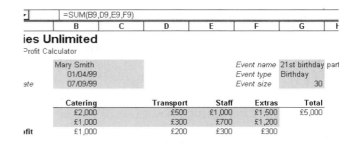

Figure 3.20 **Effect of column insertion on formula references**

values, it would now read '=B9+D9+E9+F9'. In either case, your formula would *fail* to include automatically the quote value that would be entered into the new column.

On the other hand, had your formula used a cell range, the '=SUM(B9:E9)' formula *would* change to '=SUM(B9:F9)' when the new column was inserted – exactly what you want, automatically including the new value into the formula to total the cells in row 9.

R1C1 referencing

Spreadsheet formulas usually refer to cells by a combination of column letter and row number, such as B3 or P99. If you use R1C1 referencing Excel refers to cells by row and column number instead.

The cell reference R1C1 means 'row1, column 1', which would normally be called A1. Cell M17 becomes R17C13. To switch to the R1C1 reference style', choose the 'Options' command from the 'Tools' menu, click the '**General**' tab and select '**R1C1**'.

Formula operators

Let us now consider the following operators used in formulas:

- arithmetic operators: +, -, *, /, %, ^

- relational operators: =, <, >, >=, <=, <>

- logical values: FALSE, TRUE

- text concatenation: & or +

- the use of parentheses: ( ).

The formulas we have looked at so far have used the simple arithmetic operators '+', '-', '*', and '/' — for addition, subtraction, multiplication, and division, respectively. There are a few more operators we should know about.

Powers

To raise the value in a cell to a **power,** the *exponentiation operator,* '^' is used. For example, if cell B3 contains a value that is to be squared, the formula '=B3^2' will do the trick. If it is cell A2 that contains the power to which B3 is to be raised, then the formula would read '=B3^A2'.

Concatenation

Text also can be operated upon. To combine the text in cell B5, for example, with the text in cell A3, the formula '=B5&A3' uses the **concatenation** operator, '&', to achieve the required result. Figure 3.21 illustrates the construction of a heading in cell A1 of the 'Graph' worksheet, based on the text in cells A1 and A2 of the 'Event Gross Profit' worksheet.

Notice that in this example there are three **text strings** which are concatenated, and that the middle text string, 'for', has an

invisible space before the 'f' and another after the 'r'.

Parentheses in formulas

More complicated formulas may need to use **parentheses,** sometimes wrongly called *brackets*, to ensure that values are calculated correctly. Parentheses are used in Excel formulas just as they are used in normal arithmetic. For example, the formula '=(A1+A2)*B4' ensures that the values of cells A1 and A2 are added together *before* their sum is multiplied by the value of cell B4. Without the parentheses, the multiplication of A2 and B4 would take place before adding to the result the value in A1.

Relational operators

Most of the cells in a spreadsheet will have either a numeric value or a textual value — that is, a spreadsheet consists mainly of numbers and text. Cells can have another kind of value as well, however, called a **logical** value — that is, **TRUE** or **FALSE**. It is unusual to want to *display* a cell's logical value, but quite often it is useful to be able to use its logical value in a formula or function.

We will look more closely at relational operators — the operators used to manipulate logical values — when we examine the IF() function, below, at the end of the discussion on built-in functions.

Built-in functions

Excel provides common built-in spreadsheet functions, including these eight which are explained below:

A1		='Event Gross Profit'!A2&" for "&'Event Gross Profit'!A1					
A	B	C	D	E	F	G	H
1 Event Gross Profit Calculator for Festivities Unlimited							
2							

Figure 3.21 Text concatenation

- SUM
- COUNT
- MAX
- MIN
- INT (short for 'integer')
- RAND (short for 'random number')
- DATE
- IF

These are described below; amongst the other built-in functions that you may find useful are:

- SQRT   This is the positive *square root* of a number: thus '=SQRT(4)' returns the value 2.

- MEDIAN   This is the number in the *middle* of a set of numbers.

- MODE   This is the value that occurs *most frequently* in a set of numbers.

- AVERAGE   This is the *arithmetic mean* of a set of numeric values, found by summing them and dividing by the number of values.

Much of the power of a spreadsheet comes from the use of **functions**, built-in formulas that carry out complex calculations. Excel provides a button on the taskbar which gives 'one-click' access to the functions list – see Figure 3.22.

Alternatively, the functions list can be accessed from the '**Insert**'→'**Functions**' menu item. Either way, you are presented with a functions **wizard** which helps you insert your required function into the spreadsheet. A wizard can be thought of as a set or series of dialogue boxes, designed

Figure 3.22 Function wizard toolbar button

to help you complete a more lengthy or more complicated task.

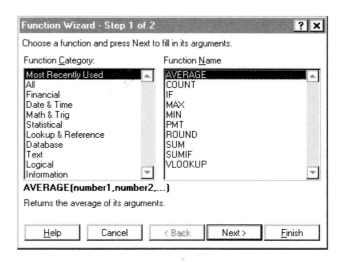

Figure 3.23 Function wizard: step 1

This particular wizard has two steps, or dialogue boxes. In the first step you select the function you require, usually by clicking on one of the function categories in the left-hand pane, and then clicking on the required function itself in the right-hand pane. Clicking the '**Next>**' button opens up the second step, in which you complete the details of the data required by the function.

The SUM() function

The **SUM**() function does the job of adding up a range of cell values. Often, the values to be added up are found in a column or in a row, but sometimes a whole block of values needs to be added up. The SUM() function is such a useful one that it has its own button on the toolbar, called '**AUTOSUM**' (Figure 3.24).

Figure 3.24 Autosum function tool bar button

We will enter the SUM() function into the FUN spreadsheet using both the AUTOSUM button and the function wizard.

AUTOSUM

Place the cursor in cell F9, and click the 'AUTOSUM' button. The result is shown in Figure 3.25.

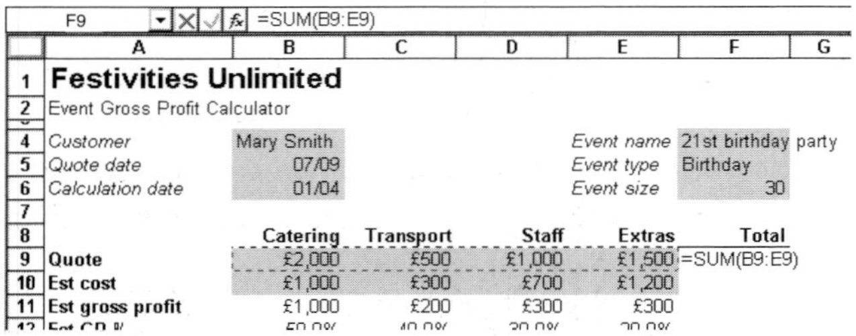

Figure 3.25 Autosum for 'Quote' values

Excel makes a 'best guess' of the cells that it thinks you want added together, and places a blinking dashed border around these cells. It shows you, in the data entry line, the formula it proposes to enter into F9: '=SUM(B9:E9)'. In this case it is correct, so you may either press the <Enter> key, or click on the 'green tick', and the entry of the SUM() function is completed. Cell F9 now displays the *cell value* of £5,000. Click on cell F9, and the data entry line shows you the *cell contents*, the formula '=SUM(B9:E9)'.

We can do the same to enter an AUTOSUM in F10, to calculate the total estimated cost.

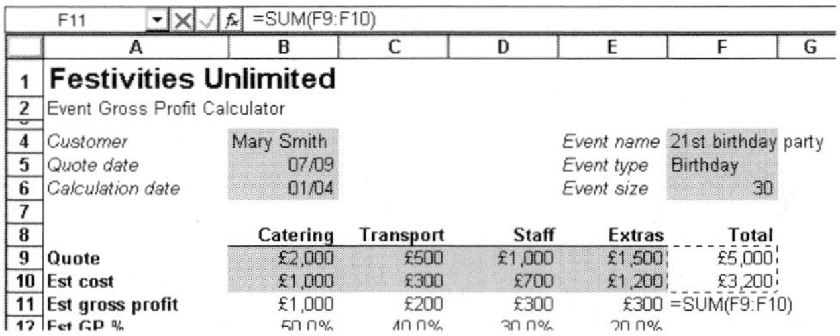

Figure 3.26 Autosum for 'Est GP' values

When we try the AUTOSUM a third time in F11, to calculate the total estimated gross profit, however, Excel behaves differently, and makes a 'best guess' which is not what we want (Figure 3.26).

Excel's 'best guess' here is to total a range of cells in column F; indeed, Excel's 'best guess' is always to suggest a column total rather than a row total if possible. To change the cell range that Excel proposes, simply highlight the required range of cells: move the mouse to the first cell of the range, and drag to the last cell of the range. The dashed line border changes to enclose the cells thus identified, as does the formula in the data entry box. Click the 'green tick' when you are satisfied.

Function wizard

We will now use the function wizard to enter the SUM() function into our formula in cell F11, to calculate the row total. Place the cursor into cell F11, and click on the 'Function Wizard' toolbar button. You may notice from the earlier screen shot of the function wizard that, as one of the most recently used functions, the SUM() function is already available in the right-hand pane. Ignore that, and look in the other function categories to find the function you want. The SUM() function belongs to the 'Math & Trig' category: click on that category, and

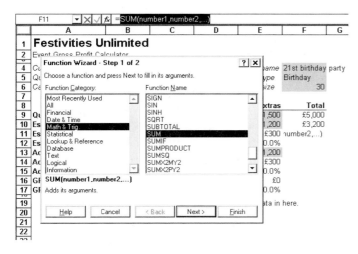

Figure 3.27 Function wizard: step 1, 'Math & Trig'

scroll the right-hand pane down until the SUM function comes into view. Click on that, and the result is as shown in Figure 3.27.

Click on the 'Next>' button, and the next dialogue box opens. The text cursor in this dialogue box is already positioned in the data entry box labelled 'number1', awaiting your input. You could type in the cell range you wish to sum, 'B11:E11'. A quicker way is to just highlight the range of cells with the mouse, and Excel will automatically fill in the cell range for you. If the dialogue box is in the way such that

you cannot highlight the required range, drag it out of the way first.

Notice that the function wizard carries out the SUM() function for you on the range of cells you indicate, and shows you the result in a box labelled 'Value:', £1,800. The wizard also shows you, in the box next to the cell range entered as 'number1', the values of the cells that are being summed – '{1000, 200, 300 …}'. These are simply aids so that you can be confident that the function is working as expected.

Function wizard: early finish

Almost all wizards can be 'finished' early. If you finish the function wizard at step 1 instead of going on to step 2, you are left with the SUM() function in the data entry line and some text that indicates where the cell range(s) must be entered (Figure 3.29).

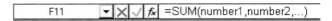

Figure 3.29 Function wizard 'finished' at step 1

You could highlight all of the text between the opening and closing parentheses here, and then highlight the range of cells for the SUM. The cell range replaces the text, and clicking on the 'green tick' completes the process.

Some useful statistical functions

COUNT()

The **COUNT()** function counts the number of numeric values that appear in the specified cell range. It is most useful when a spreadsheet is larger than the screen can comfortably fit in, and there is a need to know how many (numeric) items there are

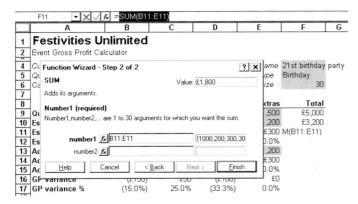

Figure 3.28 Function wizard: step 2, SUM

in a particular column or row. It ignores blank cells and text.

MIN(), MAX()

MIN() and **MAX()** find and display the smallest and largest numeric values that appear in the specified cell range.

AVERAGE(), MEDIAN(), MODE()

These functions calculate the three common measures of central tendency in a given cell range. **AVERAGE()** calculates the common arithmetic mean of a set of values. Note that blank cells and cells containing text are ignored. If you want a blank cell to be treated as having a value of zero, you will need to enter the number '0' into that cell.

MEDIAN() calculates that value which divides the range of values in half, such that 50% of the range of values is larger than the median value, and 50% of the range of values is smaller than the median value. Blank and text cells are ignored.

MODE() calculates that value which appears most frequently in the specified range. Blank and text cells are ignored.

Some useful mathematical and date functions

INT()

The **INT()** function rounds off the specified cell value to an integer. Note that when Excel displays a value, it displays it to the nearest value required by the cell format. So an actual value of, say, 11.6% held in cell F17 would be displayed as 12% if the F17 cell format specified that zero decimal places were to be shown. It is sometimes useful to have a value such as 11.6 rounded

down to 11, and 'INT(F17)' would do this. The next section illustrates another use of the INT() function.

RAND()

The **RAND()** function generates a **random number** between 0 and 1. It is useful when constructing spreadsheets to simulate real-world events. You could make a National Lottery predictor using the RAND() function, by multiplying the result of the RAND() function by 49. Figure 3.30 shows an extremely rough and ready spreadsheet to do this.

Figure 3.30 RAND() function

Notice that the value of the RAND() function, between 0 and 1, must be translated into a lottery number between 1 and 49. This requires that the RAND() number first be multiplied by 49, to generate a range between 0 and 48.9999, and then have 1 added to it, to generate a range from 1 to 49.9999. Then, the INT() function is used to prevent a value such as 49.7 being displayed as 50, which is not a valid Lottery number.

Also notice that the RAND() function does not require the specification of a cell reference inside its parentheses.

Finally, notice that functions can be **nested** inside each other.

DATE()

There are a number of date and time functions available in Excel. The basic **DATE()** function provides the way of holding a date value in a cell so that calculations can be made using it. To use the DATE() function, the year, month, and day must be specified as three values, for example '=DATE(99,4,1)' to represent 1st April 1999 (Figure 3.31).

B5	▼	=DATE(99,4,1)	
	A	**B**	**C**
1	**Festivities Unlimited**		
2	Event Gross Profit Calculator		
4	Customer	Mary Smith	
5	Quote date	01/04/99	
6	Calculation date	17/09/99	
7			

Figure 3.31 DATE() function

The example 'DATE(99,4,1)' is somewhat trivial, since the year, month, and day numbers are specified directly in the formula. Suppose you required the first day of a month held in G14 and of a year held in G12; the formula would be 'DATE(G12,G14,1)'.

Suppose you wanted to calculate the number of days between the 'Quote date' and the 'Calculation date' on the FUN spreadsheet. This would be simply done by the formula '=B6-B5'.

The IF() function

Frequently, a calculation may only need to be done when a certain condition applies, and not otherwise. The **IF()** function provides the means of having one or other of two possible values calculated, depending upon some condition or logical test. The IF() function therefore comprises three parts:

IF (Logical test, Value_if_TRUE, Value_if_FALSE)

In the FUN spreadsheet, for example, a *division by zero* error occurs if the quote value for one of the event components is £0, as illustrated in Figure 3.32.

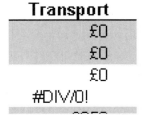

Transport
£0
£0
£0
#DIV/0!

Figure 3.32 '#DIV/0!' error

This is because in the formula for the estimated gross profit percentage, '=C11/C9', the value of cell C9 is zero. The formula needs to be changed so that the division by C9 is attempted only when the value of C9 is non-zero.

Conditions and logical tests

A condition or logical test is almost always expressed using **relational operators** ('<', '>', '=', '<>', '=<', '=>') and **logical operators** ('AND', 'OR', 'NOT'). The condition 'C9<>0' is **TRUE** if the value of C9 is non-zero, and is **FALSE** if the value of C9 is 0. Another way of establishing the same outcome is to have a condition that reads 'NOT(C9=0)'.

For the FUN spreadsheet, we can begin the IF() function needed in cell C12 with:

IF (C9<>0, Value_if_TRUE, Value_if_FALSE)

99

Value if TRUE

The second part of the IF() function is carried out if the logical test is TRUE. So, if C9 is indeed non-zero, we want to calculate the percentage by dividing cell C9 by C11, 'C9/C11'. Our IF() function is thus:

IF (C9<>0, C9/C11, Value_if_FALSE)

Value if FALSE

The third and final part of the IF() function is carried out if the logical test is FALSE. If C9 is in fact zero, we do not want to calculate the percentage at all, but what would we want to do instead? One option is to display a short text message, perhaps something like 'No value'. Our IF() function is thus

IF (C9<>0, C9/C11, "No value")

Notice that the text must be enclosed in **double quotes**. Figure 3.33 shows the IF() function used in the formula in cell C12, and the displayed result of that function.

C12		=IF(C9<>0,C11/C9,"No value")		
	A	**B**	**C**	**D**
1	**Festivities Unlimited**			
2	Event Gross Profit Calculator			
4	Customer	Mary Smith		
5	Quote date	07/09		
6	Calculation date	01/04		
7				
8		**Catering**	**Transport**	**Sta**
9	Quote	£2,000	£0	£1,00
10	Est cost	£1,000	£0	£70
11	Est gross profit	£1,000	£0	£30
12	Est GP %	50.0%	No value	30.0%
13	Actual cost	£1,150	£250	£80

Figure 3.33 IF() function

The IF() function in checking input values

The IF() function can be used to define the values of input items that are acceptable.

This point is discussed in Chapter 3.3, page 136.

Presenting spreadsheet information

We now turn to the presentation of the information in your spreadsheet. Your aim must be to convey the information in the way that is most helpful to whomever needs it.

Chapter 1.4 dealt with a large number of issues to do with presentation: this chapter covers some of the same ground, but from the perspectives of the creator and the reader of spreadsheets. As before you will need to think about how best to use computer screens and printed pages for your output, and how to use page layout, cell formats, graphs and charts as effectively as possible.

Printing and page layout

The following aspects of layout will make a difference to the *feel* of your completed spreadsheet:

- margins
- headers
- footers
- page size
- page orientation.

Page setup

The 'File'→'Page Setup...' menu item in Excel gives extensive control over the layout and printing of the spreadsheet pages (Figure 3.34).

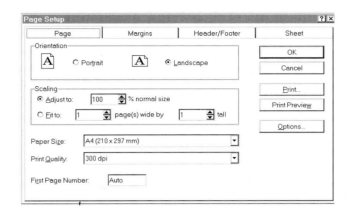

Figure 3.34 'Page Setup': 'Page' tab

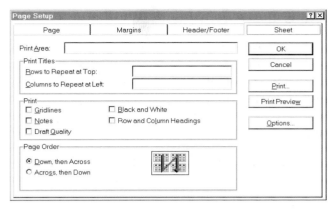

Figure 3.35 'Page Setup': 'Sheet' tab

The most important component of the '**Page**' tab in the 'Page Setup' dialogue box is the specification of the paper size. Most UK office systems employ 'A4' as their standard paper size.

The other major element of the dialogue is the specification of whether the spreadsheet should print in **portrait** or **landscape** orientation. If you are not sure which would look better, click the '**Print Preview**' button after making each choice in turn to see what you think.

The '**Margins**' tab opens a dialogue box in which you are able to specify the page side margins as well as the header and footer margins.

The '**Header/Footer**' tab opens a dialogue box in which the default page header and footer are displayed. You can click on the drop-down list boxes for header and footer items and select other formats, or you can click on the '**Custom Header**' and '**Custom Footer**' buttons and create your own.

Finally, the '**Sheet**' tab opens a dialogue box with some interesting options (Figure 3.35).

Print area

Normally, clicking on the '**Printer**' icon on the tool bar results in the whole spreadsheet being printed. If a range of cells is identified in the '**Print Area:**' edit box, however, only that range is printed. This is a useful setting to make if you expect that your users will normally only want a certain area of the spreadsheet printed: it saves them having to select the part of the spreadsheet for themselves that they want. If there are, say, three or four spreadsheet areas that are needed as printouts, you could create a set of three or four **macro** buttons that would each insert a specific cell range into the 'Print Area:' box and then initiate a printout. There is a discussion of macros in Chapter 3.2.

Print titles

Where a spreadsheet extends over a number of pages, and where the kind of information on each page is similar, it is useful to identify a set of rows, or columns, or both, that are repeated on every printed page. The rows and columns to be repeated are specified in the '**Print Titles**' dialogues.

Other print controls

To improve the look of the printed page, it is possible to suppress the spreadsheet gridlines as well as the spreadsheet row and column headings – the labels '1', '2', '3' … and 'A', 'B', 'C' … Unset these options in the '**Print**' dialogue area.

Checking the '**Black and White**' option is useful for some black-and-white printers which do not translate colours very well.

Layout control in the spreadsheet itself

To ensure that a long spreadsheet is broken up into pages appropriately, you can insert a **page break** into the spreadsheet at the point where you want following spreadsheet rows to be printed on a new page. In Figure 3.36 a page break has been inserted in cell A7.

	A	B	C	D
	FUNrev3.xls			
1	**Festivities Unlimited**			
2	Event Gross Profit Calculator			
4	Customer	Mary Smith		
5	Quote date	07-Sep		
6	Calculation date	01-Apr		
7				
8		Catering	Transport	Staff
9	Quote	£2,000	£500	£1,000

Figure 3.36 Manual page break

Click on the cell where printing should start on a new page. At the '**Insert**' menu, click on the '**Page Break**' menu item. The manually inserted page break is shown on the spreadsheet as a dashed line.

Graph and chart types

We reviewed these, apart from scatter charts, in Chapter 1.3; but here the emphasis is on graphs and charts that illustrate output arising from spreadsheets.

- line graphs
- bar charts
- pie charts
- scatter charts.

Graphs and charts can be placed into an Excel spreadsheet in either of two forms. In the first case, a graph can be 'embedded' in a worksheet. This is how the FUN spreadsheet graph has been constructed; the graph coexists in a worksheet with other worksheet cells and worksheet components, and is the result of clicking the '**Chart Wizard**' button and dragging an outline rectangle over the desired area of the spreadsheet.

In the second case, a graph can be constructed as a new worksheet itself, in which case it completely and exclusively fills the new worksheet. It is labelled with a worksheet tab called 'Chart 1' or something similar. This method is invoked by using the '**Insert**'→'**Chart**' menu item, and selecting '**As New Sheet**'. From this point, the chart wizard takes over and the steps are exactly the same as for the first case.

A picture is often said to be 'worth a thousand words' – in the case of spreadsheets, it is worth a thousand numbers. You should strive to provide an appropriate graph or chart for every major output of your spreadsheet. Fortunately, Excel provides a rich variety of graph and chart types (Figure 3.37). The construction of charts is covered in Chapter 3.2.

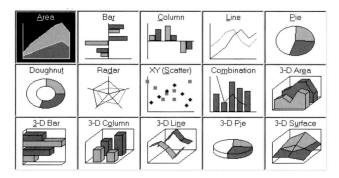

Figure 3.37 Excel charts and graphs

Data series

Central to an understanding of charts and graphs is an understanding of what Excel terms a **data series**. A single data series is a set of values that relate to some particular feature of the spreadsheet results. An example would be the estimated cost of an event, which is a particular feature of the FUN spreadsheet. There could be a data series called 'Estimated costs' that would consist of values of estimated cost for catering, transport, staff, and so on. This data series would comprise the range "Gross Profit Calculator' !$B$10:$E$10'.

Often there are two or more data series, and interest is focused on how one series compares with another. For example, the FUN spreadsheet compares the two data series of 'Estimated gross profit' against 'Actual gross profit'.

Chart types

Where there is just one data series of interest, a **pie chart** would show the proportions of each data value in that series. Alternatively, a single **bar chart** would show the actual values of each data item as the length of a bar. (Excel provides two kinds of bar chart. When the bars are laid out horizontally, it is called a *bar chart*; when the bars are laid out vertically, Excel calls it a *column chart*.) If the data values form some sort of natural sequence, or could be ordered in some way, then a **line chart** or **area chart** would show the changes in data values in sequence.

For two or more data series, a bar chart shows a comparison for data values which do not have any inherent order or sequence. Where an ordering of data values is present, then a line chart may be more appropriate. If the data series 'build' upon each other in some sense, then an area chart may be useful.

Usually, the measurements or data values in the data series are all of the same kind – amount of money, for example, or percentages. Sometimes, data series may involve measures that are of different types – for example, the height in metres, the weight in kilograms, and the ages, for a collection of children. For such data series, **scatter charts** or **radar charts** may be appropriate. These two kinds of chart allow a view of the correlation or relationship between two or more different measures.

Graph and chart formatting

For graphs and charts to be as informative and as clear as possible, it is necessary to consider all these points:

- chart or graph title
- axis titles
- legend data series labels
- category labels
- data labels
- picture markers
- axis formats

- axis values
- background
- gridlines.

These points are addressed in Chapter 3.2.

Titles and axis labels

Clearly labelled graphs and charts are essential. You should ensure that your graphs have well-thought-out titles and labels. Excel provides for a chart title, a title for each axis, a legend box which identifies each data series, and labels for the axis points. The Y-axis points are labelled the same as the legend data series labels, while Excel calls the X-axis points 'categories'.

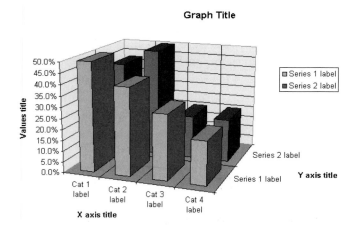

Figure 3.38 Chart titles and labels

When a chart is constructed using the chart wizard, the data series labels in the legend box and the labels for the axes data points come directly from the cells specified in the data series range. The cells that provide these labels are generally the first row and the first column of the data series cell range. The legend data series labels generally derive from the first row of the

series range, while the category labels derive from the first column of the series range.

Although the chart wizard then asks for the axes and graph titles separately, it is possible to have these refer to spreadsheet cells as well. In the edit box for the graph title, for example, type in an equals sign, '=', and then click on the cell in the spreadsheet which you want to use to provide the title text. Figure 3.39 shows the result of double-clicking on the graph title, together with the corresponding entry in the formula bar.

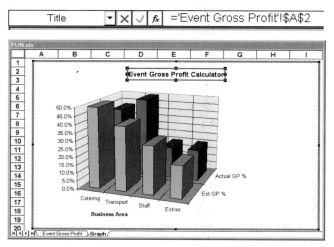

Figure 3.39 Chart title provided from a spreadsheet cell

Notice that the whole chart is first enclosed with a **bounding box,** and then within it the graph title has its own bounding box. Notice also that, in the formula bar, the graph title object has the name 'Title'. Finally, recall that any object in a bounding box can be moved, resized, and have its own formatting applied. The graph title could be moved to the bottom of the graph, for example, and formatted with a drop-shadow border coloured red, if you wished.

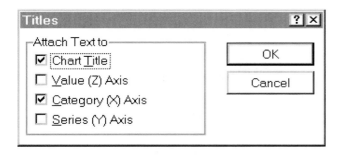

Figure 3.40 'Insert Titles' check boxes

If you did not provide one or other of the titles when the graph was first constructed, you can provide them later. Right-click on a blank part of the graph when its bounding box is visible. You are offered a menu which includes the option 'Insert Titles...'. Selecting that option brings up the check box dialogue illustrated in Figure 3.40.

When you click 'OK' and return to the graph, a single character appears inside a bounding box for each title for which you have checked 'Attach Text to'. Click on the text bounding box, and edit the text in the formula bar edit area.

Data labels

Line, scatter, and radar charts have their graph data points plotted using symbols such as circles, squares, or cross hairs. These data points can have their values attached as text labels. Also, the graphical symbol itself can be changed to something quite different, called a **picture marker**.

Figure 3.41 shows a line graph with a data label on each data point for one of the series.

The form of the data label is selected by clicking on the line or data series, and then right-clicking on the line. In the pop-up menu offered is the option to 'Insert Data Labels...' (Figure 3.42).

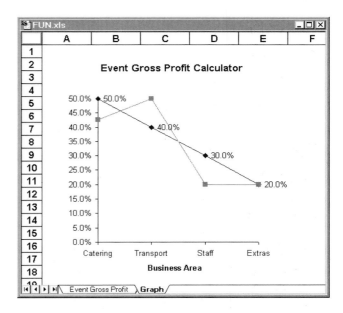

Figure 3.41 Example data labels

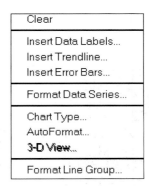

Figure 3.42 Pop-up menu

Selecting the option to 'Insert Data Labels...' brings up the dialogue in Figure 3.43.

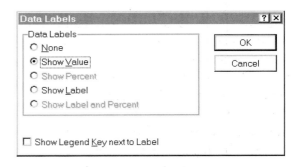

Figure 3.43 'Insert Data Labels...' dialogue

Picture markers

Instead of little squares or diamonds, a data series can be plotted using your own graphic pictures. Figure 3.44 shows Excel's help screen for such picture markers.

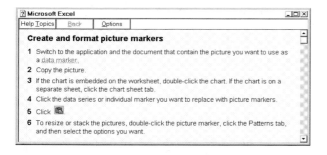

Figure 3.44 'Picture markers' Help screen

For our FUN spreadsheet line graph, let us create and use a balloon as a picture marker. Using the Paintbrush application, we create the graphic shown in Figure 3.45, and copy it to the clipboard.

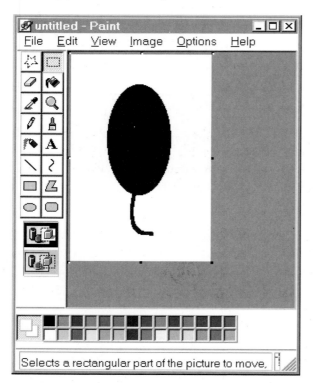

Figure 3.45 Picture marker created using Paintbrush

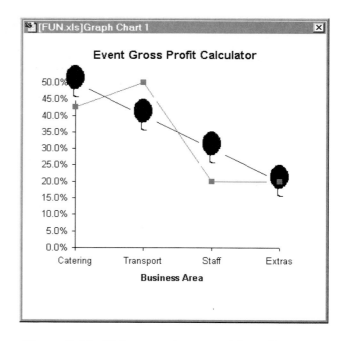

Figure 3.46 Picture markers used in a line graph

In the chart, click on the data marker, and paste from the 'Edit' menu. After some resizing of the picture, the result is as shown in Figure 3.46.

Axis formatting

Each graph axis can be formatted and adjusted in a number of ways (Figure 3.47).

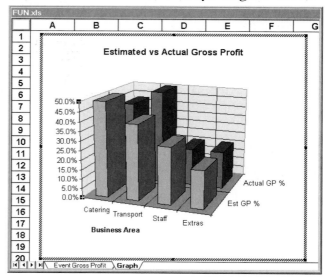

Figure 3.47 Axis selection within a graph

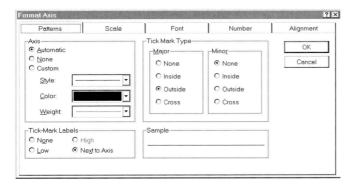

Figure 3.48 'Format Axis' tabbed dialogue box: 'Patterns' tab

With the axis selected, either double-click on it, or select the '**Format Selected Axis...**' menu item. A tabbed dialogue box allows you to change the axis parameters (Figure 3.48).

The 'Scale' dialogue is technically the most significant, since it allows you to override Excel's automatic settings for the axis and provide your own (Figure 3.49).

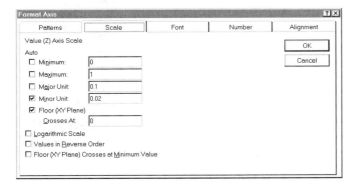

Figure 3.49 'Format Axis' tabbed dialogue box: 'Scale' tab

In Figure 3.49, the axis maximum has been set at 1 – that is, 100%.

Other graph presentation options

Backgrounds

A graph has two **background** areas – the 'chart' background and the 'plot' background. 3D charts also have '**walls**' and '**floors**'. Each of these backgrounds can have its border and colour properties set (Figure 3.50).

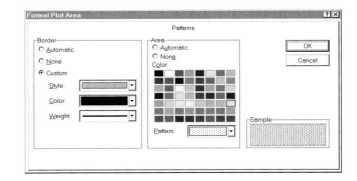

Figure 3.50 'Format Plot Area' dialogue box

Figure 3.50 illustrates the dialogue to set the plot area border and background.

Gridlines

Gridlines are linked to the axis scales, and can be turned on or off (Figure 3.51). If gridlines are turned on, their properties can be set.

The '**Format Gridlines**' dialogue box (Figure 3.52) is accessed by right-clicking on the chart. The menu that pops up offers '**Insert Grid Lines...**' as an option. There are gridlines for each of the three axes. If the '**Major Gridlines**' check box is unticked, then no gridline appears for that axis. If the check box is ticked, then the gridlines can be formatted by double-clicking on them, or by clicking on them and then selecting the '**Format Selected**

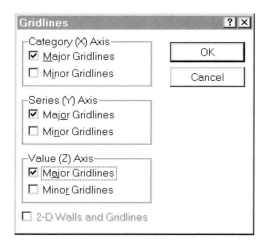

Figure 3.51 Turning gridlines on and off

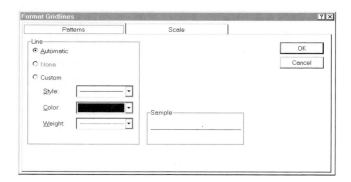

Figure 3.52 'Format Gridlines' dialogue box

Gridline' menu item. The gridline appearance and scale can be set, as illustrated in Figure 3.52.

Drawing and other graphics

You can make use of built-in drawing tools and other facilities to improve the presentation of a spreadsheet, including:

- text boxes
- graphic lines and shapes
- object positioning

- grouping objects
- object formatting
- object sizing.

Additional graphic and text objects can be placed on the spreadsheet by using Excel's drawing tools. Click on the '**Drawing**' button on the toolbar, and the '**Drawing**' tool bar appears (Figure 3.53).

Figure 3.53 'Drawing' toolbar

In the previous chapter we added a text box to the graph, and an arrow. The 'Drawing' toolbar offers a number of other objects as well: lines, rectangles, circles, arcs, and polygons.

There are times when it is difficult to select the object you require. The 'Drawing' toolbar provides a special cursor, a broad arrowhead, called the 'Drawing Selection'. This special cursor renders the rest of the spreadsheet 'dead' and responds only to drawing objects. If you find yourself wondering why nothing seems to work on the spreadsheet, it may be that you have simply forgotten to turn the drawing selection cursor off.

Object formatting

Selecting an object will change the first item on the '**Format**' menu, according to the type of object involved, and allow editing of the object's properties. Alternatively, double-clicking on the object will bring up the same 'Object Properties' dialogue box.

Two formatting buttons are provided directly on the 'Drawing' toolbar. One gives a drop shadow to any object that has a border, and the other changes the object's colour and pattern.

Object moving and sizing

If you grab the bounding box of an object you can move and position it elsewhere; while if you grab one of the control points on the bounding box, you can resize freely.

Grouping and ungrouping

Two or more objects can be grouped together, and are then treated as one. Click on the first object, and while holding down the <Shift> key, click on the other object(s) in turn. When all the required objects have been selected, click on the '**Group**' button on the 'Drawing' tool bar. The individual bounding boxes are replaced by a single, all-enclosing box. The group of objects can then be moved and resized as required.

A group of objects can be ungrouped by selecting the group and then clicking on the '**Ungroup**' button on the 'Drawing' toolbar.

Overlapping objects

Objects are **layered** on the spreadsheet, in the sense that certain objects are on top at the front, and other objects are behind at the back. Objects at the back can be partially (or completely) obscured by objects at the front, and this can produce some interesting effects.

For example, if the standard Excel drop shadow is not to your taste, you can create your own. First, draw a rectangle and give it a white fill and a thin black border. Copy the rectangle, and paste it. Move the new rectangle to one side, and give it a light grey fill with no border. It is on top of the first rectangle, so move it to the back either by clicking the '**Send to Back**' button, or by right-clicking and selecting the '**Send to Back**' item on the pop-up menu. Position it where you want behind the white rectangle, then select both rectangles and group them. Figure 3.54 shows the result when the two rectangles are positioned behind the text box (which now has no border and no fill).

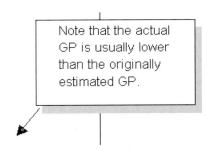

Figure 3.54 Overlapping rectangles, giving a drop-shadow effect

Try it out

The directors of FUN wish to consider possibilities for widening their range of products and services. They are keen to add to the existing operations some new events that are both more profitable and eye-catching. They have asked for a spreadsheet design that will allow the expected profitability of a range of potential events to be gauged under a variety of assumptions.

You have been asked to design a spreadsheet that will let the directors decide whether there would be a case for offering bungee-jumping events.

In this activity, you need to consider, as a group, how a spreadsheet should handle the following:

- the costs of hiring the necessary bungee-jumping equipment
- the cost of hiring a suitable site
- the cost of staff training
- the cost of insurance
- the cost of promoting the availability of bungee-jumping events
- the total costs involved in putting on this event
- the pricing structure (less in winter) for each jump
- the total income from a range of customers making, say, three jumps each
- the break-even number of jumpers and jumps in summer and winter.

You should find a way of displaying the benefits of staging the event regularly.

You need to list the Excel facilities you would use. At the end of Chapter 3.2 there is a further activity in which you have to specify and build the desired spreadsheet.

Chapter 3.2 Spreadsheet specification and development

This chapter is divided into two main parts:

- spreadsheet specification
- spreadsheet development

In addition, at the end of the chapter is the second part of the FUN spreadsheet activity.

Spreadsheet specification

When working with a user who wants a spreadsheet to behave in a particular way, you must be able to draw up and agree with that user the **specification** for the spreadsheet.

The user of your spreadsheet will want to enter data, and to be sure that the spreadsheet will process this data to produce the required output. Output may be in the form of numerical values or charts.

You need to learn how to analyse the user's requirements to determine:

- what output information is wanted
- how that information is currently obtained, if it is obtained at all
- where the data to be input is to come from
- what data capture methods can be used
- what data processing needs to be done to get the required output
- what aids can be provided to assist with data input or processing
- how the output information needs to be presented.

You will need to be able to use the answers to these questions to write down a detailed specification for the spreadsheet. You will find it helpful to discuss with others the user's requirements and how they may be met. A good specification states the user's needs in such a way that there is no ambiguity about the scope of the task and the work that has to be done. You will then need to get agreement to your specification before you begin work on developing the spreadsheet.

Drawing up a specification for a spreadsheet has many of the same requirements as drawing up any other specification: the crucial need is to understand exactly what the user or customer wants.

The specification must be sufficiently detailed for the user to be able to verify its correctness, and also sufficiently comprehensive and lucid for someone other than the user and the author of the specification to be able to build and test the spreadsheet.

Preparing the specification

A typical specification that meets these demands would probably contain some or all of the details necessary to cover the topics listed against the seven bullet points above.

What output information does the user want?

The user is likely to want to exploit the ability of the spreadsheet software to provide current or projected figures in ways that were previously slow, difficult, or even impossible to produce. The ability of a spreadsheet to extrapolate historic figures according to a variety of rules is powerful, and harnessing this strength can provide new business insights. Further, the user can call for output in graphical format – again with several choices. Examples of output formats were given in Chapter 3.1; for example, our FUN spreadsheet would calculate the required financial outcomes of gross profit, gross profit variance, and so on.

On the spreadsheet the user will also want to see headings and row titles that make clear, without taking up more space than necessary, exactly what the contents of each cell represent. For example, our FUN spreadsheet (Figure 3.2) would show the cost headings for the event gross profit calculator across each column, and the financial outcomes relating to the event gross profit would be shown as row titles.

How is that information currently obtained?

If the same output information had previously been available, the only reasons for considering the development of a spreadsheet to create it would have been to reduce the cost of generating the information, or to reduce the time taken to produce it, or to improve its accuracy – or some combination of these possible reasons.

It is more likely that some or all of the desired information was *not* previously available, because creating it in full would not have been cost-effective, or would have taken too long. If this is the case the user may need to be guided concerning what the spreadsheet could and could not do. For example, the costs information for the FUN spreadsheet is currently obtained from the

marketing manager or the sales assistant; whereas the gross profit and variance figures are not currently available, but *will* be calculated by the spreadsheet.

Where is the data to be input to come from?

The data is likely to be of an administrative or commercial nature, consisting of letters, figures, currency symbols and perhaps a few special characters. It may have been abstracted from documents that were handwritten, typed, or printed; it may have been transmitted and stored electronically, and displayed on a computer screen. It may conceivably have been dictated, or scanned into an information system. Whatever the source of the data, if this data has to entered through the keyboard to reach the spreadsheet program, the speed and accuracy of the process will be greatly influenced by the clarity of the characters making up the data.

Any opportunity for data to be passed to the spreadsheet program by **electronic transfer** within the computer system should be taken, in the interests of both speed and accuracy.

For the FUN gross profit spreadsheet, suppose that your discussions with the technical director and other staff reveal that there is already a record sheet that is sometimes used, and that the proposed spreadsheet should be based upon this record sheet (Figure 3.55).

The data needed for the application may be documented in a **data catalogue** (discussed in more detail in Chapter 3.3). The data catalogue for the FUN spreadsheet can be derived quite easily from the record sheet (Figure 3.56).

Festivities Unlimited					
Event Gross Profit Record Sheet					
Customer		Event name			
Date quote accepted		Event type			
Date GPRS updated		Event size (persons)			
	Catering	Transport	Staff	Extras	Total
Quote	£2000	£500	£1000	£1500	£5000
Est cost	£1000	£300	£700	£1200	£3200
Est gross profit	£1000	£200	£300	£300	£1800
Est GP %	50%	40%	30%	20%	36%
Actual cost	£1150	£250	£800	£1200	£3400
Actual GP	£850	£250	£200	£300	£1600
Actual GP %	47.5%	50%	20%	20%	32%
GP variance	(£150)	£50	(£100)	£0	(£200)
GP variance %	(15%)	16.7%	(14.3%)	0%	(6.3%)

Figure 3.55 Event gross profit output layout

Data item	Aliases	Data type	Min & max/ Acceptable values/ Note
Customer name		Text	40 chars
Date quote accepted		Date	
Date GPRS updated		Date	
Event name		Text	30 chars
Event type		Text	"Wedding", "Birthday", "Corporate", "Other"
Event size		Numeric	10..500
Quote		Financial	
Estimated cost		Financial	
Estimated gross profit	Est contribution	Financial	
Estimated GP %	Est contribution %	Numeric	1 decimal place
Actual cost		Financial	
Actual GP	Actual contribution	Financial	
Actual GP%	Actual contribution %	Numeric	1 decimal place
GP variance		Financial	
Gp variance %		Numeric	1 decimal place

NOTE: Financial data and financially-related numeric data, when negative, to be shown in parentheses.

Figure 3.56 Data catalogue

What data capture methods can be used?

Data set out on paper can be **captured** by a keyboard operator reading the data and entering it through the keyboard. If the data can be fed into a computer by some process – which may be wholly unrelated to the spreadsheet project – there may be an opportunity to make the data accessible to the spreadsheet program through automatic transfer within the system. For example, if part of the contents of an e-mail message consists of data needed for loading a spreadsheet, that data might be transferred to the spreadsheet very quickly and completely accurately using a direct communication route between the e-mail and the spreadsheet application packages.

In an industrial context it might be possible to move data that is logged onto a computer file straight into a spreadsheet program. For our FUN spreadsheet, however, no automated methods of data capture are appropriate.

What data processing is needed to obtain the desired output?

We introduced the Excel facilities in Chapter 3.1. Excel and other spreadsheet products contain a number of ways of presenting the user's output, which has been created by the spreadsheet using its formulas and functions. This means that the developer of a spreadsheet has to instruct the program to operate in prescribed ways on the contents of specified cells.

By way of reminder, a simple example would be for the user to require the spreadsheet to display in cell D4 the sum of the contents of cells B4 and C4. This would be achieved by entering '=B4+C4' in cell D4. The summation process can operate on rows, columns, or both simultaneously.

Other features we reviewed include statistical functions, an IF function to be used with the relational operators such as 'equal to' or 'greater than', and the use of relative and absolute addresses. The Function wizard, which is displayed by clicking on the '**Function Wizard**' button, can be used to help you enter formulas and functions.

For our FUN spreadsheet, we would need to document the formulas to be used in the calculation of the gross profit, the gross profit percentage, the variances, and so on.

For the gross profit spreadsheet, you would document the calculations as shown in Figure 3.57.

	Catering Transport Staff Extras	Total
Quote	[◄—— Input ——►]	[SUM quote]
Est cost	[◄—— Input ——►]	[SUM est cost]
Est gross profit	[= quote – est cost]	[SUM est GP]
Est GP %	[= est GP / quote]	[= est GP / quote]
Actual cost	[◄—— Input ——►]	[SUM act cost]
Actual GP	[= quote – act cost]	[SUM act GP]
Actual GP %	[= act GP / quote]	[= act GP / quote]
GP variance	[= est GP – act GP]	[SUM GP var]
GP variance %	[= GP var / est GP]	[= GP var / est GP]

Figure 3.57 Event gross profit processing

What aids will help with data input and processing?

A spreadsheet, or any other application, should be designed to make data input easy and as error-free as possible. An Excel spreadsheet can provide **prompts** to the user for input, can assist with the entry of correct data chosen from **drop-down selection boxes**, and can automate input and processing through the use of **macros** and **lookup tables**, which are discussed later. Highlighting by the use of **colour** can help both with the *input* of data and also with the *display* of data. These features of the application would be specified at this point in the specification.

Input values can be **restricted** automatically to those with acceptable values, using the IF() function described in Chapter 3.1; or else checked using testing routines.

How should output be presented?

The choice of presentation for the output should be governed by the need to provide the information in a way that is easily intelligible and, whatever else, not misleading.

Your spreadsheet program will be able to show your output as charts of various kinds: you must choose carefully which sort best meets the criteria above. Your choice may be affected by whether or not you can print the output in colour.

The kinds of chart from which you can choose probably include bar graphs, line graphs, pie charts, scatter diagrams and three-dimensional representations of data. To avoid misleading the reader concerning the significance of this information, you should carefully consider the co-ordinates of the **origin** on any graphs or bar charts. For example, the two graphs presented in Figure 3.58 tell the same story of the reported profits of a company, but at a casual glance the one on the right seems to show a much rosier picture of the progress of the business.

Remember that there may on occasion be advantages in providing the numeric values calculated by the spreadsheet as figures alone rather than as some graphical representation of them. Accountants, for example, often prefer to see the actual figures.

In Chapter 3.1 there is a full discussion of the presentation of spreadsheet output. For example, you might provide a sample

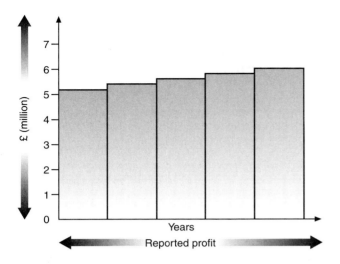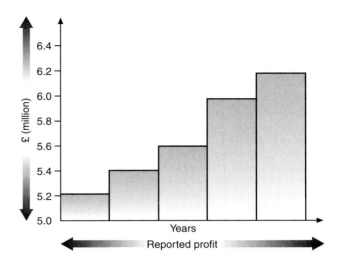

Figure 3.58 Selection of axes for graphs

spreadsheet to show the layout of the data, and a sample graph to illustrate how you propose to present the output in graphical form.

Listing requirements

All spreadsheet applications should be specified carefully in a formal way. This is especially important in the specification or large or complicated spreadsheets. The fully detailed specification should be presented in the form of a **requirements catalogue**, described in Chapter 5.2.

As an example, Table 3.1 shows some of the requirements catalogue entries for the FUN spreadsheet application. To follow this example it is useful to know that each requirement is numbered with an **identification number**, labelled 'ID' in the table. The **owner**, or stipulator, of the requirement is listed; and the **priority** given to a requirement is noted by way of a code, such as 'M'=Mandatory, 'D'=Desirable, 'O'=Optional. Each requirement will have what is called a **non-functional component** (labelled as 'Non-func. comp.'

in the table), which identifies external constraints. Finally, the requirements catalogue lists, for a given requirement, *other* **related requirements** by referring to the ID of those requirements (labelled 'Rel. req.' in Table 3.1).

Spreadsheet development

The word **development** covers all the design and other work needed to complete a new spreadsheet up to the stage at which it will be tested.

The design of the spreadsheet must make it easy to use. In creating a spreadsheet for users you should:

- present them with the simplest ways possible of entering data
- provide them with helpful prompts
- present their results in appropriate ways that will have been agreed
- use macros (described below) to simplify some of their tasks.

ID	Owner	Pr.	Requirement	Non-func. comp	Rel. req.
1	Tech Dir	M	Layout as per record sheet		6, 7
2	Off Mgr	D		Use Excel	6
3	Tech Dir	M	Bar graph for estimated vs actual gross profit	Available to view immediately the data has been entered	8, 9
4	Tech Dir	M	Spreadsheet data as per data catalogue		
5	Tech Dir	M	Calculations as per spreadsheet processing specification		
6	Tech Dir	M	Printout of spreadsheet to be available		1, 7
7	Tech Dir	O	Printout of relevant portion of spreadsheet to be done via on-screen button		1, 6
8	Tech Dir	D	Printout of graph to be available		3, 9
9	Tech Dir	O	Printout of graph to be done via on-screen button		3, 8
10	Off Mgr	D	User interface as provided by Excel		2

Table 3.1 Requirements catalogue entries for the FUN spreadsheet

Did you know?

You are not likely to run out of cells in planning any Excel spreadsheet application that occurs to you. You have 256 columns, of which you only see about 10 on a new blank spreadsheet; and 65 536 rows, of which you see only about 20 at first. That is 16 777 216 cells available to you.

Furthermore, there are three worksheets for each workbook, giving you more than 50 million cells, with the possibility of increasing further the number of worksheets.

Entering data

Provide simple but effective ways of entering data, including:

- creating worksheets that have the appearance of a conventional office form

- using data entry forms.

The key to designing an effective way of entering data is to ensure a good match between the format of the *data* to be entered and the format of the *screen* into which the data is to be entered.

As the designer of an information system, you should not restrict yourself merely to the design of the computer screen. As and where appropriate, you should consider the design of processes and forms outside the computer that are nevertheless part of the overall 'information system' with which you are concerned. It can often be easier to change the forms on which the data is captured prior to entry than to modify screen layouts to match the existing forms.

In the case of the FUN spreadsheet, the spreadsheet display has been designed to be quite similar to the original record sheet, but it must be realised that this record sheet is not a *data capture* form: it is a *data reporting* form.

For the FUN case study, and for other projects in which you are involved, it may be necessary to design data capture forms that make it easy for the user to *obtain* the data, and then to enter the data into the system. Figure 3.59 illustrates a data capture form that could be filled out for every FUN event. Notice that the data capture form is concerned only with the *input data* – there are no fields for calculations or output data.

It may be useful to create a separate worksheet as the data entry portion of the complete application. In the case of the FUN spreadsheet, you could design the first worksheet to be the data entry worksheet, the second to be the output worksheet, and the third to be the graph worksheet. The data entry worksheet would look just like the possible data capture sheet in Figure

3.59, and the calculating and output worksheet would pick up the data it required from the data entry worksheet as a set of 3D references. Figures 3.60 and 3.61 illustrate this design.

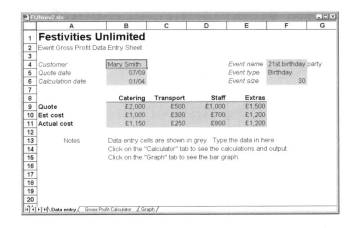

Figure 3.60 Revised FUN Spreadsheet with 'Data entry' worksheet

In more complex applications, it may be useful to create a worksheet which provides a **data entry form**, an Excel facility that allows the easy addition of data to a database which is maintained as part of the spreadsheet. This facility is not presented here in more detail, since it is almost always better to create and maintain

---

Festivities Unlimited

Event Record Sheet

Customer .... Event name ....

Date quote accepted .... Event type ....

Date GPRS updated .... Event size (persons) ....

	Catering	Transport	Staff	Extras
Quote	....	....	....	....
Est cost	....	....	....	....
Actual cost	....	....	....	....

Figure 3.59 Possible data capture sheet

Figure 3.61 Revised FUN Spreadsheet with 'Calculations' worksheet

databases using a database application such as Microsoft Access rather than a spreadsheet application such as Excel. Unit 6 covers the design and implementation of an Access database.

Prompts

The selection of suitable **prompts** can save users time and reduce mistakes. We look at two opportunities to provide such prompts:

- provision of data entry messages

- making use of data validation and associated messages.

The design of the FUN spreadsheets allows the use of colour or shading to highlight cells, and the provision of notes to guide the user of the spreadsheet. It is important to note that the spreadsheet 'tabs' have been renamed to have helpful labels, and the worksheets themselves have helpful titles and subtitles.

It is also usually necessary to have some simple **checks** made on a user's input to confirm that it is within acceptable limits, and to **alert** the user if it is not. In the FUN spreadsheet, two rows have been added, in which a check is made that the costs entered are not larger than the quote. If the cost is larger, the text display says 'Cost>Quote!'; otherwise it says 'OK' (Figure 3.62). The formula to do this is

=IF(B$10>B$9,"Cost>Quote!","OK")

Presenting results

In Chapter 1.4 we described the facilities available in Excel for presenting output in the most effective way. We now look at how some of those facilities could be applied to the presentation of the FUN results:

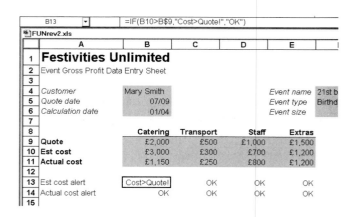

Figure 3.62 Spreadsheet with error check 'Alerts'

- cell formatting such as colour and borders

- drawing tools and graphic images

- charts and line graphs.

Figure 3.63 shows a bar graph of the event gross profit calculations, augmented with a text box showing a note and an arrow from the text box to the graph. The following paragraphs show how to use Excel's chart wizard to create graphs, how to change graphs once created, and how to add other graphic elements.

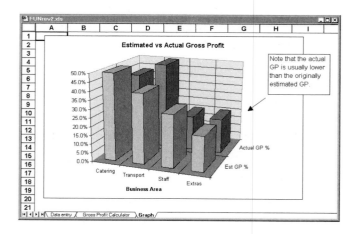

Figure 3.63 FUN spreadsheet graph

To start the chart wizard, click on its icon on the toolbar (Figure 3.64).

Figure 3.64 Toolbar chart wizard icon

The cursor turns into a cross hair with a miniature chart wizard icon attached; drag the crosshair over a section of the spreadsheet where you want the chart to appear.

Charts and graphs

Step 1

The first step is to identify those cells which contain the data you wish to show as a graph. Figure 3.65 illustrates the chart wizard dialogue for this step.

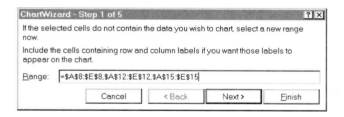

Figure 3.65 'ChartWizard': step 1

Note that the wizard suggests that labels be included in the range, if the labels are required on the chart. This is usually a good idea. A well-designed spreadsheet will have its cells well labelled already. Highlight or select those cells which contain the required data. Figure 3.66 shows the spreadsheet with three cell ranges selected (dashed lines enclose the ranges).

The first cell range, as suggested in the chart wizard dialogue box, contains the column headings. The second range, which is obtained by holding down the <Ctrl> key while selecting the relevant cells with the mouse, contains the first row of actual data for the graph, the estimated gross profit (or GP) %. Note that this row

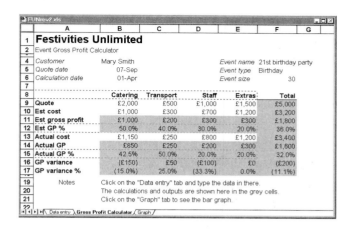

Figure 3.66 Chart ranges selected

includes as its first cell the row label. The third range contains the data for the actual GP %. When you are satisfied that the ranges have been correctly identified, click on 'Next>'.

The example graph being shown here for the FUN spreadsheet involves two rows of data ('Est GP %', and 'Actual GP %'). In general, there may be many rows of data, and the chart wizard will assign a set of graph lines or bars as needed to each row.

Step 2

In step 2, the chart wizard asks for the type of graph or chart required. Figure 3.67 shows that a '3-D Column' chart has been selected.

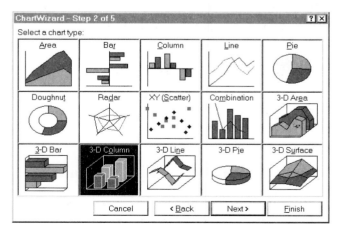

Figure 3.67 'ChartWizard': step 2

Step 3

In step 3, the chart wizard asks for the particular format or layout of the graph selected in the previous step. Figure 3.68 shows that format type '6' for the 3-D column chart has been selected.

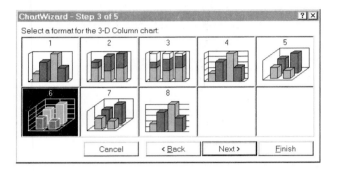

Figure 3.68 'ChartWizard': step 3

Step 4

In step 4, the chart wizard shows a sample of the specified graph, and asks for details of the data and its labels (Figure 3.69).

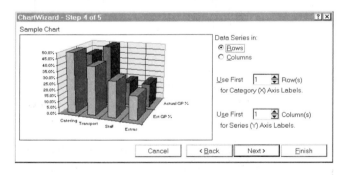

Figure 3.69 'ChartWizard': step 4

The data series from the spreadsheet are in rows, so the 'Rows' button in the dialogue box has been clicked.

Earlier, the first entry or row of data in the data range comprised the column headings, so the first row is specified to hold what the wizard calls the 'Category (X) Axis Labels'. A quick glance at the sample graph shows that these labels – 'Catering',

'Transport', 'Staff', and 'Extras' – seem to have been correctly applied.

Also, the data range specified in step 1 included the data series labels – 'Est GP %' for data series 1, and 'Actual GP %' for data series 2 – in the first cell or column, so the first column is specified as holding the 'Series (Y) Axis Labels'. Again, a glance at the sample graph shows that these series labels seem to have been correctly applied.

Step 5

In step 5, the chart wizard asks for final details about the graph to be presented (Figure 3.70).

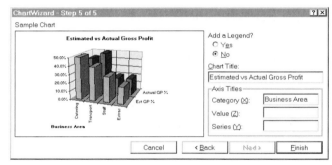

Figure 3.70 'ChartWizard': step 5

In the step 5 dialogue box, no legend has been requested. 'Estimated vs Actual Gross Profit' has been specified as the graph title; and notice that the sample graph is then adjusted to reflect the title entered. Finally, the X-axis title has been entered as 'Business Area'.

Editing a chart

Notice that the resulting graph from the chart wizard is slightly different from the graph illustrated at the start of this unit on 'Presenting results'. It is possible to change the properties of the graph by double-clicking on the graph, and then clicking on the graph element you want to edit. In

Figure 3.71 the X-axis title, 'Business Area', has been selected and moved to a different position.

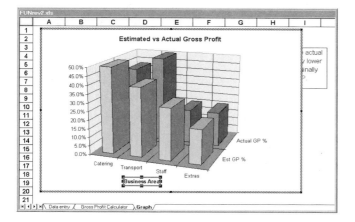

Figure 3.71 Selecting and moving a graph label

Right-clicking on a selected object on the graph brings up a tabbed dialogue box which allows you to set all the properties of that object that you consider to be relevant – colour, font, border, background, alignment, and so on.

Adding other picture elements

The drawing tools allow you to add further graphic elements to the chart or to the spreadsheet, including text boxes, arrows, circles and rectangles. The 'Drawing' toolbar is enabled by clicking on the 'Drawing' icon, found on the standard toolbar (Figure 3.72).

Figure 3.72 Toolbar 'Drawing' icon

The 'Drawing' toolbar itself is shown in Figure 3.73.

To add a graphic element, click on the required 'Drawing' toolbar button. The

Figure 3.73 'Drawing' toolbar

cursor changes to a crosshair, and in general you click and drag to create the element concerned. To move the element once created, place the cursor on the element's bounding box and drag it to where it is required. Certain elements can be resized; drag the size handles found on their bounding box. To change the properties of the element, right-click on it.

Macros

The word **macro** is an abbreviation of *macroinstruction*, meaning an instruction in a programming language that takes the place of a sequence of instructions. (The plural of macro is *macros*.) The purpose of a macro is thus to simplify the work of a user of a system by reducing the number of keystrokes to be made, and thereby saving time and improving accuracy.

The uses of macros in Excel include:

- creating single keystrokes to replace multiple key depressions for a required action

- providing a means for entering data, or simplifying an existing procedure for input

- producing printed reports, or reports displayed on screen.

In Excel macros are written in **Visual Basic**: but you do not need to be familiar with this language to be able to develop or use macros.

The user specification for the FUN spreadsheet required that negative values be shown in parentheses. Let us imagine that, after some consultation, you find out that some of the FUN staff much prefer to see negative numbers with minus signs, while other staff prefer parentheses. You thus modify the user requirement specification to give the user the option of having negative GP variance amounts and percentages shown either as numbers with a minus sign, or as numbers in parentheses.

Of course, a *user* could modify the spreadsheet by highlighting the cells involved, clicking on the 'Format Cells...' menu item, selecting the 'Number' tab in the dialogue box, selecting a 'Custom' format from the list box, scrolling down and selecting the required custom format, editing the custom format, and pressing 'OK', but that would presume the user had the necessary skills. Even if that were the case, the whole procedure would rapidly become tedious if the user wished to swap between the two formats with any regularity. Finally, a small slip by the user could make the spreadsheet unusable. It would much better to automate the process using macros.

To meet the new user requirement, you could design the spreadsheet to have two buttons. When one button is pressed, the relevant cells are formatted with minus signs; when the other button is pressed, the relevant cells are formatted with parentheses. You would then construct the spreadsheet such that the buttons activate a macro each to carry out the necessary actions. Figure 3.74 shows the revised spreadsheet.

The quickest and easiest way to develop a macro is to have Excel record your keystrokes and mouse actions and produce the macro automatically.

Recording a macro

From the 'Tools' menu, select '**Record Macro**' and then '**Record New Macro**'.

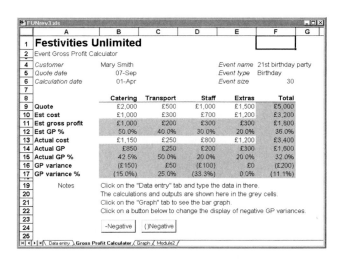

Figure 3.74 Revised FUN spreadsheet

Excel is now in 'macro record' mode – a small window opens up with a '**Stop**' button (Figure 3.76). From now on, every keystroke you make will be recorded by Excel. When you have finished performing the keystrokes you have in mind, click on the 'Stop' button, and the new macro will appear in a new worksheet called 'Module 1'.

First, we shall construct the macro that formats the 'GP variance' row with a minus sign for negative numbers. From the 'Tools' menu, select 'Record Macro' and then 'Record New Macro'. Excel opens a dialogue box for you to name the macro, and to enter a description for its actions. Figure 3.75 illustrates this dialogue.

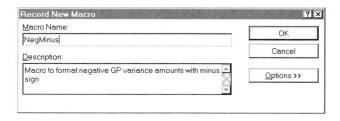

Figure 3.75 'Record New Macro' dialogue

Click on 'OK'. The 'Stop Macro Recording' button window appears, and Excel awaits your actions.

Figure 3.76 'Stop Macro Recording' button

Highlight the cells involved (B16..F16), click on the 'Format Cells…' menu item, select the 'Number' tab in the dialogue box, select a 'Custom' category from the list box, scroll down and select the required custom format (do not be concerned at this point if you can't find the exact format you require – just select something that is close), and press 'OK'. Click on a blank cell such as F1, and then click on the 'Stop Macro Recording' button. The new formatting has actually been applied to the cells, as well as being recorded.

A new worksheet called 'Module 1' (or similar) will have been added to your spreadsheet. Click on the tab for that worksheet. The display should resemble that in Figure 3.77.

```
FUNrev2.xls
'
' NegMinus Macro
' Macro to format negative GP variance amounts with minus sign
'
'
Sub NegMinus()
    Range("B16:F16").Select
    Selection.NumberFormat = "£#,##0.0;[Red]-£#,##0.0"
    Range("F1").Select
End Sub

Data entry / Gross Profit Calculator / Graph \ Module2 /
```

Figure 3.77 Recorded macro called 'NegMinus'

The first lines of the macro are comment lines, indicated by the fact that they start with a leading single quote. The description from the earlier dialogue box has been inserted.

The macro program itself is shown, starting with the key word '**Sub**', and ending with the two key words '**End Sub**'.

The key word 'Sub' identifies the macro as 'NegMinus()'.

The following three lines specify the action of the macro. The first line, 'Range("B16:F16").Select', is Visual Basic's way of recording that we highlighted cells B16 to F16. The second line, 'Selection.NumberFormat = "£#,##0.0;[Red]-£#,##0.0"', records the fact that, having navigated the 'Format' menu's dialogue box, we selected a number format of '£#,##0.0;[Red]-£#,##0.0'. This assumes that the colour 'red' is available to the user. The third line records the fact that we ended up clicking on cell F1 before stopping the recording.

Editing a macro

It turns out that we did not find exactly the right custom cell format. We clicked on a format that read '£#,##0.0[Red]-£#,##0.0' during recording. No problem: we shall edit that line in the macro to read '£#,##0;-£#,##0' shortly.

Assigning a macro to a button

We now have a macro called 'NegMinus', but no immediate way of activating it. We want to assign it to a button. On the 'Gross Profit Calculator' worksheet, bring up the 'Drawing' toolbar, and click on the '**Create Button**' button. The cursor changes to a cross-hair. On the worksheet, click and drag to create the outline of a modest button. When you release the mouse button, a dialogue box immediately opens up, asking you to identify the macro that you want assigned to your button. After clicking on the only macro currently available, 'NegMinus', you will see the dialogue shown in Figure 3.78.

123

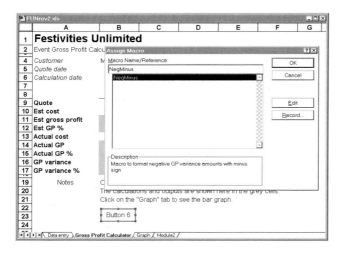

Figure 3.78 'Assign Macro' to button

Click on 'OK'. Notice that the button in the worksheet is selected. Click inside the button, and edit its default label of 'Button X' to something more meaningful, perhaps '-Negative'. The button is now ready for use.

Before you press the button to check that it works correctly, look at the worksheet carefully. Row 16 should have its negative values in red, with a minus sign, displayed with one decimal place, because that was the custom format we applied while *recording* the macro. Now move the mouse over the button, and notice that the cursor changes to a hand with outstretched finger. Press the button, and the row 16 values should be reformatted as required – no red text, no decimal places, and the negative numbers shown with minus signs.

Enhancing the macro

We now need to enhance our existing macro to format the 'GP variance %' cells appropriately as well. You do not need to know much Visual Basic to guess that we need to add the following two lines to our macro:

```
Range ("B17:F17").Select
Selection.NumberFormat = "#,##0.0%;-#,##0.0%"
```

This gives the amended macro program in the 'Module' worksheet (Figure 3.79). We have also enhanced the comments at the start of the macro.

```
'
' NegMinus Macro
' Macro to format negative GP variance amounts with minus sign
'  and negative GP variance percentages with minus sign
'
Sub NegMinus()
    Range("B16:F16").Select
    Selection.NumberFormat = "£#,##0;-£#,##0"
    Range("B17:F17").Select
    Selection.NumberFormat = "#,##0.0%;-#,##0.0%"
    Range("F1").Select
End Sub
```

Figure 3.79 Amended macro 'NegMinus'

To check that the enhanced macro works, go back to the 'Gross Profit Calculator' worksheet and click on the '-Negative' button.

Creating a macro without recording

To finish the task, we need to create another macro that formats the same cells to have negative numbers shown with parentheses, and assign that macro to a second button. Again, you do not need to know much Visual Basic to guess that we need to create a new macro program in Visual Basic that reads as follows:

```
'
' NegParen Macro
' Macro to format negative GP variance
  amounts with parentheses and negative GP
  variance percentages with parentheses
'
'
Sub  NegParen()
    Range("B16:F16").Select
    Selection.NumberFormat="£#,##0;(£#,##0)"
    Range("B17:F17").Select
    Selection.NumberFormat="#,##0.0%;(#,##0.
    0%)"
    Range("F1").Select
    End  Sub
```

On the 'Module' worksheet, highlight the 'NegMinus' lines, copy them, place the cursor on a new line at the end, and paste. Change each line in the second macro as required. On the 'Gross Profit Calculator' worksheet, create a second button next to the first, assign the 'NegParen' macro to it, and re-label the button to read '()Negative'. Click on it to check that it works.

Advanced facilities

You will need to be able to use some of the more complex spreadsheet facilities listed in Chapter 3.1, on page 94. For these you may need to make use of on-line help or instruction manuals.

Here we look at four advanced facilities, and at two further features.

Lookup tables

Some kinds of data input have certain restricted values; and a numeric input might be more usefully shown as a text value. For example, the months of the year have the restricted values 'Jan', 'Feb', and so on; 'Lun' is not a valid month of the year. For calculation purposes, it may be useful to have March represented as the number '3', but it is usually better from the user's point of view to have it *shown* as 'Mar'.

Lookup tables make it easy to accept a restricted range of input values in a spreadsheet, or to associate a certain value with some sort of 'code' value. In the FUN spreadsheet, for example, there are only four kinds of event: 'birthdays', 'weddings', 'corporate', and 'other'. It would be convenient to allow the spreadsheet user to type in a code of, say, '1', to indicate a birthday event, and have the spreadsheet supply the text 'Birthday'. This is achieved with a spreadsheet lookup function, either

HLOOKUP() or **VLOOKUP()**, as illustrated in Figure 3.80. ('H' stands for horizontal, 'V' for vertical.)

To start with, a table must be set up in an area of the spreadsheet to show the relationship between an input 'code' value, and the meaning of that code. This table is shown in G4..H7 of the FUN spreadsheet, where a code number between 1 and 4 is associated with a type of event. In this example this table is clearly visible to the user, but this is not necessary if the user if familiar with the codes in use.

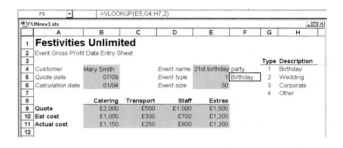

Figure 3.80 Lookup table

The lookup function is used in a formula in F5, '=VLOOKUP(E5,G4:H7,2)'. The VLOOKUP() function takes the code value entered as the event type in cell E5, and refers to the table in G4..H7, trying to find the closest match to the input value in the first column of the table. Having found the closest match to the input in the first column of the table, it then displays the contents of cell 2 of the relevant row.

In the example, the input value in cell E5 is '1'. This is a match with the first item in the first column of the table, cell G4. The content of cell 2 of the matched row is the text 'Birthday', and this is what is displayed in F5.

The number '2' in the formula using the VLOOKUP() function '=VLOOKUP(E5,G4:H7,2)' is called the '**offset**'. For larger tables, where a code value could correspond with a number of different lookup outcomes, the required column might be in the column offset '3' or '4' from the first column of the table.

Named cells and ranges

It is sometimes convenient to be able to refer to a cell not by its reference, such as F6, but by a suitable name, such as 'size'. This is most useful when a cell appears in a number of calculations in various places, where the cell usually requires an absolute reference of the form $F$6, and where enhancements of or changes to the spreadsheet at a later time may be such that you forget the significance of cell 'F6'.

In Chapter 3.1 an enhancement of the gross profit worksheet involved the calculation of the various 'per guest' values of quote, cost, and profit. In that chapter, the event size was shown as an absolute cell reference of $F$6 in the relevant calculations. It would be very useful to develop the necessary formulas to make it clear that the various totals were being divided by the event size. This may be done by **naming** cell F6 as 'size', and then constructing the formulae to refer to 'size' rather than '$F$6', as shown in Figure 3.81.

In Excel, a cell is named by clicking on the cell and entering its name in the left-hand box of the formula bar.

Templates

Where it is likely that versions of a particular spreadsheet will be created and used with a variety of data, it may be useful to create the 'original' spreadsheet as

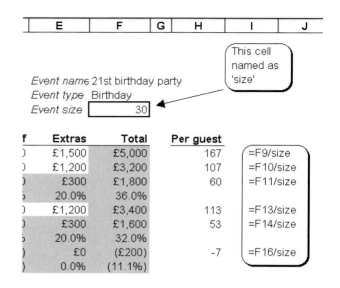

Figure 3.81 Formulas using a named cell

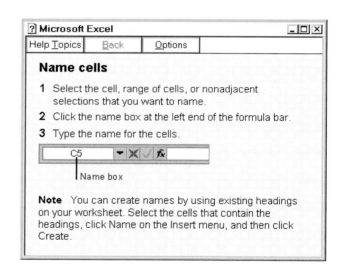

Figure 3.82 Naming a cell: Help text

a blank **template**. Particular instances of the spreadsheet can then be created and filled in as needed. This avoids the need to continually overwrite earlier versions and risk losing valuable data, or to have to begin by copying an earlier version and then saving it as a new file.

The procedure is very straightforward. The 'original' spreadsheet is 'Saved As' an Excel template file, ***.XLT**. When the time comes to create another working spreadsheet, the new spreadsheet is created using the '**File New...**' menu item (and not by clicking on the 'New' icon on the toolbar). This way, a dialogue box is opened which shows the template files available in the templates folder. Clicking on the required template then creates a new spreadsheet with all of the contents of the template.

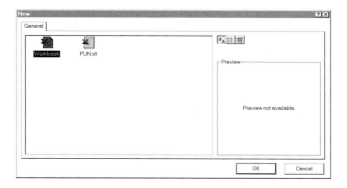

Figure 3.83 'File New...' dialogue

Protected cells

Where the expected users of a spreadsheet are perhaps not very expert, it may be useful to **protect** areas of the spreadsheet from accidental changes. There may also be a case on occasion to guard against deliberate changes that have not been sanctioned. The procedure for protecting the spreadsheet involves specifying those cells which are to be **locked**.

In EXCEL, when a worksheet is set as 'protected', by default *all* of its cells (that is those not specifically designated as 'unlocked') are locked. The procedure is therefore as follows.

The worksheet must first be unprotected if it was previously protected. Then, the cells which are to be unlocked and available for change must be selected. At the

'Format'→'Cells...''→'Protection' dialogue box, the 'Locked' box must be freed. (Figure 3.84)

Finally, the worksheet is set as 'Protected' at the '**Tools**'→'**Protection...**' menu item.

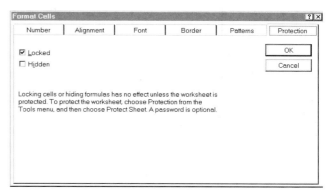

Figure 3.84 Unlocking cells

Other features

There are two further features which you might find useful.

Multiple worksheets
The complete FUN spreadsheet has been designed and developed as a number of linked worksheets contained in a single 'workbook'. This is an approach that works well in Excel, since it gives straightforward access to the various worksheets in a workbook. In particular, Excel allows the renaming of a worksheet to suit the application. Right-click on the worksheet tab, and select the '**Rename**' menu item.

Sorting
Some spreadsheets consist of a number of rows of data, and it may be useful to have the rows '**sorted**' in a particular order. In Excel, the '**Data**'→'**Sort...**' menu item offers a number of ways of sorting a range of cells into order.

Of particular interest is the fact that you can specify non-alphabetic sort sequences. The 'Options...' button on the sort dialogue allows you to sort according to the day of the week or the month of the year, for example. There are facilities for you to define your own sort sequence.

Try it out	If your group completed the bungee-jumping activity in Chapter 3.1, and if you have worked through this chapter, you will be ready for the next two tasks.
	
	1 As a group, write a specification for the spreadsheet called for by the FUN directors. Its aim is to help them determine whether or not they should offer bungee-jumping as a FUN event.
	
	    In your specification remember to make the entry of data as easy as possible for people who may have very little computer experience. You can help them with careful screen design including prompts, highlighting, and perhaps the use of colour.
	
	    Likewise the output needs to be as easy to interpret as possible, relying on graphics where you feel these would help.
	
	2 When your group is happy with the specification, work together to build the spreadsheet. Then, working individually, select some input data and print out the resulting spreadsheet.

Chapter 3.3 Spreadsheet documentation and testing

Like every ICT product, a spreadsheet is incomplete unless it has documentation. The testing of a new spreadsheet has to include the testing of its documentation. This chapter therefore falls into three parts:

- technical documentation
- user documentation
- testing a spreadsheet.

Some of the points made in this chapter are applicable to bigger projects than anything you will be working on whilst on your AVCE course. However you do need to understand the principles of system documentation and testing in general.

Technical documentation

In Chapter 2.2 we explored the relationships between *implementers*, *providers* and *users*. The technical documentation for a new product will be created by the implementers as part of the project development procedure. This documentation will be an important mechanism for communicating with the providers who will gain from it a full understanding of the way product works, which will be helpful for them in diagnosing any problems reported by the users.

As an Advanced VCE student learning how to put together a spreadsheet for a particular purpose, you can cast yourself in the role of an implementer. Writing the documentation is part of your development process.

The technical documentation for a spreadsheet would probably include the following:

- a copy of the agreed design specification
- details of the hardware, software and other resources required
- instructions for opening and configuring the spreadsheet
- details of all calculations, formulas and function used
- details of validation and verification procedures
- details of all input and output screens and printed designs
- a copy of the test specification.

The user requirements are set out in an agreed statement. As outlined in Chapter 3.2, the user requirements for a spreadsheet contain three major elements: a *data catalogue*, a set of *processing specifications*, and a *requirements catalogue* with all the associated non-functional components.

In any ICT development project the user requirements are a major outcome of systems analysis, an aspect of systems development that we shall be covering in Unit 5.

Details of hardware, software and other resources

The minimum hardware specification needed to run the spreadsheet must be stated, together with the versions of the named software that will run the spreadsheet. Other resources may not have to be spelt out unless the operating environment is especially 'hostile' in any way.

Opening and configuring the spreadsheet

Opening and configuring spreadsheets will be almost second nature to the implementers, but nonetheless the processes have to be written up fully as part of the technical documentation for the benefit of someone not familiar with the product who may be called upon to work on it, possibly at very short notice.

Calculations, formulas and functions

All this information must appear in the technical documentation so that exactly what the spreadsheet can do is set down unambiguously. The formulas are conveniently printed out by using the '**Tools Options**' menu, and checking the '**Formulas**' box in the '**Window Options**' dialogue pane of the '**View**' tab. The result is shown in Figure 3.85.

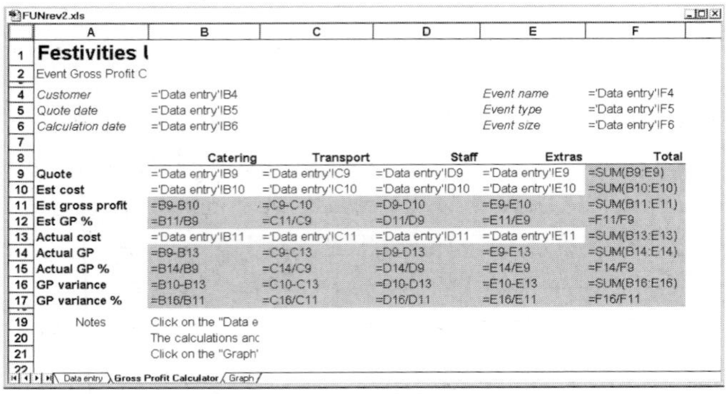

Figure 3.85 Viewing the spreadsheet formulas

Validation and verification procedures

In the discussion on testing further on in this chapter we explain the words *validation* and *verification*. They relate to the questions of whether the spreadsheet does what it is supposed to do, and whether it does it properly.

Details of input and output screens

The layout and items of information that can be displayed by all input and output screens must be shown in the technical documentation. These items can only be tested if there is clear statement of what *should* be available.

The test specification

As described later in this chapter, there must be a **test strategy** which defines the extent of testing to be carried out on a particular new product. From this strategy a **test specification** is drawn up. This consists of all the tests to be run, with each test having its collection of **test cases**.

The testing strategy must be agreed with the users. Successful testing is part of the overall acceptance procedure to be followed by the user.

Installation and training plans

Installation is covered in more detail in Unit 4. We shall see there that appropriate technical documentation includes the **schedule** for the installation of the system and for the training of the users; and any special **installation requirements**, **training materials**, and instructions for creating an appropriate **training environment**.

User documentation

User documentation helps others to use your spreadsheet. You must learn to write user instructions that are simple to understand. Your aim should be to allow users to make full use of whatever features and facilities within your spreadsheet they find relevant to their work, without having to seek further help.

User documentation is often presented as a document called a **user guide** or a **user manual**. Its contents could include:

- the scope of the specific spreadsheet program

- how to start the spreadsheet program

- routes through the spreadsheet menus

- examples of screens and data entry forms

- instructions about data entry

- advice about how to respond to error messages or conditions

- examples of data output screens and printed copy.

For the overall success of your project, writing good user documentation can be almost as important as constructing a good spreadsheet.

The requirements for the user documentation should first be planned and designed during the writing of the spreadsheet program. Following acceptance by users of the outline documentation design, the text may be written, illustrations and screen shots added, and the documentation assembled into the required medium, usually a printed booklet. The draft of the documentation should then be submitted for testing and inspection, and then reviewed through **pilot operation** of the spreadsheet by a representative of the users, before being finalised. This process is illustrated in Figure 3.86.

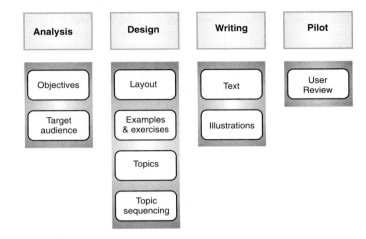

Figure 3.86 User documentation development stages

Analysis of user documentation requirements

The key to successful user documentation is a clear understanding of the users' requirements for that documentation. This way you establish the *objectives* of the user documentation.

Objectives

The objectives of the user documentation must be stated in terms of what the user is to *do*, and never in terms of what the user needs to *know*. The distinction is subtle, but vital. Your approach in developing the user documentation is to be directed towards what the user wants to *do* with the spreadsheet, not towards what the user might want to know about how it does it.

For example, the FUN spreadsheet has two worksheets, one for data entry, and one where the calculations are done. You might be tempted to write some user documentation

131

which says just that: 'The spreadsheet has two worksheets, one for data entry, and one where the calculations are done'. Some users might find that interesting, maybe even helpful, but most would not. Instead, to help the users actually *use* the spreadsheet, the same information would be presented in a different way, such as: 'Click on the "Data entry" tab of the spreadsheet and enter your data. Then click on the "Gross profit calculator" tab to see the resulting calculations.'

The result of defining the objectives of the user documentation is likely to be quite a long list, because it will include all the things that the user might at some time want to do with the system. For larger spreadsheet systems, the task of defining all the objectives is split into two parts: the first identifying the top-level, or broader, objectives; and the second breaking down each top-level objective into its components.

For example, some of the FUN spreadsheet top-level objectives might be 'Start the spreadsheet', 'Enter data', 'Change data', and 'Correct error conditions'. The top-level objective 'Enter data' would be broken down into lower-level objectives such as 'Enter event descriptions', 'Enter event quote', and 'Enter event costs'.

Table 3.2 provides a partial list of top-level and lower-level objectives for the FUN spreadsheet user documentation.

Top-level objective	Lower-level objectives
Starting the Event GPC spreadsheet	Starting EXCEL
	Opening an existing Event GPC spreadsheet
	Creating a new Event GPC spreadsheet
Entering data	Selecting the Data Entry worksheet
	Selecting the cell to receive data
	Entering the data using the formula bar
Changing data	
Correcting errors	Cells which check for entry errors
	Recognising entry errors
Viewing results	Selecting the GPC worksheet
	Selecting the Graph worksheet
Printing results	
Modifying spreadsheet appearance	Making the font smaller or larger
	Showing grid lines
	Changing the appearance of negative financial values
Quitting the Event GPC spreadsheet	Saving the current Event GPC spreadsheet
	Abandoning the current Event GPC spreadsheet
	Deleting an old Event GPC spreadsheet

Table 3.2 Sample list of documentation objectives

Target audience

During the analysis of the user documentation requirements, it is also important to characterise the intended **audience** for the documentation. This will help to ensure an appropriate design of the documentation, suitable tone and style, and the use of text, illustrations, and examples that will be clear to the reader.

Design of user documentation

Topics and topic sequencing

Following the identification of all the objectives of the user documentation, it is straightforward to move on to identifying the topics that the documentation should cover.

Usually, for every distinct objective there is a **topic** that needs to be covered. For example, in order for users to achieve the objective 'Enter data' they need to know about the actions of clicking on the required cell, typing data in at the formula bar, and pressing the <Enter> key or clicking on the 'green tick' icon.

What will require more care during design is the **sequence** in which the topics are presented in the documentation. There are no hard and fast rules. For example, should the topic dealing with correcting errors follow the topic of changing the data entered, or should it come before? Problems with topic sequencing will emerge during the pilot use of the documentation.

Examples and exercises

The second major task of designing the user documentation is designing the **examples** that will illustrate each of the topics, and designing **exercises** that illustrate to the

user how to master each of the topics. This part of user documentation usually takes the most time to construct, and hence may often be skimped. It is, however, the most valuable part of the documentation. Frequent, numerous, and rich examples and exercises are what distinguish excellent documentation from mediocre or poor documentation. The inclusion of graphs and other forms of illustration saves words and adds to the interest.

Layout

While it is often presumed that the user documentation will be in the form of a printed booklet, this is not the only way to teach the user about the spreadsheet system. For example, it could be very effective to have an **interactive tutorial** where the user sits at the computer and is guided through the spreadsheet by tutorial software.

The design of **layout** is simply the design of where material should go on the page, or screen, and how it should look. Keeping to a carefully planned layout is important if the user documentation is to be coherent and easy to use.

Writing the documentation

Writing, and presenting information, are covered in Chapters 1.3 and 1.4. If you keep the target audience in mind all the time you will produce documentation that sets an appropriate tone and style.

Pilot

Before the documentation is finalised, it should be piloted. This stage should ensure that the final version is free of errors and problems. Your selected panel of users and others will point out spelling and grammatical errors, places where the instructions are hard to follow or are ambiguous, places where you assume knowledge they do not have, and illustrations, examples, and exercises that seem inappropriate or are plain wrong.

Testing spreadsheets

Tests will have been carried out during the development of a spreadsheet. However, there must be a formal test when the development is complete, to allow users to satisfy themselves that the project has been brought to a successful conclusion. This test is usually called the **acceptance test**. Its scope and execution have to be agreed with users. Its specification forms part of the testing strategy for the spreadsheet.

Here are some of the questions an acceptance test will try to answer:

- Does your solution meet the agreed spreadsheet specification?

- Do results achieved by manual methods correspond to those produced by the program?

- Does your spreadsheet cope with normal, extreme and abnormal data?

- Can other people use your program and documentation?

- Is the program completely robust, or can it be made to fail?

Computer systems are amongst the most difficult types of system to check for correct operation. One of the reasons for this is that their processing mechanism – their software – is invisible. Checking the correct operation of machinery is much easier: you can see what is happening.

Another reason is that, during the development of a computer system, much effort goes into ensuring the system works

as required, which usually means ensuring that the system works properly with 'normal' data and 'normal' usage. It is often difficult to design and build procedures that test the full range of possibilities of abnormal or extreme usage, because of the large number of possible paths through the program.

The result of testing which is incomplete in this respect may well show that the system under test does indeed work correctly under 'normal' circumstances: but it may not disclose that there are perfectly plausible circumstances in which it will fail. Such circumstances may well be common without being covered in the testing.

There are two lessons which emerge:

- First, people other than the development team – the analyst, the designer, the programmer – must check and test the project components. All significant project components must be subject to inspection by people who did not write those components. If this process can start before the acceptance test, time may be saved.

- Second, as much as possible of the design and the development process needs to be made 'visible'. This generally means describing in writing all the components of a design, drawing diagrams and making notes, so that these items of documentation can be inspected, understood, and tested.

These principles apply to the testing of spreadsheets, just as they do to the testing of any new application development.

Quality

There is a doctrine of **quality assurance (QA)** which applies to all systems development projects. The aim of QA is to ensure that any product released from development, but before it is brought into use, is in all respects fit for its purposes. QA in large projects is conducted by teams set up especially, reporting directly to senior management. In smaller projects QA addresses the technical issues that do not form part of the acceptance testing.

QA can be thought of as having three components:

- defect prevention
- defect removal
- development process continual improvement.

These three components underlie the whole of the systems development process, as illustrated in the Figure 3.87. We have set the QA function in the context of the full development life cycle.

Defect prevention – inspection

Defect prevention covers those activities that seek to prevent errors from occurring. The major technique of defect prevention is **inspection**: checking, at each stage of development, that the design so far both matches the user requirements and conforms with the earlier analysis and design work.

Steps that could be taken to help prevent defects include involving the users in checking the requirements specification and sample screens and in experimenting with data entry to satisfy themselves that the results are as expected.

Defect removal – testing

Defect removal involves testing the software and the system for errors, and correcting whatever errors are found. This generally takes place during programming. However, this kind of testing, by definition, takes

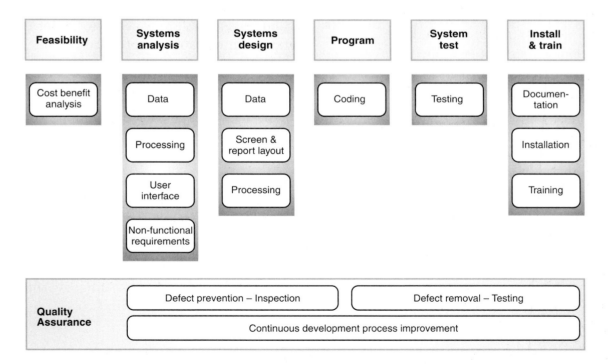

Figure 3.87 Systems development life cycle with quality assurance

place to deal with bugs and problems already in the system. It is better to prevent the defects creeping in from the start.

Development process continual improvement

Finally, while inspecting and testing will ensure that a particular project is delivered as error-free as possible, these techniques do nothing to ensure that the next project will fare better. Unless the development process itself is improved, it is likely that the same sort of problems and errors will recur.

Hence, the third component of an effective quality assurance programme consists of steps which seek to introduce continuous improvements in the way systems are designed and produced. This involves establishing a **methodology** for estimating project schedules, analysing users' requirements, designing and building programs, and testing the products which result from the development process.

The detail of this methodology should be given much thought, so that it embodies the best practice. It should then be included in the organisation's **standards** for systems work.

Test plans and checklists

You will need to be able to create a test specification that defines tests for:

- checking, independently, that all functions and formulas work correctly

- acceptable data input values (both maximum and minimum)

- unacceptable data values that should be automatically rejected

- checking that the system meets user requirements.

Independent testing

In the discussion on quality, above, we touched on the need for testing to be carried out independently. This means two things:

- First, the people who do the testing and checking must not be the people who analysed, designed, or programmed the system. The reason is quite simple, and is a result of human nature. When you produce something, it is something that 'fits' with how *you* work, how *you* solve problems, and how *you* construct solutions. It is then difficult for you to see anything wrong with your solutions, and you are naturally biased when it comes to testing your solutions. Someone *else* must test or check your work. When any changes need to be made, these changes should then be carried out by the people who originally analysed, designed, or programmed the system, as they know the system best.

- Second, where a system needs to perform certain computations or produce certain results, these computations must be performed independently, in another way and using a different system. Usually, this means doing the calculations by hand.

Validation and verification

These activities concern the data values used in testing.

Testing and checking are sometimes called, more exactly, *verifying* and *validating*. These two kinds of activity are subtly different, in that they seek to ensure two kinds of quality. The verbs are:

- **validate** – does the system do the right things?

- **verify** – does the system do what it does correctly?

Validation, for our purposes here, consists of ensuring that the spreadsheet meets the users' requirements. The process is straightforward: inspect the spreadsheet, and make sure that every user requirement that was specified is met by the spreadsheet.

Inspection

Inspections are forms of validation where two things are compared. On the one hand, as in our case, we have the spreadsheet under inspection. On the other hand, we have all the related items – documents, diagrams, programs – with which the spreadsheet program must agree.

The process of inspection looks to see whether all these items are consistent with each other. The outcome of the inspection is a list of discrepancies, which are presumed to be defects, between the spreadsheet under inspection and the other items. These discrepancies are then evaluated, and whatever action is necessary to remedy them is carried out.

A formalised version of the inspection procedure developed by M. E. Fagan, of IBM, is often followed on large projects.

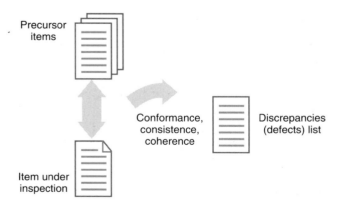

Figure 3.88 Fagan inspection

Test plans and test cases

Verification – testing proper – is covered in the remainder of this chapter. There are a number of different testing techniques, but here we shall consider a single technique called **boundary value analysis**.

A **test specification** for a given project will contain numerous individual **test plans**. A given technique of testing a spreadsheet will give rise to a test plan, covering one of the inputs and outputs of the spreadsheet under test. A test plan in turn consists of a number of **test cases**. Each test case consists of the specific input and the specific expected output involved in the test (Figure 3.89).

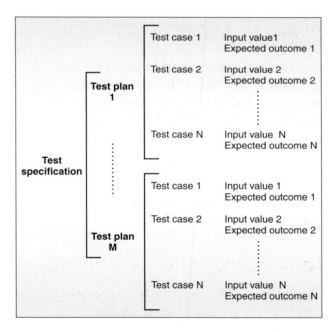

Figure 3.89 Structure of a test plan and its test cases

For the FUN spreadsheet, for example, there would be a test plan for testing that the spreadsheet processes the 'Event size' data item correctly. This test plan for the 'Event size' would specify some test cases. Each test case would involve entering a chosen value for the event size, and would specify the expected outcome which should be observed if the spreadsheet operates as intended.

Boundary value analysis

A boundary value analysis test plan specifies that there should be six test cases for a data item being tested, three of these cases being tests at the lower boundary of the data item, and three at the upper boundary. Of these three cases, assuming that we are dealing with whole numbers and not fractions, one case must involve a value for the data item one less than the boundary value, one case involves the boundary value itself, and the third test case involves a value which is one greater than the boundary value (Figure 3.90).

For example, according to the user specification, a valid 'Event size' data item has a lower boundary of 20, and an upper boundary of 500. In order to meet the user specification, the spreadsheet should refuse to process an event size smaller than 20, or

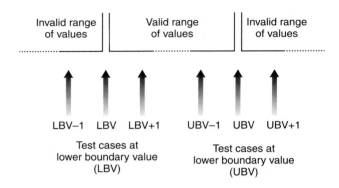

Figure 3.90 Test cases for a boundary value analysis test plan

larger than 500. A testing scheme to check this would look like Figure 3.91.

Auditing cell values

Excel provides a tool called '**Auditing**' which can be very helpful during testing. For any given cell in a spreadsheet, the tool can show the other cells which *depend* upon that cell's value, and it can show those other cells which *contribute* to that cell's value. The 'Auditing' tool is accessed from the '**Tools Auditing...**' menu item.

		TEST PLAN
		Boundary value analysis of valid values for 'Event size'
Case	Input	Expected output
1	19	Error message displayed, 'Event size too small'
2	20	Correct transfer of event size value from data entry worksheet to gross profit calculator worksheet
3	21	Correct transfer of event size value from data entry worksheet to gross profit calculator worksheet
4	499	Correct transfer of event size value from data entry worksheet to gross profit calculator worksheet
5	500	Correct transfer of event size value from data entry worksheet to gross profit calculator worksheet
6	501	Error message displayed, 'Event size too large'

Figure 3.91 Example of part of a test plan

Figure 3.92 illustrates the 'Auditing' toolbar, and the results of auditing two cells.

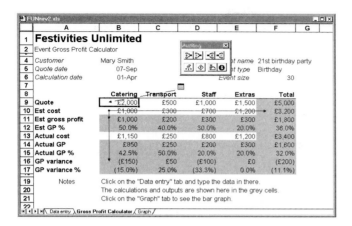

Figure 3.92 Audit traces

The screen shows – using arrows – that cell B10 has three other cells which depend

upon it: F10, B11, and B16. The screen also shows – with an icon of a worksheet – that the contents of cell B9 come from a separate worksheet.

Clicking on each cell in turn and examining the arrows that result is a first step in ensuring that the spreadsheet calculations seem to be using the values from the right places.

Some of the topics in this chapter are appropriate to the development and testing of large systems, but nonetheless there is always a case for testing with great thoroughness any ICT product that you produce.

Whatever tests are carried out, their results must be recorded.

Unit 3 Assessment

This assignment is based on the Festivities Unlimited, or FUN, case study described in the general Introduction on pages xiii and xiv.

Scenario

The amalgamation of FUN with the chain of shops known as Shop All Day, or SAD, described in Sample Assignment No. 2, has now taken place. The two businesses are now working as one, operating under the name FUN.

The directors of FUN wish to be able to assess the commercial success of the amalgamation. There are two areas of particular interest to them at present:

- the results of the customer attitude survey which FUN conducted through a questionnaire

- the value of the discounts obtained from the wholesale supplier called YARD, now used for purchasing goods throughout the FUN business.

The directors want to see the survey results displayed on a spreadsheet so that they can study the output with several different representations of the data.

They expect to want to see reports of the value of the discounts regularly, probably once a month. They therefore also want a spreadsheet prepared for this purpose.

Your tasks

1 Using the questionnaire you designed for Sample Assignment No. 1, or another similar questionnaire of about the same size, prepare a spreadsheet that shows:

- how many individuals responded to each question

- the pattern of responses to each question, with choices on how the output is to be presented: as absolute figures, as percentages, or as graphics; or as a combination of these styles.

You will have to decide what differences there ought to be for handling the responses to the open and closed questions on the questionnaire. Where the nature of the question is suitable, you should get the spreadsheet to calculate and display the average. For example, a question which asked 'How many times do you expect to order from FUN next year?' would allow you to produce a valid average.

You must provide technical information describing the formulas used.

You must write user guidance on how data is to be fed into the system, and on the ways users obtain the output formats they desire.

2 You have to specify, design, develop, document, and test a spreadsheet to provide details of the discounts given on goods received, against their list prices, from YARD. (We assume that the YARD basic prices are being monitored by FUN separately.)

First you must select and name at least twenty product lines, falling into four product groups, regularly ordered by the SAD shops before the amalgamation. For each line you must record one of the levels of order that attracted discount, and the size of the discount. For example:

Line:	Doggo, 500 gram tin
Group:	Pet Food
Order qty:	10 cases of 48 tins
Discount:	4%.

The directors want to know whether the discount structure operates more favourably now that FUN is a larger customer; how much discount is earned month by month, on each of the lines and groups being studied; and whether trends can be detected in quantities ordered and rates of discount obtained.

You have to specify a spreadsheet that will address all these matters, including the discount position, for the lines being studied, before the amalgamation, and for a rolling period of six months ending with last month.

Next you must design the spreadsheet, making it visually attractive and straightforward to use. You should look at the list of complex facilities in the extract from the Advanced VCE Specifications at the start of Chapter 3.1, pick out those that could make your spreadsheet in some way better, and incorporate them. Your design must include the input procedure, data validation, formulas, output formats and options.

You need to produce technical and user documentation.

Finally, you must plan an appropriate testing strategy for the spreadsheet, and design tests which provide evidence of correct working under normal and abnormal input. If you are tackling this assignment as a group of students, you should try to ensure that the testing is carried out by someone who was not responsible for the design of the spreadsheet.

System installation and configuration

This next three chapters address the requirements of Unit 4:

Chapter 4.1 Hardware
Chapter 4.2 Software
Chapter 4.3 System documentation and testing

The topic 'Standard ways of working' in the AVCE Specifications is covered in Chapter 1.2.

There is a large amount of detail for you to absorb in Chapters 4.1 and 4.2. You will find, however, that by becoming familiar with exactly what current hardware and software technology comprises you will be well placed to appreciate the advances that are continually taking place, and to evaluate their usefulness to your own work.

There is no requirement in the AVCE Specifications for you to know anything about magnetic tape storage. You should, however, be aware that reel-to-reel *magnetic tape* has had a role in computer systems for many years, for working storage and for archiving data. You may well come across magnetic tape cartridges which are used for archiving in some installations. You may also meet the term *streamer tape,* which is the name of a device for recording data quickly and inexpensively.

Chapter 4.1 Hardware

This part of Unit 4, which covers hardware, requires that you gain an understanding of the purposes of the main pieces of computer equipment, and of their links with other components. You will practise choosing and setting up different combinations of components for a range of different purposes and potential users.

We use the word **hardware** to mean the physical elements of a computer system, including electrical and electronic components such as devices and circuits, electromechanical components such as disk drives, and mechanical components such as the external case of a personal computer (PC).

It is convenient to describe the hardware of a computer as consisting of a **system unit** and **peripheral devices**. The *system unit* comprises a case that houses a motherboard, a power supply, and mass storage devices (such as magnetic disk drives or optical drives). The *peripheral devices* comprise input devices (such as a keyboard, a mouse, or a scanner) and output devices (including a visual display unit or VDU, a printer, or a plotter).

Some devices can function as both input and as output devices; a **sound card**, for example, can both output audio to loudspeakers or headphones, and process and sample input from a microphone.

The **motherboard** comprises the **central processing unit (CPU)**, **random access memory (RAM)**, and supporting electronics to interface with the peripheral and mass storage devices. The way in which the components of a computer are arranged and

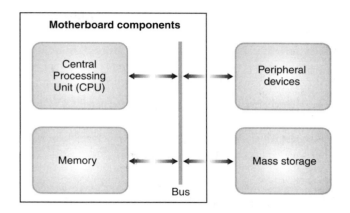

Figure 4.1 A common computer architecture

organised is called the system's **architecture**. The architecture of a typical small computer is illustrated in Figure 4.1.

The important point about this architecture is that all the devices communicate with the central processor through a **bus**. The bus is an electronic 'highway' which regulates and organises the movement of information between the central processing unit and its connected devices. It is discussed in more detail below.

Most computer systems have at least one bus, but higher-performance systems may have two or more buses. For example, the video display controller may communicate with the central processor using a **local video bus (VL-bus)** or an **accelerated graphics port (AGP)**.

Before we take a detailed look at the hardware of a typical personal computer (PC) system, we need to recall our discussion in Chapter 1.1 about the way data is held. We noted that all data in computer systems is held as binary digits, or **bits**. A set of eight bits forms a **byte**;

and it is usual to refer to storage capacity as having a certain number of bytes. There is a convention that bits are denoted by the lower-case letter **b**, and bytes with the upper-case letter **B**. Thus a thousand bytes is a **kilobyte (kB)**, a million bytes or a thousand kB is a **megabyte (MB)**, a thousand MB is a **gigabyte (GB)**, and finally a thousand GB is a **terabyte (TB)**.

? Did you know?

Strictly speaking, 1 kB is 1024 bytes, not 1000 bytes, as we mentioned in Chapter 1.1. 1 MB is 1024 kB, not 1000 kB, and so on for GB and TB. We shall not be too concerned with this issue, however, for three reasons.

First, the error introduced by using the 'round figures' approximation of 1000 instead of 1024 is between 2% and 3%, which is a modest error.

Second, the 'round figures' approximation is easier to remember, and corresponds better with other metric 'kilo' and 'mega' measures such as kilograms and kilometres, and Megastream, British Telecom's high-speed data link.

Finally, for marketing and sales reasons, computer system components such as hard drives are now often specified as having, for example, a 1 GB capacity, where what is meant is a 1 000 000 000 byte capacity, and not a 1 073 741 824 byte capacity (the result of multiplying 1024 × 1024 × 1024).

? Did you know?

In 1981 Bill Gates said: '640 K ought to be enough for anybody.'

System unit

Most personal computer systems comprise, along with a mouse and a keyboard, two main 'units': the **screen** or **visual display** unit (VDU), and the **system unit**. The system unit is usually a metal, or mixed metal and plastic case which holds a power supply, the mass storage drives, and the motherboard. On the motherboard is mounted the CPU.

Form factor

The system unit case can be provided in a variety of shapes known as **form factors**: tower, 'mini'-tower, desk unit, and 'slimline' or 'low profile' desk unit. A desk unit takes up less space but allows less internal expansion, while a tower unit takes up more space but has more capacity for internal expansion. A tower often stands on the floor, freeing some working surface, and reducing the cabling needed on the desktop.

Power supply

The power supply usually has one or two fans, whose purpose is both to cool the power supply electronics and to provide some cooling for the rest of the components in the system unit. Power supplies have a **power rating**, which is the maximum amount of electrical power they are designed to deliver. Early PC systems had power supplies rated at 135 watts, while current PC systems have power supplies rated at over 200 W, to accommodate CPUs that are more power-hungry, and more peripheral device controllers. Expanded multimedia systems might require a more highly rated power supply of around 250 W or 300 W, while dual-processor server systems would require special power supplies to satisfy their particular needs.

Motherboard

The motherboard is the heart of the system unit. Figure 4.2 shows a simple PC motherboard designed to take an Intel 80486 CPU. The terms 'ISA', 'cache', 'PCI', and 'RAM' are explained below.

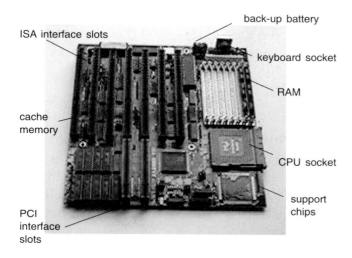

Figure 4.2 Motherboard

The major visual features of a motherboard include a large socket for the CPU, sockets for the random access memory (RAM), and a number of interface slots to the system bus. **ISA** stands for **Industry Standard Architecture**: the ISA slots are built as standard items to accept standard connectors. Other features include the socket for the keyboard on the side of the board, a small on-board battery, and a variety of support chips and other electronic components.

Motherboard form factor

The motherboard also comes in a number of shapes, or form factors. Each form factor is designed to match the case into which the board will be placed. The most popular current form factor is called the 'ATX'; older systems would probably have 'Baby

AT' form factor motherboards. These names stem from IBM's Model AT personal computer and are not, in themselves, of importance.

CPU socket

Most CPUs until recently have been provided as **PGA (pin grid array)** or **SPGA (staggered PGA)** packages, denoting the arrangement of connector pins on the bottom of the package. More recently, Pentium II and Pentium III CPUs come as **SEC (single-edge contact)** or **SEP (single-edge processor)** packages. In these cases the motherboard has a socket to accept the required CPU. Because the motherboard and CPU must be matched through the socket or slot, a given motherboard will generally only work with a restricted range of CPUs; very few motherboards have more than one CPU socket or slot.

Readers with a keen interest in details of the CPU hardware might like to know that PGA and SPGA packages are plugged into Socket 4, Socket 5, Socket 7, Socket 8, or Socket 370 motherboards; SEC or SEP packages are plugged into Slot 1 or Slot 2 motherboards.

Motherboard configuration

The motherboard is configured, or set up, using a combination of DIP switches, jumpers, and CMOS settings.

- **Dual in-line package (DIP) switches**, used to configure the motherboard, comprise a bank of small switches that have to be set on or off using a tool such as a very small screwdriver.

- **Jumpers**, also used to configure the motherboard and illustrated in Figure 4.3, comprise a bank of wire pins which are connected together as required using little plastic and metal clips. Handling the jumper clips requires a pair of pliers with very small grippers, or possibly tweezers. More advanced motherboards allow their settings to be partially or completely made using the on-board **basic input–output system (BIOS) software**. The BIOS software stores the jumper settings in battery-backed **complementary metal oxide semiconductor (CMOS) memory**. The BIOS is discussed in more detail below.

jumpers

Figure 4.3 Jumpers on motherboard

System clock

The movement of data in a computer system is regulated by a clock, usually called the **system clock**. The faster this clock 'ticks', the faster data is processed. Designing and manufacturing chips to work with fast clocks is expensive, however, which is why slower systems are cheaper than faster systems. The speed of the system clock is generally specified in **megahertz (MHz)**, so that a clock speed of, say, 100 MHz means that the clock 'ticks' one hundred million times a second, or makes that number of **cycles** a second.

The system clock is part of the motherboard. In older systems, the housing

for the crystal which regulates the speed, or **frequency,** of the system clock can usually be seen as a small silver can, about 10 mm by 15 mm. In newer systems, the crystal is integrated into the motherboard chipset, discussed below.

Older motherboards, produced for PCs before about 1995, have system clocks which run at 33 MHz, 50 MHz, or 66 MHz. Newer motherboards have system clocks which run at 100 MHz or 133 MHz.

CPU

The CPU chip is the heart of the motherboard. A number of manufacturers make PC-compatible CPUs (currently Intel, Cyrix, and AMD, for example), and each manufacturer may have a number of models of PC-compatible CPU. At the time of writing, Intel manufactures the Pentium II, the Celeron, and the Pentium III.

A given CPU is rated at a certain CPU clock speed which is different from the speed of the system clock. For example, you could purchase a Celeron 400 or a Celeron 466, where the '400' or '466' is the CPU clock speed in MHz at which the specific CPU is guaranteed to be able to work.

Older processors such as the 486 can execute an instruction every two or three clock ticks or cycles. The original Pentium processor can execute an instruction on every clock cycle. Modern Pentium III CPUs can execute four or six instructions on every clock cycle. For example, a 600 MHz Pentium III can carry out about three thousand million instructions every second.

To arrive at the processing speed of a processor, it is necessary to multiply the system clock by a factor. For a CPU rated at 266 MHz, with a system clock of 66 MHz, the factor would have to be four. The factor is determined by the internal organisation of the processor chip.

Heat generation and heat dissipation

The CPU chip generates a significant amount of heat. Early PCs relied on the fan of the power supply to pass cooling air throughout the system unit case. Later, 386, 486, and early Pentium CPUs were provided with passive heat sinks – metal 'radiators' designed to draw heat away from the CPU chip. Currently, CPUs are packaged with active heat sinks, in which a fan is mounted on top of the metal 'radiator' to cool the chip as effectively as possible, but without making too much noise.

Memory

A major distinction is made between the memory for data held on the motherboard, sometimes called **main memory**, and the memory for data held on mass storage devices such as floppy disks and CD-ROMs, which is described below.

Random-access memory.

The main memory of a computer system is called **random access memory (RAM)**, so named because any byte of RAM, wherever it resides, can be directly read or written by the CPU at any time. The data held on a disk drive, on the other hand, cannot be accessed so directly; the read/write heads of the drive must first be positioned in the right place. To read data from a disk the system must wait for the required data to pass under the read/write heads in the next revolution. The disk unit would read a 512-byte block of data into the main memory from which the data needed would have to be extracted. Similarly, data is written on to disk storage in 512-byte blocks. Fortunately for the user, the system software takes care of the transfer of data to and from disk storage.

Figure 4.4 shows a RAM **single in-line memory module (SIMM)**, such as would be plugged into the motherboard shown earlier.

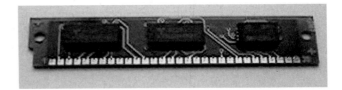

Figure 4.4   RAM SIMM

An advantage of RAM is that the effective speed of reading data from it or of writing data to it is higher than is the case with mass storage. A disadvantage of normal RAM is that it is **volatile**: the data disappears when power to the RAM is switched off. Numerous versions of RAM have been developed that are not volatile: some are discussed below.

Read-only memory.

Memory that preserves data when power is switched off is known as **read-only memory (ROM)**. Part of a PC's systems software is usually protected by holding it in ROM.

Originally, the contents of ROM were 'burned' into the ROM chip once, and thereafter could not be changed, hence the data really was 'read-only'; and not 'read or write'. This is a popular way of installing small amounts of essential software and other data on to a motherboard. It is discussed below, as the ROM BIOS.

There are some developments of ROM which allow its contents to be changed from time to time. The contents of **programmable ROM (PROM)** can be set once by using special equipment called a PROM burner. **EPROM** is a version of PROM that is **'erasable PROM'**, allowing the ROM contents to be erased by intense ultra-violet light, and reprogrammed using a strong electrical current. Finally, we have **EEPROM**, also called **flash ROM**, which is PROM whose contents can be **'electrically erased and programmed'** without using ultra-violet and a high-power current. This allows EEPROM to be installed as part of a normal circuit board such as a motherboard or controller card. All of these kinds of ROM are permanent: once the data has been programmed, power to the ROM chip can be removed, and the data remains. Their disadvantage is that they are slow in comparison with RAM.

Cache memory

Although a 200 MHz Pentium CPU might be able to carry out, say, two hundred million instructions every second, it often cannot operate quite so quickly in practice. It must wait to read data from main memory, or wait to write data out to memory, because of RAM access times.

To improve the CPU's access to data when required, a number of CPU chips have very fast on-chip memory, called **cache** memory. Cache memory is currently divided into two levels, **'level 1'**, or L1, cache; and **'level 2'**,

Variants of RAM

There is a version of RAM called **complementary metal oxide semiconductor RAM** (or **CMOS RAM**) whose contents can be preserved, provided a very modest source of battery power is provided while the main power supply is turned off. Typically, the configuration settings which are made by the ROM BIOS are stored in CMOS RAM on the motherboard. A small rechargeable battery is soldered onto the motherboard, keeping the CMOS RAM 'alive' while mains power is switched off.

Other versions of RAM include **static RAM (SRAM)**: this kind of RAM is very fast and electrically flexible, but also very expensive, and it is physically bulkier than the much more usual **dynamic RAM (DRAM)**. The main memory of almost all PCs is composed of DRAM, which itself can be provided in a number of versions: **FPM (fast page mode) DRAM**, **EDO (extended data out) DRAM**, **SDRAM (synchronous DRAM)**, or **RDRAM (Rambus DRAM)**. 'Rambus' is a proprietary name for 'random access memory bus'. Each of these versions of DRAM have features which enable faster operation in the right circumstances.

The most important performance indicator of a particular RAM chip is what is called its **access time** – the amount of time that the system must wait between making one access and making another. Because of the way RAM chips work, it is not possible to read data from them, or write data to them, instantaneously. A very short delay – the access time – is required between accessing successive bytes of data. Typically, main memory RAM would have an access time of 60 nanoseconds (60 ns). A nanosecond is one thousandth millionth of a second, and so 60 ns RAM could be read at a maximum of 16 666 667 times per second, or at about 16.7 MHz. If we had 32 MB of 60 ns RAM, and assuming nothing else was done to speed things up, it would take about two seconds just to pass the full 32 MB into the CPU.

or **L2**, cache. L1 cache memory on the CPU chip runs at the CPU 'core' speed. That is, if we have a 200 MHz CPU, its L1 cache also runs at 200 MHz, and would be rated as 5 ns RAM. Modern CPUs currently have 32 kB or 64 kB of L1 cache.

The on-chip L1 'core' speed cache memory is augmented in modern CPU designs with further L2 cache memory. L2 cache memory is usually slower than L1 cache memory, but there is more of it. In a 200 MHz Pentium system, for example, provision might be made for 512 kB of 15 ns (66 MHz) L2 cache memory on the motherboard. The latest CPU designs have moved L2 cache memory from the motherboard onto the CPU chip itself, further improving overall processor performance by reducing the lengths of the conductors.

Cache memory is used to hold the most recent data that the CPU was working on, and sometimes to hold some data that the CPU expects to need shortly. It turns out that, with a well-designed cache memory system, about 90% of the CPU's data requirements can be met from the cache, providing a valuable boost to the processing power of the system.

? Did you know?

Many computer installations install an **uninterruptable power supply** (UPS), so that in the event of an unplanned loss of electrical power. computer memory is not affected and processing can continue, at least for long enough to close systems in an orderly way.

Co-processors

The CPU can be assisted in some of its tasks by the addition of a **co-processor**. Most motherboards for the 8086, 286, and 386 CPUs also provided a socket for a matching 8087, 287, or 387 numeric co-processor to speed up mathematical operations such as multiplication and division. More recently, in designs such as the Pentium processor, the co-processor circuitry has been placed onto the CPU chip itself. Other designs of CPU allow the use of a graphics co-processor.

Bus

A PC motherboard typically has around seven **slots** for external peripheral devices. These slots comprise the interface or system bus for the system, into which **controller cards** may be plugged. A controller card or **interface card** might provide an IDE or SCSI interface (explained below) for the disk drives, for example, or it might be for the sound card for the system.

When originally launched, the PC interface slot became known as an **ISA slot**, or 'industry standard architecture' interface slot. The ISA slot started off as being an 8-bit slot (capable of moving 8 bits, or 1 byte, of data at a time), but it was soon developed into a 16-bit slot (capable of moving 2 bytes of data at a time). As systems increased in power even more, IBM developed the **MCA slot** or 'micro-channel architecture' slot; this was technically advanced but proprietary to IBM, and it failed to become popular.

An upgraded ISA interface slot called an **EISA slot**, or 'expanded ISA' slot, was designed and provided on some systems, but this slot did not find widespread acceptance. Currently, the **PCI slot**, or 'peripheral component interconnect' slot, provides a high-performance slot which allows the interface controller to have more capability than was possible with either an ISA or EISA slot.

The key performance indicator of a bus is its speed. The ISA slot is, technically, limited to a speed of 8 MHz, while the PCI slot runs at 33 MHz. These speeds imply that, for example, a 16-bit ISA interface can transfer no more than 16 MB of data per second (two bytes 8 000 000 times per second), while the 32-bit PCI slot can transfer up to about 132 MB of data a second (4 bytes 33 000 000 times per second). The implications of these limits will become apparent when we discuss disk drives and video controllers, below.

As mentioned earlier, most computer systems have other internal buses, typically for video and memory data transfers. Sometimes these internal buses are made available on a particular motherboard design for special-purpose use. In particular, the **AGP (accelerated graphics port)** is currently provided for high-performance video controllers on high-end systems. The AGP runs at 66 MHz and is 4 bytes wide. AGP2 runs at an effective 133 MHz.

Although the CPU is the heart of the motherboard, there are other functions that must be provided by the motherboard. These come from the operation of support chips. Often, these support chips are collected together into what is called a **support chipset**, which defines the capabilities and features of a particular motherboard. For example, early PCs could not automatically keep track of the date and time. A **real-time clock** was added to the PC after a while, and now this function is provided by the support chipset in conjunction with the ROM BIOS. More significantly, the AGP, PCI and ISA buses are managed by the chipset.

The '430 series' chipsets are installed on motherboards designed to support Pentium and Pentium-compatible processors, while the '440 series' supports Pentium II, III, and compatible processors. Within each chipset series, variants such as 'LX' and 'FX' have different features, such as the kind of RAM supported, the motherboard bus speed allowed, and the maximum amount of RAM that can be installed.

Try it out	As a group, collect from computer shops and from computer magazines details of performance and prices of Pentium processors being offered for sale. Make a table of what you discover. You may find big variations in the prices of identical items. Plot the best prices for a range of processors and extend the line to suggest what the prices might be for a more powerful model.

External interfaces

The motherboard provides interface slots into which **controller car**ds can be plugged. These controller cards connect the CPU and RAM to other devices such as the VDU (visual display unit). The original IBM terminology called these cards **adapters**.

Older adapter cards, called **legacy adapters**, are typically ISA cards. Currently, most adapter cards are PCI, while high-end video cards would plug into the AGP slot. Motherboards now provide a mix of ISA and PCI slots as well as an AGP slot. The **universal serial bus, (USB),** is a standard high-speed serial link. The term '**10BaseT**' which you may come across is the label for a standard form of network connection.

Some motherboard designs, particularly those for slimline desktop cases and portable computers, also have the controller electronics for video and sound built into the motherboard itself. The advantage is that much less space is needed in the case. The disadvantage is that the video or sound subsystem cannot be upgraded.

Figure 4.5 shows a typical 8-bit ISA network adapter card. It plugs into an ISA interface slot on the motherboard. Other adapter cards are broadly similar.

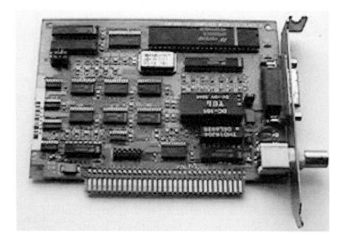

Figure 4.5 Interface card for network

Serial and parallel ports

Current motherboards always offer built-in serial and parallel ports. Some also offer the latest improvements such as USB (universal serial bus) and 'FireWire' fast serial ports. Earlier motherboards required adaptor cards to provide the serial and parallel ports.

Serial port

A **serial port** is a very simple communications port, generally used for the mouse or a modem. It sends and receives data one bit at a time, and needs just a few wires to connect the sender and receiver. The industry standard serial interface is known as RS-232C, standing for 'Reference Standard 232 Revision C'. Because data is sent one bit at a time, and because the 8 bits of a byte of data are generally sent with an extra 2 bits to indicate the start and end of the byte, standard serial port communications are relatively slow. A fast modem, for example, can send and receive data at about 56 000 bits per second, or about 5.6 kB/sec. If the modem were running at full speed, a modest data file of, say, 100 kB would thus take about 18 seconds to transmit.

Configuring a serial port
Configuring a serial port generally requires specifying to the software driver the required parameters of the port. These parameters include the speed of the port in bits per second, the number of start and stop bits per byte, and whether an error-checking **parity bit** is to be used.

Parallel port

Originally, the **parallel port** was intended to connect a printer to a computer system. It has since been developed to become a relatively fast and simple means of connecting a variety of medium-speed peripherals. As the name suggest, a parallel port transfers 8 bits of data in parallel, carrying a byte of data at a time. The original standard parallel port could achieve a transfer rate of about 150 kB/sec.

Over time, the parallel port was further developed: first, to allow bidirectional data transfers, and then to offer improved transfer rates. Current systems have an **EPP (enhanced parallel port)** that is also an **ECP (enhanced capabilities port)** parallel port, offering transfer rates of up to 2 MB/sec.

Configuring a parallel port

Because the ECP standard offers improved performance with printers and scanners, a parallel port should be configured in the BIOS as an ECP port, if that is available as an option.

Mass storage – magnetic and optical hard drives

It is convenient to divide mass storage into two types: *magnetic* (such as floppy disks, hard disks, and Zip disks), and *optical* (including CD-ROM, DVD, and CD-RW). Both types of mass storage rely on rotating disks which hold the data on their surfaces, and heads which are positioned on these rotating disks to read and write the data. Figure 4.6 shows the internal detail of a 5.25″ hard disk drive.

Mass storage – magnetic drives

The term **floppy disk** is used almost universally by everyone to refer to a standard, low-cost removable disk, although purists call it a **diskette**. Certainly it is not floppy, and any temptation to test the point should be resisted!

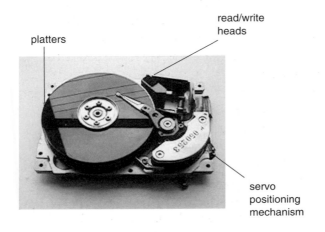

Figure 4.6 Internal detail of a hard disk drive

In general, magnetic mass storage is **read-write**, since information can be freely both read and written. Optical mass storage, on the other hand, has until recently been **read-only**, but the prices of the special drives required to write optical disks have been falling steeply and such drives are now within the reach of many users. There is an advantage to read-only storage, which is that it cannot be interfered with. All 3.5″ floppy disks have a **write-protect** slider which turns the floppy into a read-only medium if required.

The following discussion focuses on the hard drive, but the principles are applicable to all forms of rotating mass storage.

Medium

Magnetic mass storage starts with a layer of magnetic coating on a substrate, or underlying disk – in a hard disk, the substrate is aluminium; for a floppy disk, it is a tough plastic. The data is recorded onto the magnetic coating by a small **read/write head** – an electromagnet that can record tiny magnetic impressions on the coating, or detect whether or not such impressions are present.

Address

The data held on a hard drive must have an **address** to allow its correct location on the disk to be identified, and to allow data to be read and written. Data is generally held in 512-byte **blocks**. A hard drive may have one or more **platters**; each platter has two **surfaces**. On each surface there are a number of concentric **tracks**, and each track has a number of **sectors**. The data contained in one sector is a **block**. Where a drive has more than one platter, it is common to refer to a **cylinder** rather than a track, as the cylinder – tracks directly above and below each other on different surfaces –

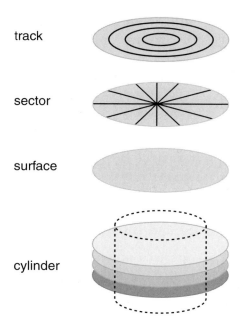

track

sector

surface

cylinder

Figure 4.7 Hard drive addressing terms

contains all the data that can be accessed by the read/write heads in a given position. Figure 4.7 illustrates these terms.

For example, an address might refer to a 512-byte block of data held on surface 1, track 562, sector 14. Fortunately the user does not normally need to be concerned about disk addresses: the systems software takes care of them.

Capacity

The **capacity** of a drive may be calculated by multiplying the number of surfaces, tracks, and sectors together to obtain the number of blocks of data, and then multiplying by 512 to obtain the total number of bytes. For example, a particular hard drive might have 2707 tracks per surface, 185 sectors per track, and 6 surfaces. This would give it a capacity of about 1.54 Gb.

Rotation speed

Older hard drives revolve at 3600 rpm; newer drives revolve at 7200 rpm or faster.

At 7200 rpm, a particular sector comes under the read/write heads 120 times every second.

Latency

If the CPU needed data from, say, track 1086, and if the read/write heads happened to be positioned on track 1086, then on average the system would have to wait for half a revolution before the data could be read. For a 7200 rpm drive, this **latency** before the data became available would be about 4 ms, 4 thousandths of a second.

Access time

If the CPU needed data from, say, track 1086, and if the read/write heads happened to be positioned on an adjacent track, track 1085 or track 1087, then the read/write heads would have to move one track before data could be transferred. The **track-to-track** positioning time might be about 2 ms, or 2 thousandths of a second. This track-to-track time is an important indicator of the hard drive's performance in situations where long streams of data need to be read or written, and where the data may be expected to occupy more than one track.

In general, of course, the read/write heads could be at any track when the requirement for track 1086 arises. In this case, the performance of the hard drive is indicated by its **average access** time, taking into account that, on average, the read/write heads would have to be moved over a large number of tracks. An average access time of 7 ms or 8 ms is typical for current drives.

Transfer rate

The most important performance indicator of a drive, however, is its **transfer rate** – the overall rate at which data can be read from or written to the drive over an extended period of time. Using our earlier example of a 1.54 GB hard drive, this rate is approximately 11.4 MB per second – 185 sectors, of 512 bytes each, would be accessed 120 times per second, though this calculation assumes no head movement.

Buffer

When the read/write heads are correctly positioned and a sector is read, the data streams in from the hard drive at a high rate – 11.4 MB/sec according to our example. Such a rate would be very difficult for the CPU to manage, and so the data would be placed in a memory **buffer** before being transferred, at a somewhat slower rate, to the CPU.

Interface

In early PC systems, the hard drive would be controlled by a controller card or interface adapter. This controller would plug into an interface slot, and connect to the hard drive through a ribbon cable. Controller electronics have been standardised over the intervening period, and now fall into two main types: **IDE or EIDE** (standing for **integrated drive electronics** and **extended IDE**), and **SCSI** (pronounced 'skuzzy', standing for **small computer systems interface**). IDE and EIDE hard drives have their controller circuitry mounted on the hard drive itself, and only the interface connector has to be mounted on the motherboard, usually built-in. A SCSI hard drive, on the other hand, requires a full SCSI interface adapter card to be plugged into a motherboard slot.

The IDE and EIDE standards are also known as the **ATA** (**AT attachment** – originally for the IBM Model AT personal computer) or **ATAPI** (**ATA packet interface**) standards. The IDE/EIDE interface provides a cost-effective high-performance interface for one or two hard drives, and has recently been enhanced into the **fast-ATA** and **ultra-ATA** standards.

The IDE interface allows up to two devices on the primary IDE channel, and two on the secondary channel.

The SCSI standard allows a number of peripheral devices to be operated by one SCSI controller, up to 8 or 16 depending upon the controller. SCSI devices are generally high-performance devices, and offer superior data transfer rates over PCI-based or EIDE-based devices. Recent enhancements to the SCSI standard include **fast-and-wide SCSI** and **ultra SCSI**.

Because the SCSI interface is better specified for the control of multiple, very high-speed devices, it is recommended that systems which include a CD-ROM writer or rewriter be SCSI based, as should systems that are designed to handle streaming video and multimedia applications.

Hard drive form factor

Hard drives come in a number of sizes, both physically and in terms of their capacity. The most common diameters, known as *form factors* and expressed in inches, are $5^{1}/_{4}''$, $3^{1}/_{2}''$, $2^{1}/_{2}''$, 1.8″, and 1″. The $3^{1}/_{2}''$ drive is most popular in desktop systems, while the $2^{1}/_{2}''$ drive is most popular in portable systems. Capacities of up to 20 Gb are readily available, and it is expected that these capacities will double about every two years for the foreseeable future.

Hard drive set-up

An IDE/EIDE drive must first be configured as either a 'master' or 'slave' unit. This is usually done with a jumper on the underside of the drive itself. If the system only uses one hard drive, it is set up as a master. If two drives are installed, one is set as the master, and the other is set as the slave. Usually it does not matter which is which, but in some older systems there may be compatibility problems, particularly if the drives are from different manufacturers, each requiring a specific arrangement.

The drive is physically installed in the system unit with screws, and its cables plugged in – a 4-pin power cable from the power supply, and a 40-pin IDE ribbon cable that terminates on the motherboard. A red stripe on the ribbon cable identifies 'pin 1', and care is needed to ensure that the cable is correctly connected to 'pin 1' both on the motherboard and on the drive unit.

When the computer system is turned on, modern systems will automatically recognise the new drive and register its settings into CMOS RAM.

The drive may now need to be **partitioned**, depending upon the operating system of the computer. The first release of Windows 95, for example, could only handle a maximum of 2 GB on any drive letter such as **C:** and if the drive was a 6 GB drive, it would need to be partitioned into three partitions, and the partitions assigned the drive letters **C:**, **D:**, and **E:**. Also, older PC systems may have a BIOS that cannot handle large drives; for example, at various times in the past there were BIOS limitations for drives larger than 504 MB, 2.1 GB, and 8.4 GB. On a PC, the software required to partition a drive is called FDISK.

Finally, the drive must be **formatted**, using the FORMAT program or command. If the drive is the only drive of the system, the PC is initiated, or booted, using a floppy disk containing the essentials of the operating system. FORMAT is then run from the floppy, and the rest of the operating system installed from CD-ROM. Modern systems can boot from the CD-ROM itself, making the process easier.

Mass storage – optical drives

We will look at **CD-ROM (compact disc read-only memory)**, **DVD (digital versatile disc)**, **CD-R (CD-ROM recordable)**, and **CD-RW (CD-ROM rewritable)**, all of which rely on optical storage technology.

Medium

Optical mass storage starts with a thin layer of reflective material that is bonded onto a plastic substrate. The reflective material has a series of tiny pits stamped or formed into it, each pit representing one bit of data. The data is read by bouncing a laser beam off the disk to detect whether a pit is present at a particular location. When the bounced beam reflects strongly, there is no pit, and a '1' is recorded; when the beam reflects weakly, a pit has interfered with the reflection, and a '0' is recorded. CD-ROMs and audio CDs are manufactured and used in exactly the same way.

Address

The data held on a CD-ROM or DVD is recorded as a very long, single spiral; almost five kilometres long on a CD. The spiral is divided into segments. The first segment of the spiral contains system data and the table of contents of the remainder of the spiral. When the CD-ROM is first loaded into the system, the first segment of data is read and the table of contents stored in RAM. Thereafter, in order to find a particular item of data, the table of contents is referenced, revealing which segment of the spiral holds the required data. A 'segment' on a CD-ROM usually comprises 2048 bytes, or 2 kB of data. Some CD-ROMs, typically video CDs, store 2324 bytes per segment.

One often hears that a CD contains a number of 'tracks'. These 'tracks' are not the same sort of tracks as exist on a magnetic disc. A CD 'track' is simply a series of segments on the spiral, each starting at a certain segment and ending a number of segments later.

Capacity

The capacity of a CD-ROM is 650 MB.

Rotation speed

Unlike magnetic disks, a CD-ROM is originally **recorded** at a variable speed – the disk spins faster when the data is being recorded on the inside tracks, and spins more slowly when data is being recorded on the outside tracks. The effect is that the data is recorded with **constant linear velocity (CLV)**, so that the data is recorded on the disk at a uniform density and at a constant rate.

Although the data is recorded on to a CD-ROM at constant linear velocity, most CD-ROM drives read the data without slowing the disk down or speeding it up according to where it is on the data spiral. Instead, most CD-ROM drives **play back** at **constant angular velocity (CAV)**. This means that the data moves past the laser at different speeds, the speed depending on where on the disk the laser is trying to read the data. Data on the outer edge of the CD is read much faster than data on the inner tracks.

Transfer rate

On an audio CD, 75 segments of data are recorded per second, and this defines the rate at which data can be read from a single-speed CD-ROM. The very earliest CD-ROM drives would read 75 segments of data per second, where each segment comprised 2 kB. This yielded a transfer rate of 150 kB/sec. This is not a very fast data rate, and later CD-ROM drives spin the CD-ROM disk faster to obtain faster

rates. A sixteen-speed (16×) CD-ROM drive, for example, has a transfer rate of 2.4 MB/sec.

However, drives rated faster than 16× currently cannot spin the disk fast enough and read the data reliably from the inner tracks of the CD; they have to slow the CD down, and can only achieve their theoretical maximum transfer rate when reading data from the outer tracks.

Access time

If the CPU needed data from an arbitrary point on the CD-ROM, a 16× CD-ROM drive would typically suffer a 90 ms access time delay. Some drives are faster, some slower.

CD-ROM drive interface

As is the case with hard drives, CD-ROM drives operate with either EIDE (ATAPI) or SCSI interfaces. And the choice between one type of interface and the other is governed by the same factors as with hard drives: cost (IDE); the requirement for high performance (SCSI); the number of mass storage drives to be connected to the system (1 or 2, IDE; 4 or more, SCSI); and the need for video (SCSI).

CD-ROM drive set-up

An ATAPI (EIDE) CD-ROM drive should be connected to the secondary channel of the EIDE interface, rather than as a slave to the primary channel. This provides for a faster transfer of data between hard drive and CD-ROM drive. If the CD-ROM drive is sharing the secondary EIDE channel with another device, it should be set to be a 'master' or 'slave' as required.

CD-R and CD-RW

There are two kinds of technology for recording on CDs, known as CD-R and CD-RW drives. They 'burn' or write a CD, providing a high-capacity recordable data storage medium very cheaply.

CD-R writes a CD disc by using a higher-power laser to melt the recordable layer and so simulate a normal CD-ROM 'pit'. The process is not reversible, and so CD-R is a 'write once, read many' (or 'WORM') device. Recent CD-R drives can record at 2× or 4× 'normal' speed, and 8× CD-R drives are available for professional use. The CD-R drive also works as, and can easily replace, a normal CD-ROM drive; currently popular CD-R drives are rated at 24× when used to play back CD-ROMs.

The CD-RW disk employs a different technology from the CD-R disk. Here the laser is fired at a high power to melt and thus change the structure of the recording layer from a polycrystalline state into an amorphous state, thereby making a pit. Alternatively, the laser is fired at a lower power to heat but not melt the recording layer, which changes any amorphous state material into the more reflective polycrystalline state, thus removing a pit.

The disadvantage of CD-RW, at present, is that the polycrystalline material is not very reflective, and most ordinary CD-ROM drives have trouble playing back CD-RW discs. The CD-RW drive acts as a CD-R drive as well as a CD-ROM drive, so if you need to play back your CD on another CD-ROM drive, it would be better to use CD-R media and produce CD-R disks rather than CD-RW disks.

DVD
Digital versatile disks (DVDs) are similar to CD-ROMs in size, appearance, and technology, but offer very much greater capacity – at least 4.7 GB against 650 MB for a CD-ROM. They pack more data by having smaller 'pits', a tighter spiral of

data, and more efficient error-correcting code so that less error-correcting data need be stored on the disk. A DVD drive can read CD-ROMs, and offers CD-ROM playback at about the same rate as a 8× CD-ROM drive, so a 2× or 4× DVD drive would be the approximate equivalent of a 16× or 32× CD-ROM drive.

In the same way that there is a difference between audio CD and CD-ROM, there is a difference between DVD-video and DVD-ROM. DVD-video disks contain only video data, and are intended to be played in a DVD player connected to a TV and hi-fi. A DVD-ROM drive can usually play DVD-video disks, but DVD-ROM discs are intended as very high-capacity mass storage.

For your DVD-ROM drive to play a DVD-video disc, it needs the additional electronics of a **motion picture experts group (MPEG)** decoder, because DVD-video is recorded onto DVD using the MPEG format. An MPEG decoder is usually provided as a separate interface card to plug into a free PCI slot, to which the DVD-ROM drive is connected, as well as providing connectors for the TV and hi-fi.

Recordable, or rewritable, DVD disk standards are still in their infancy, and at the time of writing no clear standard has emerged. DVD-RAM, DVD-R, DVD-RW, and DVD+RW are all competing standards and technologies being championed by various manufacturers.

Try it out	As a group, review the current market for storage devices, noting the technology they use, their capacities, access times, transfer rates, and prices. Select one storage technology and make a presentation to the rest of the group explaining what you have found out.

Configuring the system unit

The system unit is mainly configured using the ROM BIOS. The **BIOS**, or **basic input-output system**, is a set of software routines stored in a PROM, EPROM, or EEPROM on the motherboard. Figure 4.8 illustrates a PROM chip that has been programmed under licence from American Megatrends, Inc. (AMI), a major supplier of ROM BIOS chips. The two other major suppliers are Award Systems and Phoenix; the latter is currently the world's largest supplier.

Figure 4.8 ROM BIOS chip on motherboard

The BIOS software is a layer in the PC system that allows application and operating system software to access and use the hardware of the system in a standard way. The BIOS provides the necessary interface between the particulars of the system's hardware and the needs of the applications software to use that hardware in as independent a way as possible. If a hard drive is upgraded, it is the BIOS that registers and handles the change so that no change need be made by the application software to accommodate the upgraded hardware. The BIOS usually stores settings and parameters in CMOS RAM which is backed up by a small rechargeable battery which prevents data loss when the mains power is switched off.

Strictly speaking, the BIOS settings are usually stored on the RTC/NVRAM chip. This chip provides a **real-time clock (RTC)** for the system, and stores its date and time data into so-called **non-volatile RAM (NVRAM)** on the chip. When modern ROM BIOS software was first written, there was spare storage on the RTC/NVRAM chip, and this was used to store the BIOS parameters. The NVRAM on the RTC chip is in fact CMOS RAM, and it is only non-volatile because of the small battery used to keep it 'alive'.

POST

The ROM BIOS also contains a set of routines called the **POST**, or **power-on self-test**. This software takes control of the computer each time it switched on, to check the integrity of the system. The POST contains routines to check RAM, the keyboard, the connected mass-storage devices, and various other system components. To access CMOS RAM and configure or set up the system unit, the POST is interrupted by pressing a particular key combination. For an AMI or Award BIOS, it is <Del>; for Phoenix, it is <F2>. You are then given the BIOS set-up main menu.

BIOS set-up

The BIOS set-up menu usually allows you to specify a number of parameters. If CPU and motherboard clock speeds cannot be specified in your particular BIOS set-up, they can almost certainly be set with jumpers or DIP switches on the motherboard itself. The major parameters are as follows:

- CPU clock speed, often entered as the clock multiplier of the motherboard system clock

- system time and system date
- parallel port mode
- serial port I/O base address and interrupt channel
- power management options; boot sequence.

Peripheral units

Keyboard

The 'original' PC keyboard comprised 83 keys, and the 'original' PC-AT keyboard comprised 84 keys. Both are now obsolete. The current 'standard' keyboard is known as the 101-key 'enhanced' keyboard; a version of the 101-key keyboard has been developed by Microsoft to give a 104-key 'Windows' keyboard. Early versions of the 101-key and 104-key keyboards connected to the motherboard with a 5-pin **DIN (Deutsche industrie norm)** plug, while current versions feature the smaller 6-pin mini-DIN plug, also known as a 'PS/2' connector. Current motherboards all use the 6-pin mini-DIN, but care needs to be taken when making the connection in case the motherboard is of an older design. Adapters are readily available to convert between 5-pin DIN and 6-pin mini-DIN connectors.

Take care not to spill a drink over your keyboard – a surprisingly common event.

Mouse

A mouse usually connects to a PC through a serial interface or a dedicated mouse port. For these connections there are two types of mouse. While older PC systems generally use a mouse on a serial interface port, current systems provide a dedicated mouse port on the motherboard, also known as a

'PS/2 mouse port', using a 6-pin mini-DIN connector. The two types of mouse are not interchangeable; while they may be mechanically identical, they are electrically quite different.

Most mice have mechanical components that rather easily get dirty, causing jerky movement of the pointer on the screen. The solution is to clean the rollers inside the mouse case which transfer the ball movements to the internal circuitry.

Visual display unit

The video display of a computer system consists of two distinct components: the display screen itself, and the video controller, also known as the **graphics card**.

CRT and LCD VDUs

The screen or **visual display unit** (VDU) of a computer system is usually a **cathode ray tube (CRT)** for a desk-top system, and a **liquid crystal display (LCD)** for a portable system. A VDU is also called a **monitor**.

With a CRT monitor, the image on the screen is created by an electron beam that sweeps very rapidly over the screen. The beam moves in horizontal lines from left to right, flying back to scan the next line down from left to right, and so on from the top to the bottom of the screen. The rate at which the beam produces a dot on the screen is called the **horizontal scan frequency**, and is typically 40 kHz to 90 kHz. As the beam strikes the phosphor coating behind the CRT glass the phosphor glows briefly, and then fades rapidly. In order to maintain the glow, and hence the image, the beam must refresh the screen about 80 times per second, or at 80 Hz. This is called the **vertical scan frequency** or **refresh rate**. Refresh rates certainly need to be above 72 Hz to avoid eye strain and flickering screens; the current Video Electronics Standards Association (VESA) recommendation is 85 Hz.

With an LCD screen, the image is created by an electric current that changes the polarising orientation of a picture element, or **pixel**, at the required location. When polarised in one direction, the liquid crystal pixel allows light to pass, and so appears bright or transparent. When polarized in the other direction, the pixel blocks light, and appears dark or opaque. Because the liquid crystal pixel changes its polarisation state somewhat more slowly than the CRT phosphor dot stops glowing, an LCD screen is generally not a good choice for displaying images in which there is much movement.

Adjusting the monitor's contrast and brightness is quite different for CRT and LCD screens. For a CRT screen, you would generally set the contrast to maximum, and then adjust the brightness to suit. You'll know if the brightness is excessive if there is a misty white glow around the visible display rather than a completely black border, or if there is a misty grey background when it should be black. For an LCD screen, the adjustments are reversed: you would generally set the brightness to maximum, and then adjust the contrast to suit.

Resolution

The major difference between VDU screens lies in their **resolution**, or the detail they can show. Resolution depends partly upon the size of the screen, and partly upon the spacing between the pixels that make up the image. For PC screens, a number of standard resolutions have emerged, as shown

Resolution		Name
640 × 480	VGA	Video graphics array
800 × 600	SVGA	Super VGA
1024 × 768	XGA	Extended graphics array
1280 × 1024		

Table 4.1 PC screen resolutions

in Table 4.1. Notice that all of these resolutions are in the ratio 4:3.

Each higher resolution requires a larger sized screen for its display. The size of a monitor is measured along its diagonal, with the dimention usually expressed in inches. For CRT screens, the diagonal size is measured from the opposite corners of the CRT tube itself, which is usually an inch or two longer than the diagonal of the area that is visible once the plastic front panel has been installed. For LCD screens, the diagonal specified is the viewable diagonal.

Dot pitch

Good-quality CRTs have a smaller gap between their phosphor dots than other CRTs. For detailed work, a dot pitch of 0.26 mm or 0.25 mm is currently considered essential, while a dot pitch of 0.28 mm is acceptable for general use. If we take a dot pitch of 0.26 mm, we have a screen that shows about 97 or 98 **dots per inch (dpi)**. An XGA display on such a screen would measure about 10.48″ × 7.86″ (26.6 cm × 20.0 cm), and would have a diagonal of about 13.1″ (33.3 cm). In theory, this should make for comfortable viewing on a 15″ CRT, with 14″ viewable, but in practice would only be acceptable on a 17″ CRT. On the other hand, such an

XGA display on a 13.3″ LCD panel would provide excellent clarity.

Resolution	Minimum CRT diagonal	LCD diagonal
640 × 480	13″	10.9″
800 × 600	15″	12.1″
1024 × 768	17″	13.3″
1280 × 1024	19″	

Table 4.2 Comparison between CRT and LCD displays

Interlacing

For a number of years, low-cost CRTs and low-cost video controllers could not reach the 85 Hz refresh rate required to redraw the screen line by line. Instead, they would draw all the odd lines on one pass, and then draw all the even lines on the next pass, giving a full screen refresh rate of about 43 Hz. Such an arrangement was called 'interlaced' – half of the display was interlaced with the other half on successive passes – and it tended to provide a display with rather a high level of flicker. Currently, such interlaced displays are considered ergonomically very unsound, and only non-interlaced displays are considered acceptable.

Video display controller

The data that is displayed on the computer monitor is placed into video RAM by the application program. It is the video display controller, which is another name for the video adapter or graphics card, that takes the data from its video RAM and formats appropriate signals so that the data is shown on the VDU. At first, the very earliest video adapters could only manage

monochrome, that is black and white, displays. In these each screen pixel was represented by a bit: '0' was 'black', and '1' was 'white'. A VGA-resolution screen thus required 640 × 480 bits, or 307 200 bits. This is about 38.4 kB, and so early video RAM was specified at 64 kB.

Colour depth

Early colour video display controllers could only show 16 colours. Later this expanded to 256 colours, then 65 536 colours, and currently 16.7 million colours are available. The 16 colours of a pixel may be specified by 4 bits of data; 256 colours requires 8 bits per pixel; 65 536 colours, 16 bits; and 16.7 million colours, 24 bits. A display resolution of 1280 × 1024 involves 1 310 720 pixels; with a 24-bit colour depth, that is 3 bytes per pixel, the amount of video RAM required is 3 932 160 bytes, or about 4 MB.

Resolution	Colours	Colour depth	Video RAM required
640 × 480	16	4 bits	256 kB
800 × 600	256	8 bits	512 kB
1024 × 768	65 536	16 bits	2 MB
1280 × 1024	16.7 million	24 bits	4 MB

Table 4.3 Video RAM requirements

Configuring the display

Setting up the screen correctly in a PC involves knowing the resolution of the VDU, and knowing the amount of video RAM installed on the video controller. Given the resolution and the video RAM, the highest attainable colour depth can be calculated, and the video driver software can then be set to use the VDU resolution at the calculated colour depth.

Printers and plotters

There are three types of printer, making use of the three main printing technologies, for use with PCs – laser, inkjet, and dot matrix. There are two kinds of plotter – flatbed and drum – both of which are mainly used for engineering applications.

Printers

Laser printer

A laser printer works by firing a laser beam onto a photosensitive drum. The parts of the drum affected by the beam become electrically charged, and attract the very fine particles of toner. As the drum rotates, it transfers the toner to the paper, and the toner is then fused in place by passing the paper through a set of heated rollers. The technology employed is identical to that used in office photocopiers, except that the image source is through a laser from a

computer data file, rather than from a brightly illuminated paper original and a lens system.

A laser printer gives excellent print quality. There are really only two areas in which a different printing technology has benefits: inexpensive colour printing is better provided by an inkjet printer; and multi-part business forms are better printed on a dot-matrix printer.

Inkjet printer

An inkjet printer works by ejecting tiny drops of ink on to the page. Almost all current inkjet printers are colour printers, and they provide very good colour prints, particularly when used with good-quality paper.

Dot-matrix printer

A dot-matrix printer works by firing a set of pins in its print head against a carbon or inked ribbon positioned next to the paper. Because of this mechanical printing action, multiple copies can be printed at once using **multi-part forms**, and this is the only remaining area in which dot-matrix printers offer any advantage over other types of printer.

Resolution

The major measure of the quality of print output is the **resolution** – the number of dots per inch that the printer can place on the page. The more dots per inch (dpi), the better the resulting image. Inexpensive laser printers currently offer 600 dpi, while inexpensive inkjet printers offer 300 dpi. For comparison, book publishers would currently use printers that have a resolution of 2 400 dpi. A 24-pin dot matrix printer provides about 180 dpi.

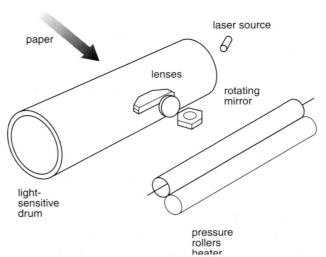

Figure 4.9 Laser printer major components

Speed

The other major measure of printer performance is speed. Inexpensive laser printers offer 4 or 6 **pages per minute (ppm)** when printing in monochrome. Inkjet printers typically give 3 ppm and dot matrix printers 2 to 4 ppm. Their speed drops very significantly when printing in colour. More expensive work-group, network, and departmental printers would offer 16 ppm.

Colour

Colour on a page is most commonly achieved by using four colours, and overlaying different quantities of each colour to achieve the desired effect. Both colour laser printers and colour inkjet printers use four colours of toners or inks: **cyan, magenta, yellow, and black (CMYK)**. Some inkjets use six ink colours in addition to black to provide better near-photographic quality output.

Printer memory

A laser printer generally needs the whole of the page to be available before printing can start, while an inkjet or dot-matrix printer can stop half-way down a page if necessary and allow the computer to 'catch up' with generating the output image. A whole page comprises a prodigious amount of data when expressed as bits, particularly if it involves 24-bit colour depth. For example, an A4 page is approximately $8'' \times 11.5''$; at 600 dpi, there are about 33 million dots. If each dot requires 24-bit colour, approximately 100 MB of memory would be needed to hold the image; if each dot was part of a 256-greyscale image, then 8 bits would be needed, implying a 33 MB image file.

Most laser printers today have 2 MB or 4 MB of memory, and could not possibly hold a 100 MB or even a 33 MB image. Instead, a variety of **compression** techniques are used by the printer driver and by the printer electronics to squeeze the 100 MB or 33 MB of raw data into available memory. There are, naturally, limits to the degree to which any file of data can be compressed.

Interface

Most printers connect to the PC through a parallel port interface. Some older printers might use a serial interface, while more recently a network interface allows a printer to be easily shared by a number of users. An A4 600 dpi 24-bit colour image, when compressed, might occupy 10 MB, and so a laser printer printing at 8 ppm would require about 80 MB per minute, or an interface that could comfortably sustain a transfer rate of about 1.25 MB/sec. This is within the operating parameters of an enhanced parallel port, and so a more sophisticated interface would not be necessary.

Drivers

All printers require a software driver of some kind. Some printers can provide basic text printing without a driver, but the current trend is towards printers that do not work at all without driver software.

Plotters

The printers discussed above are all 'digital' in the sense that they create text and images from individual dots. A plotter, on the other hand, is a printout device that creates text and images by 'drawing' – moving a pen over paper to create the

Try it out	As a group, make a survey of printers that can work with personal computers. For each printing technology, note the printing speed, the print resolution, the availability of colour, the sizes and types of paper that can be handled, and the prices. Try to find out how much printing can be carried out before a replacement toner cartridge, ink container, or ribbon is needed.

output. Plotters are currently only used in specialist applications, such as the production of engineering drawings or architectural schematics. An interesting niche application of a plotter is as a 'cutter' – the pen is replaced by a small sharp scalpel blade, and the cutter then cuts out shapes from rolls of special, usually plastic, materials. Such cutters are used for signwriting, sail-making, and dressmaking.

Scanners

A scanner is an image capture device, turning text and drawings into computer-usable data files. Most scanners are currently either inexpensive hand-held devices, or desktop flatbed devices. In either case, a scanner works by illuminating the original and sensing the reflected light to determine the tones of the image.

Resolution, colour, speed

As with a printer, the major parameters of a scanner's performance and quality are its resolution, speed, and colour capability. Most **small office and home (SOHO) scanners** can offer 300 dpi or 600 dpi resolution, and such resolution is generally a good match for the SOHO inkjet or laser

printer that will eventually print out the results. Similarly, most SOHO scanners can scan in colour, offering 8-bit resolution for each of the primary colours of red, green, and blue, giving a 24-bit colour depth overall. Scanning speed varies from about one page every two minutes to about one page in ten seconds, depending upon the resolution and colour depth required, and the money available.

Compression and image file formats

The amount of data that results from a 600 dpi scan of an A4 page in 24-bit colour is huge. As calculated for the laser printer, above, it is about 100 MB. Even the very largest hard drives would soon fill up if scanned images also were not compressed into smaller data files. There are several image file formats which store the image data as compressed data. The most common formats are the **JPG** or **JPEG (joint photographic experts group)** format for photographic types of image, and the GIF **(graphics interchange format)** file for line art and cartoon or clip-art types of image.

Interface

As a scanner scans, large amounts of data are generated, which have to handled by the computer system as the data is produced. SOHO scanners do not have much internal sophistication, and simply transfer the data stream straight to the computer for processing. If the data stream comprises a 100 MB image that is being scanned at, say, two pages per minute, the interface and computer must be capable of comfortably handling a transfer rate of about 3 MB/sec or 4 MB/sec. Such a rate is well outside the capability of an enhanced parallel port, and if such data rates are required, then a SCSI interface is needed.

Most scanners are, in fact, connected to an enhanced parallel port, and so either they must scan more slowly, at about one page every two minutes, or they must periodically pause in their scan to allow the computer to 'catch up'.

Configuration

For a scanner to be used where accurate colours are required, the scanner must be **calibrated**, usually at the same time as the printer and the VDU. Calibration starts with a known, high-quality colour test image which the scanner scans. The calibration software then compares the scan results with the data it has about the test image, and is able to suggest changes that the image-editing software should make to other scanned images to improve their colour accuracy. The scanned test image is then displayed to allow the VDU to be adjusted, and finally it is printed out so that the characteristics of the printer can be assessed and any further adjustments made.

Audio

A multimedia PC requires a **sound card** to complement its video display capabilities. Although the audio adapter is mainly used to play back sound files, it generally can also record sounds and music from a microphone or from its audio inputs.

Sounds and music can be held in a data file in one of two basic formats. The first type of sound data file is a waveform file, where 'normal' analogue sound recordings are **digitised** into formats such as WAV and VOC, and may then be **compressed** to a format such as MP3. These names, WAV, VOC, and MP3, are simply labels identifying different formats of waveform sound recording.

The second type of sound data file is a **MIDI (musical instrument digital interface)** file. The contents of such a file are completely different from a waveform file; in this case the file data specify instructions for the playback device to create the sounds required. In this respect, a MIDI file is like a musical score, specifying the notes to be played, their duration, and their characteristics, so that the audio synthesiser can create the required sounds.

Waveform data

The quality of a waveform sound file depends upon the rate at which the original sound was sampled or digitised. Low-quality sound would be sampled at about 11 kHz and digitised into an 8-bit sample, yielding files about 11 kB in size for every second of sound. High-quality sound, such as CD sound, would be sampled at 44 kHz and digitised into a 16-bit sample, yielding files of about 170 kB in size for every second of sound. A 60-second sound track at CD quality, for example, would result in a 10 MB data file.

Currently, the MP3 file format allows significant compression of a waveform file, typically by as much as 90%. A 10 MB WAV file, for example, would become a 1 MB MP3 file. The MP3 format derives from the MPEG standards for video compression, using just the sound part of that standard.

Playback of a waveform file requires a relatively simple digital-to-analogue converter (DAC) that feeds an ordinary audio amplifier. If the waveform file is a compressed file, such as MP3, then playback software has to decompress the file before conversion to analogue format.

MIDI data

MIDI files are very much smaller than waveform files. Composing a MIDI track requires some form of sequencing software, and usually a MIDI-compatible musical keyboard. The drawback of a MIDI file is that, to be played back, a synthesiser is required, and the quality of the output depends directly on the quality of the synthesiser. While all sound cards have a synthesiser, it is generally not as good as stand-alone music synthesisers.

Interface

A sound card is plugged into a motherboard interface slot, and requires software drivers to provide its facilities for recording and the two kinds of playback, waveform and MIDI. Additionally, it may require hardware connections to the CD-ROM drive, and will require loudspeakers or headphones. Optionally, it may provide for a microphone input and hi-fi audio inputs and outputs.

Other components
Cabling

We have mentioned hardware connections and cables, and there is a wide variety of both. Particular kinds of cable are associated with particular kinds of connection requirements. Table 4.4 lists the major kinds of cable.

Connectors

Associated with each kind of cable is a particular kind of connector. Table 4.5 lists the major connectors (plugs and sockets).

Consumables

The final matter to remember about all this computer hardware is the consumable materials needed to keep the system running.

Paper

Most laser printers are perfectly happy with 80 gsm (**grams per square metre**) photocopier-grade paper. However, a good

Try it out	As a group of three or four, pick two of the following four outline situations and consider what hardware you would suggest, and why:

- Mrs A., 76, coping on a very limited budget, wants to be able to e-mail her son and his family who live in Sydney. She would like to be able to receive photos, if possible, and print them.

- School pupil B., 15, is doing GCSEs, and surfs the Internet most days to do research for homework. She word-processes assignments; next year she will be doing AVCE in ICT and A-level Business; and she wants to be able to download music from the Internet.

- Mr and Mrs C. run a newsagent and confectionery business. They want to be able to prepare their budgets, keep their accounts, bill their customers, and occasionally word-process letters.

- Mr D., 50, is a full-time author of technical books. He needs to be able to keep successive versions of his books, both as he is drafting them and as new editions are published from time to time. He must be able to print and store diagrams and drawings obtained from a variety of sources.

Cable type	Known as	Description	Application
Shielded copper wire		General cable, from about 4 to 40 copper wires. Wire bundled within a metal mesh. Mesh provides electromagnetic shielding from interference, and mechanical strength.	Cable for SCSI device, printer, scanner, modem, keyboard, mouse, etc.
Shielded twisted pair	STP	Generally 4 copper wires. Wires twisted together in pairs. Bundled within a shielding mesh.	USB
Unshielded twisted pair	UTP, 10BaseT	Generally 4 copper wires. Wires twisted together in pairs. No shielding mesh. Bundled within a plastic sheath.	Short-run network cable
Coaxial	Thin coax, thick coax	Single copper wire insulated within a thin or thick mesh braid. Thin or thick plastic sheath.	Medium- or long-run network cable
Ribbon		General cable, from about 4 to 80 copper wires. Wires laid flat. No shielding.	Very short-run device connection; IDE, EIDE, ATAPI device
Optical fibre		Single or bundle of glass threads within a sheath.	Long-run high-speed network cable

Table 4.4 Major kinds of cable

quality output on an inkjet printer, especially a colour output, will require higher-quality paper. This paper is generally glossier, slightly heavier at 100 gsm, and has a surface treatment designed to prevent the ink **bleeding**.

Floppy disks

For PC-compatible systems, the 'standard' floppy disk is the 1.44 MB 3.5″ double-sided high-density disk. These are now available pre-formatted.

Toner

Most laser printers require a new toner cartridge every 2 000 to 20 000 pages. Some

also require a new drum unit every 10 000–50 000 pages.

Ink cartridges

Inkjet printers require ink cartridges. These are usually black, three-colour, four-colour, or six-colour cartridges, depending upon the printer and the way it is used.

CD-R and CD-RW media

For back-up and distribution purposes, recordable or rewritable CDs are very useful. Note that CD-R and CD-RW media are completely different; you should be careful to choose the right one.

Cable type	Connector	Application
Copper wire	6-pin P8 Burndy connector 6-pin P9 Burndy connector	Power, older motherboard to power supply
	20-pin ATX Molex connector	Power, ATX motherboard to power supply
	4-pin AMP	Power to internal drive
	4-pin mini-AMP	Power to 3.5" floppy drive
Shielded copper wire	'Alternative 2' 50-pin Centronics 68-pin high density 'squeeze to release' 'Alternative 4' 80-pin	SCSI device
	DB-25 (at source), IEEE 1284-A Centronics (at device), IEEE 1284-B 'Mini-Centronics', IEEE 1284-C	Printer, scanner, other parallel interface device
	15-pin high density D-type	VDU
	DB-9, DB-25	External modem, serial mouse
	5-pin DIN 6-pin mini-DIN	Keyboard, PS/2 port Mouse (mini-DIN only)
Shielded twisted pair	Series 'A' Series 'B'	USB
Unshielded twisted pair		RJ45 Network
Thick coax	DB-15	Network
Thin coax	BNC	Network
Ribbon	40-pin ribbon header	IDE/EIDE/ATAPI device
Optical fibre	ST	Network

Table 4.5 Kinds of connector

Chapter 4.2 Software

A useful way of looking at the various kinds of software used in a computer system is illustrated in Figure 4.10.

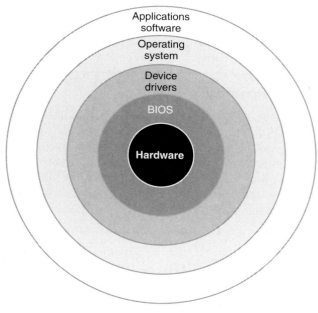

Figure 4.10 Software layers around the hardware core

At the lowest level, the hardware of the computer is accessed by the **basic input-output system (BIOS)** software and the BIOS settings held in CMOS RAM. At the next level are the **device drivers**, elements of the systems software that are designed to communicate with particular hardware devices, such as printers. Device drivers usually work through the BIOS and CMOS RAM settings in order to manage and operate their specific devices. At the highest system level, the **operating system** offers facilities to the user to configure the device drivers and other components of the computer system, and it also offers facilities to all **applications programs** to give them access to systems resources such as memory and peripheral devices.

Notice that the various layers of software are broadly divided into **system software**, comprising the BIOS, device drivers, and the operating system, and **applications software**. Associated with this division is a distinction that is commonly made between *systems* programming and *applications* programming. This distinction identifies the requirements of each kind of programming and operating environment.

The computer user may be required to operate the computer through any of a variety of interfaces. The most popular interface at present is the **graphical user interface (GUI)**, generally characterised by the use of windows, icons, drop-down menus, and a pointing device such as a mouse, sometimes called collectively 'WIMP'. Usually, a GUI operating system provides the low-level routines needed for applications software to use a GUI; but in some cases an application may use its own GUI routines in conjunction with a non-GUI operating system. In either case, the routines and functions of the operating system are made available to the application software through a set of standards and conventions known as the **applications program interface (API)**.

User interfaces are discussed more fully on page 265.

ROM and BIOS software

The BIOS was introduced in the chapter on hardware, Chapter 4.1. In addition to the hardware-related functions discussed there, the BIOS also performs some systems software-related functions which are discussed below.

Boot devices

The BIOS set-up allows you to specify which device should be used to load, start up, or boot, the operating system. More usefully, the BIOS set-up should also allow you to specify a list of possible boot devices, and the order in which each device should be tried.

So that you can boot from a floppy disk in an emergency, set the floppy drive (A:) as the first boot drive. Then, you may wish to be able to boot from a CD-ROM, particularly if you have an operating system that allows you to do so, so you would set the CD-ROM drive letter as the second

boot device. If you have a CD-R or CD-RW device, it may be more convenient to burn a CD-ROM as an emergency boot disk, rather than rely on a floppy disk. Finally, you would set the hard drive (C:) as the third device. The hard drive is effectively the default device, used to boot the system, provided that neither a floppy disk nor a CD-ROM is inserted in the appropriate drive at start-up.

New hard drive

With early PCs, it was necessary to enter a hard drive's parameters in the BIOS set-up, and have them stored in CMOS RAM. With current PCs using IDE hard drives, the BIOS can detect and set up the drive automatically. SCSI drives have specific set-up procedures that depend upon the SCSI adapter in use, and instructions should always accompany the adapter and hard drive involved.

Set password

Most current BIOS set-up software allows the specification of a password before any, some, or all of the CMOS RAM settings can be altered. The details of how the password is set up, changed, or deleted depend upon the options provided by the BIOS manufacturer and the motherboard manufacturer. Note that other passwords –

for access to the network, for example – are entered and managed using operating system routines rather than BIOS routines.

Configure new interface card

Most current BIOS software and most current interface cards allow the automatic detection and set-up of the interface card and device parameters. More precise control of the device settings is done through the operating system which gives access to the relevant device driver. This facility is known as 'plug and play', or PnP.

In early PCs, it was commonly necessary to set the parallel and serial port parameters through the BIOS set-up; using the Windows operating system, however, these parameters are automatically set by PnP, and the CMOS RAM modified, if necessary, through the Windows port device drivers.

Operating systems

An operating system provides two main classes of service. On the one hand, through its device drivers, it links with and extends the BIOS to provide access to the computer hardware and peripheral devices. On the other hand, through its API, it provides facilities to applications software for the display, printing, communication, and storage of data.

Major operating systems currently support one or both of two main methods of giving the user access to systems software and the computer system, through a command line interface (CLI) or a graphical user interface (GUI). The Windows operating system primarily provides a GUI, while the older Disk Operating System (DOS) and the

more recently developed Linux operating system, a version of UNIX, provide a CLI. Windows 95 and Windows 98 also support a DOS-mode CLI which can be used if required.

A CLI requires you to type a command into the computer system in order to perform a function. For example, you might type DIR to see a listing of the files in given disk directory, or MODE to set the video display to a specific resolution.

We shall next illustrate the configuration and management of a PC under the Windows 95 operating system.

Most of the configuration and control utilities of Windows 95 are collected together into a subsystem called the control panel. The control panel can be accessed from the 'Start' menu, moving the cursor to the 'Settings' menu item, and clicking on 'Control Panel'. Another route to the control panel is to double-click on the 'My Computer' icon on the desktop, and to double-click on the 'Control Panel' entry in the resulting display. The control panel for a computer used by one of the authors is illustrated in Figure 4.11.

Figure 4.11 Windows 'Control Panel'

Memory management

Earlier personal computers based on the Intel x86 CPU needed careful setting up in DOS because of limitations that were built into the x86 family of chips. Currently, most personal computers are based on the Intel Pentium and compatible CPUs, running the Windows 9x and Windows NT operating systems under which the problems of memory management have all but disappeared. Windows 2000 can be seen as an enhancement of Windows NT.

For example, the only memory-related configuration control in Windows 95 relates to the amount of disk space that Windows should use as 'virtual' RAM, should the *actual* RAM space become fully used. Figure 4.12 illustrates the dialogue box that is available from double-clicking on the 'System' icon in the control panel, then clicking on the 'Performance' tab and clicking on the 'Virtual memory' advanced setting. If you do not select the option to allow Windows to manage virtual memory, you can then specify how much space on a hard drive should be used.

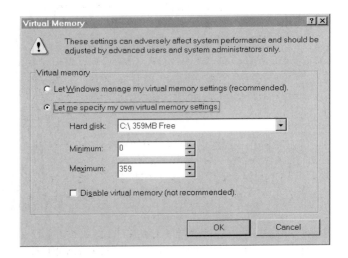

Figure 4.12 Specifying virtual memory

Date and time

The control panel offers a simple dialogue box to set the system date and time. Double-click on the 'Date/Time' icon, and Figure 4.13 illustrates the result.

The month and year are selected from the appropriate data entry boxes, and the day is selected by clicking on the calendar. The time is set by typing the desired time into the relevant data entry box as well. Clicking 'OK' then resets the clock.

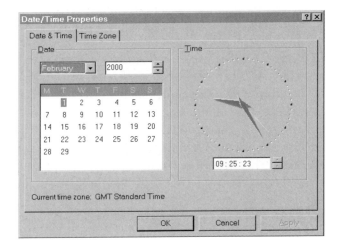

Figure 4.13 Specifying date and time

Passwords

When a PC starts up in Windows 95, the user is asked for a password. This password can be changed by using the 'Passwords' application found in the control panel. Double-clicking on the 'Passwords' icon brings up the options shown in dialogue box Figure 4.14.

If you click on the 'Change Windows Password...' button, you are asked to enter your old password, then your new password (twice), in a dialogue box shown in Figure 4.15.

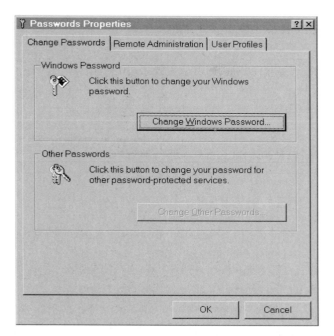

Figure 4.14 Password options

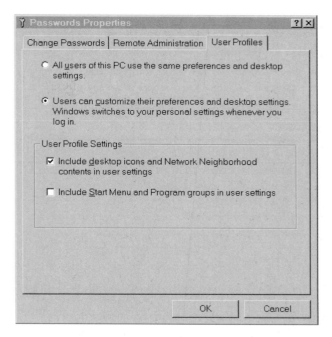

Figure 4.16 Specifying user profile settings

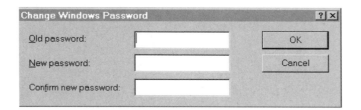

Figure 4.15 Specifying a new password

User profiles

A significant feature added to the Windows 9x operating systems, and given added significance in Windows NT, is the ability to configure a given system differently, depending upon the needs of different users. The result is the 'user profile'.

When you use the PC, you log on as a particular user with your own user ID and password. The system remembers and restores your settings, which may well be quite different from those of another user, even though you are both using the same PC. Figure 4.16 is a screen shot of the

'user profiles' setting available in Windows 95, accessed from the 'Passwords' icon in the control panel.

Batch file operation

A **batch file** is a file of commands to the computer system, usually to be executed without user intervention. In particular, when a computer system starts up a number of processes must be initiated to set the computer up in the required way, and it is convenient to have these processes initiated from a batch file.

Older PCs running a version of DOS used two user-definable files called AUTOEXEC.BAT and CONFIG.SYS to define the start-up configuration of each PC. Strictly speaking, only AUTOEXEC.BAT was a batch file of commands to the system; CONFIG.SYS was a file of device settings and device drivers. Under Windows, these two files can still be used if you wish to open a

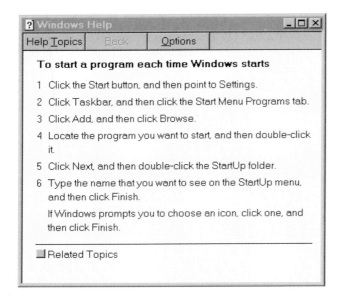

Figure 4.17 Specifying start-up programs

non-standard DOS window or run the PC in DOS mode.

Current PCs running the Windows operating system do not use batch files or device configuration files in the same way. Instead, Windows allows you to configure your system by specifying any programs you wish to run at start-up in the 'Start' menu. The 'Help' box shown in Figure 4.17

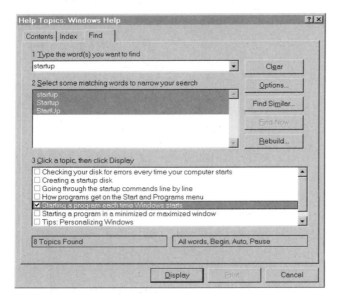

Figure 4.18 Control panel help topics for 'Startup'

explains how to add a program to the start-up sequence.

This particular help was found by using the 'Help' menu item from the control panel, as illustrated in the screen shot Figure 4.18.

Anti-virus software

A very common type of program that you would want to run automatically whenever the system starts would be **anti-virus software**. The screen shot in Figure 4.19 illustrates the configuration settings available for one of the more popular anti-virus programs, called 'Dr Solomon'.

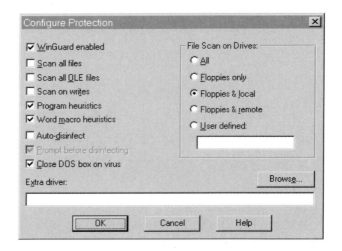

Figure 4.19 Anti-virus configuration settings

Directory structure facilities

With a newly-installed operating system, or a new hard drive, it is useful to construct a tailored directory structure to hold the data files that will gradually fill up the available storage space. An operating system will provide the necessary software tools to create and delete directories and sub-directories, and to move, copy, or delete data files within directories. Figure 4.20 shows the Windows 95 application called

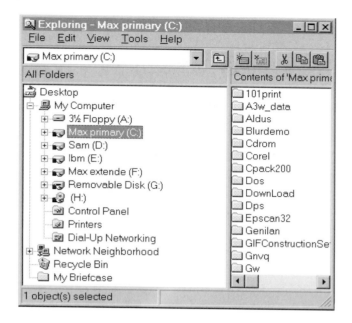

Figure 4.20 Sample directory structure in
Windows Explorer

'Windows Explorer' that is used for this
purpose.

Peripheral configurations

Software will be provided to configure most
of the peripheral devices of a computer
system. If a device is of a type that is widely
used, the configuration software may well be
provided by the operating system itself.
Usually, a device requires its own specific
driver software, and either the device driver
or specific configuration software is used to
set up and manage the device.

The example shown in Figure 4.21 is of
one of the configuration screens for the
Windows 95 'Standard modem', accessed
from the 'Modem' icon of the control
panel, or the 'System' icon. The first screen
shot shows the result of accessing the
'System' icon, clicking on the 'Device
Manager' tab, and double-clicking on the
small 'Modem' icon, to reveal the
'Standard 28 800 bps Modem'.

Try it out Figures 4.21–4.31 display
different aspects of the control
you can exercise over your
systems through Windows
facilities. On your own
computer you should bring up
each of the screens illustrated,
and become familiar with it.

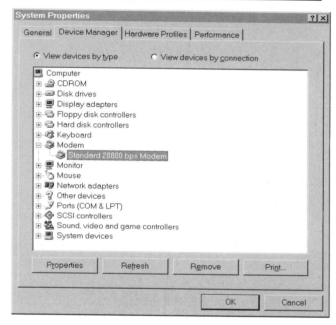

Figure 4.21 Sample list of 'System' devices in
Windows 95

Clicking on the 'Properties' button brings
up the device configuration dialogue. One of
its screens is illustrated in Figure 4.22.

Similar configuration dialogues are available
for the VDU, keyboard, mouse, and other
peripherals. The following paragraphs describe
how to configure the VDU, or 'Display'.

Desktop appearance

Right-clicking on a blank part of the screen
in Windows and clicking on 'Properties', or
clicking on the 'Display' icon in the
control panel, brings up the configuration
dialogues for the desktop background,

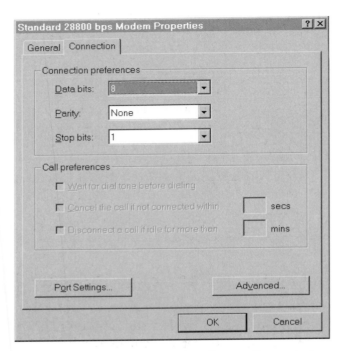

Figure 4.22 Setting the data bits, parity, and stop bits for the modem

Figure 4.24 Setting the desktop appearance in Windows 95

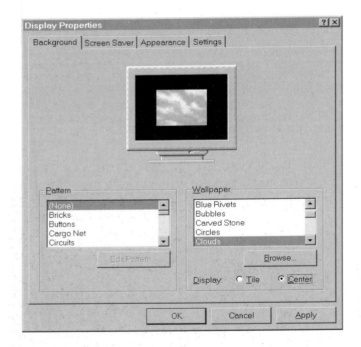

Figure 4.23 Setting desktop background in Windows 95

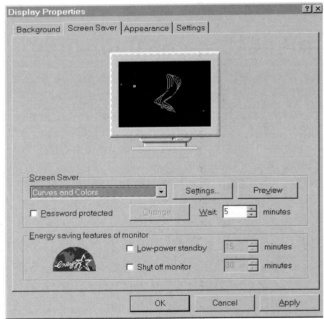

Figure 4.25 Setting the screen saver in Windows 95

appearance, screen saver, and VDU settings. The four screen shots in Figures 4.23–4.26

illustrate each of these dialogues in turn.

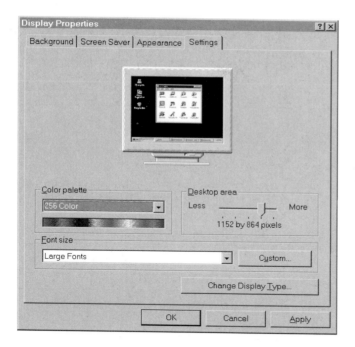

Figure 4.26 Setting the VDU parameters in Windows 95

The '**Settings**' tab of the display properties dialogue box is the most important of the display properties. When the system is first assembled, or when a new video adapter card or new VDU screen is added to the system, the '**Change Display Type**' dialogue is accessed to define the adapter card and the VDU. This dialogue is shown in Figure 4.27.

Given these selections for the adapter card and the VDU, the settings of the display properties are then constrained to offering only those settings that are possible. For example, the Hansol 701P VDU cannot display at any resolution above 1280 × 1024, and so a higher resolution such as 1600 × 1200 would not be offered as a possible size for the desktop area. Similarly, the S3 Trio PCI controller card only has 2 MB RAM installed, and so cannot provide 16-bit or 24-bit colour at the selected resolution of 1152 × 864.

Screen prompt appearance

In earlier PCs that run under DOS, and in the '**DOS box**' provided by Windows, it may be useful to set certain of the properties of the screen prompt. This is done by using the '**SET PROMPT**' command in the AUTOEXEC.BAT file, as illustrated in Figure 4.28.

The DOS box was initialised with a prompt which was set to show the current directory and a '>' sign, using the 'SET PROMPT=PG' string shown in the AUTOEXEC.BAT listing. The prompt is

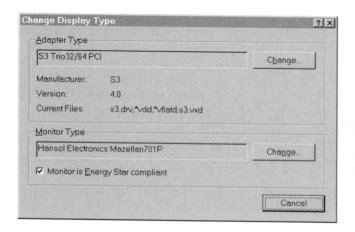

Figure 4.27 Identifying the adapter card and the VDU

Figure 4.28 The 'DOS box' in Windows 95

then set to show just the '>' sign, as specified by the 'set prompt=$G' command. The parameter '$P' specifies that the prompt should show the current directory. The parameter '$G' specifies that the prompt should show the '>' symbol.

Application software icons

Usually a different icon can be substituted for the default icon of an application. Figures 4.29 and 4.30 show this process in Windows 95. First, right-click on the icon to be changed, and click on the 'Properties' item in the resulting menu. This will bring up a tabbed dialogue box. Click on the 'Program' tab.

Clicking on the 'Change Icon...' button brings up a list of different icons, found in the additional icons file called PIFMGR.DLL. Click on the desired icon, and click the 'OK' button. If you have other icon files, you might wish to browse them to select another icon for the application.

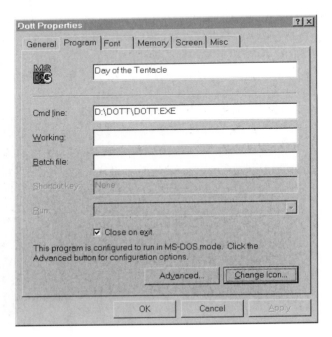

Figure 4.29 An icon 'Properties' display box

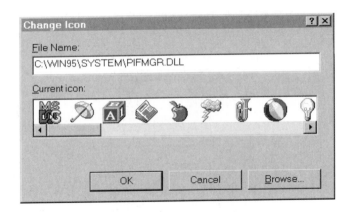

Figure 4.30 Changing an icon

Disk management

The two major tasks of disk management are the backing-up of data files, and the checking for, and correction of, disk errors. An operating system may provide tools to help with these operations, but it is common to purchase and use third-party tools instead. In the case of back-ups, for example, third-party tools usually provide for restoring the files even if there is a change of operating system; this is not usually the case for a back-up utility that is specific to one operating system.

Figure 4.31 illustrates the built-in disk management tools provided with Windows 95; the tools are accessed from Windows Explorer by selecting 'Properties' from the 'File' menu.

Besides the essentials of error detection and correction, and back-up, Windows 95 provides a tool to 'defragment' a hard drive. **Fragmentation** occurs on a hard drive as files are deleted and new files are added. When a file is deleted, the space it had occupied is released and re-used when a new file is added. Usually, the new file is a different size from the deleted file, and so does not take up the same space – it may require less space, or it may require more

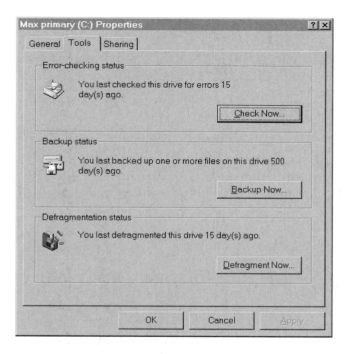

Figure 4.31 Windows 95 disk management tools

space. As time goes on, the contents of a particular file may become scattered across the disk, or **fragmented**.

A fragmented file takes longer to read into the system. Instead of the file contents being in adjacent disk sectors on adjacent tracks, the contents are likely to be scattered. The read heads must therefore be moved successively to positions over whichever tracks hold the data; these tracks may be far apart from one another, resulting in prolonged access times. If high performance is a priority, then periodic **defragmentation** of the files on a disk drive is required. It is activated by clicking on the 'Defragment now...' button.

Network facilities

A typical application program may have to make frequent requests of its operating system that data be sent to or received from a remote system. The application may be, for example, a word-processing program, a file management program, or a web browser. The operating system software needed for this task is called the **network client** software.

The data that is sent from one computer to another, or received by one computer from another, is structured according to a given protocol by the protocol software, often called a **protocol stack**. The protocol stack takes a request for data from the network client, constructs an appropriate data packet, and passes the packet to the **network interface card (NIC) driver**. The NIC driver, in turn, controls the **adapter card** that physically sends and receives the network data.

At the remote system, the adapter card physically receives the data packet. The NIC driver passes the received data packet to the protocol stack, which extracts its contents, and passes the properly structured contents to the network client.

For the network to function, therefore, three layers of software are required, as well as the network hardware or adapter card. These three layers of software are installed and set up in Windows 95 by clicking on the '**Network**' icon in the control panel. Figure 4.32 shows the result.

This screen shot shows that the required three software components have been installed. The network client is called 'Client for Microsoft Networks', the protocol stack is called 'TCP/IP', and the network interface card driver is shown as belonging to the 'GE2500II PCI Ethernet Adapter'.

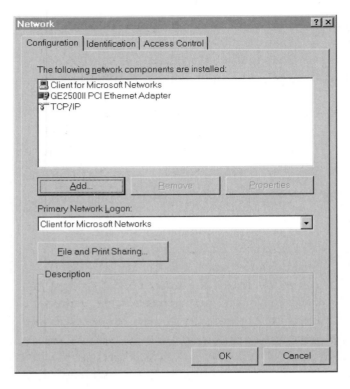

Figure 4.32 Windows 95 'Network' icon display

Commentary

When files of data are to be passed between a number of networked computers, the computers need to agree on how to communicate. An agreed method of communicating is called a **protocol**. There are a large number of different protocols, but two stand out as being the most popular and best supported: Transmission Control Protocol/Internet Protocol (**TCP/IP**), and Internet Packet Exchange/Server Packet Exchange (**IPX/SPX**).

A protocol needs to deal with a number of issues in computer communications. The first issue is called **flow control**, a method of regulating the flow of data from one computer to another. Typically, the receiving system is not able to accept the data at precisely the instant that the sending system is ready to send it. Hence,

the protocol must provide a method by which receiver and sender can each signal that they are either ready or not ready to send, and are either ready or not ready to receive.

Associated with the issue of flow control is some management of the **amount of data** that can be sent at any one time. A protocol must define how the data is to be divided up into manageable chunks called **blocks** or packets, and the maximum size of each such block or packet of data. A popular choice for this maximum is 1 kB.

A second issue is that of **error detection and correction**. There must be an agreed method by which a data packet or block can be checked for errors, and an agreed method by which any errors can be corrected. An almost universal method of error detection is called a **cyclic redundancy check (CRC)**. Given that an error has been detected, a common, simple method of error correction is to request re-transmission of the faulty data packet.

A third issue is one of **addressing**. Where a number of computers are networked, a particular transmission of data requires an address so that only the recipient computer, and no other, accepts the transmission. Again, the protocol specifies the way in which a data packet is **labelled** with the proper destination address.

The network client configuration dialogue box is illustrated in Figure 4.33. It is accessed by highlighting the 'Client for Microsoft Networks' component and clicking on the 'Properties' button in the network display. The client configuration dialogue offers few options for customisation, mainly because the Windows 95 Network Client is relatively simple in the functions it performs.

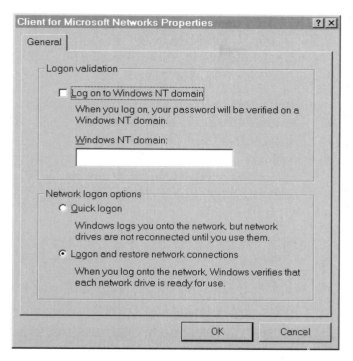

Figure 4.33 Windows 95 network client configuration

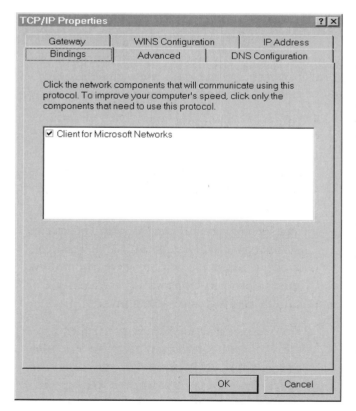

Figure 4.34 Windows 95 TCP/IP protocol stack configuration

The protocol stack configuration dialogue box offers six tabs to set the required network parameters. It is accessed by highlighting the 'TCP/IP' component and clicking on the 'Properties' button in the network display. The tab illustrated in Figure 4.34 is the '**Bindings**' tab, which shows that the TCP/IP protocol stack in the system we are looking at is connected or 'bound' to the network client that is installed, the 'Client for Microsoft Networks'.

Figure 4.35 shows the properties of the NIC installed in the system. It is accessed by highlighting the 'GE2500II PCI Ethernet Adapter' component and clicking on the 'Properties' button in the network display. The tab labelled '**Driver Type**' gives information about the NIC driver software. The tab illustrated is the 'Bindings' tab, which shows that the NIC driver is connected or 'bound' to the TCP/IP protocol stack.

Figure 4.35 Windows 95 NIC driver configuration

Finally, control over allowing other network users access to your own system is provided in Windows 95 by the 'File and Print Sharing' button on the 'Network' display, as shown in Figure 4.36.

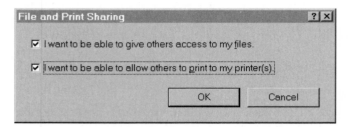

Figure 4.36 Windows 95 file and printer sharing configuration

Applications software

Types of applications

An information system may be considered as consisting of two components: **data,** and the **processes** that accept, transform, and store that data. The choice of what applications to use in a particular system must thus be guided by considering first the nature of the data, and second the nature of the required processing.

A required application may have an off-the-shelf software solution, or it may need bespoke development. Off-the-shelf solutions are currently available for most mainstream popular business and personal application requirements. Bespoke software may need to be developed when an application is unusual or new, or when existing packages do not have the required features and facilities. The development of a bespoke solution will usually require the use of a programming language such as Pascal, COBOL, or Java.

There are various ways to classify 'data'. We shall not attempt to define these various

ways, but instead we shall simply illustrate the major kinds of data by providing examples and suggesting appropriate applications to process them.

- **Text**. Where the data is mainly pages of text for printing, then a **word-processing** application would be suitable. If the text is enhanced by many images or needs to be laid out in unusual ways, a **desktop publishing** application may be preferable.

- **Display**. The data might be mainly screens of text and images for display, where the text was prepared in a word-processor, and the images were prepared in a graphics package. If the display is to be used in the context of a meeting of some sort, then a **presentation** application would be suitable for group viewing. If the display is for individual or small group viewing, then a **multimedia** applications generator would be suitable, possibly coupled to a **web browser** if the data were held on the Internet or on an intranet.

- **Images**. Diagrams, cartoons, or photo-quality pictures divide into two kinds of image: vector and bit-mapped. **Vector** image data consists of numbers which describe the data in terms of its geometry: points, lines, curves, and so on. Vector images are seen in diagrams, engineering drawings, and in graphics such as cartoons, and require their own specific application which is usually called '**draw-type**' software.

  Bit-mapped image data consist of an array of bits such that each bit encodes a rather small area of the image in terms of its colour and shading. Bit-mapped images are used to hold all forms of photographic images, and require a different application, usually called **'paint-type' software.**

- **Records.** The data might involve a set of records, such as customer records, product details, or financial transactions. Wherever data consists of records, a **database** application is required.

- **Calculations.** Finally, the data might involve mathematical or statistical calculations, perhaps requiring the production of graphs, to analyse, model, or predict the results of certain scenarios or processes. A **spreadsheet** application would be most suited to such work.

Of course, items of real data are not so easily categorised. The database records you would like to keep might well involve images, or require extensive statistical analysis. You might want to provide web-based displays of information from desktop published documents or from spreadsheets. While it is becoming more and more straightforward to integrate various kinds of data and various kinds of processing, it is most likely that you will find that five kinds of basic application will cover your business processing requirements:

- word-processing for text
- a database for keeping records
- a spreadsheet for modelling numerical outcomes
- a draw-type application for diagrams
- a paint-type application for photographic-quality images.

Configuring applications

Most applications can be set up, and configured, or customised, in a variety of ways. The chapters on spreadsheets, Chapters 3.1–3.3, and on databases, Chapters 6.1–6.7, illustrate a number of these customisations.

Almost every applications software product has an 'Options' menu item which allows you to set preferences, such as where the data files are kept, what the start-up default settings of the application are to be, whether the application should periodically save the work, and so on. Most Windows applications have a further menu item called 'Customise' which allows you to change the windows layouts, the menu structures, the toolbar layouts, and the grouping of icons. Also, most applications can have some of their operations automated by the use of macros. Macros are discussed in the units on spreadsheets and databases, Units 3 and 6.

One way in which you can help a user make immediate use of an application is though the preparation of data **templates.** Some applications, such as Microsoft Word and Excel, explicitly provide facilities for the use of templates. A template is a partially-finished product, such as the skeleton of a frequently-needed letter or monthly sales analysis, that just requires particular data to be entered to complete it. A set of thoughtfully prepared templates allows a user to get on with the main job of completing letters or reports without first having to learn all the details of the application.

Try it out	Return to the four scenarios described in the 'Activity' in Chapter 4.1, on page 166, if possible in the same groups.
	Look again at the hardware you decided to suggest in the two cases you considered. Now focus on the applications software the users would need in order to be able to do what they wanted to do. List the types of application software each would need; and try to identify particular products, noting the sources, capabilities and optional features, and prices.

Chapter 4.3 System documentation and testing

This chapter is concerned with:

- recording the details of the hardware and software of a PC system when it is first installed

- following up faults that are detected or reported, by trying to deduce the causes of the faults, and then testing in a rational way those that seem to be the most likely

- identifying the causes of faults, whether in hardware or software, and documenting both the faults and the solutions that were found for them.

Documenting the initial configuration

The hardware configuration of a particular computer system is not easy to see. Even taking the lid off the system unit may not reveal everything you need to know.

Documenting a system's configuration is most easily done by using utility software. Of course, this utility software needs to be loaded and usable on the system in the first place if it is also to help later in diagnosing problems. It is therefore good practice to use such software when the system is first set up. Records should be made of the configuration of the system as soon as it is working as intended.

Control panel

The control panel in Windows (Figure 4.37) provides some basic utility software which detects and reports on the system

settings. Double-click on the 'System' icon to access details of these settings. (You may remember that the Windows control panel can be accessed from the 'Start' menu.)

Figure 4.37 Windows 'Control Panel'

Figure 4.38 'Performance' properties of the system

Figure 4.38 shows the '**Performance**' tab of the resulting '**Systems Properties**' display. Amongst other matters, it specifies that the system has 32 MB of RAM installed.

Other utilities

If Windows is not installed or is not working, then other utility software may be used to identify important configuration details. Microsoft issued a utility called '**MSD**', Microsoft Diagnostics, which is useful for earlier DOS and Windows 3.x systems. Figure 4.39 shows a screen shot of the main MSD display for a system.

Figure 4.40 Norton Utilities display of a system configuration

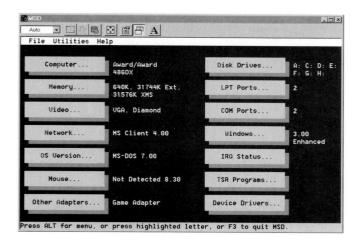

Figure 4.39 MSD display of a system configuration

Other suppliers provide utility software for the same purpose. The 'Norton Utilities' are particularly well regarded, and the screen shot in Figure 4.40 shows one of the Norton Utility 'SysInfo' displays for a DOS-based system.

At the time of initial system set-up, it is very desirable to prepare a record of relevant details, based on the items in the list below:

- Date of initial configuration.
- System hardware, including:

○ make of motherboard and its chipset
○ motherboard jumper settings
○ make and version/revision level of BIOS
○ non-standard CMOS RAM settings
○ make and speed rating of processor; whether a processor fan was fitted
○ amount, type, and speed rating of RAM
○ make and size of hard drive; whether IDE or SCSI interface
○ make of video interface card, video chipset, amount of video RAM, video driver resolution set, video driver number of colours set
○ make of VDU, refresh rate at selected resolution
○ make and details of other peripherals: mouse, keyboard, network interface card, sound card, printer, scanner, CD-ROM, DVD-ROM, modem
○ for each interface card, whether ISA or PCI.

- Operating system, including:
○ version/revision level
○ special or downloaded drivers
○ special or extra fonts.
- Any faults and problems experienced at initial installation, including:
○ defects at delivery

o solutions applied
o support services accessed
o diagnostic software used.

It may also be useful to record relevant output from the displays of whatever utility software was used. All the manuals and documentation that were provided with the system and its components should be kept where they can be reached easily. Particular care should be taken with original software. It would be wise to take immediate back-ups of any floppy disks containing original drivers.

Documenting configuration changes

Every time the system is changed it is important to prepare a record of relevant details, since it is usually at a time of change that problems and difficulties arise. Most changes involve an upgrade or update of the system, but some changes involve the removal or deletion of system components which can have unexpected consequences. Make a record of changes along the following lines.

- Date of change.

- Hardware change details, including changes to CMOS RAM settings, involving any of the motherboard, processor, RAM, hard drives, video interface, or other peripherals such as sound card, printer, CD-ROM, DVD-ROM, or modem.

- Software change details, involving new drivers or driver settings, new or upgraded applications software, or any other software-related changes.

- Any faults and problems experienced during the change, including solutions provided.

Documenting faults

Dealing with a fault involves a process of identifying and collecting symptoms, making hypotheses about the causes of the fault, testing these hypotheses through a variety of troubleshooting and investigative procedures, identifying the probable cause, identifying a variety of possible treatments, and then selecting and applying one of these treatments as the 'fix'. This process is illustrated in Figure 4.41.

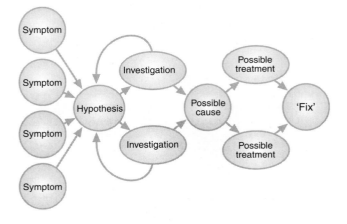

Figure 4.41 Fixing a fault

Symptoms

Fault symptoms materialise at one of three times during the use of a system.

- When the system is first switched on, the power-on self-test (POST) software of the BIOS conducts some basic tests of the system hardware. The results of these tests are usually displayed on the VDU, but are sometimes given as a series of beeps. If you hear more than one beep, you will need to refer to technical documentation to decode the beep message to identify the symptom being reported. That should help you identify the item at fault. The POST, if error-free, gives you some confidence that the basic hardware of the system is functioning correctly.

- Then, during the boot-up of the operating system, symptoms can be detected and reported. These faults are usually set-up or configuration faults rather than hardware faults. They would be corrected by changing, for example, driver parameters.

- Finally, fault symptoms may occur when running an application. These can sometimes prove very difficult to reproduce.

The basic technique of dealing with fault symptoms is first to document them, and then to be able to reproduce them upon demand. A reproducible symptom makes fault-finding very much easier.

Investigation

The key to finding the probable cause of a fault is to isolate it.

If the fault seems to be related to hardware, troubleshooting usually involves making a reasoned guess as to the cause of the symptoms observed, substituting for the suspect one a replacement part that is known to be working, and seeing whether the symptoms disappear.

If the fault seems to be related to software, troubleshooting usually involves making a reasoned guess as to the cause of the symptoms observed and then changing a set-up parameter, a configuration file, or a device driver to see whether the symptoms disappear. It may be necessary to delete the offending application completely, and then reinstall it with default parameters.

In either case, be sure to change only one thing at a time. Diagnostic hardware and software can sometimes help. Specialised manufacturers provide plug-in sockets and interface cards to help diagnose hardware problems, and diagnostic software to help

with software problems. Microsoft Windows 9x has the 'ScanDisk' utility which can check a hard drive for errors, for example, while Norton Utilities has its own data-recovery software.

Random faults or symptoms that cannot be reproduced as required are particularly difficult to deal with. In these circumstances, it is necessary to extend the details recorded to include features of the operating environment and system usage that could have a bearing on the fault.

As you do not at first know what may prove to be important, you should note matters such as the time of day, the number of hours after switch-on, the office temperature and humidity, whether static discharges occur, whether more than one user has regular access to the system, what other applications were running at the time of the error and just beforehand, and the details of the exact situation in which the fault occurred.

If a problem is especially hard to track down there may be a need to record details of several occurrences of it. As the log of the sets of details grows, a pattern to prompt further hypotheses and investigations will emerge.

This process of investigation should be documented, with a list of the various substitutions or changes tried and the outcome of each.

The 'fix'

The final fix of the fault should, of course, be carefully documented, to help with any future occurrence or with any future upgrades that may conflict with the solution provided. Where the solution of a problem is thought to be potentially of interest to the users of other systems, you should arrange to circulate the details to them.

Unit 4 Assessment

This assignment has a rather different character from the other five sample assignments in that it is heavily dependent upon the resources available in your centre.

The extent to which you can select PC components and cabling is limited by the quantity and variety of items that can be provided for you to use in assembling or modifying a computer system.

The work you can do to install or modify software products is constrained by the products that are available. As examples of software you might be able to use in this assignment, there could be a spreadsheet that was produced in response to the requirements of Unit 3; or you may be able to obtain access to some other piece of software already in your centre.

You will need the teaching team to guide you in what you can sensibly undertake and complete. If you do some of the work as a member of a group, you must be sure you that you can identify your own distinctive contribution.

Your tasks

1 You or your group must build a PC system from the components supplied to meet a specification given to you, or else modify an existing system to satisfy a given requirement. Later you must show that you can restore the system to its starting configuration.

2 You must access the ROM-BIOS parameters, and make a note of their values. If necessary, you must select new values to suit the devices installed in the system and the requirements of the new system. For example, you should be able to set the current date and time through the BIOS.

You must install and configure the operating system, including all device drivers. For example, you should be able to set a variety of VDU settings for various display resolutions and colour depths.

You must select the applications software necessary to provide the facilities specified; and then install it, reviewing the options offered and choosing those you need to meet the specification.

3 You must devise and run a test to satisfy yourself that the system you have built does meet the specified requirements.

4 Throughout all this work you must keep a log of all the actions you took, and include comments on any problems you experienced.

Systems analysis

The development of a spreadsheet, such as the FUN spreadsheet we have already considered, is an example of the development of an information system to meet the needs of a user or group of users. The development of any information system should proceed in stages that are supported by all those involved. These stages form what is known as the *systems development life cycle* (or *sDLC*), presented in Figure 5.1.

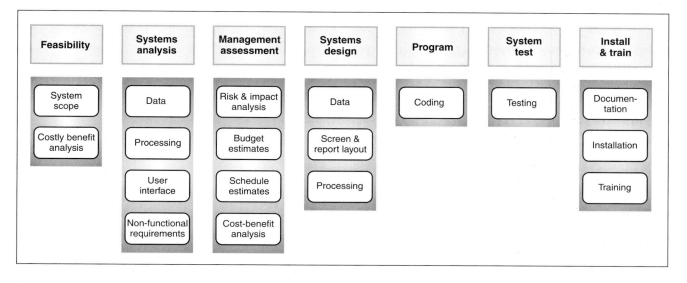

Figure 5.1 Systems development life cycle

One purpose of adopting the structure of the systems development life cycle is to maintain throughout the planning and preparation of a new ICT system a balance between the investment made in a prospective new project and the understanding of the project's business and technical characteristics. There is danger in committing substantial resources before the full facts are known.

More generally, the components of the SDLC form an accepted sequence to be followed in the development of a computer system. They thus impart a standard structure to the work, and help those involved in a development project to avoid misunderstandings when communicating with each other.

In pursuing this approach we follow the line that the feasibility study is carried out, and its findings considered, before there is a decision to embark on full systems analysis. The feasibility study is thus not part of the systems analysis process, but a necessary preliminary to it.

This unit is presented as three chapters:

Chapter 5.1   Investigation and feasibility study

Chapter 5.2   Structured analysis

Chapter 5.3   System specification

Investigation and feasibility study

Where there is an existing ICT system which, it is thought, could with advantage be replaced, the feasibility of replacing it by any proposed new system must be established before the organisation becomes committed to the cost of making the change. A preliminary activity in this case is the accumulation of information about the *existing* system.

If the proposal is for the implementation of a completely new system – one that is not intended to replace any existing system – there is still a need for investigation. This is because, unless the organisation is about to go into a wholly new field of business, the activities to be carried out by the proposed new system must be being carried out already by some process, even if that process cannot be generally recognised as a 'system'.

Part of determining the feasibility of even a very modest project, such as the design and development of a new spreadsheet, involves estimating the costs of the development, estimating the benefits, and comparing these values in a *cost-benefit analysis* (*CBA*). In order to do this, of course, estimates must be made of the size and scope of the proposed system, and the planned timing of its introduction.

Once the feasibility study has determined that the proposed system has an encouraging CBA, and that it is expected to confer net advantages over the current system, management can decide whether or not to go ahead with the implementation of the proposed system. If management decide that it is desirable to have the new system, the detailed work of undertaking a full systems analysis can begin.

We shall introduce in Chapter 5.1 the *context diagram*, also known as a high-level *data flow diagram*, as the main technical product of the feasibility study; and the cost-benefit analysis as the main business product for management.

Structured analysis

The first stage of technical work is *systems analysis*. Essentially, systems analysis involves the specification of the user's requirements: that is, the specification of what the proposed system should do, and an outline description of the processing system that would be required to do it.

Figure 5.2 illustrates the components of an information system – processing, data, and interfaces – that need to be specified as part of the user's requirements.

An important outcome of the systems analysis is often called a *requirements specification*, or sometimes a *functional requirements specification* or a *user requirements specification*. One of the key issues

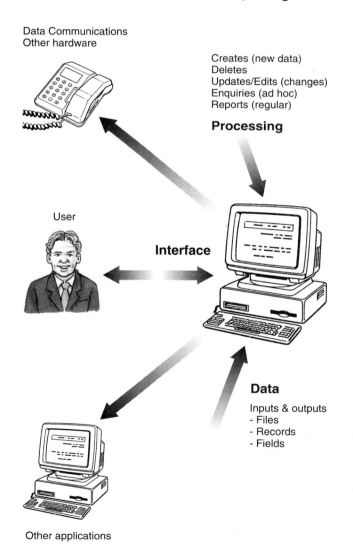

Data Communications
Other hardware

Creates (new data)
Deletes
Updates/Edits (changes)
Enquiries (ad hoc)
Reports (regular)

Processing

User

Interface

Data

Inputs & outputs
- Files
- Records
- Fields

Other applications

Figure 5.2   Components of an information system

in the life-cycle approach to systems development is the distinction between what the proposed system should do, and how the system would do it. Systems analysis is concerned with what the system should do, described in a requirements specification. System design is concerned with designing an information system to do it.

In Chapter 5.2 we present three major technical components of the requirements specification: low-level *data flow diagrams* to extend the context diagram of the feasibility study; the *data dictionary*; and the *requirements catalogue*.

System specification

Chapter 5.3 covers two main topics: the specification of the proposed new system, and the way the risks associated with the development project should be assessed.

By considering these two issues together the systems analysis team should be able to arrive at their conclusions about the proposal, and make recommendations to the organisation on whether or not it should proceed.

Chapter 5.1 Investigation and feasibility study

As mentioned in the introduction to this unit, the AVCE Specifications for Unit 5 treat feasibility studies as if they lay within the systems analysis process. However, many writers, teachers, and most ICT managers prefer to treat a feasibility study as a preliminary activity whose successful outcome can be regarded as the trigger for carrying out systems analysis.

Systems analysis of a large processing system is expensive. Therefore before it is commissioned, the investigation of the system in question, and a feasibility study of it, should be carried out sufficiently thoroughly for the case for undertaking the systems analysis to be clear.

Let us first think about the investigation that we shall have to make before we are ready to launch into a feasibility study. The purpose of the feasibility study, discussed below on page 199, is to examine an existing system, consider the characteristics of a proposed replacement system, and compare the two to see whether the proposed new system would be in some way better. The purpose of the investigation is to assemble all the facts we need to allow the feasibility study to go ahead without delays or distraction.

This chapter is divided into two parts:

- investigation
- feasibility study.

Investigation

There are three issues that will concern us during systems investigation:

- the kind of information we should be seeking

- the techniques that can be used to help ensure that we obtain the information we need

- interpersonal issues that may be significant during interviews and when asking for help from others.

Kinds of information

We have seen earlier that an information system broadly consists of three components: *data, processing,* and *interfaces.* These then are the areas in which we should be seeking information. As we look for this information about the functionality of both the existing system and the proposed system, we must also be aware of, and on the look-out for, information about non-functional requirements and constraints, examples of which are mentioned below.

Data

When we speak about the 'data' that an information system processes, we are generally speaking about one of two things. First, there are the entities about which the system keeps data, such as 'customer' or 'product'. Each of these is called a **data entity**. Second, there are the various items of data which we might hold about a

---

Commentary

You will often find users talking about 'files' of data, and it is usually the case that a 'file' corresponds to a data entity; for example, the 'customer file' or the 'product file'. You may also come across users talking about a 'database'. Sometimes they just mean a 'file', but at other times they may mean a 'collection of files'. The 'marketing database', for example, might consist of data entities such as 'customer', 'product', and 'order'.

particular data entity, such as customer name, customer ID, customer phone number, and so on. These individual items of data are called **data attributes**.

During the gathering of information on the data of a system, you would naturally first focus on identifying the various data entities involved in that system. Then, for each data entity, you would focus on identifying its data attributes. For each data attribute, it would be important to establish its allowed values: the largest and smallest permissible value if it is a number, the minimum and maximum number of characters if it is textual, and so on.

While gathering information about the data of a system, you would also document the sources of data and the data-capture methods used to obtain the data in the first place, the documents used in the system on which data is recorded and processed, and the storage methods used to provide access to the data.

In Chapter 5.2 we shall review how the data of a system is documented in a **data dictionary**.

Processes

While gathering information about the data of the system, you will naturally gather information about how that data is processed. In general, there are four kinds of processing that are applied to a data entity: **create**, **read**, **update**, or **delete** (often formed into the acronym **CRUD**). A data entity is said to be 'read' when its data is used without updating for outputs, either for routine reports or for *ad hoc* enquiries.

As you investigate processing, it is very useful to find out when, where, and how a particular data entity is created, updated, deleted, and used for reports or *ad hoc*

enquiries. As you identify the various processes of the system, you establish the flow of information from one process to another, the decisions taken by a process (usually an update process), and whether the process involves manual operations or automated operations.

In the next chapter we shall review how the processing of a system is documented in a set of **data flow diagrams**.

Interfaces

As you investigate data and processing, you will also need to establish where and how the system interfaces with the outside world: with its users and with other systems.

It is important to list all the personnel involved in the system, the roles each person plays, and the particular responsibilities each has for data entry, for checking data, and for making decisions.

It is also important to identify where the system connects to other systems, and the extent to which the system under investigation needs to be synchronised or kept in step with other systems.

The interface requirements are documented in the **requirements catalogue**, to be reviewed in the next chapter.

Non-functional requirements and constraints

Finally, as you investigate the data, processing, and interfaces of the system, you will uncover a wide variety of non-functional issues to do with constraints, speed of processing, response times, volumes of data, security, access, service levels, and system availability. All these non-functional requirements have to be documented in the requirements catalogue.

Techniques of information gathering

There are five techniques we discuss here (Table 5.1):

- interviews
- observations
- questionnaires
- documents inspection
- records sampling.

Interviews

The most obvious way of gathering information about a given processing system is to interview people about the system. If an interview is planned beforehand and questions are prepared, it is called a **structured interview**. If, on the other hand, there are no prepared questions and the interviewer simply follows whatever line of investigation seems appropriate at the time, it is an **unstructured interview**.

Between the two, of course, is the **semi-structured interview**. In many

circumstances this is the kind of interview that works best. It combines the advantages of both the main types of interview: the ability to build rapport and a communication link between interviewer and interviewee while capturing the essential information, and the ability to branch off and follow an interesting or significant line of investigation that was not anticipated.

The major disadvantage of the interview is that it is exceptionally time-consuming for both parties.

Observation

Observation is how the investigator 'sees what's actually going on', rather than relying on information provided by others. Without suggesting that your informants will be trying to mislead you or give you false information, it is almost always wise to have some kind of cross-check on the information you are given. Like interviews, observations can be structured, unstructured, or semi-structured, with much the same advantages and disadvantages. Often semi-

Techniques	Advantages	Disadvantages
Interviews	Follow unexpected lines Establish rapport	Time-consuming
Questionnaires	Saves time Anonymous replies	Low response rate Difficult to judge reply quality
Observations	See what's 'really' going on	Crucial, low-frequency events may be missed
Records sampling	Useful for large data sets	Statistical expertise required
Documents inspection	Manuals, plans, etc. readily available	May not be up to date or actually implemented

Table 5.1 Techniques of information gathering

structured observations combine the strength of a structured and planned approach with the ability to investigate the unexpected.

The disadvantage of observation is that unless it is continuous, important events that occur irregularly or rarely may be missed.

Questionnaires

A **questionnaire** is a list of questions, planned and written, that can be duplicated and given to a number of informants. The technique was discussed in Chapter 1.3, on page 25. It is much quicker than an interview in acquiring the same amount of information; and it may also be anonymous, which on occasion may be a great advantage.

On the other hand, responses to questionnaires are notoriously easy to falsify, and the quality of the information gathered may need checking. Where large numbers of questionnaires are distributed by post or in some other impersonal way, for example to learn the views of customers, a low return rate may also affect the quality of the result.

Document inspection

Another other major source of information is the documents in use in the business. You may want to start with an organisational structure chart. It will tell you who is responsible for what.

You will then need to read the minutes from relevant meetings; the aids, manuals, and guides that have been produced to help staff do their jobs; information packs for new staff or newly-transferred staff to orientate them in their new job;

departmental and progress reports, which are usually produced monthly or quarterly; and plans for improvements and development of the various business functions. And you will be interested in documents that give the sizes of major files, and the volumes and rates of transactions related to those files.

Such documentation is almost always easily available, though it may be incomplete or out of date; or, worse, may not exactly reflect the actual behaviour of the organisation.

Records sampling

Finally, most organisations will have numerous **records** that are relevant to the system, probably dating back a number of years. These could include customer lists, product details, monthly accounts, and other papers recording trading history. The technique used for **sampling** these records, especially if there are large numbers of them, is important. You will need a method of systematically sampling these records to derive an accurate picture of their contents and the various kinds of data they contain. Sampling, and the statistical analysis of sample data, requires some expertise. If you do not have such expertise, you will need to get help in acquiring it.

Interpersonal issues when gathering information

There are a few general points that need to be made about information gathering. Because it is an activity that directly involves people, and hence directly involves their interests, motivations, attitudes and values, there are many ways of failing to obtain the information you require, of failing to obtain such information with

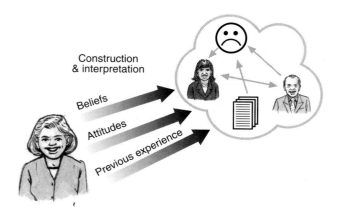

Figure 5.3 The construction and interpretation of 'facts'

sufficient reliability and validity, and of annoying others while you are trying to gather what you need!

The constructive nature of 'reality'

It is not normally obvious, but what we take as 'fact' may not actually and literally *be* fact. This is because perception varies from individual to individual. The variation may be small, but we should nonetheless be aware of it. The reason for these differences is that, as humans, we automatically interpret what we see and hear so that it makes sense for us. This act of interpretation involves personal beliefs, values, attitudes, and experience that others do not and cannot completely share.

During your information gathering, therefore, you need to be aware both that you are interpreting the information you gather, and that the information you are gathering is itself already the result of interpretations and personal understandings. This can make it very difficult to obtain a clear, consistent picture of a system, particularly if the system is at all complex (Figure 5.3).

Assertive investigation and respect

During your information gathering, you may well feel that the attitudes and interpretations of others are somehow hindering your progress. While it is almost certainly true that the attitudes and interpretations of others will pose some challenges to you, they need not hinder you, and it may be useful to identify some ways of dealing with the frustrations and difficulties that will occur.

Asking for help

The first step is to recognise that some of the people you work with are probably feeling the same way as you do, albeit for different reasons. This means that you need to respect their views and feelings, in the same way that you hope they will respect yours. Table 5.2 lists some ideas on asking for help.

Don't apologise	'I'm very sorry to bother you and I hope I'm not...'
Be direct (don't hint)	'I'd really like the data by Friday; can that be done?'
Keep it short!	Long-winded explanations get confusing
Don't justify yourself	'I wouldn't normally ask, but Ann's not here and...'
Give a (genuine) reason for asking	
Don't 'sell' your request	'You're just the right person and I'm sure you'll...'
Don't play on others' good nature	'Be a pal and...'
Don't take a refusal personally	
Respect the other's right to say 'No'	Give more information, clarify your request. Attempt problem-solving

Table 5.2 Asking for help

Rights and responsibilities at work

The second step is to be clear about what is reasonable for you to expect from others – and, of course, what it is reasonable for others to expect from you (Table 5.3).

To be clear about what is expected of you

To get on with your job in your own way, once objectives and constraints have been agreed

To ask for (not demand) assistance

To refuse a request you feel is unreasonable (but your contract may not have granted you this right)

To make mistakes from time to time

To be consulted on matters which affect you

To expect work of a certain standard from others

Table 5.3 Reasonable expectations at work

If you accept that you have certain rights at work, you also need to accept the consequential responsibilities (Table 5.4).

To do what is expected of you

To acknowledge a mistake, not to blame others; to put it right; to learn from it (not to repeat it)

To provide work of a certain standard yourself; to let others know what the standards are

To criticise assertively, not aggressively

To recognise there may be good reasons for below-standard work

To abide by the agreed constraints and work towards the agreed objectives

Table 5.4 Responsibilities at work

Thinking positively

The third step is to correct any 'faulty thinking' with 'sound inner dialogue' (Table 5.5). That a particular set of circumstances seems to be a problem is perhaps only because you think it so. You can think differently about the circumstances, and therefore think positively and constructively about the 'problem'. This is the core idea behind **NLP** (**neuro-linguistic programming**), a common business technique for addressing this question of thinking round a problem.

NLP claims that if you change the language that you instinctively use concerning your perception of some issue, you can alter your patterns of behaviour in response to that issue (Table 5.5).

Resolving conflict

The final step is to deal with conflict in a problem-solving way. The key step in resolving conflict is to accept that there is sure to be conflict, or at least tension, and to accept that this arises quite naturally because your needs are different from those of the other person (Table 5.6).

Recording the results of investigation

When you are carrying out an investigation you must be sure to end up with a record of what you found out. You should always assume that you will not be able to ask the

Faulty thinking	Sound inner dialogue
He doesn't care	He might not care, but that need not hinder my work.
He'll make an excuse and fob me off	He may make excuses, but that need not fob me off. There may be good reasons behind them.
I can't allow that	I can allow it if I choose to.
I'll have to show him	I can point out the effects of his behaviour without getting mad.
He has got to give me the information I want	It would be helpful if he would give me the information, but I can get it elsewhere. He'll have to take responsibility for his own behaviour.

Table 5.5 Thinking positively and constructively

Identify *needs*	Make your own needs clear Seek information on the other's needs Ask for clarification of the other's needs Check your understanding of the other's needs
Check for and accept any *conflict* of needs	State your acceptance of their needs Gain their acceptance of your needs
Come up with and agree *solutions*	Seek suggestions Make suggestions Develop suggestions Seek reactions Summarise State your acceptance of the solution Gain their acceptance of the solution

Table 5.6 Resolving conflict

same questions again just because you have forgotten what was said.

You do, however, have to strike a balance between distracting or alarming someone you are interviewing by making your recording of what is said too obtrusive, and by trying to commit everything to memory so that you can maintain conspicuous interest in the person speaking and provide plenty of eye contact.

At one extreme you can ask if you might make a tape recording of an interview, or even key the responses of the person being interviewed into a laptop computer: at the other extreme you can appear to be doing nothing. You have to try and match the style of note-taking to the seniority and availability of the person concerned, how much you already know (or think you know), about what is going to be said, and the physical surroundings. If you happen to be competent in shorthand a middle course is immediately open to you. Most interviewers rely on writing in longhand in a notebook, but are apt out of courtesy to avoid using it during an interview, sometimes with damaging results.

Before ending an interview you should make an appointment to return to run over your record of the points that arose, to check that you have understood them and that the detail is correct.

Feasibility study

The central purpose of a feasibility study is to consider whether there are net benefits to be obtained from replacing a current processing system by a different system. The information collected by the earlier investigation is now crucial in deciding the answer to this question. If the answer is 'No' there is nothing to be done. If it is 'Yes' the task becomes one of deciding which of all the possible types of replacement system is the most desirable.

Normally the answer is 'Yes', for otherwise the call for a feasibility study would quickly have been shown unnecessary. Very often there will be little doubt as to the correct choice, and that is the assumption underlying the rest of this chapter. If, however, there is doubt about the selection of one of several plausible possibilities, a feasibility study would have to be carried out for each.

In many ways, a feasibility study is a small version of a full systems study that would be required after a decision to go ahead had been taken. The purpose of making the feasibility study first is to find out, before committing substantial resources, whether or not the proposed new system will yield the necessary net benefits. In the feasibility study you therefore need to describe the proposed system in much the same way as you have to for the implementation of the full system.

As an essential part of the feasibility study activity you need to produce a **cost-benefit analysis (CBA)**, which is like a financial assessment of the proposed system. The CBA will provide the financial evaluation of the whole development project that is necessary for the implementation of the proposed new system. In order to carry out a CBA, you need to draw up a draft budget for the proposed system, based on your forecast of the timings of the various elements of expenditure and of financial benefit. The method of conducting a CBA is discussed below and in Appendix B. (You do not need to grasp all the detail in Appendix B unless you are set on obtaining an 'A' grade.)

Chapter 5.3 refers to Appendix B to provide more discussion on project sizing, project budgets, and project schedules; and also to Appendix D on issues of project risk and project impact which are usually closely connected with the analysis of project feasibility.

In this chapter, we will present a technique called the **context diagram** which defines the scope of the proposed system. The context diagram is a simple version of a data flow diagram, which is covered in detail in the next chapter.

Case study

We will continue with our use of the company, Festivities Unlimited (FUN). They wish to convert their current manual events bookings system – pencilled entries in a diary – to a computerised version of the same system. FUN management feel that a computerised bookings system will be able to give them quick, accurate

> **Commentary**
>
> In formal systems analysis the word 'event' has a specific meaning, but to avoid confusion within this book as a whole we continue to use the word 'event' in a normal, non-technical way.

management information that they currently do not have. In particular, the Marketing Director would like to be able to find out easily and quickly, at any time, how much capacity to mount events is still available.

> **Commentary**
>
> You may come across the term structured **systems analysis and design method (SSADM)**, which is the methodology used in many system development projects in the UK, and is demanded in all government and military ICT development contracts.
>
> The approach adopted by SSADM is formal, and the methods are especially suited to large projects, and for those reasons it is not usually covered in Advanced VCE courses.

It is relatively easy for FUN managers to find out how many events they have booked, how many staff will be needed for these events, and what other resources will be needed. But it is more difficult for them to know how many more events could be sold before they were full up; this is one of the major reasons for wanting a computerised system.

Purpose
Statement of purpose

The feasibility study report should begin with a brief statement of the *purpose* of the system. Laying down the purpose of any proposed system is very important. If it is inaccurate or unclear, priorities may be allocated wrongly and inappropriate technical issues addressed. The purpose of a system is an answer to the question 'Why is this system wanted?' It is a rather different question from 'What is the *scope* of the proposed system?'

The purpose of a proposed system is usually a political, commercial, or broad organisational issue. The scope of a proposed system is usually a technical issue. The purpose comes first and determines the system scope. The technology needs to be subordinate to business purpose in almost all cases.

For the FUN party booking system, the major purpose of the proposed computerised system is to provide management information about the company's free capacity to mount parties above its current level of bookings. There are other purposes of the system, of course, but this particular purpose focuses attention on what is considered most important from the business point of view, rather than on what is technologically possible.

Statement of deficiencies

Often, the purpose of a proposed system is to overcome the deficiencies of an existing system, or the lack of any system. It may be useful to list the deficiencies as a separate statement.

Statement of user requirements

When we arrive at the systems analysis stage, defining and listing the user requirements is done in a systematic way. For the feasibility study, however, the user requirements are implied through the statement of purpose, through the statement of deficiencies, if there are any, and through the context diagram which represents the scope of the proposed system. If it is thought important to list the user requirements separately, perhaps because there are significant non-functional components or constraints that are not otherwise obvious, then the technique of

requirements cataloguing, discussed in Chapter 5.2, may be used.

Scope – the context diagram

The scope of a system can be conveniently captured in a **context diagram**. This diagram consists of three components.

- At the centre of the context diagram is a rectangular **system box** which represents the proposed system.

- Arranged around the system box are a number of ovals representing the **external entities**: those people, organisations, or other systems that provide input data to the system, and that take output data from the system.

- Each item of input and output data is itself shown as an arrow representing a **data flow** between an external entity and the system.

This notation is standard. You will find it helpful to recognise the components easily whenever you see them, so they are illustrated in Figure 5.4.

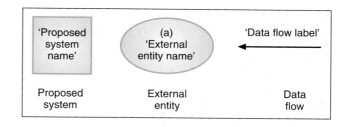

Figure 5.4 Context diagram notation

Note that the system box should be very carefully labelled with the exact name or description of the proposed system. Note also that the external entity, as well as having a name, is also given an identifying label such as (a).

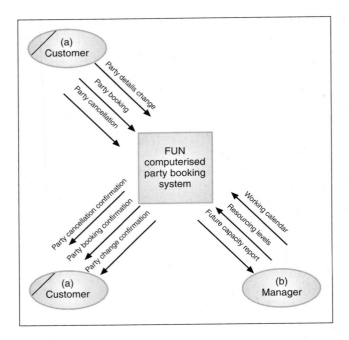

Figure 5.5 FUN booking system: context diagram

Figure 5.5 is an example of a context diagram being developed for the FUN booking system. From the point of view of notation, notice that a diagonal line has been placed across the upper left of external entity (a). This diagonal line on the external entity is called a **duplication line**, and is shown on any entity that is repeated within the diagram. It serves to remind you, in this case, that there are not two 'Customer' external entities, just one, and that the duplication of the external entity is to make the layout of the diagram clear in this respect.

As far as it goes (because a real bookings system would be somewhat more complex), the context diagram shows that the scope of the proposed FUN bookings system involves nine data flows: three input data flows from the customer about the booked party; three output flows to the customer which confirm aspects of the party; two input data flows from a manager which relate to FUN's capacity to mount a party; and one output

data flow to a manager which reports on the future capacity of the company to manage parties.

Now for some details about the components of the context diagram.

External entities

An **external entity** is a person, organisation, or separate system that provides data to the proposed system or receives data from it. What is significant is that this external entity is *external* to the system, not a part of it. For example, a computerised booking system would require a clerk to type in the party bookings, but the clerk *is* part of the system, and so is *not* shown as an external entity; whereas a travel agent making a booking enquiry for a client would be an external entity.

The external entities identify the interfaces that must be provided between the system and its environment.

Sometimes there is difficulty in deciding whether something is external to a system or not. If the question 'Is that part of the system, or not?' remains difficult to answer, then you can try the technical definition of 'external entity': an external entity is something that is the original source of data to the system, or something that is the final destination – the sink – of data from the system.

As we have just seen, the clerk typing party bookings data into the system is *not* the original source of that data and therefore is not an external entity. However, the sales assistant sitting in the office taking a new party booking over the telephone, and jotting down the details for the clerk, *is* an external entity who just happens to be in the same room.

The name provided for an external entity is always a noun – it is always a 'thing'. It is also conventional to ensure that the name of the external entity is shown in the singular form, and not the plural form – 'Customer', for example, rather than 'Customers'.

Data flows

A particular data flow is a specific collection of data items which are input to the system, or output from it, as a result of an **event**. In this sense, a data flow on the context diagram is as much an indication of an event that the system must process as it is a description of the data that flows as a result of that event.

The label or name given to a data flow must state as clearly as possible the data that is flowing. Because data is a 'thing', data flow labels are always nouns. For example, when the customer makes a party booking, the data that flows would not be labelled 'Make booking', because that is the name of a process, and the label contains a verb or 'action word'. Again, it is conventional to ensure that the label of the data flow is shown in the singular form, and not the plural – 'Party booking', for example, rather than 'Party bookings'.

Cost-benefit analysis

In most circumstances the financial expectations of a prospective new system are of crucial importance: they are likely to be the outcome of the feasibility study that will determine whether or not the proposed system will be implemented. The organisation commissioning or carrying out the feasibility study will insist on knowing how the feasibility study team rate the expected costs and benefits.

Usually the director or manager setting up the feasibility study will have some idea of the expected outcome. If FUN had asked for a feasibility study into the possible purchase of three new computers and bespoke software, and the engaging and training of a new employee, the study team might quickly discover that the expected costs would far outweigh any conceivable benefit. That could hardly have been the expected outcome, or the study would not have been started. The team should therefore immediately report their preliminary finding and ask whether to carry on or not.

This forecast of costs and benefits, and the analysis of their relationship one with another, is the cost-benefit analysis. It can be complicated, and it can also be subtle in the sense that it involves timing as well as predicted cash flows. You can find out more about cost-benefit analysis in Appendix B.

The implementation of the proposed new system may involve the design and development of special-purpose software, and the cost and delivery time of such bespoke software are always hard to forecast. This is because by definition bespoke software is being built for the first time, and it therefore has some of the uncertainties of a research project. Furthermore, the cost of this software is likely to make up a large proportion of total costs.

There are several techniques for estimating the cost or duration of creating a bespoke system. One popular method is called **function point analysis (FPA)**. FPA addresses one component, albeit possibly the most important one, of the expected costs of the proposed system being studied. There is a description of FPA in Appendix C. (As with Appendix B, you may find the notes on FPA in Appendix C rather heavy going: do not worry about the detail unless you are consciously working for an 'A' grade.)

The outcome of the CBA will be the main factor determining the recommendation given by the feasibility study team on whether or not the proposed new system should be implemented. There are sometimes other factors that override the findings and recommendations of the CBA – for example, the need to react quickly and therefore perhaps in a way that is not the most cost-effective, for fear that the organisation is about to become the target of an imminent, hostile attempt to take it over; or to snatch an unexpected, desirable overseas marketing opportunity – but such exceptions are rare.

Conclusions of the feasibility study

The recommendations made by the feasibility study team have to take into account the team's assessment of the risks to which the project is exposed. The question of how these risks should be quantified is considered in Chapter 5.3 and Appendix D.

We can usefully summarise the usual outputs of the feasibility study. They are:

- statement of purpose
- list of deficiencies
- statement of user requirements
- context diagram
- CBA results
- risk analysis
- provisional conclusions.

The person calling for the feasibility study will indicate how much time is to be spent on the study and how substantial the report containing the findings ought to be.

Chapter 5.2 Structured analysis

High-level (contextual view) data flow diagrams

The **context diagram**, or high-level **data flow diagram (DFD)**, was introduced in Chapter 5.1 as one of the major outcomes of a feasibility study. The context diagram shows the system under study as a single systems box. The processes and data inside the system are shown in a set of detailed, low-level DFDs.

Low-level (detailed view) data flow diagrams

Notation

The symbols and notation used in a data flow diagram are shown in Figure 5.6. The **document flow** arrow, a 'fat' arrow, is not found in a finished DFD, but can be used during the initial development of a DFD. Users often discuss the data that flows between system processes in terms of the document or form on which that data is printed. It is your job as the systems analyst to identify the actual data that is flowing, rather than just the name of the form.

The symbol used in a DFD to indicate a **data store** is an open-ended box containing the name of the data being stored.

Level 1 DFD

Your first DFD would probably be developed from your context diagram. One

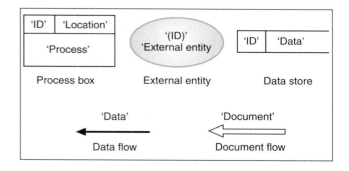

Figure 5.6 DFD notation

way to develop a DFD from a context diagram is to consider each context data flow in turn, and then to define the processes that would handle those context data flows. As you develop a set of processes, you will see where data may need to flow between one process and another, and you will see where data may need to be shown as being stored in a data store that is accessible to other processes. Often, the data stores may be conveniently shown in the centre of the DFD.

If we follow this approach using the FUN event booking system context diagram, the result might look like Figure 5.7. It would be called the **level 1 DFD**.

Each **process** has been given an identifying number, as has each data store. Each process has additionally been annotated with the location where it takes place. Each process has been named, and the name given – such as 'Accept and confirm party booking' – is clearly a *process* name in that it describes an *action*. Each **data flow** has also been named with a label that identifies the data being input or output to the process.

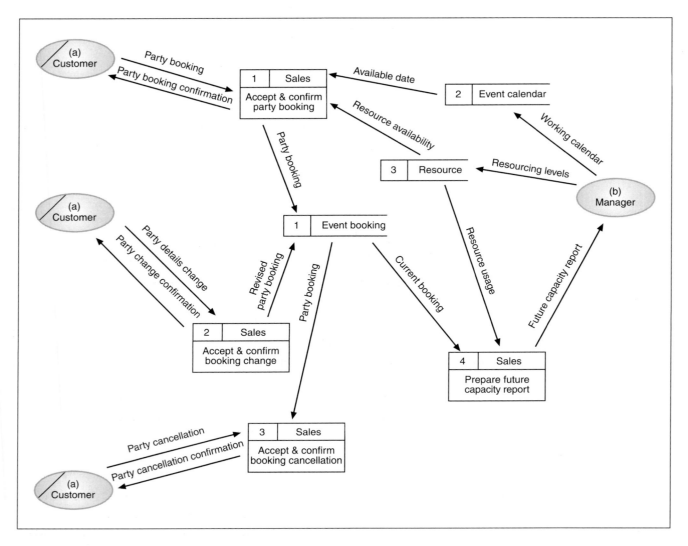

Figure 5.7 FUN booking system: level 1 DFD

Decomposition of processes

The key idea behind data flow diagramming is that the various processes of a system can be decomposed into finer detail in lower-level DFDs. When you compare the context diagram (Figure 5.5) with the level 1 DFD (Figure 5.7), you can see that the external entities and the context data flows are the same in both. What has happened is that the 'system box' of the context diagram has been decomposed into four processes, along with some internal data flows and three data stores.

In a similar way, each of the four processes of the level 1 DFD can be decomposed into finer detail in the lower-level DFDs. The lower-level DFD resulting from the decomposition of a level 1 process is known as a **level 2 DFD**. Figure 5.8 illustrates the level 2 DFD corresponding to the decomposition of process 1 in the level 1 DFD in Figure 5.7. Notice that the data flows to and from process 1 remain and are shown on the level 2 diagram, and that

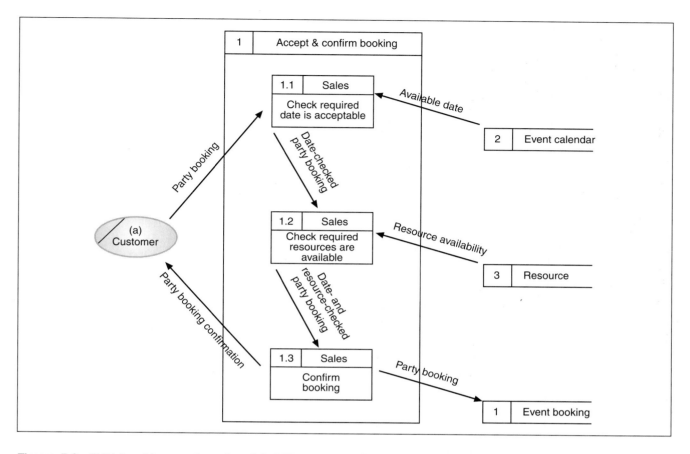

Figure 5.8 FUN booking system: level 2 DFD

process 1 has been decomposed into three level 2 processes and some internal data flows. Finally, notice that, in the decomposition of process 1 into the three level 2 processes, these level 2 processes are numbered 1.x, where the '1' refers to process 1, the decomposed process, and 'x' is a new identifying number for each of the resulting level 2 processes.

In principle, each of the level 2 DFD processes could be further decomposed in to **level 3 DFD**s. This may well be useful in a large system, but would be unusual in a smaller system. A process need only be decomposed to the point where the processing and data involved is clearly understood by all concerned with the project.

It may be useful to recognise that a data flow diagram, despite its name, is in fact a diagram which primarily details the *processes* and *processing* within the system. The documentation of the *data* objects within a system is provided by other diagrams.

Process specification

Although each process shown in a set of DFDs may seem clear and unambiguous, it is necessary to provide a detailed **process specification** for each DFD process. Such a detailed process specification is always required when programming of the process is undertaken, but may also be required during analysis and design if the process employs particular formulas or complicated methods, or involves numerous decisions.

A detailed process specification is usually provided as a **structured English specification**: it may sometimes be provided as a **decision table**, or very rarely, as **flow charts**.

Structured English

Structured English is a way of using a limited set of English words to describe the logical flow of a process.

A structured English process specification provides the **sequence** of actions and operations that define a given process. It is set out to make evident, and clear, any **iteration** or **selection** demanded by the logic of the process. These words – *sequence*, *iteration*, and *selection* – have precise meanings in describing processes, and are explained below.

Structured English has proved to provide a reliable, unambiguous, and compact means of describing a process. Any process can be defined by using the operations of sequence, iteration, and selection.

Sequence

Let us examine 'making tea' as an example. We could construct a simple structured English process specification for tea-making that involved operations such as 'put teabag into mug' and 'boil kettle'. The result is shown in Figure 5.9.

Selection; IF

The above structured English process specification illustrates a simple sequence of operations, starting at the top and ending at the bottom. A more complex process specification would recognise that there are

```
Put teabag into mug
Boil kettle
Pour boiled water into mug
Wait two minutes
Remove teabag from mug
Add milk
Add sugar
Stir
```

Figure 5.9 Simple structured English sequence for 'Making tea'

points at which some *decisions* must be made, where a **selection** needs to be made of the appropriate operation to carry out. These selections might be, for example, of weak or strong tea, and of tea with or without milk.

Selection is indicated by using the structured English **key words IF..THEN..ELSE..ENDIF**.

Examine the structured English specification in Figure 5.10.

Notice that the operation that is carried out as a result of making the selection, such as

```
Put teabag into mug
Boil kettle
Pour boiled water into mug
IF weak tea is wanted THEN
     Wait 20 seconds
ELSE
     Wait 2 minutes
ENDIF
Remove teabag from mug
IF white tea is required THEN
     Add milk
ENDIF
If sweetened tea is required THEN
     Add sugar
ENDIF
Stir
```

Figure 5.10 Structured English showing selection using IF

'Add milk', is indented in the list of operations. This convention makes the overall structure of the process specification clearer to the human eye, and so easier to grasp accurately. Notice also that there are some selections that do not involve an ELSE; this part of the selection may be omitted.

| **Try it out** | Write instructions in structured English for boiling an egg. |
| | Then modify the instructions to define the process of boiling two eggs, started together but with one intended to be medium-soft and the other medium-hard. |

Selection: CASE

The IF..THEN..ELSE..ENDIF structure offers a choice between only two options. Some selections need a choice to be made between more than two options. In these situations the **CASE SELECT..END SELECT** structure is necessary.

For example, we could imagine three ways of making a cup of tea, as shown in Figure 5.11.

The CASE SELECT key words indicate the basis on which the selection is to be made. In the example, this basis is 'type of tea'. For each 'type of tea', we have the CASE key word for each particular tea type: 'teabag', 'loose tea leaves', and 'tea concentrate'. Finally, the CASE structure is terminated with the END SELECT key words.

It is sometimes useful to have a 'CASE' that covers a situation other than one of those listed. This is done by including the CASE ELSE key words, followed by the operations to undertake in this situation. The CASE ELSE set of operations is usually put last in the list of CASEs.

Again, notice how the indenting makes the structure of the process specification clearer and easier to follow. This layout using

```
Boil kettle
CASE SELECT type of tea
    CASE teabag
        Put teabag into mug
        Pour boiled water into
          mug
        Wait two minutes
    CASE loose tea leaves
        Prepare teapot
        Put two teaspoons tea
          leaves into teapot
        Pour boiled water into
          teapot
        Wait two minutes
        Pour tea from teapot into
          mug
    CASE tea concentrate
        Put one teaspoon
          concentrate into mug
        Pour boiled water into
          mug
END SELECT
Add milk
Add sugar
Stir
```

Figure 5.11 Structured English showing selection using CASE

indentation creates blocks of structured English, and the resulting process specification is often described as **block-structured**.

Iteration: DO..REPEAT UNTIL

The third component of a process specification is iteration, in which a set of operations is carried out repeatedly. Iteration may be shown by using the structured English key words **DO, REPEAT,** and **UNTIL.** Such an iteration is often called a **DO loop**.

Imagine that you are making tea for a tea party, rather than just a single cup for yourself. You then need to iterate, or repeat, the making of a number of cups of tea. Figure 5.12 shows a structured English specification which might be used.

```
Count Number_of_Guests
Put Number_of_Guests+2 teabags into
   teapot
COMMENT Add one teabag for
   yourself, and one 'for the pot',
   as they say
Boil kettle
Pour boiled water into teapot
Wait two minutes
DO
   Pour tea from teapot into mug
   Add milk
   Add sugar
   Stir
REPEAT UNTIL Number_of_Guests+1
   mugs of tea have been made
Distribute the mugs to the guests,
   and keep one for yourself
```

Figure 5.12 Structured English showing iteration

The important thing about this iteration is that it is always carried out *at least once*. This is because the test to check whether all the required iterations have been made is placed at the *end* of the DO loop.

Notice another key word, **COMMENT**, which distinguishes any remarks you may want to make about the process specification and ensures that these are not confused with the operations of the process themselves.

Iteration: DO UNTIL..REPEAT

Sometimes it is necessary to have a DO loop that might not be carried out at all, depending upon the circumstances. For example, consider Figure 5.13, which defines how to sweeten the cup of tea.

The important thing about this iteration is that it might *never* be carried out. This is because the test to check whether all the required iterations have been made is placed at the *start* of the DO loop.

Finally, notice that the structured English key words are shown in upper case, while the remainder of the process specification is largely in lower case. This is another convention which serves to highlight the structure of the process.

```
Ask Number_of_Spoons_of_Sugar
   required
COMMENT Find out how many teaspoons
   of sugar are wanted
DO UNTIL Number_of_spoons_of_Sugar
   have been added
      Add a teaspoon of sugar
REPEAT
```

Figure 5.13 Structured English showing alternative iteration

Try it out	Write the instructions in structured English for blow-drying your hair. Assume that the hair starts wet, and that you want to blow it until it is dry, without blowing it for longer than necessary. You need to test your hair now and again to find out how the drying process is coming along, turning the dryer off while you do so.
	You could test the dryness every minute until you think it is nearly done, then every half minute.

Relational and logical operators

Iteration and selection always involve a test of some kind – for example, is the kind of tea we are making today loose leaf tea? More complex tests involve questions as to whether some quantity is larger or smaller than some other quantity, or whether a situation involves both one item and another item.

Questions or tests about a quantity being larger or smaller are expressed using the symbols '<', '=', and '>' to construct a set of **relational operators**. These tests, and their corresponding operators, are shown in Table 5.7.

Test	Relational operator
Less than	<
Less than or equal to	<=
Equal to	=
Not equal to	<>
Greater than or equal to	=>
Greater than	>

Table 5.7 Relational operators

For example, to test whether sufficient cups of tea have been made, we would have the 'equals' relational operator in the UNTIL test (Figure 5.14).

```
DO
      Pour tea from teapot into a
        mug
      Add milk
      Add sugar
      Stir
REPEAT UNTIL Mugs_of_Tea_Made =
  Number_of_Guests
```

Figure 5.14 Test using relational operator

Questions about whether an item *and* another item are present, or whether an item *or* another item are present, or whether an item is *not* present, are made using the logical operators 'AND', 'OR', and 'NOT' (Figure 5.15).

```
IF Time_of_Day = 'morning' AND
  Number_of_Guests <= 2 THEN
        Make tea using teabags and
          mugs
ELSE
        Make tea using loose leaf
          tea and teapot
ENDIF
```

Figure 5.15 Test using relational and logical operators

Commentary

When a process specification takes more than a page to write out, it is probably time to break it down into separate modules which are brought into the flow of the process description required using the key word **CALL**.

For example, we need to 'Add milk' in a number of places, as well as sugar. Instead of inserting the structured English operations for adding milk and adding sugar in every place in which they arise, we could specify the process once, and then note where these parts of the overall process are to be used. We would begin by defining 'Add milk' and 'Add sugar' as separate processes, and then specifying with the CALL key word the process that is to be included – see Figure 5.16.

```
PROCESS Add_Milk
        Find out how dark the tea
          should be
        DO UNTIL tea is correctly
          milked
            Add some milk
        REPEAT
END PROCESS
PROCESS Add_Sugar
        Ask Number_of_Spoons_of_
          Sugar required
        DO UNTIL Number_of_Spoons_
          of_Sugar have been added
            Add a teaspoon of sugar
        REPEAT
END PROCESS
.DO
        Pour tea from teapot into
          a mug
        CALL Add_Milk
        CALL Add_Sugar
        Stir
REPEAT UNTIL Mugs_of_Tea_Made =
  Number_of_Guests
```

Figure 5.16 Defining separate processes

Decision tables

A *decision table* is a device which makes explicit all the various possible outcomes of a decision-making process.

For example, Festivities Unlimited allows a 5% discount on an event booking if it is budgeted to cost less than £5000 and is booked by a customer who has enjoyed a FUN event in the past year; an 8% discount if it is budgeted to cost more than £5000; and a 10% discount if it is budgeted to cost more than £5000 and is booked at least three months in advance.

Each of these possible situations is known as a **condition**. These conditions are independent of each other so the full range of possibilities must be considered, each combination leading to a particular outcome. Each distinct set of conditions is called a **rule**. The decision table which results from the FUN detail above is shown in Figure 5.17 and explained below.

		Rule							
		1	2	3	4	5	6	7	8
Condition									
Cost > £5000?		N	Y	N	Y	N	Y	N	Y
Event in past year?		N	N	Y	Y	N	N	Y	Y
Booked in advance?		N	N	N	N	Y	Y	Y	Y
Action									
No discount		X				X			
5% discount				X				X	
8% discount					X	X			
10% discount								X	X

Figure 5.17 Decision table for event discount

To construct such a decision table, you first need to identify the various conditions or choices that are involved, and to ensure that these choices are phrased as 'either/or', 'true/false', or 'yes/no'. That is to say that each must have only one or other of two possible **values**. In the example table, three conditions have been identified and phrased as 'yes/no' conditions: 'Is the event cost greater than £5000?' 'Has the customer had an event in the past year?' And, 'Is the event booked in advance?'

Then, you need to identify all the possible outcomes, also known as **actions**, or decisions, that could occur. In the example table, four possible decisions are identified: 'No discount', '5% discount', '8% discount' and '10% discount'. Note that every possible action must be exclusive of every other action. It should not be possible, for example, to give both 'No discount' and '8% discount'.

Third, you need to develop the set of rules which govern the decision being tabulated. A rule is one particular combination of conditions, and the full set of rules is developed by systematically varying the answer to each condition.

How many rules are there in a 'full set'? We have said that there are to be only two possible values for each condition. In our case there are three conditions that can apply, each of which is restricted to either one or the other of two values. The number of possible combinations, which is the same as the number of rules, is therefore two raised to the power of three: that is, eight.

In general, if there are C conditions, each of which can take on two values, then there must always be 2^c rules. In the example table, there are 3 conditions, so there are $2^3 = 8$ rules.

Finally, for every rule, you need to identify the single action or decision which results from it, placing an 'X' in the appropriate place.

The value of a decision table for anything more than a very simple decision is that it requires you to be very precise about all aspects of the decisions involved: what the various conditions are, exactly how many possibilities there are, and what the various exclusive actions are.

Commentary

You will sometimes find it useful to review the full decision table and then **reduce** it to its smallest possible size, by combining rules which lead to the same action. Such a reduced decision table developed from our example above is shown in the Figure 5.18, where the '–' indicates 'don't care', or 'either Y or N'.

	Reduced Rule			
	1	2	3	4
Condition				
Cost > £5000?	N	Y	N	Y
Event in past year?	N	–	Y	–
Booked in advance?	–	N	–	N
Action				
No discount	X			
5% discount			X	
8% discount		X		
10% discount				X

Figure 5.18 Reduced decision table for event discount

The value of a reduced table is that it makes clear which combination of conditions result in a given action, and which conditions have no effect upon that action. For example, the action 'No discount' occurs when the cost is less than £5000 and the customer has not had an event in the past year, regardless of whether the event is booked in advance or not.

Some decision tables may need to be large and complicated, and there may be difficulty in identifying all the conditions, actions, and rules that are involved. Software packages called **decision table processors** can be used in such cases.

Try it out Construct a decision table to reflect your choices in the following situation. You have agreed to take part in a sponsored walk, but you know little about what you have let yourself in for. You decide that:

(a) if the route is to be rough you will wear boots

(b) if the weather forecast is poor you will take your anorak, and wear boots

(c) if the length is more than 10 miles you will take food, and the anorak to sit on

(d) if your trainers are not back from the menders you will wear boots.

Can you reduce the size of your table?

Entity relationship diagrams

Terminology

In the same way that we analysed and documented the processing of a system using data flow diagrams, we document the data of a system using a technique called **data modelling** and a diagram called the **entity relationship diagram (ERD)**. There is a fuller discussion of these topics in Chapter 6.2.

Figure 5.19 illustrates a very simple ERD.

We begin by noting that your investigation of a system will generally reveal that there are several objects in the system about which data is kept. For example, there might be customers, and for each customer we would probably record their name, address, telephone number, and so on; there

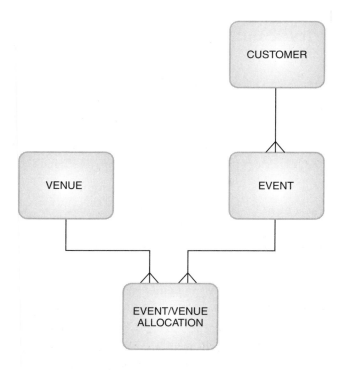

Figure 5.19 Example ERD

might be venues, and for each venue we would probably record the venue code, the venue name, its address, its seating capacity, and whether it has a dance floor.

The abstract object for which we would keep data is called a **data entity**, and the individual items of data are called **attributes**. For the purpose of building up a database, an object is only of interest if it has *many occurrences*; that is, for example, if there are many customers, or many

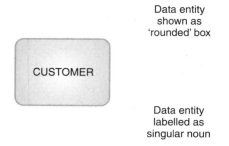

Data entity shown as 'rounded' box

Data entity labelled as singular noun

Figure 5.20 Data entity notation in ERD

products. There is little point constructing a database that contains only one occurrence of an object.

Each data entity in the ERD is shown as a 'rounded box', as specified in Figure 5.20.

The attributes of a data entity are most useful if they are **atomic**: this means that the attributes in question cannot be broken down any further into constituent parts. For example, we said earlier that 'Address' is an attribute of the 'Customer' data entity. For small or limited systems, this might be fine, but an address is not an atomic attribute. For larger systems, we would probably break an address down into attributes such as 'House number', 'Street name', 'Town', 'County', and 'Postcode'.

It is convenient to think of, and to lay out, the data we hold about an object as a **table** (Figure 5.21). Each *row* of the table is a particular occurrence of the abstract object, and each *column* of the table corresponds to an attribute. A particular phone number, 01234 56789, for example, is the particular *value* of the 'customer phone number' attribute.

If the data about the customers were to be stored in a *simple* computer filing system, we would have a **file** of customer records. Each **record** would correspond to a table row, and within each record there would be fields of data, each **field** corresponding to an attribute.

Shortly we will explore the relationship between data entities or tables – in this context, it is common to refer to a data entity or a table as a **relation**. This concept and others in the following paragraphs are developed further in the chapters of Unit 6, which is devoted to database design.

Notice that the label for a data entity, table or relation is almost always a noun in the

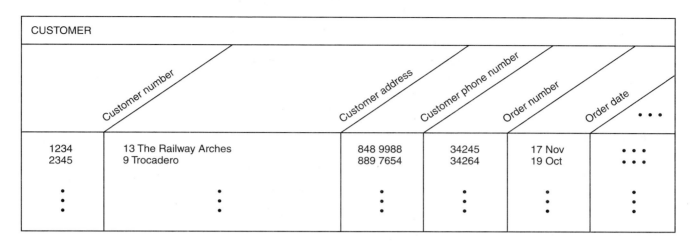

Figure 5.21 Example table of data

singular, not the plural. We often talk of the file of customers, but we are talking of the many occurrences of the 'customer' object.

Keys

Every occurrence of a data entity needs to be identifiable in such a way that no occurrence can be confused with any other. This requirement is expressed by saying that each occurrence of a data entity must be *uniquely identifiable*. The requirement is also expressed by saying that at least one column in the table must have unique values. An attribute that has unique values over all occurrences is known as a **key** attribute, or 'key' for short.

In some tables, there may be a number of attributes each of which has unique values; such attributes are said to be **candidate keys**. For the purpose of constructing a database, one of these candidate keys is selected to be the **primary key** for the table, and the remaining candidate keys are designated **alternate keys**. Of course, if the table has only one attribute with unique values, that attribute is necessarily the primary key.

Some tables may not have any one column that contains unique values. In order to satisfy the requirement that a table must have uniquely identifiable rows, it may be necessary to combine two or more columns into a **composite key**, which is a key that consists of more than one attribute.

For example, we would probably want to record customer details in our FUN event bookings system. The rows in the customer table might be uniquely identifiable just by using 'Surname' as the primary key, but this would be rather unlikely if FUN had more than a few customers. Then, we might be able to identify customers uniquely by using a composite key of 'Surname, First name', but we would soon have two identical composite keys, say 'Jo Bloggs'. We could expand our composite key to include 'Date of birth', but not even that would guarantee uniqueness. The way out, of course, would be to create a new attribute called 'Customer number': we could then ensure that every customer has a unique number, and have that attribute as our primary key.

Finally, a table may have as one of its columns an attribute that is the primary key of another table; this would be called a **foreign key**. For example, FUN may mount certain events at one of a selected number of venues. There would be a table which would list all the venues, where 'Venue code' would be the venue table's primary key. The table of events would most probably have a column labelled 'Venue code', being the venue code for a particular event, so as to provide a cross-reference to the venue table. In the event table, then, 'Venue code' is a foreign key.

Relationships

A customer may have one or more events booked with FUN. There is thus a **relationship** between the 'customer' entity and the 'event' entity. We have just expressed this relationship in one way – 'A customer may have one or more events' – and we can express the relationship in a second way – 'An event must be booked by one and only one customer'. A relationship really contains connections between two entities.

Two data entities have a relationship if there is some direct connection between the. They do not have a relationship if there is no direct connection. For example, there is no direct connection between 'customer' and 'venue'. Any relationship we feel may exist between 'customer' and 'venue' is really a relationship between 'event' and 'venue'. For example, perhaps: 'An event must take place at one or more venues' and 'A venue may host one or more events'.

For our limited introduction to ERDs, the most important aspect of a relationship is the number of occurrences of the one data entity that are related to the other. A customer may book many events, and this is a **one-to-many connection** from the

'customer' to the 'event' data entities. An event must be booked by one and only one customer, so this is a **one-to-one connection** from the 'event' to the 'customer' data entities. Finally, a **many-to-many relationship** is shown by the relationship between 'event' and 'venue': an event may take place at many venues and a venue may host many events.

Figure 5.22 illustrates how these relationships are shown on the ERD. Two data entities which have a relationship are connected by a **relationship line**, and the way the line is terminated indicates the kind of relationship. The 'many' terminator of a relationship line is known as a **crow's foot**.

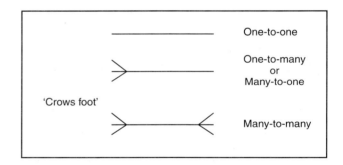

Figure 5.22 Relationship notation for ERD

One of the main reasons for undertaking data modelling is to identify any many-to-many relationships, and to take steps to resolve them. This is because it turns out that many-to-many relationships cannot be satisfactorily computerised. The solution is to introduce a new data entity which breaks the many-to-many relationship into two one-to-many relationships. This new data entity is often called an **allocation** or **link** entity. If referred to as a table, it is called an **intersection table**. In our example FUN event bookings ERD, in Figure 5.19, the many-to-many relationship between 'event' and 'venue' has been replaced by an entity called 'event/venue allocation' and two one-to-many relationship lines, one to the 'event' entity, and the other to the 'venue' entity. Notice that the allocation relationships are 'a venue has one or more event/venue allocations' and 'an event has one or more event/venue allocations'.

The second important aspect of a relationship is whether an occurrence of one data entity must be related to an occurrence of the other. A customer may book many events, and this indicates an **optional relationship** – a particular customer need not book any events at all. On the other hand, an event must be booked by one and only one customer, so this is a **mandatory relationship** from the 'event' to the 'customer' data entities: if there is an event, there must be a customer who has booked it. On the ERD, whether a relationship is optional or mandatory is shown by making the relationship line dashed or solid, as illustrated in Figure 5.23.

To summarise, the purpose of producing ERDs is to provide the clearest possible representation of the data entities and their relationships for a particular system. For this reason ERDs make a valuable contribution to the clarity of any systems analysis report.

If the system that is the subject of systems analysis involves a database, as is likely to be the case, the use of the ERD in the design of the database will be essential.

Chapter 6.2 shows how to make use of the ERD in designing your database.

Normalisation – first normal form

Normalisation is the process which ensures that data is held in a database in a way that has eliminated redundancy and

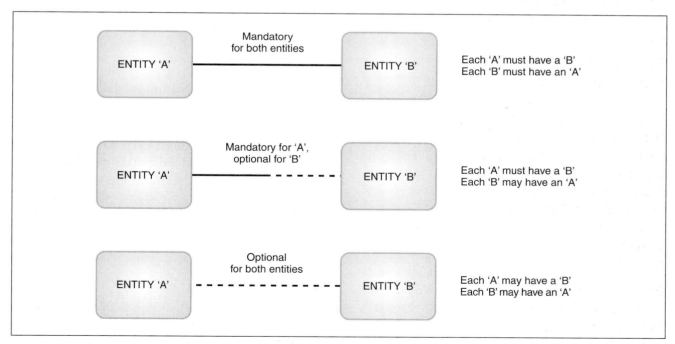

Figure 5.23 Relationship notation for ERD

achieved complete consistency, allowing efficient and accurate processing of the data. Normalisation is carried out by stages, arranging the data in a succession of **normal forms**, starting with **first normal form**. These next paragraphs introduce first normal form. The ideas are expanded in Chapter 6.3.

An important issue when developing the ERD is deciding whether a certain set of attributes defines one data entity, or whether the attributes would be better divided between two data entities. For example, a FUN event might involve some stage turns, such as a magician and a juggler. It would be understandable if, to begin with, you listed some of the attributes for the 'event' data entity as in Table 5.8.

```
EVENT
    Customer reference number
    Event reference number
    Event date
    Venue code
    Name of stage turn 1
    Duration of stage turn 1
    Cost of stage turn 1
    Name of stage turn 2
    Duration of stage turn 2
    Cost of stage turn 2
    Name of stage turn 3
    Duration of stage turn 3
    Cost of stage turn 3
```

Table 5.8 Attributes to one entity

Notice that the primary key of the data entity has been underlined, to follow a well-established notational convention, and that in this instance the primary key is a composite key.

However, the 'stage turn' comprises what is called a **repeating group** – a group of attributes which are repeated for each stage turn that might be booked. Whenever you find a repeating group, you need to extract that group of attributes from the data entity and create a new data entity using those attributes.

As you do so, you will also need to copy to the new data entity the primary key of the parent entity, and then to create the primary key of the new data entity by adding to the parent primary key a further attribute that will make the new composite key unique (Table 5.9).

```
EVENT
    Customer reference number
    Event reference number
    Event date
    Venue code
STAGE TURN
    Customer reference number
    Event reference number
    ST Name
    ST Duration
    ST Cost
```

Table 5.9 Attributes divided between two entities

We note that 'ST Name' is the new primary key for the stage turn, but we still need the composite primary key of the event because the stage turn provided for an event depends upon both the customer requirements and the make-up of the event of which it is part.

In this example, the repeating group 'stage turn name, stage turn duration, stage turn cost' have been removed from the 'event' entity and transferred to a new entity which we have called 'stage turn'. The primary key of the 'event' entity has been copied to the new 'stage turn' entity, and the primary key of the new entity has been created by adding a third attribute, 'ST name'.

The process of identifying a repeating group in the list of an entity's attributes, and of extracting those attributes to create a second entity with an appropriate primary key, is called **normalising** to **first normal form (1NF)**. In Chapter 6.3 you will find descriptions of routine normalisations that go to **second** and **third normal form**. Some complicated database applications, which we shall not be considering, may require that normalisation pass through to fourth, fifth, and sixth normal form.

The advantage of having your data in first normal form is that, at the least, you have identified a basic set of data entities for further analysis, design, and programming.

Data dictionary

A **data dictionary** is a record of all the data in the system. Each data entity, and each attribute, is listed and defined. Cross-references are provided between the data stores and data flows of the data flow diagrams, and the attributes and data entities, documented earlier.

Every data entity is listed, giving its name, a description, and a note of any aliases by which it may be known. For each data entity, its attributes are noted. Its primary key is generally indicated by underlining the attribute or attributes concerned, and each attribute that is a foreign key is

generally indicated by an asterisk, '*'. For example, the 'event' data entity for the FUN event bookings system might be entered in the data dictionary as shown in Table 5.10.

Every attribute is listed, giving its name, a description, a note of any aliases by which it may be known, its type, its size, and its maximum and minimum permitted values, or a list of its allowed values. The **type** of an attribute is its 'data type': integer, real, financial, string, date, time, or Boolean. The size of an attribute is generally expressed as the number of bytes which are needed to store the attribute. (Chapter 6 gives further details.) For example, Table 5.11 shows some attributes that might be found in the FUN events booking system.

Every data flow in the DFDs is listed and named. For each data flow, there is a cross-reference list of the data entities, or attributes of which it is composed.

Every data store in the DFDs is listed and named. For each data store, there is a cross-reference list of the data entities or attributes of which it is composed. It is usual to find that a data store simply corresponds to one or two data entities, and it may be useful to lay out the data stores entry as a cross-reference table (Table 5.12). Each data store is named as a column heading, each data entity is named as a row,

Name	Description	Aliases	Attributes
EVENT	Table of data relating to each booked event	Party, 'Do'	<u>Cust-ref-no</u> <u>Event-ref-no</u> Event description Event date Event type *Venue code *Salesperson code Price

Table 5.10 Data dictionary: data entities list

Name	Description	Aliases	Type	Size	Allowed values
Cust-ref-no	The unique reference number given to each customer	Customer code, Customer reference, Customer number	Integer	4	Min. 100,000, max. 890,000
Event type			String	9	'Birthday', 'Corporate', 'Wedding', 'Party', 'Other'
Event date	Date on which the event is due to take place	Party date	Date	4	No event may be booked more than 2 years in advance
Price	The amount quoted to the customer	Quotation value, Quote, Estimated price	Financial	8	

Table 5.11 Data dictionary: attributes list

and an 'X' is placed in the table where a particular entity is stored in a given data store. Such a table makes it easy to find out whether there is a data store that doesn't seem to involve a known data entity, and whether there is a data entity that doesn't seem to be stored in any data store.

Table 5.12 suggests that our analysis is incomplete: we have not yet defined a data entity for resources or the event calendar.

Requirements catalogue

Any systems analysis report for any processing application is likely to need a **requirements catalogue**. Its object is to display in a formal way the outputs to be provided by the system about to be implemented. The requirements catalogue is therefore a crucial part of the system documentation.

		Data store				
		Customer	Resource	Event booking	Event calendar	Venue
Entity	Customer	X				
	Event			X		
	Venue					X
	Event/venue allocation			X		

Table 5.12 Data dictionary: data entity/data store cross-reference

An example of a requirements catalogue is given in Chapter 3.2, which covers spreadsheet design. For each aspect of the proposed system there must be:

- a requirement identifier

- the name of the 'owner' of the requirement

- the priority, or importance, of the requirement

- a brief description of the requirement

- any non-functional component of the requirement

- a note of related requirements.

Try it out	The example in Chapter 3.2 relates to the requirements of the FUN spreadsheet. You should think about any other system you know about, such as the one that keeps records of borrowers using the school or college library. Work out who needs what information from the system, and build your own requirements catalogue for this system.

An understanding of the purpose and structure of a requirements catalogue is part of the assessment evidence you will have to provide for this unit.

Chapter 5.3 System specification and conclusion

This chapter covers the creation of the system specification for the proposed system, and introduces the evaluation of project risks, which are considered more fully in Appendix D. Together with the other study outcomes, these allow the team to arrive at a conclusion about the merit of going ahead with system design.

Provided that the team *do* see merit in going ahead, it is usual that there is commitment to implement the system from this point onwards, subject to scheduled reviews of progress.

The chapter is divided into two parts:

- system specification

- arriving at a conclusion.

System specification

A system specification comprises all the information resulting from the investigation, the feasibility study report, and the structured analysis with statements about the input and output needs of the system. You will need to be able to produce a simple system specification that comprises:

- a high-level (context view) DFD

- low-level DFDs

- an entity relationship diagram (in 1NF)

- a data dictionary

- process specifications

- input specifications

- output specifications

- details of resource implications.

The result of systems analysis is a document called the **system specification**. (Sometimes it is called a **requirements specification**, a **functional requirements specification**, or simply a **functional specification**). Its key purpose is to set out exactly what is required of the system to be developed. Following systems analysis is the stage of system design, where a specific solution is designed to meet the requirements expressed in the specification.

The system specification contains the eight components listed above. The input and output specifications are covered below; the remaining six components will already have been produced as a result of the investigation of the current system and of the feasibility study. During the work of the systems analysis study, these components are updated and expanded to form parts of the specification document. Table 5.13 lists the components of the system specification, the source of each, and the chapters of this book in which they are introduced.

The resource implications of the project were initially considered during the feasibility study to allow the cost-benefit analysis to be carried out. The project costings need to be reviewed at the end of the systems analysis stage, by which stage more is known about the proposed project, and new estimates of project budget and schedule devised. These revised budgets and schedules form part of the conclusions, discussed later in this chapter.

Input specifications

The inputs to the proposed system are conveniently derived from the context diagram. Each context diagram data flow is either an input to or an output from the

Component	Chapter	Page	Source
Context diagram	5.1, 5.2	201; 205	Feasibility study
Data flow diagrams	5.2	205	Investigation
Process specifications	5.2	207	Investigation
Entity-relationship diagram	5.2; also 6.2	213; 231	Investigation
Data dictionary	5.2	219	Investigation
Input specifications	5.3	222	Investigation
Output specifications	5.3	224	Investigation
Resource implications	5.1	200	Feasibility study (CBA)

Table 5.13 Components of the system specification

system, and it is a relatively simple matter to extract and list the data flows into the system. It is useful to produce a list which identifies, for each input data flow:

- the data source

- the data attributes

- the method(s) of data capture

- the nature and method(s) of validation and verification

- the data input form or screen layout(s).

Data source

Given each input data flow, the context diagram readily identifies the source of the data as that external entity which originates the data flow. For example, from the FUN context diagram of Figure 5.5 on page 202, we see that the customer is the source of a party booking.

Data attibutes

The composition of the input data must be specified, with reference to the data

attributes which are listed in the data dictionary. For example, a FUN party booking would probably comprise a 'customer address' whose attributes would include 'street', 'town', 'county', and 'postcode'.

Data capture

The next issue to consider is how the data is obtained or captured for entry into the system. There may be an existing form, such as an order form, whose data is to be keyed in. The required data may already exist in machine-readable form, such as an account number on the magnetic strip of a credit card. Or, the data may be entered as required by the operator or user of the system into an on-screen data-entry form. Of course, there may be a mix of capture types. In a supermarket checkout, for example, product barcodes are automatically read by a laser scanner, the operator presses a key to add up the costs of the transactions, and the customer's credit card is swiped through the card reader.

In our FUN party booking system, it is possible that the party booking from the customer arrives in the form of a letter. It is also likely that some customers will wish to make party bookings on the phone. In both cases, no 'standard' paper-based booking form has been filled in, so the data must be entered into an on-screen data-entry form.

One of the issues in deciding upon the most desirable pattern for data capture is to consider whether the data needs to be held separately from the computer system for a period of time, for legal or security reasons. If it does, it may be useful to have a paper-based form which is filled in, from which the data is then keyed into the system.

Validation and verification

The input usually needs to be checked, and this part of the input specification lays down the checks that should be made. The exact nature of the checks depends upon the characteristics of the input. At the least, we would turn to the data dictionary and, referring to the data attributes of the input data flow, note the type, size, and allowed values of the input data.

For example, according to the data dictionary prepared earlier for the FUN party booking system, the proposed party date would be checked to make sure it is no more than two years in advance. We could also make sure that it is not a date that has already passed.

Data-input form or screen layout

If a paper-based data-input form exists, then it is relatively easy to specify the matching input screen to be used when the data is keyed in, and often the layout and content of this screen require little attention. If a data-input form does not exist, then you must decide whether to write the data onto a paper-based form first, and then key it in to the system from that form; or to capture the data directly into the system for display on its screen.

In the first case, the paper input form needs to be specified. In the second case, the screen layout needs to be specified, and considerably more attention must be given to the correct placement of input fields, facilities to help the operator with unusual data possibilities, and the provision of lists from which the operator can pick particular values of data items.

In either case, the input form or screen layout should be cross-referenced to the list of data attributes specified earlier. This ensures that all the required data has in fact been considered, and that unnecessary data has been eliminated.

Output specifications

In a very similar way, the outputs from the proposed system are conveniently derived from the context diagram. It is a relatively simple matter to extract and list those data flows which constitute outputs from the system. It is useful to produce a list that identifies, for each output data flow:

- the data attributes
- the method(s) of data output
- the output screen layout(s) or printed layout(s).

Data attributes

The composition of the output data should be specified with reference to the data attributes listed in the data dictionary.

Data output methods

Output from the system will be one or other of these three kinds: displayed on a screen, printed in a report, or recorded as a machine-readable file.

In our FUN party booking system, the party booking confirmation is most likely to be a printed letter to the customer. It is also likely that the 'future capacity report' to the manager would be provided both as an on-screen display and as a printed report.

Again, one of the issues in deciding upon the form of data output is whether the data needs to be held separately from the computer system for a period of time. If not, an on-screen display may be sufficient.

Output report or screen layout

If there is an existing report form, or an output form such as a letter, then it is relatively easy to specify the required computer output report or screen layout. If no existing report or other form is available, then a good method of proceeding is to model the required report on something similar that does exist.

In either case, the screen or report layout should be cross-referenced to the data attributes mentioned earlier, both to ensure that nothing has been left out, and to ensure that unnecessary data has not been included.

Arriving at a conclusion: the business case

Resources

The hardware, software, and human resources needed for the implementation of the proposed project were estimated during the feasibility study, mentioned in Chapter 5.1 and discussed in detail in Appendix B. The cost-benefit analysis will have made use of these resource estimates. It will also have taken account of whatever constraints were foreseen at that stage.

At the completion of the systems analysis study, all these estimates will have been updated to reflect the fuller understanding of the project gained during systems analysis.

Try it out	Without going into detail, make notes on the factors you would consider in forming your estimates of the resources that would be required for the following.
	FUN proposes to install a PC in its catering department, in the corner premises which was previously a fish-and-chip shop. The purpose of the new system will be to run a stock-control application for all the items purchased for the catering department, allowing the production director, Sandra, to monitor catering stocks held, and all the receipts and issues of items.
	Apart from installing the new software, FUN will need to modify its procedures to enable the details of deliveries to be fed into the computer system, and to ensure that details of all catering issues are also available as input. There will have to be periodic checks to compare the physical stock in the store with the totals held in the PC's database.
	The catering manager will operate the stock-control system personally, having first been on a training course. The reports wanted from the system will have to be designed.

The management of the organisation for which the project is being evaluated will want to know the strength of the business case for going ahead with full implementation. The business case to be presented to the organisation must end with a clear recommendation, and must cover the following:

- the current proposal, including updated estimates of hardware, software, and personnel; any constraints; and the outline timetable for implementation, acceptance testing, and handover to the users.

- the expected project costs and the forecast expenditure profile, updated from the estimates prepared for the cost-benefit analysis during the feasibility study

- possible alternative solutions for meeting the requirements that were considered and rejected – the reasons for rejection should be explained

- the project benefits, updated and quantified in the way explained in Chapter 5.1 and Appendix B

- a cost-benefit analysis, carried out on the same basis as that in the feasibility study, using the techniques discussed in Appendix B

- a risk analysis of the proposed project, discussed below, and using the techniques given in Appendix D

- a statement of the effect that the outcome of the risk analysis should have on the cost-benefit analysis for the whole project

- the recommendations.

Risk analysis

All ICT development projects are at risk from many directions. The risks are especially acute for the development of bespoke software. The assessment of such risks, and their quantification, are crucial preliminaries to taking a decision on whether or not a given project should go ahead. Appendix D looks carefully at risk assessment.

The final recommendations of the systems analysis team on the strength of the business case for implementing the project will be strongly affected by the risk analysis.

Unit 5 Assessment

This assignment can be used as practice for the externally set assignment.

This assignment is based on the Festivities Unlimited, or FUN, case study described in the general Introduction on pages xiii and xiv at the front of the book.

Scenario

As part of its survey of possible organisations to take over or merge with, FUN decided to look at a business which hires out crockery, cutlery, folding chairs and tables, portable stoves and barbecues, cooking utensils, and small marquees. The business in question is called Catering Universal Product Supplies, or CUPS, and is based in Putney, just across the river from FUN.

At present CUPS makes no use of computers except for word-processing. FUN wants to be sure that if it joins with CUPS full use could be made of computers in the combined business. CUPS has agreed that FUN can make a cost-benefit analysis of computerising the CUPS operation to see whether computer working would be economically attractive.

CUPS hires out its items on a day rate which falls after the first three days; and charges for delivery at one rate for the first thirty kilometres of a return journey, falling to a lower rate beyond that distance. There are discounts for large orders and for prompt payment. Four office staff are employed to run this system and handle all the paperwork.

Your tasks

You have been asked to take charge of the investigation into the possible use of computers by CUPS. You must make plausible assumptions about the scale of the CUPS operation, about the charging scheme for the different types of item that CUPS hires out, and about the skills of the office staff, and their wages and other costs.

You must also make, and state, assumptions about the availability and cost of software to do the work that you think could be transferred to computer, and the cost of the minimum necessary computer equipment; and also about the cost of specifying, designing, building, documenting, and testing whatever bespoke software you think will be needed.

You must assess the cost and timing of any recruitment you feel will be necessary, and the cost of essential training.

You must work out the extent and timing of the savings and other benefits you expect to be available to CUPS as a result of adopting computer systems to replace the current manual systems.

Taking all your assumptions, you must set out a cost-benefit analysis, showing:

- annual and cumulative cash-flows of expenditure, the annual and cumulative value of the benefits, and the net differences; and the timing of break-even (ignoring interest on borrowed money, and discounting)

- the discounted cash-flow position at the end of year four (using the Excel DCF feature).

You must make a risk appraisal of the project, and give your recommendations to the FUN directors on whether or not conversion to computer working within CUPS would be cost-effective.

Database design

Unit 6 of this book, devoted to database design, is longer than the other units of the book. Students are, however, expected to allocate approximately the same amount of time and effort to each unit, so, in principle, Unit 6 itself is not larger or more demanding than the other five units. There are two reasons for this unit's length:

- Most modern business computer systems have at least some of their applications built around a database. It is therefore important that all aspects of database design are treated with thoroughness.

- The requirements of the Advanced VCE Specifications for Unit 6 include a large number of database topics, some of which are intangible or not intuitively obvious, and some of which are generally not explained accurately and carefully in the literature. We have therefore sought to apply rigour to the definitions and descriptions needed in the chapter, and to provide extensive examples, drawn from the case study, to illustrate all the points covered.

This unit contains eight chapters:

Chapter 6.1   Database concepts
Chapter 6.2   Logical data modelling
Chapter 6.3   Normalisation
Chapter 6.4   Relational database structures and construction
Chapter 6.5   Data entry forms
Chapter 6.6   Reports
Chapter 6.7   Database documentation and testing

A database is a homogenous data structure made up of one or more data files, or tables of data. You may come across the term *data warehouse*, meaning a structure consisting of one or more databases. Its characteristic is to present to the user an interface of the kind that would be presented by the database management system (DBMS) handling a single database.

The databases forming the data warehouse could be mounted on incompatible platforms, managed by different DBMS products, in various locations – yet, thanks to the data warehouse software, give the user the illusion that there is just a single database. This is a powerful facility.

Chapter 6.1 Database concepts

Data

Data comes in a very wide variety of forms, such as pictures, sounds, and text. Our discussion of databases will focus on structuring and organising the data which relates to a number of similar objects that a given information system must process.

Did you know?

We have pointed to several organisations that hold huge masses of data, but consider one category that has special storage requirements that are growing at rates that far exceed those of the ICT world as a whole.

Spare a thought for Internet service providers (ISPs). The more customers they attract, the more traffic they have to handle, and the more need they have for storage and back-up facilities. One ISP company, Planet Online, estimates that its storage needs, already large in order to serve 4 000 UK customers, are growing at more than 1500% a year. Web hosts have hefty demands for the storage of data, graphics, video, sound, and other information.

A database, that is, a collection of data, is often managed in a computer system by a **database management system (DBMS)**. The DBMS software usually provides facilities to add, delete, and generally organise the data. It is discussed more fully in Chapter 6.2.

The types of object about which we hold data are called **data entities**. In the following discussion we shall refer to 'data entities' simply as 'entities', but it is important to remember that there are other objects in the computer system that are also called 'entities', specifically the external entities of a data flow diagram (DFD), which are discussed in Unit 5, on page 205.

For example, a database for our FUN case study might involve the 'Customer', 'Event' and 'Supplier' entities or types of data object. It is usual to refer to an entity in the singular: a 'Customer' data entity, for example, rather than the 'Customers' entity.

Given an entity, there will normally be a number of **instances** or **occurrences** of that entity. For example, there would be numerous particular FUN customers, there would be a number of specific forthcoming events to be arranged, and there would be various suppliers who would be involved in the events.

In our use of the term 'entity' in the analysis and design of a database, we shall assume that the abstract object we call an entity in fact stands for all the *instances* of that entity in the system.

The particular items of data held for an entity are known as the **attributes** of that entity. For example, the 'Customer' entity would have attributes of 'First name', 'Surname', and 'Phone number'.

An attribute is the smallest possible item of data, and is regarded as **atomic**. Consider a customer's address, for example, such as '1 The Railway Arches, Littlefen, LF16 6QW'. This address contains a number of attributes: 'House number', 'Street', 'Town', and 'Postcode', for example. An 'address' in this analysis is thus *not* an attribute, because it can be divided into smaller items of atomic data.

Another way of talking about data involves files, records, and fields. We often talk about a **file** of records, such as the file of customer records, or the file of forthcoming events. The file is almost always a file for a given entity, such as 'Customer'. A file contains **records**, such that there is one record for what we have called an instance or occurrence of that entity, such as a customer. Each record contains a number of **fields** of information, and these fields are what we have been calling attributes. A database can be thought of as consisting of a number of files; that is, a database consists of a number of entities.

There is yet a third way of talking about data, involving tables, rows, and columns. A **table** of data usually involves the data for a particular data entity, and so is somewhat similar to a file of data. The **rows** of the table correspond to the records of a file, where each row contains the data relevant to a particular instance of the data concerned. Finally, each **column** of the table corresponds to a field or attribute. Figure 6.1 illustrates the terminology.

Criteria for entities

For an entity to be sensibly part of a database or held as a computer file, it must usually meet the following criteria.

- The data entity must be *of interest* or *of use* to the information system. It should be obvious that there is no point in

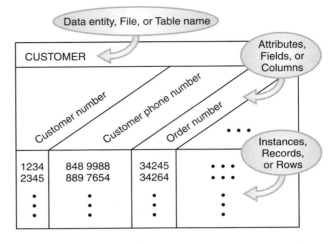

Figure 6.1 Ways of referring to database data

storing data that will never be called for. For example, a database constructed for our FUN case study might hold data about customers, events, and suppliers, but would not hold data about satellites orbiting in space.

- If the entity is to form part of a database, there should be *a number of instances* of the entity about which data is to be gathered and stored. A database would not normally be constructed to hold data about just one instance of an entity.

- An entity must have *a number of attributes*. There must be a number of items of data which it is sensible to hold

Try it out	Wal-Mart
	US giant and the world's largest retailer, Wal-Mart, is flexing its muscles in Europe. It has acquired the British chain ASDA. Wal-Mart has a history of investing vigorously in computer technology and now boasts impressive operating statistics. It runs the world's biggest retail database to underpin the company's delivery systems, allowing the business to replenish any of its stores within 24 hours. That is a good deal more promptly than its main competitors can do the same job.
	As a group, think about the task of fulfilling an order from one of Wal-Mart's stores. Limit your thoughts to one specific product line held at all three of the warehouses which together serve, say, 100 stores. What tables would be used in the database? What attributes would each record hold? How do you think the delivery is organised to allow the smoothest path from warehouse to store?

about a given entity. If a potential entity seems to have only one attribute, it is unlikely to be a true entity.

- Each instance or occurrence of an entity must be *uniquely identifiable*. Every instance must be labelled in a way that makes it unique or different from every other instance.

If it is a record in a computer system, each instance must be unique so that it can be retrieved, otherwise the computer would not be able to locate the required data. Suppose, for example, that a corporate customer called 'Exploits International' asks FUN to arrange its monthly sales conference on the first Monday of every month for the next year. In a sense, these are all instances of the 'same' event, a monthly sales conference. In order to store these events in a database, however, each event must be distinguishable from every other event, and so each instance must be distinguished by the month in which it occurs, such as the 'June monthly sales conference', and probably also by the customer for the event, so it would be the 'Exploits International June monthly sales conference', to make it different, for example, from the 'Impex June monthly sales conference'.

The 'label' that makes an instance of an entity uniquely identifiable is called a **key**. Much of the work of the database designer involves ensuring that each entity has a well-constructed key.

- The data must in some sense be *permanent*, not temporary or transient. A database would only be constructed to hold data entities whose attributes would be needed for a significant period of time and which would probably need to be accessed often over that period.

Did you know?

One of the largest and most notable databases in the world is operated by the Mormons at Salt Lake City, Utah, in the United States. The Mormons are a religious sect founded in 1830, and properly known as 'The Church of Jesus Christ of the Latter-day Saints'. For many years they have accumulated and stored details of the family trees of people all over the world, and are consequently consulted by those engaged in genealogy research – whether for social and recreational purposes, or in the pursuit of solutions to crime.

Entities and relationships

The terminology of *entities*, *instances* and *attributes* is generally used by software engineers during the analysis and design of larger systems. The terminology of *files*, *records* and *fields* is commonly used by analyst/programmers during the development of smaller systems for which a database is not used. The terminology of *tables*, *rows* and *columns* is generally used by database designers and implementers where the system under development is overwhelmingly a database type of system. We shall use all these terms freely; sometimes mixing them, and referring, for example, to tables whose instances have particular fields.

The data for a given information system may be held in a database or a set of computer files. In a database, as distinct from a simple set of files, we explicitly identify the **relationships** between the entities, and much of the work of a database designer is focused upon these relationships.

A very simple FUN database, for example, might involve the entities of 'Customer', 'Event', and 'Supplier', such that there were relationships between the 'Customer' and the 'Event' entities, and between the 'Event' and the 'Supplier' entities. This is because an event involves a customer, and an event involves one or more suppliers. The entities and their relationships are diagrammed in a **logical data structure** or **entity relationship diagram (ERD)**; this type of diagram is introduced in Chapter 6.2.

Try it out	In pairs or groups, see if you can arrange to visit an organisation that operates a computer database. Ask questions about the entities that underlie the database, and about the relationships between them. In this way, studying a real-life example of a working database, you will start to get a feel for the preliminary steps to be taken in designing a database. Also the differences between a database and a set of files holding the same data will become clear.

Attributes

The data attributes, or data fields, that make up a data record, or an instance of an entity, come in a variety of types and formats.

Data types

An attribute must be one of the following data types: *text* or *string*; *numeric*; *date*; *time*; *currency*; or *logical*. It is necessary to identify the data type of an attribute so that the computer system can store and process the data appropriately.

Text or string

A **text or string** data type consists of a sequence of characters. For example, a 'Surname' attribute would be a text data type, as might be the 'Event description'. Text would be held in the computer as a number of bytes, usually one character per byte. Operations applicable to text would include joining two strings together to make one string, an operation called **concatenation**, and extracting a sub-string from a given larger string.

Numeric

A **numeric** data type is what we would call a number; when printed out, this usually consists of the digits 0 to 9 as well as the characters '+', '−' and '.' (decimal point). In the computer, though unseen by the user, a numeric data type would usually be held not as a string of digits, but as a binary number in one, two, four, or eight bytes. This format allows arithmetic and mathematical calculations to be readily performed on the data.

A number may be one of two data types, **integer** or **real**. An integer number is a 'whole' number without any decimal point or fractional part, and is held exactly within a certain limited range of values. A *short integer* would be held in one byte, and has the range of positive values 0 to 255, reflecting the 256 different ways in which the eight bits in the byte can be arranged. A *'normal'* integer would be held in two bytes, giving a range of signed values −32768 to +32767, where one of the 16 bits is used to denote the positive or negative value of the remaining bits. A *'long'* integer would be held in four bytes, allowing numbers up to about two billion.

A *'real'* number, sometimes known as a **floating point** number, is a decimal number, held in either four bytes in **'standard'** precision or eight bytes in **'double'** precision. A double precision real numeric, also called a *'long real'*, offers up to 15 significant digits of accuracy for numbers as large as 10 to the power 307.

Depending upon the database management software, a numeric data type could be declared to be an **auto-incrementing** numeric. Such a data type is managed by the DBMS. For every new instance in which it appears, it is automatically set to the next number in the sequence.

Date and time

Date and **time** data types would, when printed out, be shown as digits and certain characters, such as '10 Jan 2001' or '10:24 a.m.' In the computer, these data types would be held as binary numbers. A date might be represented, though not seen by the user, as the number of days since 1st January 1900, for example, while a time could be held as the number of seconds since midnight. Operations on dates or times are restricted to simple addition and subtraction.

Currency

A **currency** data type is a number which is held in the computer in such a way that the quantity is exact. In contrast, a numeric data type usually has a limited accuracy: this is not a problem for most ordinary calculations when the data needs only to be accurate to, say, four or six significant digits. In certain business applications, however, the pounds and pence, and other currency amounts, must add up exactly; approximate results are not acceptable. In these cases, the FUN 'Event cost' attribute, for example, would be a currency data type. Operations on currency data types essentially involve four-function arithmetic – addition, subtraction, multiplication, and division.

Logical

A **logical** data type is used where an attribute has the values 'True' or 'False'. For example, there might be an attribute 'First time customer' that would be a logical, or **Boolean,** data type. The main operators available for logical data types are NOT, AND, and OR.

Data formats

A particular data type may be printed or displayed in a variety of formats, though the data is held and processed in the computer in just one standard binary representation.

- Text could be formatted to be shown all in lower case, for example, or all in upper case. It could be formatted to show only the first specified number of characters in a string. It could also be formatted to be shown in a certain colour, or in bold or italic; and there are other choices that could be made.

- Numeric data types may be displayed in formats in which only a specified number of decimal places are shown, where the '+' sign is always placed in front of a positive number, where leading zeroes are always displayed, and so on.

- Dates and times may be shown in a wide variety of formats. The order of the day, month, and year may be chosen, as may the number of digits in the year; the punctuation between the date components; whether a 12-hour or 24-hour clock, the punctuation between the time elements; and other options.

- Currency data types generally offer formats which allow you to specify the currency symbol and its placement before or after the digits, whether negative values should be shown in parentheses, whether there should be leading '*' to fill up blank spaces to the left of the amount, and so on.

Data verification

Associated with each data type are certain kinds of verification which the database system should allow you to implement.

Text data could be checked and restricted to a specified number of characters, for example. Certain characters could be excluded from permitted input, such as '$' or '%'.

Numeric data could be restricted to fall between certain values, while dates and times could be restricted to certain ranges. Data verification is discussed further in Chapter 6.7.

Chapter 6.2 Logical data modelling

In Chapter 6.1, we introduced the concepts of 'entity' and 'attribute'. We now need to consider how we are to identify uniquely the instances of an entity by the use of a **key** attribute.

Keys

Each row of a table must be unique. In general, at least one column, or *combination* of columns, of the table must hold values that are different for every row. Some tables may have a number of columns, each of which has unique values for each row.

Where a table has a number of columns whose values are different for each row, these columns are called **candidate keys**. One column or one combination of columns is then chosen as the **primary key**, and the other candidate keys are then known as **alternate keys**. For example, the 'Suppliers' table in a FUN database might have columns labelled 'Supplier ID', 'Supplier Postcode', 'Supplier VAT Number', and 'Supplier Company Registration Number'. It is almost certain that each of these columns contains values that are unique to a given supplier, and so each column would be a candidate key. Because the 'Supplier ID' is a unique identification given to the supplier by FUN, it is likely that this would be designated the primary key, and the other columns would become alternate keys.

Where just one column provides a key, the key is said to be a **simple key**: it consists of one attribute. Where two or more columns must be combined into a key in order to yield a uniquely identifiable row, the key is said to be a **composite key**: it consists of a number of attributes combined together.

For example, an 'Events' table in a FUN database would have many rows relating to various events: a particular event would probably have to be uniquely identified by a combination of customer name and event date as its composite key. Because it is always easier to work with a simple key than with a composite key, a database designer would be inclined to create an 'Event ID' attribute for each event and make that attribute the primary key for the 'Event' table.

Where a table happens to have a column, or combination of columns, that is also the primary key of *another* table, that column or combination of columns is called a **foreign key**. For example, consider an 'Event' table whose primary key was 'Event ID', and which had a column that was 'Customer Name' or 'Customer ID'. This column would be a foreign key in the 'Event' table, because 'Customer Name' or 'Customer ID' would be the primary key of the 'Customer' table. In this way, the 'Event' table and the 'Customer' table are related by a common column.

Notice that a table might have a composite primary key such that one or other of the composite columns was also a primary key of another table. In this case, the relevant column could also be thought of as a foreign key, but it is not usually referred to as such. This is because the column is part of the key of the current table, and confusion might arise if it were referred to as a foreign key as well.

For example, consider an 'Event' table whose primary key was a composite key

235

comprising 'Customer ID' and a column called 'Event Date'. The column 'Customer ID' is also the primary key in the 'Customer' table, and in this way the 'Event' table and the 'Customer' table are again related by a common column.

We are now in a position to say more clearly what we mean when we say there is a **relationship** between two entities or two tables: two *tables* are related by having one or more *columns* in common, and two *entities* are related by having one or more *attributes* in common, where the column or attribute is a key or part of a key in either or both tables or entities. The discussion in this chapter and in Chapter 6.3 illustrates these points with diagrams.

Try it out	As a group, try to identify at least two possible applications for computer databases. Don't worry about whether or not the transfer from the present systems would be cost-effective: just look for examples, such as the newspaper delivery service operated by your local newsagent, with its routes, delivery boys and girls, and range of newspaper titles.
	Make lists of the entities, attributes, and relationships.

First draft logical data model

The first step in the design of a database, and also one of the first steps in the design of any information system, is the drafting of a **logical data model** (LDM). The LDM comprises two components: a **data dictionary** (DD), and an **entity-relationship diagram** (ERD).

The data dictionary component of the LDM identifies all the data entities of the system and all the attributes of each entity, together with the data type of each attribute, its format, its range of values or size, any validation rules that are applicable, and any **aliases**, or alternative names, by which any attribute or entity may be known. The DD is discussed more fully in Chapter 5.2.

An entity-relationship diagram is a diagram that shows the data entities of the system and the relationships between them, using a particular notation. The ERD is also discussed in Chapter 5.2.

? Did you know?

In the 1960s IBM produced a very expensive computer called the IBM 3090, commonly known as 'STRETCH'. It had a number of novel features in its hardware and software, to help it achieve design objectives which included fast processing for scientific applications and rapid access to its main file of data. The data was held in words each of 64 bits so as to provide the great precision needed for the application; and it was held on a single disk unit with 32 recording surfaces.

To read or write a word of data a comb of 32 read-write heads would be moved over the required cylinder of tracks, and two data bits transferred to or from each surface. Forty years on such an arrangement seems utterly bizarre, though at the time it was seen as a pioneering breakthrough. Alas, though, IBM sold only 14 of these machines.

Entity relationship diagram (ERD)

A data entity is shown on an ERD as a labelled rounded box, as illustrated in Figure 6.2.

Figure 6.2 Data entity notation for an ERD

A relationship between two entities is shown by a *line*. Figure 6.3 illustrates two entities joined by a relationship line. A relationship is shown between two entities if they have one or more attributes in common, where the common attribute is a key or part of a key for one or both entities.

The nature of a relationship between two entities may take a number of forms. We will be concerned here with one of these

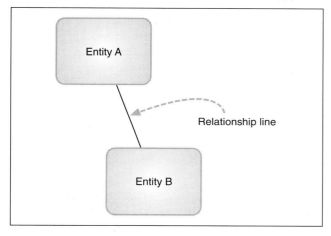

Figure 6.3 Relationship line in an ERD

forms, known as the **degree** of the relationship, which is most easily explained by way of an example. Consider a lending library with a computerised database of library members and of library books. A library member could borrow a number of books, but a book could only be borrowed at any one time by one member. The key concept here is that the

relationship between member and book is **'one to many'** – one member can borrow many books – and this is what is meant by the *degree* of the relationship. A 'one to many' relationship is often written as '1:m'.

Now consider a library database which holds details of the books in the library, and of the authors of those books. A particular author could be the author of a number of books, and a particular book could be written by more than one author. The degree of the relationship between author and book is 'many to many', and could be written as '**m:n**'. The third kind of relationship degree is 'one to one'. Suppose our library had a rule that restricted members to being able to borrow only one book at any one time. In this case, the degree of the relationship between a member and a book would be 'one to one', written as '1:1'.

Commentary

It is sometimes suggested that each relationship be named or labelled to identify its nature, and this may be useful in some circumstances. In general, however, we do not feel such a practice is a necessary step in the development of an ERD or of the data dictionary component of the LDM. Where a relationship is to be named, this is generally done by providing short phrases to describe the nature of the relationship at each end of the relationship line. In the example of the lending library, the relationship between a member and a book may be named at one end as 'borrow', and at the other end as 'borrowed by': a member may 'borrow' a book, and a book may be 'borrowed by' a member.

On the ERD, the way in which the relationship line is terminated at either data entity shows the degree of the relationship. Figure 6.4 illustrates the terminating symbol, called a **crow's foot**, which shows that the relationship has a 'many' component. The crow's foot is placed on that data entity of which there may be 'many'. If the relationship has a 'one' component, then there is no crow's foot, just a straight line placed on that data entity of which there may only be 'one'.

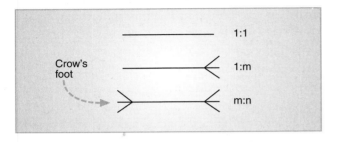

Figure 6.4 Relationship degree

A simple example of an ERD for a FUN database might show the entities of 'Customer', 'Event' and 'Supplier', and the relationships between them, as illustrated in Figure 6.5.

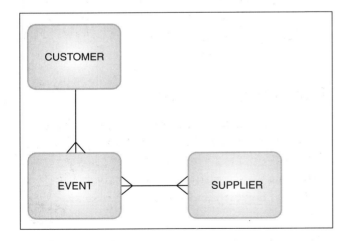

Figure 6.5 Simple first draft ERD

We would read the relationships shown in this ERD as follows. First, there is a relationship between a customer and an event. The relationship is of degree 'one to many', or '1:m', where a particular customer may have one or more events booked, while a specific event is booked by one and only one customer. Secondly, there is a relationship between an event and a supplier, of degree 'many to many', or 'm:n'. This means that a specific event may involve one or more suppliers, and a given supplier may be involved in one or more events.

Commentary

Another aspect of the relationship between two data entities concerns what is called the **optionality** of the relationship. Given a FUN customer, for example, we may note that the customer may have an event booked, or he or she may not. From the point of view of a customer, the existence of an event is **optional**. On the other hand, given a specific booked event, we may note that there *must* be a customer for that event. From the point of view of an event, the existence of a customer is **mandatory**. We cannot sensibly conceive of the booking of an event without also knowing who the customer is. The software that manages a database will always need to know whether, given an instance of entity A, there must always be an associated instance of entity B; or whether there may or may not be an instance of entity B.

This aspect of a relationship between two entities is discussed in more detail later in this chapter, dealing with the implementation of a database in a database management system such as Access.

Resolving m:n and 1:1 relationships

An ERD is generally developed in a number of stages over a period of time. The ERD we have developed here is a 'first draft' ERD, and it is generally permitted for a first draft ERD to have relationships with degrees both of 1:1 and of m:n, as well as the more common 1:m relationships. However, by the time the final ERD is developed, it is necessary that *all* m:n relationships are **resolved** into two 1:m relationships, and that 1:1 relationships are minimised.

The reason that an m:n relationship is undesirable in the final ERD is that it causes difficulties when the time comes to construct a database which is based on that data model. An m:n relationship implies that each of the entities involved must have an array of attributes which store the many keys to the other entity. For example, the 'Event' entity would have to store an indeterminate number of supplier IDs; and the 'Supplier' entity would have to have an array of attributes to store an indeterminate number of event IDs. This is not a manageable situation for database management software.

An m:n relationship is usually easily resolved by creating a new entity, called a

link entity. The link entity *separates* the two entities involved in the m:n relationship, such that these two entities each have a 1:m relationship to the link entity. The resolution for our first draft FUN ERD is illustrated in Figure 6.6.

A 1:1 relationship is problematic for a rather different reason. Where two entities are in a 1:1 relationship, the question arises as to why they need to be distinct. Sometimes further analysis reveals that what originally seemed to be two different entities are in fact one and the same; or that the data items being held in the one entity could just as easily be held in the other, simplifying the data model by reducing the entity count.

Of course, there may be good reasons why the two entities in a 1:1 relationship need to be distinct, in which case such a relationship would be allowed to remain.

Identifying the necessary entities, identifying their primary keys, and resolving both m:n and 1:1 relationships in a more structured and clearer manner, are the topics of Chapter 6.3, on relational data analysis and normalisation.

Drawing an ERD

There are a few comments to make about drawing an ERD. The first is fairly obvious: if possible, the ERD should be drawn so that relationship lines do not cross. This makes the diagram clearer and easier to read.

The second point is that, if possible, the entities should be arranged so that all relationship lines have their '1' end higher up the page than their 'm' end. Again, this is to aid the reader's quick understanding of the diagram. The arrangement is usually said to produce an ERD 'without dead

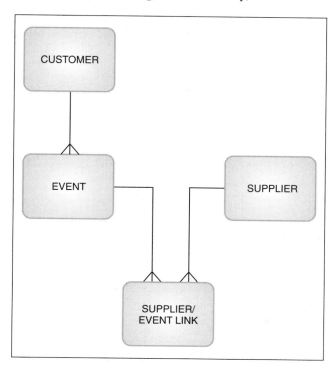

Figure 6.6 Second draft ERD with link entity

crows'! Figure 6.7 illustrates an ERD with undesirable dead crows – that is, where the relationship lines have their '1' end lower on the page than their 'm' end.

The reason for avoiding dead crows is that the entity at the '1' end of the 1:m relationship is, in some sense, usually the more important entity or the more permanent entity; and the entity at the 'm' end is usually likely to be derived from it. Often, the entity at the '1' end is called the **master**, and the entity at the 'm' end is called the **detail**. Sometimes the master entity is called the **parent** entity, and the detail entity is called the **child** entity. Given this situation, it is easier to read and understand the ERD from top to bottom if the master or parent entities are towards the top of the page, and the detail or child entities are nearer the bottom. The entities are thus arranged in a hierarchy.

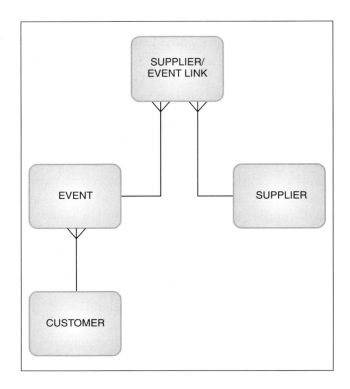

Figure 6.7 Poorly drawn ERD with 'dead crows'

Chapter 6.3 Normalisation

Authors' note

You will probably notice differences between the words used to describe normalisation in the text that follows and the way **normalisation** is defined in the AVCE Specifications which you may have downloaded.

You should not allow these differences to trouble you. They arise because we have chosen to use the words that we believe provide a full and rigorous interpretation of the issues, and these words are also used widely in education and business.

Refining the data model

In Chapter 6.2 we constructed a 'first draft' logical data model (LDM) of the data to be held in our application's database. The LDM consists of a data dictionary, and an entity-relationship diagram. The concepts of DD, ERD, and database keys were introduced in Chapter 5.2.

The data dictionary lists all the data entities of the system, and lists the attributes of each. One or more attributes of a data entity comprise its **primary key**. These are identified, along with any **foreign keys**. Foreign keys are the attributes which happen to be keys of other data entities. For each attribute, the DD would note its data type, its format, and any validation rules that were applicable.

The ERD shows all the data entities of the system and the relationships between them. Two data entities have a relationship if they have a key attribute in common, and the degree of the relationship is identified as 1:1, 1:m, or m:n.

While the first draft LDM was based on an initial round of investigation and analysis, the final data model needs to be based on a more formal and more rigorous analysis of the data. This rigorous and formal analysis is called **relational data analysis (RDA)**, and involves a technique of data analysis called **normalisation**. Normalisation can be carried out to a variety of depths known as **normal forms**. Chapter 5.2 introduced the concept of normalisation, and discussed normalisation to first normal form.

The effect of normalising the data making up a database is to ensure that the resulting database is consistent and is as free from error as possible. It also ensures that the database will have what is called **referential integrity** – that is, that it will remain error-free and robust when data is added, changed, or deleted.

The essence of ensuring referential integrity is the elimination, as far as possible, of *duplicate* data. This process is called **eliminating redundancy**. Amongst other matters, this means having data items stored once only, in a single appropriate table, and having these data items accessed as necessary through a well-defined primary key.

We shall analyse our data using the first three forms of normalisation to arrive at what is called **third normal form**. We shall start with un-normalised data, and proceed to normalise the data to first, second, and finally third normal form.

Source of data to normalise

While normalisation can be carried out on any chosen set of data, the resulting tables and logical data model are particular to that set of data. It is therefore usual to normalise a number of particular sets of data for a computer system, and then to integrate the various resulting tables and logical data models into one overall final data model. The best place to find sets of data to normalise in any system is to look at the inputs to, or outputs from, the system.

We shall use our FUN example of an events database, and normalise one of the forms or sheets currently used by FUN to plan an event. This sheet is shown in Figure 6.8.

Festivities Unlimited
Event Planning Form

Event ID _____   Event date _____

Event size (persons) _____   Event type _____

Event components

Component   Cost   Duration

_____   _____   _____

_____   _____   _____

_____   _____   _____

_____   _____   _____

Customer

Customer ID _____   Name _____

Phone _____   E-mail _____

Suppliers

Supplier ID   Contact name

_____   _____

_____   _____

_____   _____

Figure 6.8 FUN event planning sheet

This event planning sheet is used by FUN staff to identify the components of the

event concerned – such as 'Pre-dinner drinks', 'Dinner', and 'Disco' – and to identify any external suppliers that may be required by the event.

During the analysis and design stages of any computer system, a number of different forms, data entry sheets, or reports would be normalised in order to obtain as complete a logical data model as possible.

Un-normalised form

The first step in normalising a set of data is to construct a list of the attributes of that data set. This list of attributes is constructed in a particular way, and is known as the **un-normalised form (UNF)**. It is illustrated in Figure 6.9. UNF is the listing of all attributes to be normalised, ensuring that each attribute is atomic.

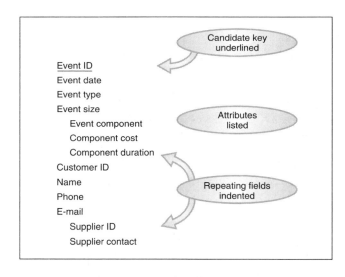

Figure 6.9 UNF for the FUN event planning sheet

When listing the attributes, care should be taken to ensure that these are atomic – that is, that no one attribute can sensibly be broken down into other attributes.

For most data sets, certain of the attributes in the data set 'repeat': that is, a particular attribute may occur a number of times in the data set. For example, provision is made on the FUN event planning sheet for listing up to three suppliers, noting the 'Supplier ID' of each, and the name of the person at that supplier who is the first point of contact, the 'Supplier contact'. This **group of repeating attributes** must be indented when listed, to help with the next stage of normalisation.

Lastly, a **candidate key** should be selected for the UNF list. This key should be underlined, and by convention it is placed at the top of the list.

We are now ready to begin the process of normalisation. This process entails progressing through the forms of normalisation, one at a time, up to third normal form.

Commentary

This concept of un-normalised data seems, in the abstract, to be extraordinarily boring! But as soon as you have real data before you it will come to life. If you look, for example, at the vehicles in your school or college car park, you will quickly realise that the makes and models are unlikely to be unique, but that the registration marks on the number plates *are* unique.

First normal form

The UNF list of attributes, with the candidate key identified is, in fact, a crude table which we now refine. When we refine the UNF table to **first normal form** (**1NF**), we move all repeating groups of attributes into separate tables, and give each new table an appropriate key.

1NF is the separation of repeating groups.

Put simply, the reason for moving repeating groups of attributes into separate tables is that in a well-designed database no attribute appears more than once in a data record. If a record seems to require an attribute or group of attributes to be repeated, there are three immediate difficulties.

- First, there is the problem of exactly how many repeating attributes should be allowed in the record – usually it is impossible for a record to store an indefinite number of attributes.

- Second, there is the problem of access to individual instances of the repeated data – direct individual access to just part of a record is usually impossible.

- Third, there is the issue of duplication of data.

These difficulties are discussed by way of examples below.

To refine the UNF to a 1NF set of tables, we begin by copying out the UNF table to make the first 1NF table, starting with the candidate key.

At the point where we encounter a repeating group of attributes, we move the repeating group into a new, separate, table. For this new table, we construct its key by first copying the candidate key from the UNF table, and then identifying a *second* attribute of the new table to combine with it to form a *composite* key. It is sometimes necessary to identify and combine a third and even a fourth attribute in order to ensure the uniqueness of the key for each row of the table. By convention, the components of the key are all underlined.

Having moved a repeating group of attributes to a new table, we resume copying out the rest of the UNF attributes to the first 1NF table until there are no further attributes or until we encounter another group of repeating attributes. In this latter case, we again move the repeating group to its own new table.

Figure 6.10 illustrates the creation of the 1NF tables from the UNF table for our FUN event planning sheet.

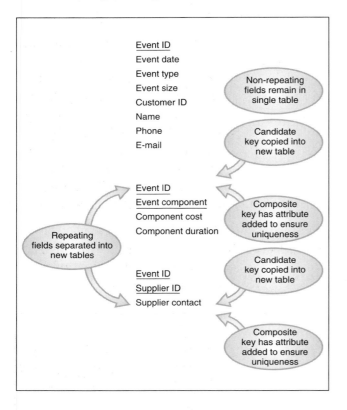

Figure 6.10 1NF for the FUN event planning sheet

As a result of moving the repeating groups of attributes, we have created three tables in 1NF, of which two are *new* tables. In the first new table, we have taken the repeating group of attributes to do with the event components, and have given this table a composite key of 'Event ID, Event component'. In the second new table, we have the repeating group of supplier attributes with a composite key of 'Event ID, Supplier ID'.

All the other, non-repeating attributes have been left in the first table.

What has 1NF achieved for the FUN event planning data? Consider the supplier attributes in this data, 'Supplier ID' and 'Supplier contact'. If we had *not* moved the supplier details into a separate table, we would have been required to keep these details with the 'Event' record, and the difficulties we mentioned earlier would immediately have arisen, namely:

- First, how many suppliers would we have to allow in the 'Event' record? Although the planning sheet shows room for three suppliers, a specific large event could well have many more. Would we have to reserve space in the 'Event' record for, say, up to 10 suppliers? What would happen if, for some unusual event, 11 suppliers were involved? Yet, most of the smaller FUN events would have no outside suppliers involved at all, and so we have significant waste of space in the database, reserving storage unnecessarily for up to 10 suppliers for every event. When supplier attributes are separated into a separate table, these problems disappear. We do not have to make space in the 'Event' record for these details; instead we keep supplier records in a separate table, which holds as many supplier contacts as we need.

- Second, how would we find out the events for which a given supplier was involved? We would have to read the whole 'Event' table, record by record, looking in each 'Event' record for a specific supplier ID; a somewhat laborious process. By separating out the supplier attributes, we can easily look up all the records of a particular supplier in the new table and identify the events in which that supplier is involved.

- Third, the same details of the supplier ID and contact name would be repeatedly duplicated in the various 'Event' records. While there might be a moderate penalty paid in storage requirements for this duplication, there is a more significant threat to database security, which is discussed in the following paragraphs on *second normal form*.

Second normal form

To refine the 1NF tables to **second normal form (2NF)**, we consider all tables with composite keys, and move into separate tables any attributes that do not depend upon the *whole* of the composite key, but only upon one or other *part* of the composite. The key to the new table is just that part of the composite key on which the attributes of the table depend.

When we ask whether an attribute depends upon a part of a key or on the whole key, we are really asking whether that attribute would change its value if *any part* of the key changed its value; or whether the attribute would only change its value when a *certain part* of the key changed, and not when some other part of the key changed. Examples of such dependency are discussed below when we take the FUN event planning data to 2NF.

The reason for creating separate tables for attributes that depend only upon part of a key is that there would otherwise be duplicated data in tables. Holding duplicated data usually causes only a small problem from the point of view of needing enough storage space, but it presents a much more serious problem from the point of view of ensuring that the database is error-free, secure, and robust. Again, examples are discussed below in the context of the FUN event planning data.

2NF is the separation of part-key dependencies.

To refine the 1NF set to a 2NF set of tables we begin by copying out the 1NF tables. The first table is copied out in full: it has a simple key, not a composite key, and so is not relevant to the 2NF procedures. The remaining tables each have composite keys, and are therefore subject to the 2NF refinements. For each such table, we begin by copying its composite key, and then consider each attribute of the table in turn.

For each attribute of a table with a composite key, we ask whether the attribute depends upon the *whole* composite key, or upon only one or other *part* of the composite key. If the attribute depends upon the whole of the key, it is copied over into the table headed by that composite key. On the other hand, if the attribute depends upon just a part of the composite key, we move the attribute into a *new* table, whose key is just the relevant part of the composite key.

Figure 6.11 illustrates the result of the 2NF procedure when applied to the 1NF tables of the FUN event planning data.

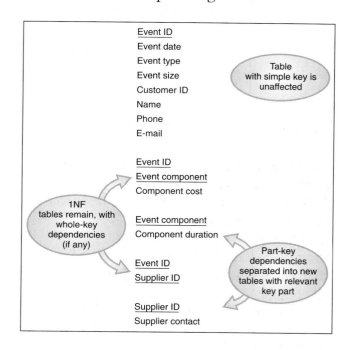

Figure 6.11 2NF for the FUN event planning sheet

The 1NF table involving the attributes 'Event ID', 'Event component', 'Component cost', and 'Component duration' has been separated into two tables. The 1NF table remains with the attributes 'Event ID', 'Event component', and 'Component cost', while 'Component duration' has been moved into a new table whose key is 'Event component'.

The reasoning was as follows. In following the 2NF procedure, we first copied out the composite key of the 1NF table 'Event ID', 'Event component', and then looked at the first attribute of this 1NF table, 'Component cost', to see whether it depended on only part of the composite key. The composite key has two parts, 'Event ID', and 'Event component'. Suppose, for instance, that the 'Event ID' part of the key changed: would the component cost change? Yes; if the component was 'Dinner', for example, this might cost £200 for an event called, say, ID 347, but might cost £1000 for event ID 348, probably because the two events were of different sizes.

Suppose that the 'Event component' part of the key changed: would the component cost then change? Yes; if the component changed from 'Dinner' to 'Disco', for example, there would be a change in the cost of that component. So the attribute 'Component cost' depends upon the whole of the composite key – that is, it depends upon all parts of the key – and it is therefore copied over into the same table as that composite key.

Then we consider the second attribute, 'Component duration', and ask whether this depends only upon part of the key.

To make the point here, let us imagine that FUN organises its events so that, for example, dinner always takes 2 hours; pre-dinner drinks always take 1 hour; and a disco is always provided for 3 hours. In such circumstances, what happens to the component duration if we change the event ID – would the component duration change? No; if the component was 'Dinner', for example, for both event 347 and event 348, the component duration would remain the same, 2 hours regardless of the event.

But what happens to the component duration if we change the 'Event component' from dinner, say, to pre-dinner drinks? Then the component duration certainly does change, from 2 hours to 1 hour. We have thus established that the attribute 'Component duration' depends only upon 'Event component', and not at all upon 'Event ID' – that is, it depends only upon one part of the composite key, and not upon any other parts. In this case, we create a new table with a key of 'Event component', and move 'Component duration' into this new table.

The 1NF table involving 'Event ID', 'Supplier ID' and 'Supplier contact' has been separated into two 2NF tables, one involving 'Event ID' and 'Supplier ID', and the other involving 'Supplier ID' and 'Supplier contact'. This means that we have determined that 'Supplier contact' is dependent on only part of the key, 'Supplier ID', and not upon the other part of the key, 'Event ID'.

Note that this would only be true if FUN used just one specific contact person for a given supplier. Another business might have a different business policy which allowed different contact people for different events: for such a business we would not have separated 'Supplier contact' into a new table.

Similarly, we need to be aware of the possibility that FUN might change its own business policy in the future; for example, FUN could decide to plan 'Dinner' with a number of different durations, rather than only ever using a 'standard' 2-hour duration. In this case, 'Component duration' would become dependent upon both 'Event component' and 'Event ID', and we would have to re-engineer our logical data model accordingly.

Commentary

As an organisation grows or changes, it is very common for the structure of its data to change in ways that make the structure of its database out of date. Re-engineering the organisation's logical data model and bringing its database up to date is a continuous maintenance problem.

A commercial example could involve a distribution database. Suppose that an oil company decided to start using fewer, larger bowsers for refilling the underground fuel tanks at service stations. There would be changes to the maximum delivery quantities, to the number of vehicles, to the number of drivers, to the schedules, and to the routes followed by the vehicles.

In our example of the FUN event component duration, we could temporarily avoid having to restructure the database if we advised FUN to create different kinds of event component, rather than allowing an event component to have different durations. For example, instead of the single event component called 'Dinner' being allowed to have durations of 1, 1.5 or 2 hours, we might advise them to create the components called 'Dinner (1 hr)', 'Dinner (1.5 hr)', and 'Dinner (2 hr)'. This would allow us to retain the existing database structure which assigns a fixed component duration to a given component.

Finally, note that we have created a rather curious table: one that consists entirely of a composite key and no other attributes. This is a fairly common outcome of 2NF; we have created a 'pure' link table, one whose function is simply to link or connect together the instances of one data entity with the instances of another. The table with the key 'Event ID, Supplier ID' serves to link a particular supplier with a particular event.

To see what we have gained by having our database tables in 2NF, consider the attributes of the event components, 'Event component', 'Component cost', and 'Component duration'. If we had not separated 'Component duration' into its own table with a key of 'Event component', we would have to store the duration of the component with every table row where we recorded which components were needed for every event.

Because these durations are all the same for a given component, the result would be repeated duplication of data. We would therefore be wasting storage space with such duplications – though thanks to falling storage costs, this consideration of wasted space is much less significant than it once was.

Much more importantly, duplicated data is always a threat to the security and integrity of a database, and hence to the operations of the organisation. Suppose in our FUN example that we used 1NF instead of 2NF for the database tables, such that when recording the components of a given event a FUN computer operator recorded 'Event component', 'Component cost', and 'Component duration' together on one record. This would allow a FUN user to set by accident a duration of, perhaps, 22 hours for a dinner for a certain event, when all other events had their dinner component correctly specified as 2 hours.

If the error was not caught in time, there might be a lot of food left over at the event in question! Had the database been set up using 2NF tables, this kind of error would not occur so easily because the database structure would ensure that all dinners had the same specified duration.

Third normal form

We take our 2NF tables to **third normal form (3NF)** by creating new tables for attributes which do not depend upon their candidate key, but which depend instead upon other non-key attributes in their 2NF table.

Again, when we ask whether an attribute depends upon the candidate key of its table or on some other non-key attribute, we are really asking whether that attribute would change its value if the *key* changed its value, or whether the attribute would only change its value when some other attribute in the table was changed. Examples of these dependencies are discussed below when we take the FUN event planning data to 3NF.

The reason for creating separate tables for attributes which depend on each other rather than upon the key of their current table is that, as discussed in 1NF and 2NF, there would otherwise be extensive duplicated data. At 3NF, though, we are also ensuring that we are creating truly independent tables, and thus enhancing referential integrity.

3NF is the separation of non-key dependencies.

Again, examples are discussed below in the context of the FUN event planning data.

To refine the 2NF set to a 3NF set of tables we begin by copying out the 2NF tables. For each table, we begin by copying its key, and then consider each attribute of

the table in turn. Does the attribute depend upon the key of the table, or upon some other attribute in the table? If the attribute depends upon the key, it is copied over into the table headed by that key. On the other hand, if the attribute depends upon some other attribute in the table and not upon the key, we must create a new table.

We copy the dependent attributes into a new table, and examine the remainder of the original table, looking for further attributes which depend upon the attributes of the new table, and adding any that we find to the new table. When we are satisfied that all dependent attributes have been moved from the original table into the new table, we construct a candidate key for the new table. Finally, and most importantly, we copy this key back into the original table, and mark it with an '*' as a foreign key in that table.

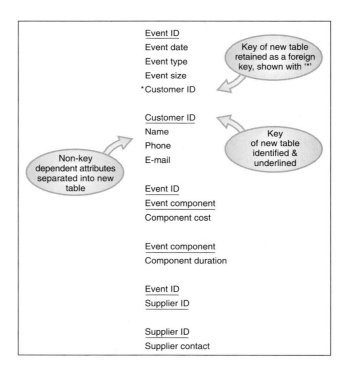

Figure 6.12 3NF for the FUN event planning sheet

Figure 6.12 illustrates the result of the 3NF procedure upon the 2NF tables of the FUN event planning data.

Notice that we have created a new table involving the customer attributes, identified the key to this new table as 'Customer ID', and retained this attribute in the original table, now showing it as a foreign key.

The argument was as follows. As we copied over the first 2NF table into its 3NF form, we copied over the 'Event ID' as the key, and then the event attributes of date, size, and type, since it was obvious that an event's date, size, and type are dependent upon the 'Event ID'. If the 'Event ID' were to change, so would the other event attributes. Then we reached the 'Customer ID' attribute, and noticed that there were other attributes to do with the customer, such as name, phone number, and e-mail **universal (or uniform) resource locator (URL)**.

It is clear that a customer's name, phone number and e-mail address depend much more upon the 'Customer ID' than upon the 'Event ID'. If the 'Event ID' were to change, the customer details would not change too; after all, a customer could have booked more than one event. On the other hand, if the 'Customer ID' were to change, then a completely different set of customer attribute values would necessarily occur. The result is the creation of a new table of customer details, and the 'Customer ID' is left behind in the original table as a foreign key.

Notice also that no other new tables have been created. Sometimes the reason for this is that there are insufficient attributes in a table, and 3NF cannot be applied. Specifically, if a table does not have at least two non-key attributes, it cannot be strictly determined whether the single non-key attribute that it *does* contain is dependent upon the key or upon some other attribute which is not present. This point is made to suggest that normalisation works best when there is a full variety of attributes to analyse.

What have we gained by having our tables in 3NF? Suppose we constructed a database with tables that were just in 2NF. As our FUN example shows, we would have to store customer details with every event record. Again, this is a duplication of data, since we would store the same customer data for every event that a particular customer had booked. And again, this duplication is a waste of storage space. But there is a much more serious problem.

By storing duplicated customer data through the 'Event' table, we are at much greater risk from erroneous data that would be difficult to track down and correct. Suppose FUN's most popular customer had booked 10 or 12 events, and so the FUN database users would have to enter the same customer details 10 or 12 times. Not too serious, perhaps; but now imagine that this customer's phone number changes from, say, 0181 *xxx-xxxx* to 0208 *xxx-xxxx*. There is no easy way to change all 10 or 12 occurrences of the phone number automatically. Over time, it is likely that customer details would acquire errors.

On the other hand, if the customer details were all held in one place – in one 'Customer' table, as suggested by 3NF – the phone number would appear once and thus have to be changed just once. After that, every event would be able to access the correct and most up-to-date customer details through the 'Customer ID' foreign key. This is exactly what we mean by ensuring that there is no redundant or duplicated data in the database.

Normalised ERD

Given the normalisation carried out to 3NF, we are now able to review and revise our first draft ERD. The first step is to consider the various tables that have arisen from the normalisation, and then to give each table a name. By giving the table a name, we are also naming the data entity it represents, so that we can relate the tables of normalised data to the data entities of the ERD.

Next we draw each data entity with both its name and its keys. The keys for a particular data entity are as shown in its table, where we show both the primary key attribute (or attributes, if a composite key) and any foreign keys. Figure 6.13 illustrates the enhanced notational conventions used in the final ERD.

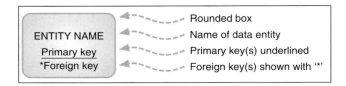

Figure 6.13 ERD notation

The normalisation to 3NF of the FUN event planning sheet resulted in six tables. Four of these tables concern data entities we would call 'Customer', 'Event', 'Supplier', and 'Event component'; two tables are link entities, one which links an event and a supplier, and the other which links an event and its components.

These named tables are illustrated in the Figure 6.14.

To construct the final ERD, we connect two data entities with a relationship line if they have a key in common. Then, we consider whether the relationship is 1:1, 1:m or m:n, and place crows' feet accordingly. We would probably have to redraw the ERD as a

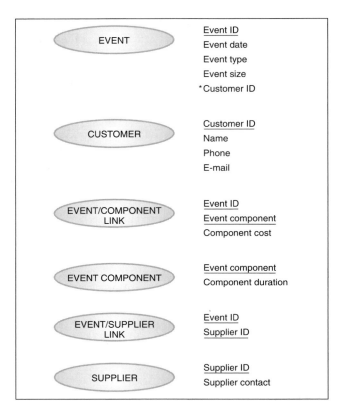

Figure 6.14 The 3NF tables named

result, to ensure that there were no 'dead crows'. The result would be the final ERD. For our FUN data, it would look like Figure 16.5.

Note that if normalisation was carried out successfully on a sufficiently rich set of data attributes, we would not find m:n relationships in the final ERD, and it would be unusual to find 1:1 relationships.

With a computer system more substantial than FUN's, we would in practice undertake a number of normalisations, and the result would be a number of 'final' ERDs, one for each normalisation. The last step in constructing the logical data model for such a system then would be to merge the various ERDs into one, comprehensive, overall 'final' ERD, and that would form the basis of the database for the system in question.

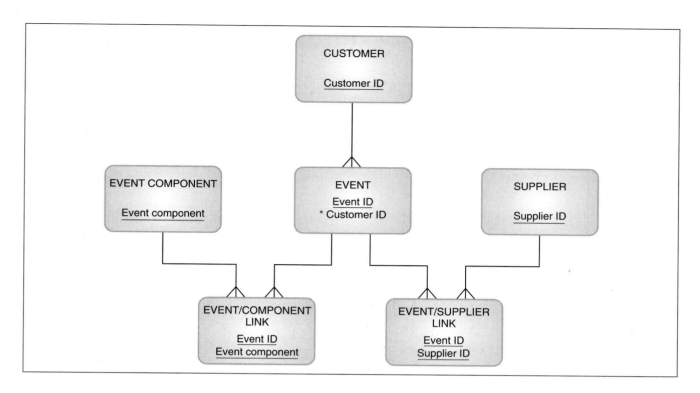

Figure 6.15 Final FUN ERD

Chapter 6.4 Relational database structures and construction

Relational database structures

We are now ready to consider the creation of a computer database. A software package that allows the user to create databases is called a **database management system (DBMS)** if it provides the tools needed to create, maintain, and use the resulting database. It would be called a **relational database management system (RDBMS)** if the databases that it supports are 'relational' databases, which are explained below. This chapter uses Microsoft Access to illustrate the construction of a database: Access is an RDBMS.

Commentary

It is possible to construct a relational database, of course, without using a relational database management system. Although it is possible, however, it would be extremely time-consuming, because it would involve the programming of a large number of routines and utilities to do what an RDBMS does. While such programming was necessary in the early days of computer databases, it is almost never done any more. Most businesses rely upon an RDBMS such as Access for smaller systems, or Oracle for larger systems.

A *relational database* is exactly the sort of database that we have been analysing and designing in the chapters of this unit. 'Relational' refers to the fact that the database has been designed using the principles of **relational data analysis (RDA)**, meaning that a relational database consists of a number of carefully normalised

tables with carefully constructed primary, composite, and foreign keys. Such a set of normalised tables minimises duplicated data. A database with normalised tables provides a robust database that is likely to remain error-free as new data is added, current data is changed, and old data deleted.

Various DBMS and RDBMS software packages use slightly differing terminology to describe the components of a database. It is useful to recall the different terms that apply to a table of data (Figure 6.16).

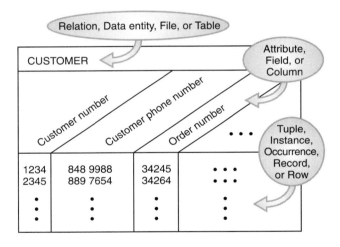

Figure 6.16 Database and file terminology

As a result of constructing a normalised ERD and a data dictionary, we have our database design ready for entry into the RDBMS. Its components are as follows. The finalised and normalised ERD is a diagram that shows the data entities of the system and the relationships between them. Its main purpose is to illustrate what the tables of the system are; what the keys in the tables are; and how one table relates,

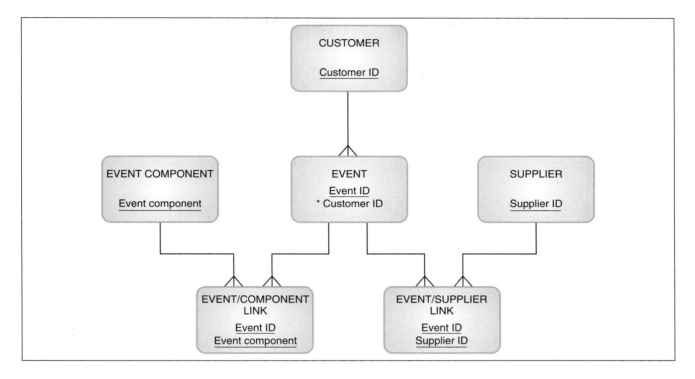

Figure 6.17 Normalised ERD for the FUN event bookings database

through its keys, to other tables with matching keys. The relationship lines indicate, for the rows of a table, relationships with rows of other tables. The ERD we shall implement is illustrated in Figure 6.17.

The data dictionary contains the details of all the data in the system. Each data entity is defined, its keys identified, and all of its attributes listed. For each attribute, a note is made of the data type of the attribute, its allowed size or length, and any validation operations that may be relevant to that attribute. It is the data dictionary that provides the input to the RDBMS in the implementation of the database design in the computer.

Table 6.1 provides some of the data dictionary entries for the various attributes in our FUN event booking database. The

data dictionary shown is illustrative, not exhaustive. A real database would hold many more attributes than those listed.

Relational database construction

The first step in the construction of a database is to define the *tables*, *attributes*, *keys* and *relationships* using the tools provided by the RDBMS. The next step is to define the *data entry forms* that will be used to enter data into the database. The third step is to define the various *standard reports* that are required, and the range of queries that may have to be answered. The final step is to *populate the database* and *test its operation*. All of these matters are addressed in the remaining chapters of Unit 6.

Entity	Key	Attribute	Data type	Size	Validation
CUSTOMER	Primary	Customer ID	Numeric	5 digits	Between 10,001 and 99,999
		First name	Text	15 chars	
		Last name	Text	20 chars	
		Phone number	Text	12 chars	
		E-mail address	Text	30 chars	Must have an '@' symbol somewhere within the string
EVENT	Primary	Event ID	Numeric	6 digits	Between 1 and 999,999
	Foreign	Customer ID	Numeric	5 digits	
		Event date	Date		Between 'Today' and 1 year's time
		Event time	Time		Between 6 am and midnight
		Event duration	Numeric	2 digits	Between 1 and 48
		Event size	Numeric	4 digits	Between 5 and 2000
EVENT COMPONENT	Primary	Event component	Text	15 chars	'Dinner' 'Drinks' 'Disco' 'Other'
		Duration	Numeric	1 digit	
		Component cost	Financial		Between £1.00 and £1,000.00
SUPPLIER	Primary	Supplier ID	Numeric	4 digits	
		Contact name	Text	30 chars	
EVENT/ COMPONENT LINK	Primary Primary	Event ID Event component			
EVENT/ SUPPLIER LINK	Primary Primary	Event ID Supplier ID			

Table 6.1   Data dictionary entries for the FUN event bookings database

New database creation wizard

The **Access wizard** takes the user through the creation of a new database. When you start up Access, it asks whether you have an existing database to open, or whether you want to create a new database (Figure 6.18). To use the database wizard to create the new database, click on the 'OK' button to continue.

Figure 6.18   Access opening screen

The new database could be created without the wizard, simply by opening a 'blank' database and starting from there. This approach is illustrated later in the chapter.

The wizard then asks where to save the new database, and what filename to give it. By default, it offers the 'My Documents' folder as the location of the database; this can be changed to place the database files in any other chosen folder. Figure 6.19 shows the name of the database file changed to 'FUNevb'; the standard file extension used by Access to identify a file as an Access database file, '.mdb', is retained. Click on the 'Create' button to continue.

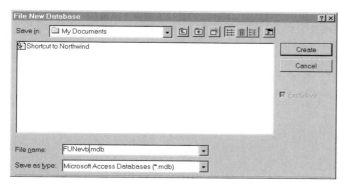

Figure 6.19 Create 'New Database' wizard: database location

Creating a database from a pre-defined template

The wizard then offers a selection of pre-designed **database templates** which could be used as the basis of the database. Clicking on the 'Event Management' template, for example, followed by the 'OK' button, would yield the following sequence of dialogue boxes (Figure 6.20–6.25): by working through these the user can tailor the database template to suit individual taste.

The dialogue boxes are largely self-explanatory, but it is worth reading through each of them in sequence to see what the

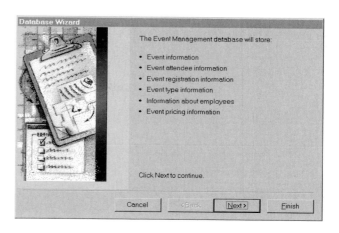

Figure 6.20 'Event Management' template database: screen 1

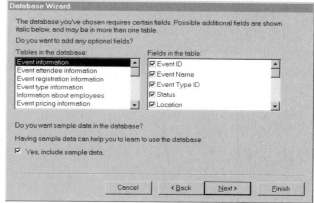

Figure 6.21 'Event Management' template database: screen 2

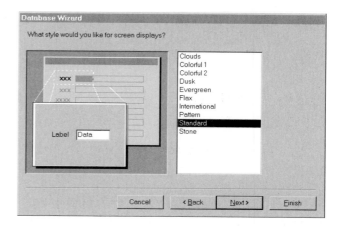

Figure 6.22 'Event Management' template database: screen 3

255

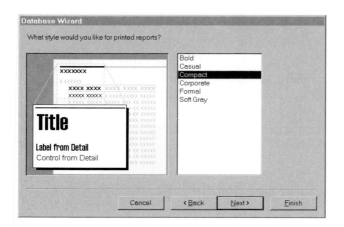

Figure 6.23 'Event Management' template database: screen 4

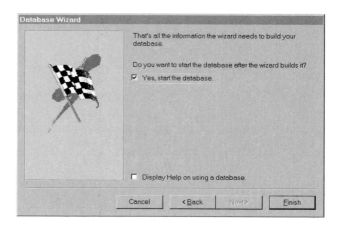

Figure 6.25 'Event Management' template database: screen 6

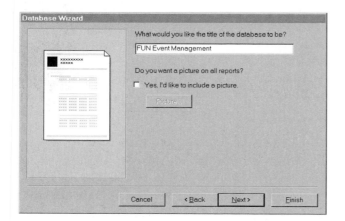

Figure 6.24 'Event Management' template database: screen 5

The database creation wizard provides what Access calls a **switchboard** – a menu listing the various things that can now be done with the database. This menu provides an easy way into the database for the new or novice user. (Switchboards can also be created 'manually', as discussed later in the chapter.)

You will notice a *minimised taskbar* at the bottom left of the Access display. This is the Access **database window**, which the wizard has tucked out of the way. Clicking on this taskbar restores it.

wizard is doing and what choices are offered when creating a database using a pre-defined template.

After the 'Finish' button has been clicked, the wizard spends a little time creating the database, displaying a set of progress bars and text indicators to keep the user informed of progress. If you have asked for the database to be started or opened upon completion, the wizard finishes by returning you to the Access screen with a custom 'switchboard' on display for your newly created 'Event Management' database (Figure 6.26).

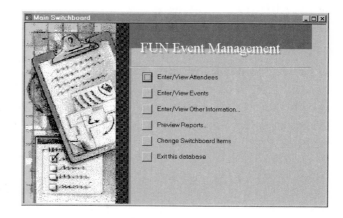

Figure 6.26 'Event Management' template database: the 'switchboard'

For the experienced user or the database developer, the Access database window is actually a tabbed display box which lists all of the components of the database. The database tables are shown in the 'Tables' tab display, as shown in Figure 6.27. Other components include data entry forms and reports, explored later in the chapter.

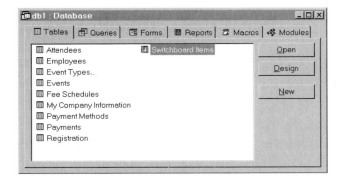

Figure 6.27 The Access 'Database' window with the 'Tables' tab displayed

Creating a database from a 'blank' database

Instead of relying on one of the pre-designed database templates, the user is free to create a new database with its own design. To begin doing this, when the wizard displays the templates, click on the '**General**' tab and select a '**Blank**

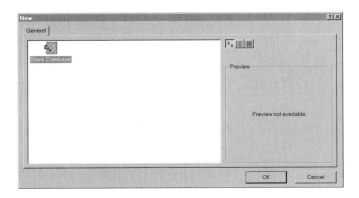

Figure 6.28 Create 'New' database wizard: 'Blank Database' template

Database', then click 'OK' to continue (Figure 6.28).

The result is a blank 'Database' window: having selected a 'Blank Database' template, you will now have to build all the database components you require for the FUN event bookings database. The empty database window is shown in Figure 6.29, within the Access desktop window.

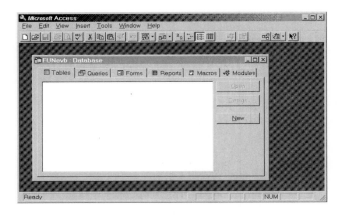

Figure 6.29 Blank 'Database' window in the Access desktop

Creating tables

The second step in building the FUN database is to construct the tables for 'Customer', 'Event', and so on. It would be quite possible to take the pre-defined 'Event Management' database and modify its tables – we will see how to modify tables later in the chapter – but for illustrative purposes we will build our own.

With the '**Tables**' tab of the database window displayed, click on the '**New**' button to create a new table. There are five options (Figure 6.30). There are two ways of creating a table directly, using either the '**Datasheet View**' or the '**Design View**'; there is an option to create a table using the '**Table Wizard**'; there is an option

257

'**Import Table**' to use an existing table from elsewhere; and finally there is an option '**Link Table**' to create a special kind of table that links the database to an external file of data. We shall first illustrate the construction of a new table using the 'Table Wizard'. Later in the chapter we shall illustrate the construction of a new table using the 'Design View' option.

Select 'Table Wizard' and click on the 'OK' button.

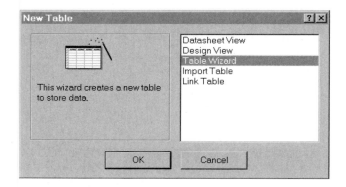

Figure 6.30   Selecting a method of table creation

Table creation with the table wizard

The table wizard now offers a list of pre-designed tables, for the user to select and then adapt (Figure 6.31).

In our example, the data dictionary identifies a Customer table, so we can select the 'Customers' table from the list of '**Sample Tables**'. In the middle list, '**Sample Fields**', the wizard shows attributes that could be included in the table. Suitable attributes for our database will be 'CustomerID', 'ContactFirstName', 'ContactLastName', 'PhoneNumber' and 'EmailAddress' – these displayed fields are the closest matches to the attributes specified in our data dictionary. For each attribute selected in the middle list, click

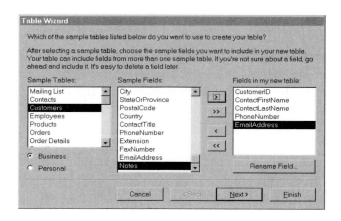

Figure 6.31   Pre-designed tables in the 'Table Wizard'

on the '>' button to transfer that attribute to the list of '**Fields in my new table**', the list of attributes that will make up the Customer table.

The attribute names in the Access database should exactly match the attribute names in the data dictionary. In this case, therefore, it is necessary to rename two fields in the 'Customer' table, changing them from 'ContactFirstName' and 'ContactLastName' to 'FirstName' and 'LastName'.

To do this, select the field to rename in the right-hand list and click on the '**Rename Field...**' button. A small dialogue window appears (Figure 6.32), in which the new name can be typed. Clicking on the 'OK' button returns the user to the earlier display.

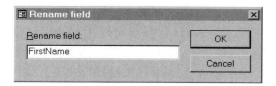

Figure 6.32   Renaming an attribute

Once the fields of the new table are correct, click on the '**Next>**' button. The table wizard then asks for the name of the new table, and asks whether you wish to specify the primary key yourself. In this case, the table is to be called 'Customer', and you do wish to specify the primary key (Figure 6.33). Click on the 'Next>' button.

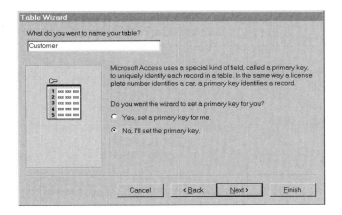

Figure 6.33 Naming the table

The data dictionary specifies that the 'CustomerID' is to be the primary key of the 'Customer' table, so this is entered in the table wizard's dialogue box (Figure 6.34). The wizard also asks about the *structure* of the key, and offers three choices.

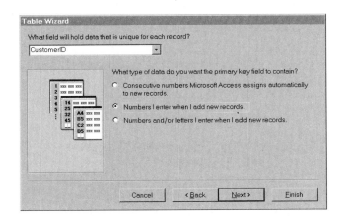

Figure 6.34 Specifying the table key

Access can provide a key that automatically **increments** every time a new customer

record is added. This is often a useful feature, but in this case it is not appropriate – according to the data dictionary, customer IDs must start from 10001, whereas an *auto-incrementing* field would start from 1. Access also offers us, as the third choice, the ability to mix letters and numbers: this is a popular choice for many businesses. The 'Customer' table key will simply be a number, entered by the user.

When the 'Next>' button is clicked, the wizard tells us that it is about to finish creating the 'Customer' table, and asks whether you want to modify the table when it has done so (Figure 6.35). Select this option to see the processes involved in modifying any Access table.

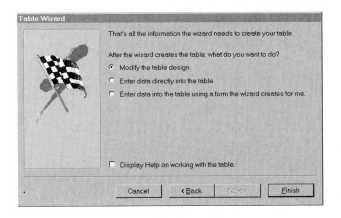

Figure 6.35 Finishing the table creation

Notice that the table wizard offers to create a data entry form for the table: data entry forms and their creation are considered later in the chapter.

Clicking on the 'Finish' button tells the wizard to create the 'Customer' table. If you have asked to modify the table, the wizard will take you directly to the appropriate window.

Modifying a table

The usual route to modifying a table is to display 'Tables' in the tabbed database window, select the table you want to modify, and click on the 'Design' button. The result is a display of table attributes, and of the properties of the selected attribute within the table.

Figure 6.36 shows the 'Customer' table, and the properties of the 'CustomerID' attribute. Access calls this view of the table the 'Design View'.

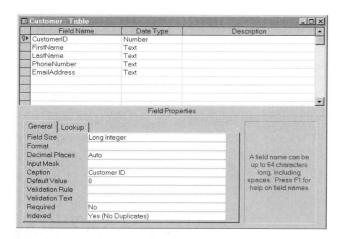

Figure 6.36 The 'Customer' table shown in 'Design View'

Access offers extensive attribute or field properties. Consider the validation rule in the data dictionary that the 'CustomerID' must be between 10 001 and 99 999. To implement this, place the cursor in the 'Validation Rule' field property box and click on the '...' button which appears next to the property. This opens a dialogue box, shown in Figure 6.37. (In the figure, the required validation rule is expressed as '>10000 And <100000': it could equally have been specified as '>=10001 And <=99999'.)

Note that the '<', '>', and 'And' operators are obtained by clicking on the relevant button, just below the entry area, or by selecting the required operator from the list and clicking on the 'Paste' button.

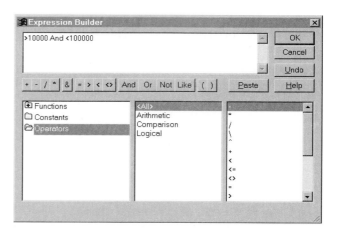

Figure 6.37 The 'Validation Rule' field property dialogue box

Clicking 'OK' returns you to the design view of the 'Customer' table, with the new validation rule for 'CustomerID' shown.

Also needed is a validation rule for the customer's e-mail address. In Access, a text field is validated using the 'Like' operator, which is followed by a special text string to identify the characters that are required (Figure 6.38).

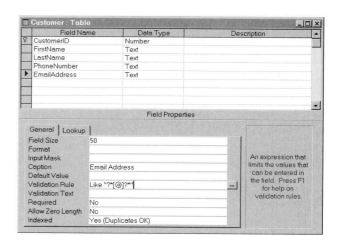

Figure 6.38 The field properties of 'EmailAddress'

Construction of a 'Like' expression is explained in the 'Like' help topic of Access, part of which is shown in Figure 6.39.

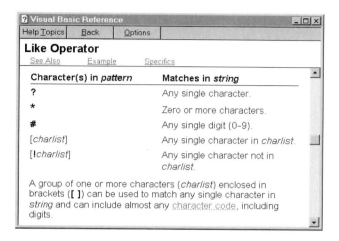

Figure 6.39 The characters used to construct a 'Like' validation rule

To complete modification of the 'Customer' table, ensure that its attributes have the lengths specified in the data dictionary. Then click on the 'X' button on the taskbar to finish. A confirmation box is displayed (Figure 6.40).

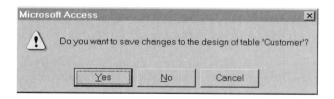

Figure 6.40 Confirmation box for changes to the 'Customer' table

Creating a table without the wizard

The remaining tables of the FUN database must now be created: 'Event', 'Event Component', 'Supplier', 'Event/Component Link', and 'Event/Supplier Link'.

To create the 'Event' table, click on the 'New' button in the tabbed database

window with the database tables shown, and select the 'Design View' for table creation (rather than the table wizard), as in Figure 6.41.

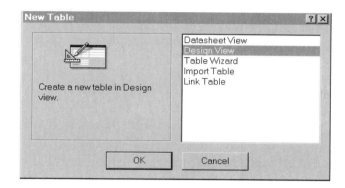

Figure 6.41 Creating a new table using 'Design View'

Into the blank design view, enter the fields of the Event table – 'EventID', 'CustomerID', 'EventDate', 'EventTime', 'EventDuration', and 'EventSize' (Figure 6.42). For each field, set the properties required, such as the field's caption, any validation rule, and so on. The final task,

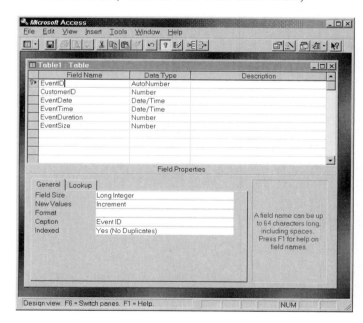

Figure 6.42 Identifying 'EventID' as the table primary key

261

which earlier the table wizard arranged for us, is to designate the table's primary key.

To designate the 'EventID' as the primary key, select the 'EventID' attribute row and click on the button in the Access toolbar that has a small key symbol. A matching symbol appears next to the 'EventID' entry in the table design.

Note that the 'EventID' is specified to be incremented automatically, as an '**AutoNumber**'. This number is managed by Access: every time a new event is entered into the database, it is automatically given the next available event number as its identification. Because it is specified as 'AutoNumber', no validation rule is needed.

When the 'Event' table has been fully constructed, close the window by clicking on the 'X' button, and give the table a name (Figure 6.43).

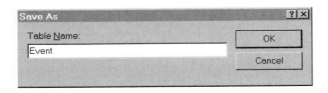

Figure 6.43 Naming the new 'Event' table

The result is shown in the database window (Figure 6.44). There are now two tables,

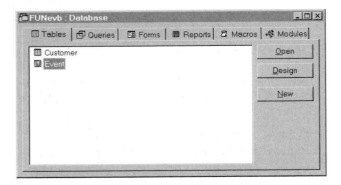

Figure 6.44 Database window showing two tables

and the other tables required by the FUN database are created in the same way.

Creating composite keys

In creating the 'Event/Component Link' table it became apparent that a composite key was required. To implement this in Access, display this table in design view, then select *both* of the relevant two fields – 'EventID' and 'EventComponent' – and click on the key button on the Access toolbar. (Alternatively, select 'Primary key' from the 'Edit' menu.)

A composite key is also needed for the 'Event/Supplier Link' table.

Creating lookup field contents

The 'Event Component' table requires the event component to be restricted to one or other of four specified components: 'Dinner', 'Drinks', 'Disco', and 'Other'. In Access this restriction can be enforced by creating a **lookup column**. The 'EventComponent' field is a text field, as declared when it was created (Figure 6.45).

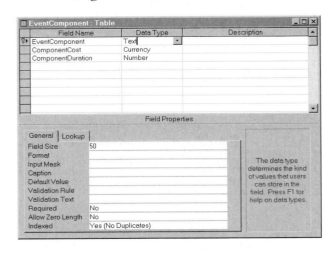

Figure 6.45 Database window showing the 'EventComponent' field

Also in the list of data types for the 'EventComponent' field is an item labelled **'Lookup Wizard...'**; clicking on this now initiates the lookup wizard. The wizard offers a choice between linking this field to another table which will supply these values, or specifying allowable values for the field. Although we will supply the values in this case, in general it is wise to place such values in a separate table, and link them.

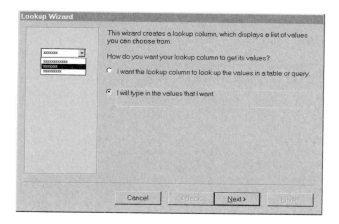

Figure 6.46 'Lookup Wizard' dialogue

Click on the 'Next>' button. The wizard now requests the specific values allowed for the field. For the 'EventComponent' field only one column of values is required; these are entered in order, pressing the <Tab>

key to advance to the next value (Figure 6.47).

When all values have been entered, click on the 'Next' button. The final dialogue box offers the chance to change the label of the lookup column (Figure 6.48).

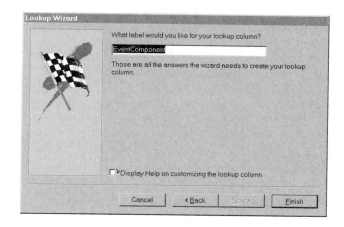

Figure 6.48 'Lookup Wizard': choosing a label

Specifying relationships

Having created the tables, it is now necessary to tell Access what their relationships are. To do this, click on the **'Relationships'** item in the **'Tools'** menu. The 'Relationships' window opens, and a dialogue box asks you to select tables to be added to the window. Select each table as appropriate, and click on the **'Add'** button – the result is shown in Figure 6.49. Finally, click on the **'Close'** button of the **'Show Table'** display.

To specify that two tables are related, click on the key of the primary or master table, and drag that key over to the same-name field in the secondary or detail table. Suppose, for example, that the label for the 'EventID' field in the 'Event' table is dragged over the 'EventID' field in the 'Event/Component Link' table. A

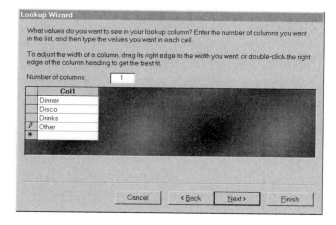

Figure 6.47 'Lookup Wizard': entering values for the 'EventComponent' field

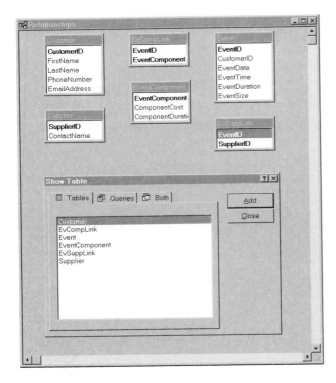

Figure 6.49 'Relationships': identifying tables to be linked

'Relationships' dialogue box will open, showing the two tables involved and listing their common field, as shown in Figure 6.50.

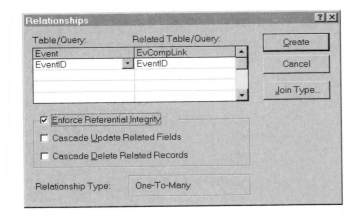

Figure 6.50 Relating two tables

Check the '**Enforce Referential Integrity**' check box: this ensures that when any event components are added to or deleted from a specific event, these changes will be made securely and without error. Referential integrity is discussed in Chapter 6.5, page 274, and Chapter 6.7, page 304, where examples are provided. Now click the '**Create**' button, and the 'Relationship' window updates to show the 1:m relationship that has been created between the 'Event' table and the 'Event/Component Link' table.

In a similar way, create the remaining relationships. The resulting Access equivalent of the FUN database ERD is shown in Figure 6.51.

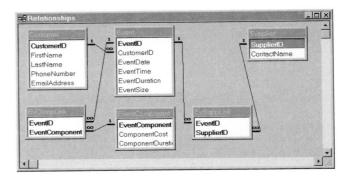

Figure 6.51 Access equivalent of the FUN ERD

Chapter 6.5 Data entry forms

Creating a form using the form wizard

Having constructed the database, we must now provide ways of adding data, changing existing data, and deleting old data. These operations are most easily done by way of **data forms**.

Clicking on the '**Forms**' tab of the Access database window shows us that no forms have yet been defined. Click on the '**New**' button to begin to create a form to enter customer details. In the resulting '**New Form**' dialogue box, select the '**Form Wizard**', and in the drop-down list box identify the 'Customer' table as the basis for the form. These selections are illustrated in Figure 6.52. Click on 'OK' to continue.

On page 267 we illustrate the creation of a new form using the 'Design View' option.

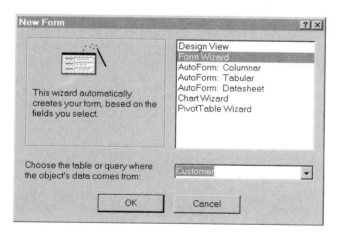

Figure 6.52 Starting the 'Form Wizard' for the 'Customer' table

In the next dialogue, the form wizard lists the available fields in the 'Customer' table. The user can select and transfer some or all of these fields into the new form, as well as selecting and transferring fields from other tables. To add to the list of fields displayed on the form, select a field in the left-hand list and click on the '>' button. To remove a previously-selected field from the right-hand list, select it, and press the '<' button. Figure 6.53 shows that two fields have been moved into the right-hand list. We want *all* the 'Customer' fields in our form: a quick way to transfer all the fields from the left- to the right-hand list is to click on the '>>' button. Click the 'Next>' button to continue building the form.

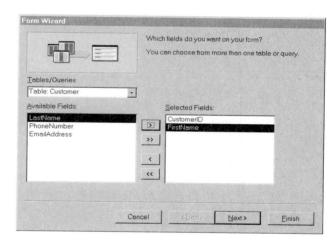

Figure 6.53 Selecting the form fields

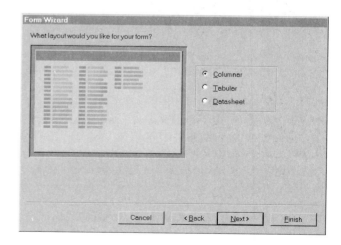

Figure 6.54 Selecting the form layout

The form wizard then offers a choice of form layouts (Figure 6.54). Choose the '**Columnar**' layout, and click on 'Next>' to continue. Other possibilities are '**Tabular**' and '**Datasheet**'.

The form wizard then gives us a choice of form styles (Figure 6.55). Choose the '**Standard**' style, and click on 'Next>' to continue.

Commentary

Access offers you various colour and background styles which you can use to make your screen distinctive and interesting; but almost all the choices other than 'Standard' really do hurt the performance by slowing down the filling of the screen. The only exceptions are 'Colorful' and 'Stone'.

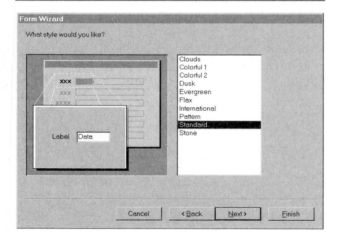

Figure 6.55 Selecting the form style

Just before we finish, the wizard asks us for a title for the form, and offers the name of the table as a default title. Figure 6.56 shows the word 'Details' added to 'Customer', as this will be clearer to the user of the form.

The wizard offers options to modify the form design immediately, and to ask for help. Neither of these options is activated

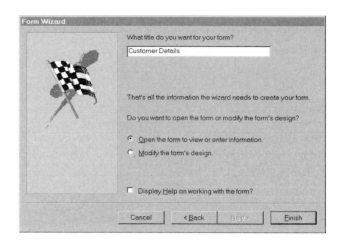

Figure 6.56 Finishing the form

in Figure 6.56, which simply asks to open the form. Click on 'Finish' to do this.

The wizard works for a few seconds, and then displays the resulting form for use (Figure 6.57). There are no 'Customer' records in the database at the moment, so the form invites us to enter the first customer, with an ID of 0. At the bottom of the form is the standard Access **navigation panel**, which shows the record number on display, and provides buttons to go forward or back one record, to move to the start or the end of the table, or to add a new record.

Notice that each field has been labelled with the attribute name taken from the 'Customer' table. These attribute names have been retained because they are already

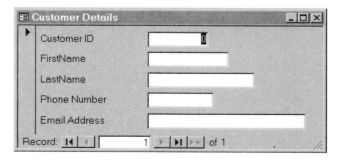

Figure 6.57 The resulting 'Customer Details' form

clear to the form user, but it would be possible to modify the form and improve the labels provided for the fields. Notice also that the fields have been sized according to the settings made when the 'Customer' table was originally created.

We will modify this form later, but we shall first illustrate the creation of a form without the form wizard.

Creating a form using the 'Design View'

The next form to create is the 'Event' form, allowing the user to create a new event booking and edit existing event bookings. 'Design View' can be used to create this form from scratch.

Looking at the Access database window with the 'Forms' tab on display, you can see the new 'Customer Details' form shown (Figure 6.58). Click on the 'New' button to start a new form.

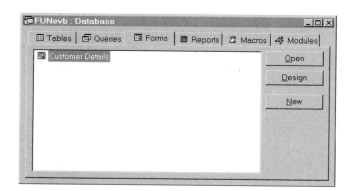

Figure 6.58 'Database' window showing forms created so far

In the 'New Form' dialogue box (Figure 6.59), we select 'Design View' as the creation method, and identify the 'Event' table as the source of the form's fields. Click on 'OK' to continue.

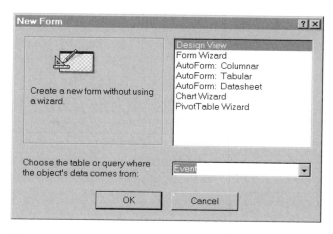

Figure 6.59 Creating the 'Event' form using 'Design View'

The screen display now changes (Figure 6.60). First, the standard Access menu bar is modified: a second row of icons is added, and on the first row some new icons are displayed.

Figure 6.60 Access menu bars for forms design

By default, the '**Toolbar**' button is depressed on the Access menu bar. This button controls the display of the forms design view toolbox (Figure 6.61).

Figure 6.61 Toolbox for forms design

267

This toolbox is the second addition to the screen, and contains a variety of tools used in the design and modification of a form.

The third new addition to the screen is a blank form (Figure 6.62), with a grey grid in place to help in positioning the various form elements on the form.

Next to the 'Toolbox' button on the Access

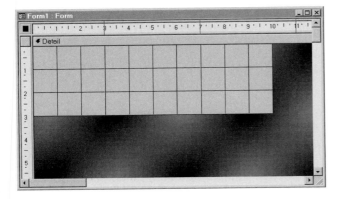

Figure 6.62 The blank form

screen is a button called '**Field list**'. Click this and a list of all the fields in the 'Event' table is shown (Figure 6.63). This list will be needed for the forthcoming design activities.

Figure 6.63 The field list for the 'Event' table

The last button to click is the '**Form Properties**' button on the Access menu bar. This displays a tabbed window of details about the form being designed (Figure 6.64).

To begin the form, place the 'EventID' field on it. To do this, select the field in the

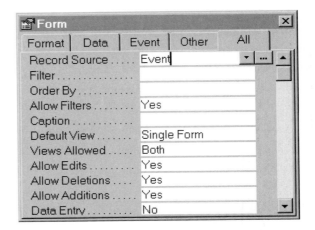

Figure 6.64 The 'Form' properties tabbed display

field list, drag it over to the form, and release it in the required location. The result is two objects placed on the form: a label for the 'EventID' field, and a data entry box for the 'EventID' data itself. Both objects are selected by default, and can be moved as a group to another position if desired. These objects are called **controls**, and much of form design is concerned with the arrangement and working of the form's controls. In Figure 6.65, the 'EventID' label has a single **selection handle**, while the 'EventID' data entry box has both a selection handle and a set of eight **resize handles**.

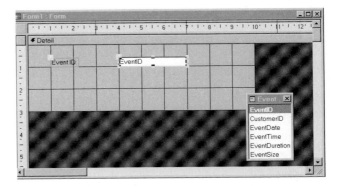

Figure 6.65 The form with the 'EventID' field dragged over

The 'EventID' data entry box or control has been sized according to the size of the attribute we specified in the previous chapter, when we set up the 'Event' table. To make the field a different size on the form, simply grab one of the resize handles and drag it until the box is the size required.

Associated with each control is a comprehensive set of **properties**. Figure 6.66 illustrates the default properties shown for the 'EventID' data entry box control in the form properties sheet. There are over seventy properties that can be set for a single control; below we explore only a few of these.

'Format' properties of a control

The '**Format**' properties of a control manage how that control looks on the form.

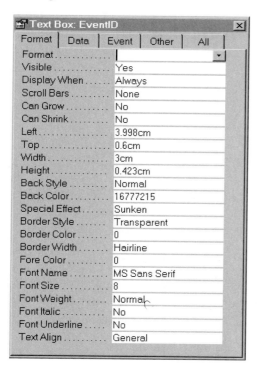

Figure 6.66 Default 'Format' properties of a control

While all of the format properties of a control can be set using this property sheet, the most commonly customised format properties can be more easily set using the format menu bar (the second row of menu bar icons shown in Figure 6.66).

Figure 6.67 illustrates the effect on the control of changing the '**Font Size**' property to '14', setting '**Font Italic**' to 'Yes', having a 4-point '**Border Width**', and giving the box a '**Drop Shadow**'. (Double-click on the lower left selection handle of the field to resize it to suit the new properties.)

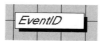

Figure 6.67 The 'EventID' control with modified format properties

'Data' properties of a control

The default values of the '**Data**' properties of the 'EventID' control are shown in Figure 6.68. The default values of '**Enabled**' ('Yes') and '**Locked**' ('No') specify that the field can be copied and edited.

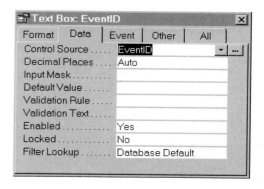

Figure 6.68 Default 'Data' properties

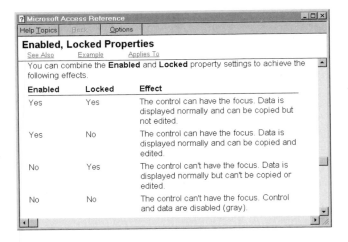

Figure 6.69 Access help on the 'Enabled' and 'Locked' properties

Because the EventID is an automatically generated number, the database user should not be able to edit it. To prevent this, change 'Enabled' and 'Locked' properties to 'No' and 'Yes' respectively. Figure 6.69 shows an excerpt from the Access help system, displayed by asking for help on these elements of the properties sheet; it explains the use of the 'Enabled' and 'Locked' properties.

'Event' properties of a control

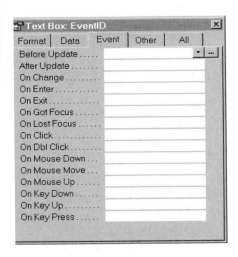

Figure 6.70 The default 'Event' properties

The 'Event' properties of the 'EventID' control are blank by default (Figure 6.70). These properties are used to trigger special processing when the event that is specified occurs. For example, if the data in the control is changed, the 'On Change' event could trigger a Visual Basic program to undertake more complex validation processing than could normally be undertaken using a validation rule.

'Other' properties of a control

The 'Other' properties of the EventID control allow help and instruction to be provided for the database user when an event is entered into the database (Figure 6.71).

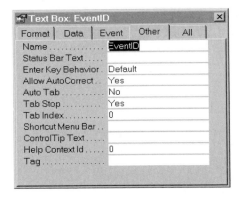

Figure 6.71 Default 'Other' properties

For example, a 'ControlTip' could be provided for the user which displayed the message 'Event ID is automatically calculated' when the mouse cursor was placed over the Event ID data entry box (Figure 6.72). This would be particularly useful because, as the 'Enabled' property has been set to 'No', the user cannot click inside the data entry box and enter or modify the automatically generated EventID number. The inability to edit the EventID might puzzle a user, and a control tip could

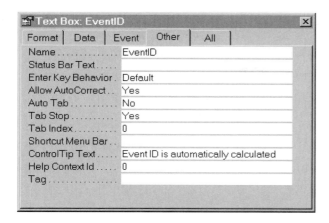

Figure 6.72 Modified 'Other' properties for the 'EventID' control

explain this. Setting the message simply involves typing it in as the value of the 'ControlTip Text' property.

Another good idea would be to set the background, or '**Back Style**', of this control to '**Transparent**', using the formatting menu bar: this would make it appear to be un-editable. This is done by going back to the 'Format' tab of the property sheet, as shown in Figure 6.73.

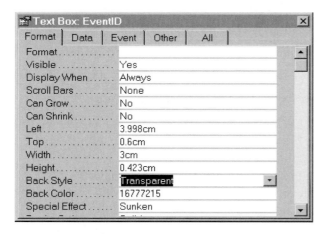

Figure 6.73 Making the background 'Transparent' for the 'EventID' control

Finally, we can change the label for each control. Click on the control's label, and the properties window shows the label

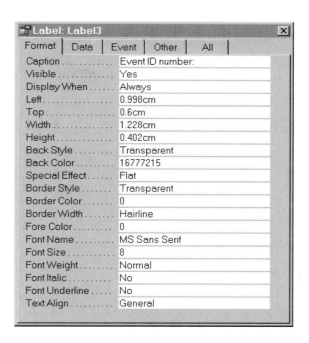

Figure 6.74 Changing the label (or caption) for the 'EventID' control

properties. Click on the 'Format' tab, and type in the required label as the '**Caption**' property. Figure 6.74 shows that the caption has been changed to 'Event ID number:'. It is desirable to give labels which are as meaningful to the user as possible.

Having added the 'Event ID' control to the form, the remaining fields are added to the form in the same way.

Setting defaults with the 'Expression Builder'

One further property of a control is worth mentioning – being able to specify its **default** or **initial value**. For example, you might decide that the database user should be offered a default value of the 'EventDate' field that is seven days in the future; that is, today's date plus seven days. To do this, select the 'Data' tab of the property sheet for the 'EventDate' field, place the cursor in the 'Default Value' property, and click on the '...' button that appears in the right of the property box. This brings up the 'Expression Builder' dialogue window.

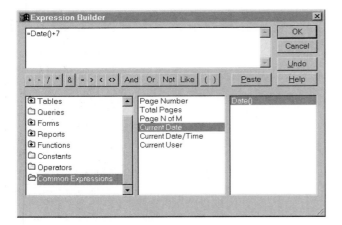

Figure 6.75 Using the 'Expression Builder'

The expression builder allows the user to define a variety of values that can be provided for a field. Click on the 'Common Expressions' item in the left-hand list, and select 'Current Date' from the middle list. The only expression listed for 'Current Date' is shown in the right-hand box as 'Date()' (Figure 6.75). We click on the 'Paste' button, and the expression 'Date()' is placed into the expression builder's editing window. Add '+7', and click 'OK'.

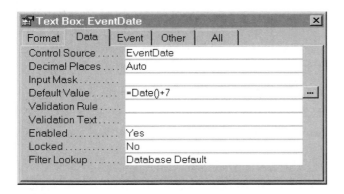

Figure 6.76 Modified 'Default Value' set for 'Event Date'

The result is shown in Figure 6.76. The default property for the 'Event Date' field is to be today's date, expressed by 'Date()', plus seven days, expressed by '+7'.

Setting validation rules with the 'Expression Builder'

In the same way that you can set a default value for a particular field, you can also set a **validation rule**. This is a 'Data' property of the control, and is set using the expression builder. In Figure 6.77 the rule specifies that an event must always have an 'EventSize' greater than 9.

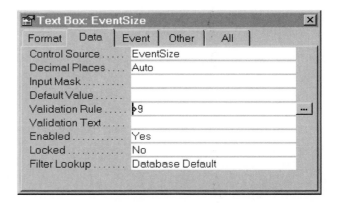

Figure 6.77 'Validation Rule' set for 'Event Size'

If the database user tried to enter an event size less than 10, the window shown in Figure 6.78 would pop up:

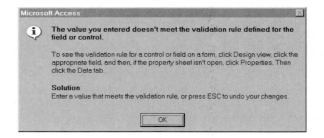

Figure 6.78 Message displayed for a validation rule violation

Adding text labels to a form

The validation rule violation message would not be a particularly helpful message if it were to appear in front of a new user. It would be better, for example, to have some information on the form itself warning the user that the event size needs to be greater than 9. This can be done by placing a label on the form itself.

Labels can be added to a form by using the 'Label' tool from the toolbox; it is the capital 'A' icon. Click on the 'A', then click on the form where you want the label placed. You can, of course, move it around afterwards. Type into the resulting box the label you want.

Notice that the properties window has changed to show you the properties of your new label. The results are illustrated in Figure 6.79.

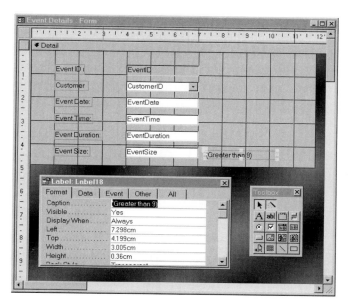

Figure 6.79 Informative label added to a form

Properties for a form

Figure 6.80 shows the first draft of the 'Event' form as shown in the design window. We shall modify this form later.

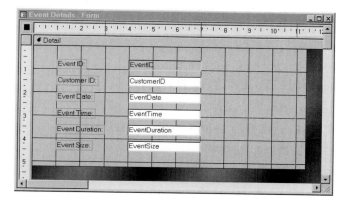

Figure 6.80 First draft of the finished 'Event' form

For the moment, note that the form as a whole has a number of properties, quite apart from the properties enjoyed by its various controls. Some of these are discussed below.

To see the properties of a form as a whole, as opposed to the properties of its details, click on the square in the top left corner of the form window. The property sheet window, which previously showed the properties of a control, now shows the properties of the form. There are more than

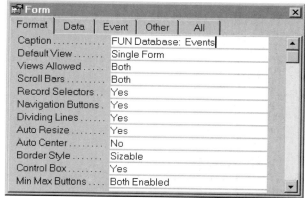

Figure 6.81 Modified 'Format' property sheet for the 'Event' form

seventy properties for the form as a whole. In this case it is necessary to provide a caption for the form. As illustrated in Figure 6.81, the caption 'FUN Database: Events' is entered into the 'Caption' property on the 'Format' tab of the properties sheet for the form.

Saving the form

The 'Event' form is now complete. Closing the design window brings up a dialogue box asking what the form is to be called (Figure 6.82).

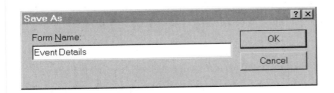

Figure 6.82 Naming a new form

The form is now listed in the database window, with this name (Figure 6.83).

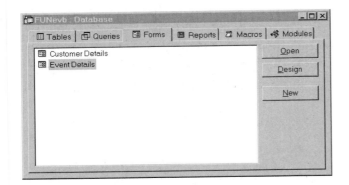

Figure 6.83 'Event' form listed in database window

Viewing the form

Finally, selecting 'Event Details' and clicking on the 'Open' button displays the newly created form, ready to accept new

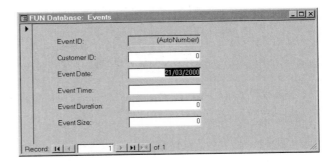

Figure 6.84 First use of the 'Event Details' form

event records (Figure 6.84). Notice that the form caption reads 'FUN Database: Events', as set earlier (Figure 6.81).

Notice that the 'Event ID' field has a background which is the same colour as the body of the form, not white. This signals that it is not an editable field, as arranged earlier when we set the 'Format' properties of this control. Notice that Access displays the text '(AutoNumber)' for any field that is automatically allocated a number.

Note also that the 'Event Date' shows a default value of '21/03/2000': this is seven days ahead of the date at which this form was first displayed. Again, this value results from the 'Default Value'→'Data' property of the 'Event Date' control, as set earlier.

Modifying a form

The forms created so far are the 'Customer' form and the 'Event' form. It is now necessary to provide an explicit link in the 'Event' form so that any new 'Event' record always links to an existing 'Customer' record. This ensures that the details of a customer are always present before any events are created for that customer.

Access already knows that an event must be linked to a customer; this was specified in the relationship between the 'Customer' and 'Event' tables. If the user attempted to add

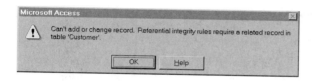

Figure 6.85 Attempting to add an event for a non-existent customer

a new event record for a non-existent customer, Access would generate an error message explaining that this violated referential integrity (Figure 6.85).

The necessary link between an 'Event' and a 'Customer' is thus already present. However, this is not a very user-friendly error message, and there is nothing in the 'Event' form that helps the user select the right customer when the event record is being created.

The 'Event' form can be modified so that the 'CustomerID' field allows the user to select an existing customer from the 'Customer' table, without needing to remember that customer's ID number. The control required is known as a **combo box** control.

Selecting an existing customer from a list

The combo box is a control that allows the user to select an item from a drop-down list. The **Combo Box Wizard** allows you to produce such boxes quickly and easily. We will use the wizard to produce a combo box of customers on the 'Event' form, so that when the user selects a particular customer, the 'Customer ID' is placed in the 'Event' record.

The combo box wizard is accessed from the Toolbox, which is displayed when a form is designed. Select the 'Event Details' form in the database window, and click on the 'Design' button. The 'Event' form is

displayed, along with the toolbox, the form properties, and the 'Event' field list.

Select the existing 'Customer ID' control on the event form, and delete it and its label. Then click on the 'Combo Box' button in the toolbox. The cursor changes to a combo box icon. Move the cursor over to the 'Event' form, and click where you want the combo box to be positioned – probably where the deleted 'CustomerID' control was. The combo box wizard then opens up, and asks you to identify where the combo box values (which the user selects) come from (Figure 6.86). In the case of our 'Customer' combo box, the values should come from a table (the 'Customer' table, in fact). Select that option and click on the 'Next>' button.

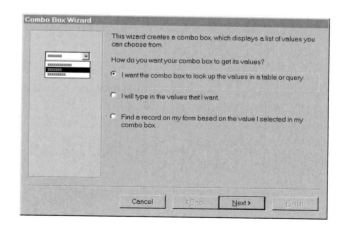

Figure 6.86 Starting the 'Combo Box Wizard'

The next wizard dialogue asks you to identify the table or query which will supply the values for the combo box. This is the 'Customer' table, in our case. Select the 'Customer' table from the list supplied, make sure that the '**Table**' button is selected, and click on the 'Next>' button.

Having identified the 'Customer' table as the source of values for the combo box, the wizard then asks which of the fields in the Customer table to use (Figure 6.88).

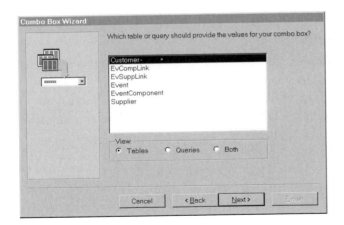

Figure 6.87 **Selecting the combo box data source**

We need the 'CustomerID' and the 'LastName' fields to be shown, so select each field in turn from the left-hand list of available fields and click on the '>' button to transfer that field over to the right-hand list of selected fields. Click on the 'Next>' button to continue.

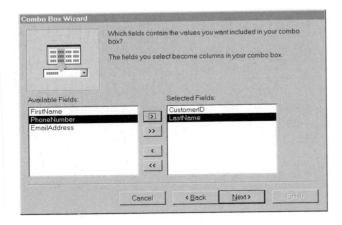

Figure 6.88 **Selecting the combo box display fields**

The wizard then shows an approximate view of what the combo box contents would look like when opened by the user (Figure 6.89). By default, the wizard suggests that the key field be hidden. In our case, we remove the tick from this check box, so that the

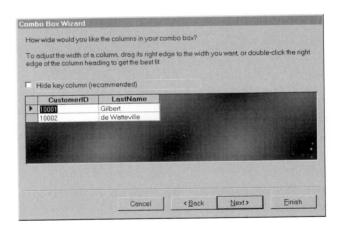

Figure 6.89 **Laying out the combo box display**

'CustomerID' is indeed shown along with the 'LastName'. The wizard also allows you make any adjustments to the width of the combo box display by adjusting each column.

When you have set the combo box contents as desired, click on 'Next>' to continue.

Here we come to the real point of the combo box. The wizard asks which field you want when the user clicks on a given row in the combo box. What we want to know is the 'CustomerID' of the customer row data that the user selects, so select 'CustomerID' from the list of combo box fields, and click on 'Next>' (Figure 6.90). It

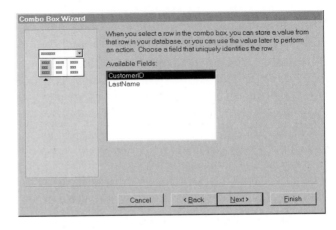

Figure 6.90 **Identifying the required field from the selected row**

is important to be clear that, at this point, the wizard is asking us about the field that we want to *use* from the 'Customer' table when the user selects a particular customer in the combo box.

The wizard then asks whether you want to do some calculations with the user-selected value, or simply to store that value. Select the button to store the value; in fact, it needs to be stored in the 'CustomerID' field of the 'Event' table (Figure 6.91).

The drop-down list in the wizard dialogue box lists all the fields of the 'Event' table. Again, it is important to be clear: at this point, the wizard is asking in which field of the 'Event' table the selected 'CustomerID' from the 'Customer' table is to be stored. Click on the down-arrow of the list box to see all the fields in the 'Event' table, and select 'CustomerID' from this list. Click on 'Next>'. The effect will be that the 'CustomerID' from the 'Customer' record will be inserted as the 'CustomerID' of the 'Event' record.

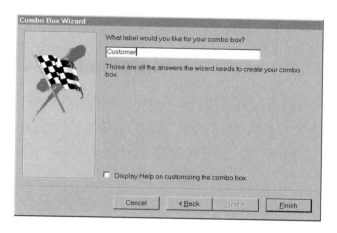

Figure 6.92 Providing the label for the combo box

label of 'Customer', and click on the 'Finish' button (Figure 6.92).

The result of using the combo box wizard is a 'Customer' combo box placed on the 'Event' form, illustrated in the Figure 6.93. You can drag the box around if it is not in the correct position.

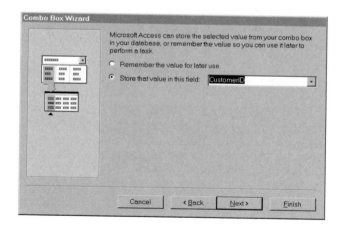

Figure 6.91 Identifying the field to receive the value from the selected row

The last wizard dialogue box asks us to provide the label for the combo box that will be shown on the 'Event' form. Enter a

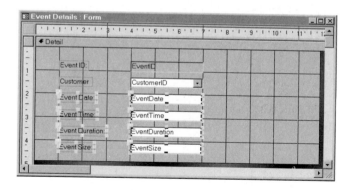

Figure 6.93 Resulting combo box on the 'Event' form

If we were now to try out our modified 'Event' form, we would notice that the combo box worked well (assuming, of course, that customers had already been added to the 'Customer' table), except that the combo box would list the customers in 'CustomerID' order rather than alphabetical order. The properties of the combo box can be modified so that the box shows customers in alphabetical order.

Changing the sort order of a combo box control

Open the 'Event' form in 'Design' view, and click on the 'Customer' combo box. The properties of this combo box are then shown in the properties table, as in Figure 6.94. Select the **Row Source** property of the combo box. A '...' button is shown, indicating that we can edit this property using a dialogue box of some sort. It is the 'Row Source' property that establishes the order in which the combo box items are displayed.

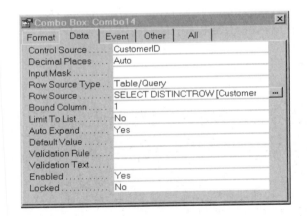

Figure 6.94 'Row Source' property of the combo box

Clicking on the '...' button of the 'Row Source' property of the 'Customer' combo box brings up the 'Query Builder'; in particular, the 'SQL Statement' query builder. It turns out that the combo box contents are established by an SQL statement which reads:

```
SELECT DISTINCTROW
    Customer.CustomerID,
Customer.LastName FROM Customer;
```

SQL (pronouced 'see-quel') stands for **Structured Query Language**, which is an industry-standard language for manipulating databases. We are now able to modify the SQL statement that produces the combo box contents, using the SQL query builder dialogue.

The 'SQL Statement: Query Builder' dialogue shows that two fields are involved in this combo box, that both fields come from the 'Customer' table, and that neither field is sorted. Click in the 'Sort' row of the 'LastName' column and a drop-down list box appears. Click on the down-arrow and select **Ascending** as the sort order. The result is as shown in Figure 6.95: the combo box contents are now sorted by 'LastName'.

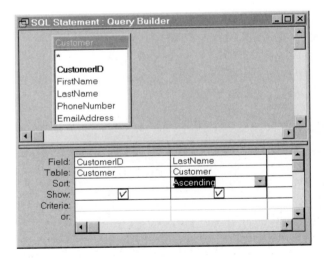

Figure 6.95 Setting a sort order in the SQL combo box statement

Click on the 'X' button of the SQL query builder, and Access asks you to confirm that you do indeed want the SQL statement modified. Click 'Yes' (Figure 6.96).

You might be interested to see the modified SQL statement:

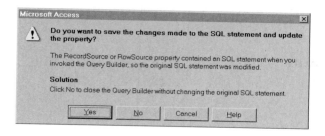

Figure 6.96 Confirmation of SQL statement change

```
SELECT DISTINCTROW
Customer.CustomerID,
Customer.LastName FROM Customer
ORDER BY Customer.LastName;
```

Exit from the 'Design' view of the 'Event' form. Access may well ask you to confirm your changes again.

Now when you open the 'Event Details' form and click on the 'Customer' combo box, existing customers are shown in alphabetical (ascending) order. This is illustrated in Figure 6.97 for a database containing two customers.

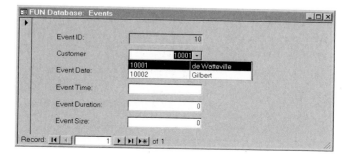

Figure 6.97 'Event Details' form with 'Customer' combo box

Multiple tables in one form

Although the 'Event Details' form reasonably shows the overall details of an event, we know that an event generally

consists of dinner, drinks, perhaps a disco, and other components. In fact, we have a table of these 'Event Components' specifically set up to maintain a set of standard event component details. These components must now be offered as part of the 'Event Details' form.

We also know that the components for an event are identified, for a particular event, through an 'Event/Component Link' table. What we want to do is to construct entries in the 'Event/Component Link' table for a particular event, so that the required components are linked to the event.

The first step is to construct a form corresponding to the 'Event/Component Link' table. The form in Figure 6.98 is the result of using the form wizard, and requesting that it construct a form for the 'EvCompLink' table using the **Datasheet** layout. You will see shortly why the datasheet (or tabular) layout, rather than the columnar layout, is preferred in this case.

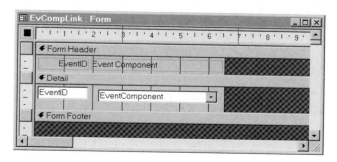

Figure 6.98 The design of the 'Event/Component Link' form

Note that on the 'EvCompLink' form the 'Event Component' control is a combo box whose contents have been taken from the 'Event Component' table. The standard event components are thus selected from the list provided in the combo box.

Now that we have the 'Event/Component Link' form, we may insert it into the 'Event

Details' form using the '**Subform/ Subreport Wizard**', and thereby create a form that involves two tables. The subform wizard arranges for the components of the event to be linked, via the 'Event/Component Link' table, to the 'Event' table.

Begin by opening the 'Event Details' form in 'Design' view. To make space for the forthcoming 'Event/Component Link form', rearrange the fields on the form, as shown in Figure 6.99.

The subform wizard is an icon on the toolbox. Click on the wizard icon, and the cursor changes into the wizard icon as well. Move the cursor into the 'Event Details' form, and drag a rectangle outline in a blank area. The subform Wizard dialogue box opens up, and the result on the 'Event Details' form is as shown in Figure 6.99.

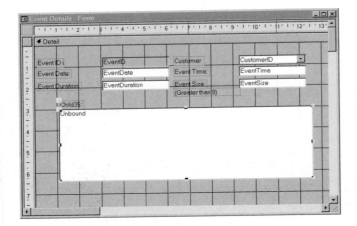

Figure 6.99 'Event Details' form at the start of the subform wizard

The wizard first asks whether there is an existing form to insert. We do have an existing form, but there would be no problem if we had not; the wizard would construct it for us. Identify the 'EvCompLink' form as the form to insert, and click on 'Next>' to continue (Figure 6.100).

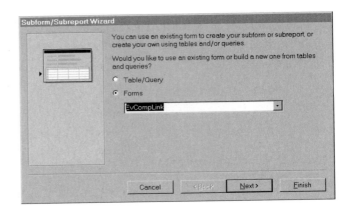

Figure 6.100 'Subform/Subreport Wizard': selecting an existing form to insert

The key dialogue of the subform wizard is shown in the next box. Having selected the 'EvCompLink' form to insert into the 'Event Details' form, the wizard is able to detect, through the relationships that we declared earlier, that the 'Event' table has a one-to-many relationship with the 'Event/Component Link' table, using 'EventID' as the key field. This relationship is highlighted; click on 'Next>' to continue.

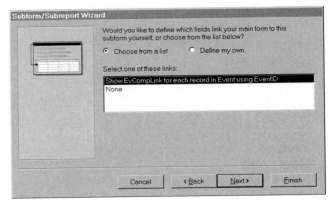

Figure 6.101 'Subform/Subreport Wizard': confirming the link between 'Event' and 'Event Component'

If, in this dialogue box, the wizard had failed to notice the link between the two tables involved, you would have been asked

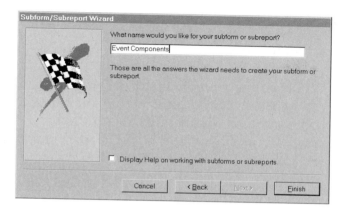

Figure 6.102 'Subform/Subreport Wizard': naming the subform

to define your own link. This would indicate that you had not defined the relationships correctly, or that you had not defined the tables correctly, in the earlier design of the database.

Having identified the link between the two tables involved, the wizard is ready to finish. It asks for the title to place on the form to be inserted. You could call the resulting subform 'Event Components', and click on 'Finish' (Figure 6.102).

When the wizard has finished working, the resulting 'Event Details' form is as shown in Figure 6.103. Nothing much seems to have happened; there is just a reserved space

where the 'EvCompLink' form will go when the 'Event Details' form is actually used.

The final screen shot of this chapter, Figure 6.104, shows the 'Event Details' form in use. You can now see that the 'EvCompLink' subform shows, in this example, that three components have been specified for this event, for which EventID = 10, for CustomerID = 10001.

The subform has a datasheet layout, which allows it to show more than one event component at a time; three are actually displayed, and there is room for another two or so before **scroll bars** would be provided automatically to allow more. A *tabular* layout would give the same effect; but a *columnar* layout would only show one component at a time, and would not be suitable for this application.

You can also see that each event component is implemented as a drop-down list. It is clearly easier for the user to select the component from a list, rather than having to type 'Dinner' or 'Drinks' every time.

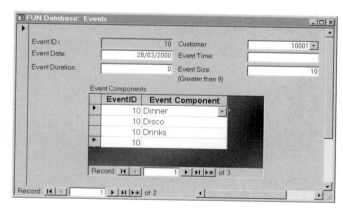

Figure 6.104 Resulting form with subform

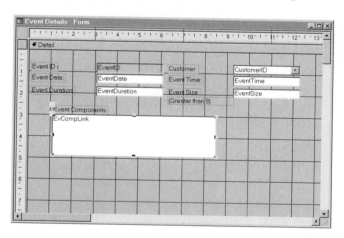

Figure 6.103 'Event Details' form with 'EvCompLink' subform inserted

Chapter 6.6 Reports

Producing reports from computer databases

A **report** is a way of displaying summary data from the records in a database. In Access, there is no significant distinction between a report that is shown on the screen and a report that is printed. In both cases, a requested report automatically displays on the screen. Clicking on the printer icon sends the report to the printer for printing.

Figure 6.105 shows the Access desktop when a report is on display. The desktop is a 'preview' desktop with icons relevant to preview shown on the Access taskbar.

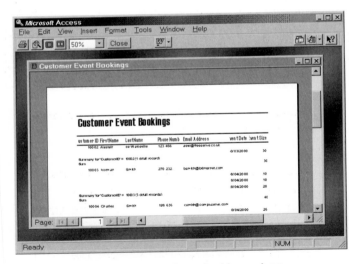

Figure 6.105 Access preview desktop when viewing a report

Associated with any report is a **query**, a statement or instruction which extracts the required data from the database for that report. In a sense, a report *is* a query, the answer to which is attractively arranged for viewing.

Constructing a report involves two components: firstly, constructing the query appropriate to the required report; and secondly, specifying the layout of the report, the grouping of the data records extracted, and the calculation of totals and subtotals.

We will begin by constructing a simple report using the **report wizard**. Then we will construct a more complex report from scratch. Constructing and using reports is very similar to constructing and using forms.

A new report using the report wizard

The first report will list, for each customer, the event or events booked. The report will include the customer details, and for each customer, the date and size of the booked events. It will total the event sizes for each customer, and give a grand total for *all* customers.

To start, click on the '**Report**' tab of the database window. There should be no reports listed, and only the 'New' button should be available. Click on it, and a dialogue box opens (Figure 6.106).

Select the '**Report Wizard**' as the desired method of creating the report, and choose the 'Customer' table as the source of the report's data.

You will want to add data from the 'Event' table as well; this will be possible in the next dialogue box. Click on the 'OK' button, and the report wizard will present the next dialogue box.

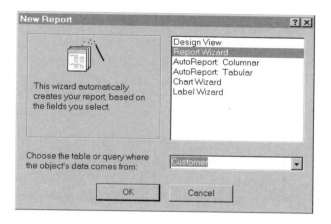

Figure 6.106 Creating a 'New Report'

Here, you can identify the various fields you want on the report. Identify the table that holds the required fields in the drop-down list box, select from the fields shown in the left-hand list box, and click on the '>' button to move the selected field into the right-hand list box (Figure 6.107).

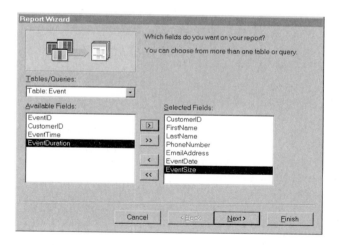

Figure 6.107 Selecting the fields for the report

Figure 6.107 shows all the fields from the 'Customer' table, and 'EventDate' and 'EventSize' fields from the 'Event' table. Click on the 'Next>' button.

The report wizard now shows us how it proposes to list the data in the report. In Figure 6.108 the wizard suggests that the

customer data is shown first, followed by the event data in an indented section. The wizard makes this suggestion because fields have been selected from both the 'Customer' and 'Event' tables, and it knows that we have specified a 1:m relationship between the 'Customer' and 'Event' entities. It therefore assumes that each customer record will be a master record, and that each event record will be a detail record of that master; on this basis it lays out the report accordingly.

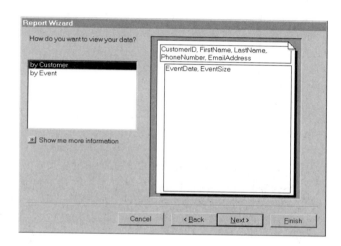

Figure 6.108 'Report Wizard': the proposed form of data listing

You could click on the 'Show me more information' button to see various examples of report layouts. For the time being, click on the 'Next>' button.

The next dialogue box asks whether you want any 'grouping' of the report data (Figure 6.109). It offers the fields of the report which you could select as the basis of any such grouping.

No grouping is required for this report; but you could, for example, ask for the report to be grouped by 'LastName'. The effect of this would be to gather together on the report all the customer records which had

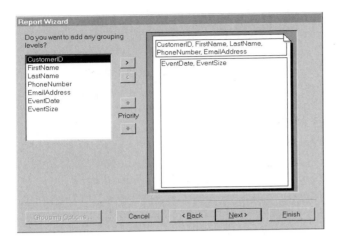

Figure 6.109 Report grouping

the same surname, along with their related event records. Click on the 'Next>' button.

The report wizard now asks about the detail records – that is, the event records for a particular customer (Figure 6.110). For these records, you can select how they are to be sorted, and what summary information should be calculated. Notice that the wizard has not asked how you want the customer or master records sorted; the wizard simply stipulates that the report contents will be sorted on the primary key of the 'Customer' table.

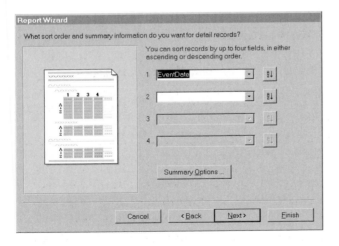

Figure 6.110 The sort order for records, and calculation options

To ensure that the individual event records for a customer are sorted in date order, click on the drop-down list box and select 'EventDate' as the sort field. Check that the sort order button reads 'A-Z' and not 'Z-A'. Click on the 'Summary Options...' button.

The 'Summary Options' dialogue box (Figure 6.111) shows the remaining fields in the detail records you are listing, and offers four options for making calculations using the fields. Check the 'Sum' box for the 'EventSize' field. This will cause the report to show the total number of places booked by a customer over all that customer's booked events.

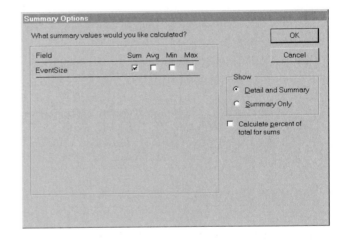

Figure 6.111 'Summary Options' for calculations on detail records

On the right-hand side of the dialogue box, two button options are offered: to show the calculation selected – 'Sum' of 'EventSize' – either at both the 'Detail and Summary' level, or at the 'Summary Only' level. Select the 'Detail and Summary' level, which will cause the report to show the total places for the events of a particular customer, as well as the total places for all customers. If we had selected 'Summary Only', then the report would not show the event places totals per customer. Click on the 'OK' button to exit the 'Summary Options' dialogue, and then click on the 'Next>' button to move on to the next report wizard dialogue.

The remaining wizard dialogues offer some layout options. In the following dialogue (Figure 6.112), there are options for the **'Layout'** style, and options for the page **'Orientation'**. You can experiment with each to see the effects; the screenshot shows selection of a **'Stepped'** layout and a **'Portrait'** page orientation.

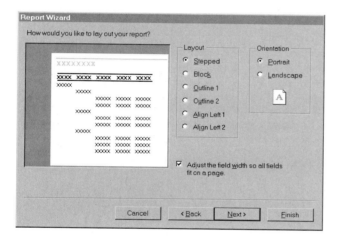

Figure 6.112 Report layout

Click on the 'Next>' button. The wizard offers us a choice of text styles, colours, fonts, and weights (Figure 6.113).

Choose the 'Compact' style, and click on the 'Next>' button. All that remains is to provide a title for the report, and the report is finished (Figure 6.114).

Enter a title of 'Customer Event Bookings', and click on 'Finish'. As the button to 'Preview the report' is selected, when the wizard finishes it displays the report you have just constructed. Figure 6.115 shows a screen shot of the resulting report.

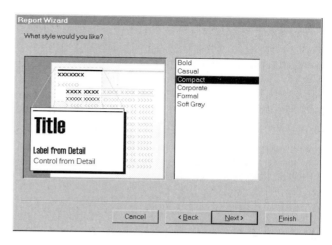

Figure 6.113 Report styles

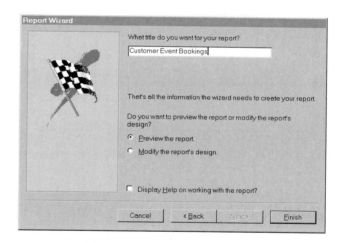

Figure 6.114 Report title

Commentary

There are six pre-set report styles from which you can choose. You can get an idea of what each looks like in the little window, and then select the one you like best: there is no right or wrong.

You will notice immediately that it is not perfect; in particular, not enough space is available for the column headings, and for some of the data. The wizard has not selected appropriate font sizes. You will see later how to modify a report: it is easy to change these and other aspects of any report as you wish. Close the report preview window by clicking on the 'X' button.

You can now see that the report has been added to the list of available reports in the database window (Figure 6.116).

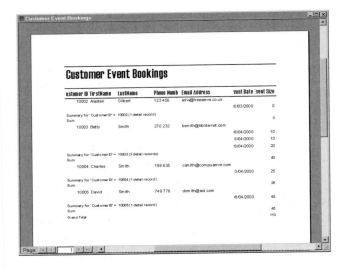

Figure 6.115 Preview of the first, imperfect report

It is instructive to look at the details of the report that the wizard produced. With the 'Customer Event Bookings' report highlighted, click on the 'Design' button. The result is the design screen for the report, complete with the toolbox, the list of fields used in the report, and the report

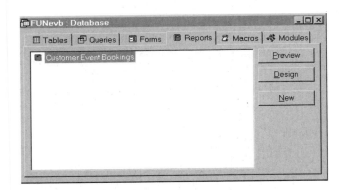

Figure 6.116 Report added to the 'Reports' tab of the database window

properties table. Figure 6.117 shows the report design screen itself.

Associated with the report design is the report properties display. With the whole report selected, the 'Data' tab of the properties shows us the most important feature, the 'Record Source' (Figure 6.118).

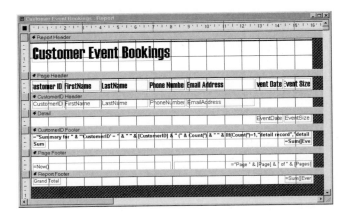

Figure 6.117 Report design screen

Figure 6.118 Report properties, 'Data' tab display

The 'Record Source' is the SQL query which extracts the required records from the database for display in the report. In full, the 'Record Source' reads as follows:

```
SELECT DISTINCTROW
[ Customer] .[ CustomerID] ,
[ Customer] .[ FirstName] ,
[ Customer] .[ LastName] ,
[ Customer] .[ PhoneNumber] ,
[ Customer] .[ EmailAddress] ,
[ Event] .[ EventDate] ,
[ Event] .[ EventSize] FROM
([ Customer]  INNER JOIN [ Event]  ON
[ Customer] .[ CustomerID]
=[ Event] .[ CustomerID] );
```

This is the SQL query or statement which 'drives' the report. Without trying to understand too much about SQL, it may be worth getting some idea about what the query statement says.

The first part of this SQL query is:

```
SELECT DISTINCTROW
[ Customer] .[ CustomerID] ,
[ Customer] .[ FirstName] ,
[ Customer] .[ LastName] ,
[ Customer] .[ PhoneNumber] ,
[ Customer] .[ EmailAddress] ,
[ Event] .[ EventDate] ,
[ Event] .[ EventSize]
```

This part of the query identifies the fields to extract from the records it finds.

The next part of the SQL query is

```
FROM ([ Customer]  INNER JOIN
[ Event] ON
[ Customer] .[ CustomerID]
=[ Event] .[ CustomerID] )
```

This part of the query identifies the required records to extract from the database. The required records are those from the combination of the 'Customer' and 'Event' tables – their 'inner join' – where a given CustomerID has an event booking recorded.

In summary, the report wizard has constructed the two report components needed: it has provided the SQL query statement on which the report is based; and it has laid out the resulting data according to various layout, style, and format options previously specified.

Constructing a new report from scratch involves these same two components. First, you need to construct the SQL query statement which extracts the data you require from the database. Secondly you will use the report design view to lay out the query results as you would like.

A new report from scratch: constructing the SQL query

The report to be made here is a report that lists all the event components which are booked for the next seven days. That is, the report will show all the 'Dinner' components booked, all the 'Disco' components, all the 'Drinks', and all the 'Other' components. For each component, the report will show the event ID, the date, and the event size.

Such a report would be wanted frequently by Sandra, FUN's Production Director, who must constantly check that all the resources needed to stage the events that have been negotiated can be made available at the correct times and places. Sandra must have enough notice to be able to book agency staff if necessary, and so she will always press Steve, the Commercial Director, to take bookings well ahead.

The first task in constructing a new report from scratch is to construct its underlying SQL query statement. To do this, click on the '**Query**' tab of the database window, and then click on the 'New' button. The resulting dialogue box, shown in Figure 6.119, asks how you would like to go about creating the new query.

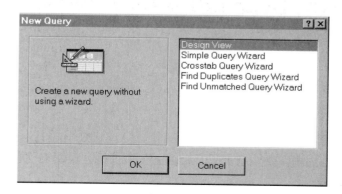

Figure 6.119 Creating a new query

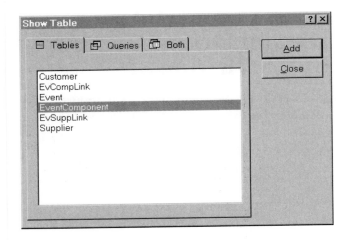

Figure 6.120 Tables to be selected for the query

Select 'Design View', and click 'OK'. Access opens two windows. The first is a dialogue box, 'Show Table', shown in Figure 6.120, which allows you to select the tables that will be queried for the required data.

When you select a required table and click on 'Add', the table fields are shown in the second window, the SQL query builder window (Figure 6.121). Select and add these tables: 'EventComponent', 'EvCompLink', and 'Event'. Close the 'Show Table' dialogue box. The SQL query builder window now has the three required tables shown in its upper panel, complete with their relationships.

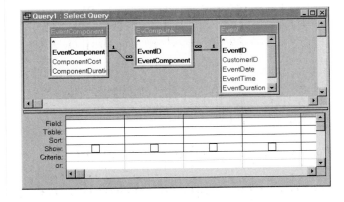

Figure 6.121 SQL query builder window with required tables displayed

The SQL query is built in the lower pane of the window. Click on the fields required from the tables on display, and drag them one by one into the 'Field' row of the next blank column. The resulting display is shown in Figure 6.122, after dragging in the 'EventComponent' field from the 'EventComponent' table, the 'EventID' from the 'EvCompLink' table, and the 'EventDate' and 'EventSize' fields from the 'Event' table.

Notice what has been done. In order to find all the events for a particular event

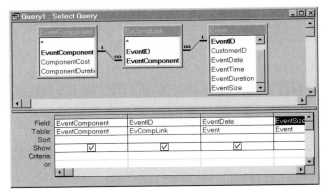

Figure 6.122 Building the SQL query

component, you have specified that, for a given event component from the 'Event Component' table, Access must look up the event ID from the 'EvCompLink' table that uses that component, and then look up the event date and size from the record in the 'Event' table that corresponds to that event.

Finally, you need to specify that you only want records of events due in the next seven days (Figure 6.123).

This is done by specifying, in the 'Criteria:' row of the 'EventDate' column, that the event date must be less than today's date plus seven days. The expression to do this is '<Now()+7'.

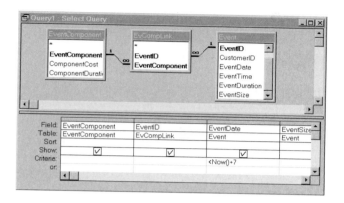

Figure 6.123 Specifying criteria for the records to be extracted

Having finished building your query, click on the 'X' of the query builder window to bring up the dialogue box in Figure 6.124.

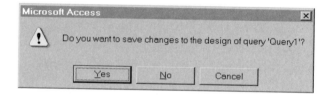

Figure 6.124 'Save changes' dialogue box

Click the 'Yes' button, and then supply a name for the query (Figure 6.125).

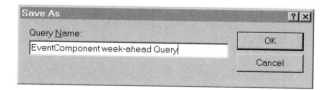

Figure 6.125 Naming the new query

The new query is now shown in the database window (Figure 6.126).

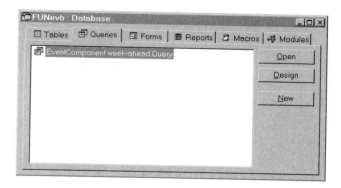

Figure 6.126 Database window, 'Queries' tab display

Try it out	Suppose the date is 30th October and Sandra wants to know what bookings there are for FUN to put on firework parties within the next seven days; and, of those, how many are linked to a disco the same evening. See whether you can build the query she will have to use.

A new report from scratch: laying out the report in 'Design View'

We have already constructed the required query for the report: extract all event records from the database that are due in the next seven days, and group them under each type of event component. This query can now be used as the basis for a report.

Begin by clicking on the 'Reports' tab of the database window and then on the 'New' button.

In the resulting dialogue box (Figure 6.127), make sure that 'Design View' is selected as the method of constructing the report. In the drop-down list box, select our newly-created query 'Event Component

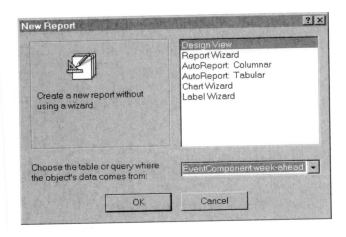

Figure 6.127   Creating a 'New Report'

week-ahead Query' as the source of the data for forthcoming report. Click on the 'OK' button to continue.

The design view for creating or amending a report is a fairly busy one, with five windows or components. These windows are illustrated in Figure 6.128.

Not all of these windows appear automatically. It may be necessary to go to the 'View' menu item and make sure there is a check mark against each of the required components, or to click on the relevant

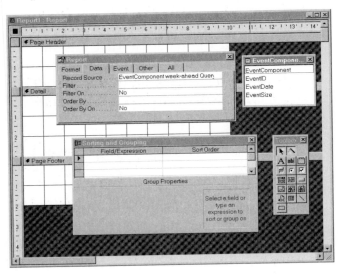

Figure 6.128   Creating a new report in 'Design View'

icons on the Access report toolbar. A portion of the toolbar is shown in Figure 6.129, with the relevant icons depressed.

Figure 6.129   Access report toolbar

The large main window is the design screen itself, where you lay out the report headings, fields, and so on. It is divided, by default, into three sections, allowing you to put information into the report page header, the page footer, and the body or 'detail' of the report itself.

Associated with the report is its tabbed report properties dialogue box, with the now-familiar tabs of 'Format', 'Data', 'Events', 'Other', and 'All'. Figure 6.128 shows that the 'Record Source' property shown under the 'Data' tab of the report properties is the query we specified, 'EventComponent week-ahead Query'.

Next to the properties window in the screen shot is a field list window, showing all the data fields which are involved in the query selected. This list will be used shortly to drag each field over to the layout window and position it as required.

Towards the bottom of the screen is the 'Sorting and Grouping' dialogue box. This allows you to specify how the report data is to be grouped and sorted.

Finally, there is the 'Toolbox' window. Components of the toolbox were used in constructing forms earlier; tools will also be helpful with this report design.

Dropping the fields into the report

The first step is to click on each of the fields in the field list, and drag and drop it to the report layout screen. Figure 6.130 shows the 'EventComponent', 'EventID', 'EventDate' and 'EventSize' fields dropped into the 'Detail' section.

Notice that a text label box comes with each field control, and that the 'EventComponent' comes with the combo box control specified earlier when the 'EventComponent' table was designed.

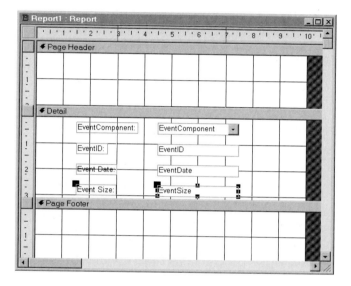

Figure 6.130 Dragging and dropping the fields into the report

Grouping the fields into a report section

The next step is to gather together the report data into groups, to make the report easier to read and its layout more logical. Event data should be grouped according to the event component, to give all events with 'Dinner' listed in one group, then all events with 'Disco' listed in another group, and so on. To achieve this, you can use the **'Sorting and Grouping'** window.

In the field list, click on the field that controls the grouping: in this case it is the 'EventComponent' field. Drag this field over

to the 'Sorting and Grouping' window, and drop it into the first row under the 'Field/Expression' column heading. The result is shown in Figure 6.131.

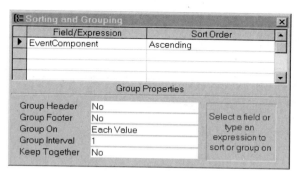

Figure 6.131 Grouping by 'EventComponent' field

Notice that you are given ascending sort order by default. Components will therefore be listed in the following order: 'Dinner', 'Disco', 'Drinks' and 'Other'.

Having arranged for the required data to be extracted from the database and listed in the report, it is now time to improve the layout of the report. The next task is to provide a clear heading for the event records which will be grouped under each event component. At the 'Sorting and Grouping' window, change the **'Group Header'** setting from 'No' to 'Yes' (Figure 6.132).

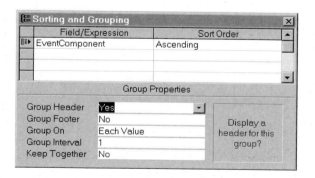

Figure 6.132 Providing a group header in the report

The report layout screen immediately changes, and a new section is added, titled 'EventComponent Header' (Figure 6.133). Whatever you put into this new header will be printed on the report whenever the records for the next event component are shown.

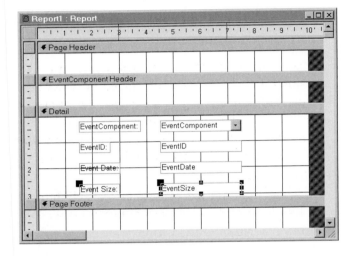

Figure 6.133 'EventComponent' header

Improving the report layout

Figure 6.134 illustrates some improvements to the report layout.

The 'Event Component' control has been dragged and positioned in the relevant header section. The title text has an

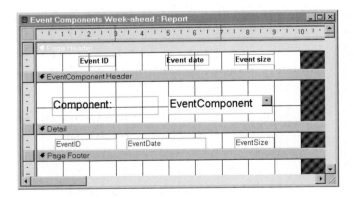

Figure 6.134 Improving the report layout

increased font size, has been rendered as bold, and has been changed to read simply 'Component:'.

Additional label boxes have been added to the page header, to serve as column headings for the following detail records. Each label box was created by using the 'Label' tool from the toolbox. The labels have been set as bold, and positioned towards the right so that they line up with the data columns.

In the detail section, the labels for the controls have been deleted; all that remains are the controls for the fields themselves. The detail section has also been narrowed so that the detail records are displayed closer together.

Many other improvements could also be made, of course. It would be useful to have the date of the report shown in the footer, perhaps, along with a page number. It would be useful to have a thin horizontal line separating successive event components; and so on.

However, the present version will serve as an example. Click on the 'X' of the report layout screen. Access asks whether you want to save the changes (Figure 6.135).

Click on the 'Yes' button, and then supply a name for the report (Figure 6.136).

Figure 6.135 Saving the changes

The new report is added to the list of reports shown in the database window (Figure 6.137).

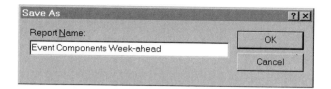

Figure 6.136 Naming the new report

To see what our report looks like, select it in the database window, and click on the '**Preview**' button. Figure 6.138 shows the result.

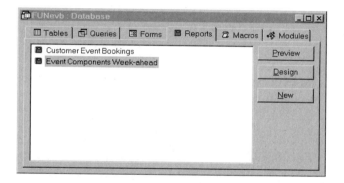

Figure 6.137 Reports shown in the database window

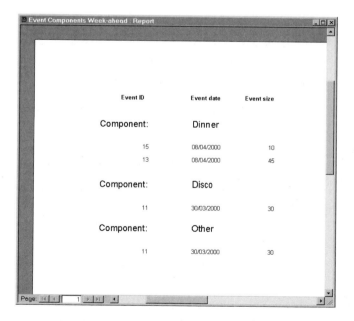

Figure 6.138 The new 'Event Components Week-ahead' report

Amending a report

An existing report can be changed. An example is to amend the 'Event Components' report, by adding a subtotals field so that the report shows the total number of places booked in the week ahead for each event component.

Select the report, and click on the 'Design' button.

The subtotal of the event places for an event component can be placed in a footer section for each component. As yet there is no footer section: to request one, set '**Group Footer**' to 'Yes' in the 'Sorting and Groups' window, as shown in Figure 6.139.

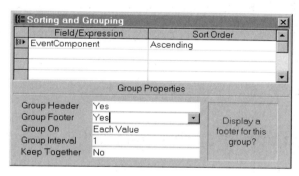

Figure 6.139 Creating a footer section for each event component

The new footer section is shown immediately in the report layout screen.

In order to place a subtotal in the new footer section, create a **text box control**, and insert into the control a formula to calculate the required value.

Click on the '**Text Box**' control icon in the toolbox. Move the cursor into the footer section, where it changes into a cross-hair. Drag the cross-hair cursor to create a rectangular box, and release the mouse button. The result is a text box control, comprising a label component, and the text box itself with the word 'Unbound' inside. The label component will have a name such as 'Text12' or similar.

Edit the label to read 'Total:'. Click on the text box itself, and select the 'Data' tab on the properties sheet. In the '**Control Source**' property, enter the formula '=Sum([EventSize])'. The result is as shown in Figure 6.140.

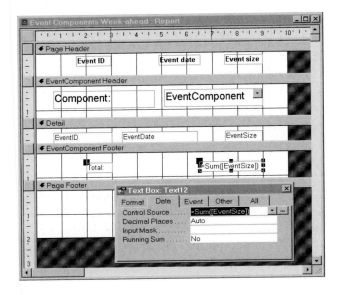

Figure 6.140   Text box control to give subtotals of 'Event Size'

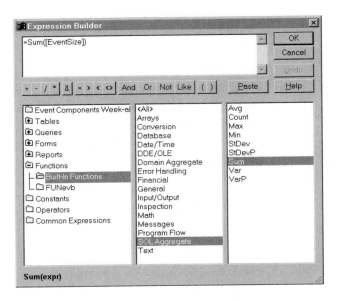

Figure 6.141   The 'Expression Builder' being used to create the formula for the subtotal

If you are not sure of a formula to enter, click on the '...' button next to the 'Control Source' property. This brings up the 'Expression Builder' window, where you can create the formula or expression that you need from the components presented to you (Figure 6.141).

Figure 6.141 shows that the 'Sum()' function is listed under the '**SQL Aggregate**' built-in function. Any necessary field names would be found by expanding the 'Tables' list.

Chapter 6.7 Database documentation and testing

As with the earlier topics of spreadsheets and system installation and configuration, we cover documentation and testing in a single chapter. 'Testing' comes after 'documentation' because documentation itself must be subject to testing.

Documentation

This part of this chapter is divided into:

- technical documentation
- user documentation.

Technical documentation

As discussed in Chapter 3.3, on documentation of a spreadsheet, the systems development life cycle provides a convenient framework for the technical documentation of any software development project, including a database project. Each major phase of the life cycle involves the development of a set of products which represent the work of that phase. These products constitute the technical documentation of the project. They are listed in Figure 6.142 and discussed below.

User requirements

The **user requirements** for a database are documented in two major products: a *data catalogue* (also known as a *data dictionary*), and an *entity-relationship diagram*. Unit 5 introduced these concepts. For a more complex database, it is also useful to document the processing specifications by way of a *context diagram* and one or more *data flow diagrams*, and to provide a *requirements catalogue* with all associated non-functional components. The user requirements are the major outcome of the systems analysis phase.

Inspection procedures

As discussed in Chapter 3.3, on testing spreadsheets, validation may be carried out using the technique of Fagan inspection. A brief statement of the procedures involved should be part of the products for the systems analysis phase.

Layouts

Although *data entry*, *enquiry* and *report layouts* would have been started in systems analysis, they would be more fully detailed

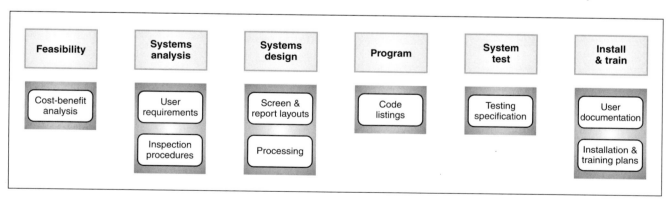

Figure 6.142 Development products and technical documentation

during system design. They constitute one of the two major outcomes of the systems design phase.

Processing

The other major documentation product of systems design is the detailed design of the processing that the database application will do: the *data entry procedures* and *checks*, details of any *calculations* to be made; and the production of *reports* and *enquiries*.

Code listings

Printouts of all **program code** should be provided. This allows someone to check what version of a program is in use; and also, in the event of a query, to clarify exactly what the program does.

Testing specification

If you have covered Chapter 3.3, you will have seen that the testing specification consists of all the *test plans*, and that each test plan has its collection of *test cases*. The same applies here, with databases.

Installation and training plans

Appropriate technical documentation includes the **schedule** for the **installation** of the system and the **training** of the users, along with any special installation requirements, training materials, and instructions for creating an appropriate *training environment*.

User documentation

As noted in Chapter 3.3, writing good user documentation can be almost as important to the overall success of your project as constructing a good database.

One way of writing good *user* documentation – as opposed to technical documentation, which is of very little relevance to users – is to treat this as a mini-development project in itself. The requirements for the user documentation should first be analysed during an analysis phase.

Then, following acceptance of the documentation requirements, the required user documentation should be designed

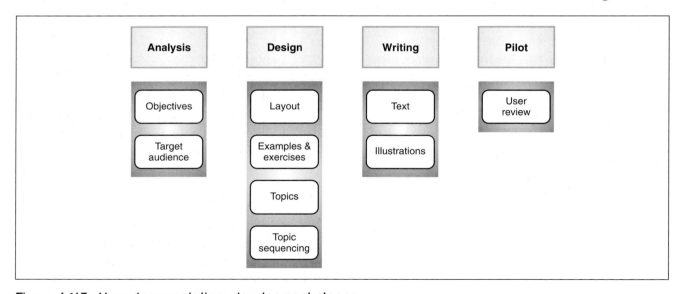

Figure 6.143 User documentation: development stages

during a design phase. Following acceptance of the user documentation design, the text may be written, illustrations drawn and screen shots recorded, and the documentation assembled into the required medium, usually a printed booklet. The draft of the documentation should then be submitted for testing, checking, inspection, and review through **pilot usage** by a representative **panel of users**, before being finalised. This process is illustrated in Figure 6.143.

Analysis of user documentation requirements

The key to successful user documentation is a clear understanding of the *user's requirements* for that documentation. This is the first task of analysis, in which you establish the **objectives** of the user documentation.

Objectives

The objectives of the user documentation must be stated in terms of what the user is to be able to *do*, and never in terms of what the user needs to *know*. The distinction is subtle, but vital: your approach in developing the user documentation must be orientated towards what the user wants to do with the database, not towards what the user might want to know *about* it.

For example, the FUN events database has a number of tables, some forms, and some reports. You might be tempted to write some user documentation which says just that:

The events database has a number of tables, some forms, and some reports.

Some users might find that interesting, maybe even helpful, but most would not. Instead, to help the users actually *use* the database, the same information would be presented in a different way. For example: Click on the 'Forms' tab of the database window, select the 'Customer', 'Event', or 'Supplier' form, and click on the 'Open' button to enter your data. Click on the 'Reports' tab to see what output information is available for event bookings.

As always, the golden rule is to put yourself in the users' shoes and picture what detail you would like to see in the documentation.

The result of defining the objectives of the user documentation is likely to be quite a long list, because it will list all the things that the user *might* want to do with the system. For larger systems, the task of defining all the objectives is split into two parts: first identify the top-level or broader objectives, and then break down each top-level objective into its components. For example, some of the FUN database top-level objectives might be 'Start the database application', 'Enter data', 'Change data', and 'Print reports'. The top-level objective 'Enter data' would be broken down into lower-level objectives such as 'Enter customer details', 'Enter event bookings', and 'Enter supplier details'.

Table 6.2 provides a partial list of top-level and lower-level objectives for the FUN database user documentation.

Target audience

During the analysis of the user documentation requirements, it is also important to characterise the intended **audience** for the documentation. This will

Top-level objective	Lower-level objectives
Starting the 'Event Bookings' database	Starting Access Opening the 'Event Bookings' database
Entering data	Selecting the required data entry form Entering data using the data entry form
Changing data	
Correcting errors	Validation checks on data items Checks for non-existent customers and other records
Printing reports	Selecting the required report Printing the report
Quitting the 'Event Bookings' database	

Table 6.2 Documentation objectives

help to ensure an appropriate design of the documentation, and the use of appropriate text, illustrations, and examples.

Design of user documentation

Topics and topic sequencing

Having identified all the *objectives* of the user documentation, it is then very easy to identify the **topics** that the documentation should cover. Usually, for each distinct objective, there is a topic that needs to be covered. For example, in order for users to achieve the objective 'Enter data', they need to know about the topics of opening the required form, typing data into the form's fields, and pressing the <Enter> key to add the new data to the database.

What will require more care during design is the **sequence** in which the topics are presented in the documentation. There are no hard and fast rules. For example, should the topic dealing with correcting errors follow the topic of changing the data entered, or should it come before? Mistakes or problems with topic sequencing will emerge during the piloting of the documentation.

Examples and exercises

The second major task of designing the user documentation is designing the **examples** which will illustrate each of the topics, and the **exercises** which will help the user to learn each of the topic activities.

This part of user documentation is usually the most time-consuming to construct, and hence is often skimped. It is, however, the most valuable part of the documentation. Frequent, numerous and rich examples and exercises distinguish excellent documentation from poor documentation.

Layout

While it is often presumed that the user documentation will be in the form of a

printed booklet, this is not the only way to teach the user about the system. In the case of a database form, for example, it might be more effective to have an **interactive tutorial** so that the user could actually sit at the computer and be guided by tutorial software through filling in the form.

Designing the layout simply involves choosing where material should go on the page, and how it should look. Keeping to a specified layout design is important: it makes the user documentation coherent and thus easier to use.

Writing the documentation

Writing is covered in Units 1 and 2. Keep in mind the target audience whom you identified during the user documentation analysis: this will help you set an appropriate tone and style.

Pilot

Before the documentation is finalised, it should be piloted. This is a vital stage to ensure the final materials are as error-free and problem-free as possible. Your selected panel of users and others will point out spelling and grammatical errors, places where instructions are hard to follow, places where you assume knowledge they do not (yet) have, and illustrations, examples, and exercises that seem inappropriate or plain wrong.

Testing

As explained in Unit 3, on spreadsheets, computer systems are some of the most difficult systems to check for correct operation. One of the reasons for this is that their working parts – the software –

are invisible. Checking the correct operation of machinery, for example, is much easier: you can see what is happening. (Similarly, when the design for a database exists only inside the designer's head, it is very difficult to check that the design is likely to work properly.)

Another factor is that during the development of a database, much effort goes into ensuring that the database works as required, which usually means ensuring that it works with 'normal' data and 'normal' usage. It is usually difficult to design and build procedures and programs that can withstand abnormal or extreme usage, because it is difficult to imagine *all* the alternative possibilities to the 'normal' or 'usual'. In a very real sense, there is usually one way to process the data in a database correctly, but an infinite number of ways to do so incorrectly! The result is often a database that works correctly under 'normal' circumstances, but that fails when faced with particular other circumstances – some of these 'unusual' circumstances may in fact be quite common, but not ones that the designer thought of as 'normal'.

Two lessons emerge. First, people other than the development team – analyst, designer, programmer – must check and test the database design and implementation. These components must be subject to inspection and review by people who did not originate the components themselves.

Secondly, as much as possible of the design and the development process needs to made as 'visible' and accessible. This generally means writing down all of the components of a design, drawing diagrams and making notes, so that these concrete development products can be checked, inspected, reviewed, and tested.

Quality

In a general sense, **quality assurance** in a database development project can be thought of as comprising three components:

- defect prevention
- defect removal
- development process continual improvement.

These three components underlie the whole of the systems development life cycle, as illustrated in Figure 6.144.

Defect removal – testing

Defect removal involves testing the database for errors, and fixing any problems. It generally takes place during and after implementation. However, testing can only take place after the errors and problems have found their way in the first place *into* the database. It is more efficient and more effective if you can prevent the defects from creeping in at all.

Defect prevention – inspection

Defect prevention covers those activities that seek to prevent errors occurring. The major technique of defect prevention is inspection: checking that, at each stage of development, the database design so far both matches the user requirements and conforms with the earlier analysis and design work. Inspection and review generally occurs during feasibility, analysis, and design.

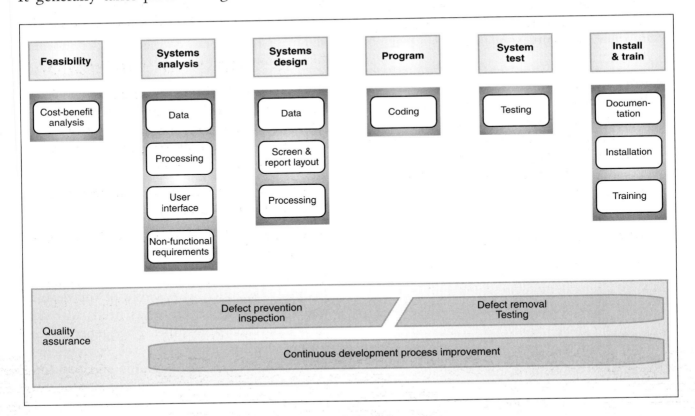

Figure 6.144 Systems development life cycle with quality assurance

Development process continual improvement

Finally, although inspecting and testing will ensure that a particular database is delivered as error-free as possible, these techniques do nothing to ensure that the next *project* will fare better. It is more than likely that the same sort of problems and errors will recur.

Hence, the third component of an effective quality assurance programme is to seek continuous improvements in the *development process* itself.

- Firstly, this involves looking for better ways to manage the project: better ways to estimate the project schedule and budget; better ways to identify the tasks that must be done; better ways to identify which tasks can overlap, and which must be properly signed-off before the next tasks can begin; and better ways to set, agree, and carry out reviews of progress.

- Secondly, improvements in the development process involve setting standards that need to be met for a good-quality requirements specification, a good-quality design of the proposed solution, and a good quality of database implementation.

Independent testing

The testing and checking of any system needs to be done independently. This means two things.

First, the people who do the testing and checking must not be the same people who analysed, designed, or implemented the database. The reason is quite simple, and is a result of human nature. When *you* produce something, it is something that 'fits' with how *you* work, how *you* solve problems, and how *you* construct solutions. Being used to your own way of working, it is then difficult for you to see anything wrong with your own approach, and so you are naturally biased when it comes to testing your solutions.

Someone else must test or check your work. As and when any changes need to be made, these changes should then be carried out by the same people who originally analysed, designed, or implemented the database – it is they who know the database best, after all.

Secondly, where the database needs to perform certain computations or produce certain results, these computations must be performed in another way and using a different system, independently. Usually, this means doing the calculations by hand.

Validation and verification

Testing and checking are sometimes called, more exactly, **verifying** and **validating**. These two kinds of activity are subtly different, in that they seek to ensure two different kinds of quality.

- *Verification*: whatever the database does, does it do it correctly?

- *Validation*: does the database do the right things?

Validation, for our purposes here, consists of ensuring that the database meets the user's specified requirements. The process is extremely straightforward: inspect the database, look through the requirements catalogue (Chapter 5.2), and check that every user requirement is in fact met by the database.

Inspection and review

Inspections and reviews are a form of quality assurance. The inspection or review of any item involves two things. On the one hand, we have the item itself which is under inspection. On the other hand, we have numerous precursor items – documents, diagrams, specifications, standards, checklists – with which the item under inspection must agree.

The process of inspection compares the item under inspection with the precursor items, and checks that the item under inspection is coherent with, consistent with, and conforms to, the precursor items. The outcome of the inspection is a list of **discrepancies** (presumed defects) between the item under inspection and the precursor items. These discrepancies are then addressed and eliminated. Often, it is one of the precursor items that needs attention rather than the item currently under inspection.

This outline of the inspection process is that developed by M. E. Fagan, working at IBM, and is illustrated in Figure 6.145.

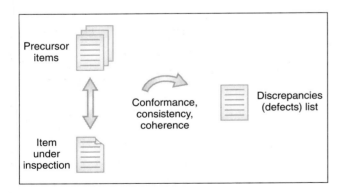

Figure 6.145 Fagan inspection

Test plans and test cases

Verification – testing proper – is covered in the remainder of this chapter. These points have also been discussed in Unit 3, on spreadsheets.

There are a number of different testing techniques. We will consider a single technique of testing called **boundary value analysis**.

A **test specification** for a given project will contain numerous individual test plans.

A given technique of testing will give rise to a **test plan**, covering one of the inputs or outputs of the database under test. A test plan in turn consists of a number of **test cases**. Each test case consists of the input and expected output involved in the test (Figure 6.146).

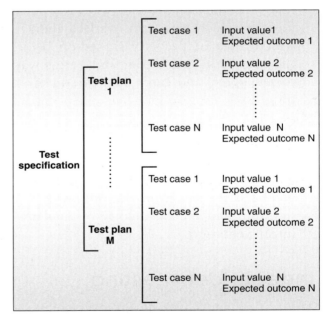

Figure 6.146 Structure of a test plan and its test cases

For the FUN event database, for example, there would be a test plan for testing that the database accepts and stores the 'Event size' data item correctly. This test plan for the 'Event size' would specify some test cases. Each test case would involve feeding in a value for the event size, and would specify the expected outcome: what will be observed if the database has operated correctly.

Boundary value analysis

In general, a data item has a range of valid values that occur between two boundaries. For example, suppose that a valid 'Event Size' is any number between 10 and 500. In this case, the value '10' is the lower boundary, and '500' is the upper boundary.

A **boundary value analysis test plan** specifies that there should be *six* test cases for a data item being tested, three of these cases being tests at the lower boundary of the data item, and three at the upper boundary (Figure 6.147). Of these three cases at a given boundary, one case must involve a value for the data item one less than the boundary value, one case involves the boundary value itself, and the third test case involves a value which is one greater than the boundary value.

The database should only accept event sizes between 10 and 500, and should not accept any other values. In this case, a boundary

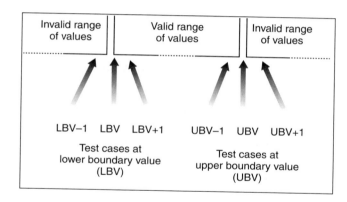

Figure 6.147 Test cases for a boundary value analysis test plan

value analysis would involve test cases with event sizes of 9, 10, 11, 499, 500, and 501. So the test plan is as shown in Table 6.3.

Testing issues specific to databases

A database application typically comprises a number of elements which are common to almost all database applications: a *main menu* and *sub-menus*; *data entry forms*; *facilities to update and delete records*; *standard reports and enquiries*. Each of these elements should be the focus of a set of test plans.

TEST PLAN		
Boundary value analysis of valid values for 'Event Size'		
Case	Input	Expected output
1	9	Error message displayed, 'Event Size too small'
2	10	Event Size value accepted
3	11	Event Size value accepted
4	499	Event Size value accepted
5	500	Event Size value accepted
6	501	Error message displayed, 'Event Size too large'

Table 6.3 Test plan

Testing menus

Testing a menu system involves a number of checks. The following list indicates tests that are likely to be relevant.

- Each item on the menu, when selected, is correctly accessed or activated.

- Each item on the menu is well labelled, and its function perfectly clear.

- Where a menu has items that are sometimes available, and sometimes not, the availability of each item must be clearly shown and distinguishable.

- The menu items are listed and/or grouped logically. (For example, it is useful to have the items of every menu arranged according to the sequence 'create–amend–enquire–report–delete–exit'.)

- Use of colour, fonts, and emphasis is consistent.

- There is a 'Help' facility for complex menus.

- Having used a menu item, the user is returned at completion to the relevant menu.

- As the user moves from menu item to menu item, it is perfectly clear where the user is in the menu structure.

- There is a clearly labelled and easily accessible facility to exit from a menu item which may have been entered accidentally.

Testing data entry forms

Much of the testing in data entry involves the test plans discussed earlier, particularly boundary value analysis, whereby every attempt is made to see that the application only accepts data that is within valid ranges.

In addition, tests must be carried out to check that *referential integrity* in the database is maintained. When creating new data records, an attempt should be made to create a new detail record for which the relevant master record does not exist. (This is shown, of course, by a 1:m relationship between these two tables.) For example, as a test you should attempt to enter the details of a FUN event for a non-existent customer. Normally in such circumstances an error message would appear (in this case specifying that the customer must first be recorded before any events can be booked for that customer), but in a more sophisticated application the user might be allowed to create the necessary customer record then and there.

Finally, as for all presentations of information, these are some of the considerations for *data entry forms.* They should offer:

- Clear, informative titles.

- Clear, useful, and relevant supporting text and/or pictures.

- Clear field labels.

- Useful help facilities.

- Clear, useful error messages.

- Abort facilities.

- Consistency of layout, use of colour, font, and emphasis.

- An ordering of data fields that reflects the 'normal' or 'natural' order in which data is to be input.

- Data fields whose content is for information only should be clearly non-editable.

- Data fields where data entry is required should be clearly identified.

- Data fields in which only certain restricted data may be entered should have user-friendly support to ensure that valid data only can be entered

- The default value for a data field should be carefully considered so that changes to this value are the exception rather than the norm. If changes would be frequent, no default value should be offered.

- The value shown or entered for any data field that is empty, blank, or non-existent should be carefully considered. In particular, the value in a 'blank' field should be clearly different from any actual data value, such as zero or its equivalent in date, time, or text terms.

Testing updates and deletes

Referential integrity must also be checked during updates and deletions.

First, an attempt should be made to change the values of a master record while entering data into the detail record. For example, while entering the details of, say, the third event booking for a customer, you should attempt to change the customer name, and then the customer address. Depending upon the application, at least the first, and perhaps both, of these attempts should be blocked.

Secondly, an attempt should be made to delete a master record while there are still valid detail records associated with that master. For example, you might attempt to delete a FUN customer who has an event currently booked. Depending upon how the user wishes the data to be processed, this might be permitted after a warning message has been displayed, or it might be blocked.

Testing standard reports and enquiries

Every report and enquiry available in the application should be tested.

The technique is to populate the database with a small number of carefully constructed records, and then to request the relevant reports and enquiries.

Every report and enquiry should have two test records specifically constructed and inserted into the database for that report or enquiry. One test record should have data values which ensure that it *does* appear in the relevant report or enquiry, and the second test record should have data such that it should *not* appear.

Four test runs are then made with the particular report or enquiry:

- for the first test run, *both* test records are present in the database

- for the second test run, just one of the test records is present, and the other is removed

- for the third test run, the other test record is present, and the first is removed

- for the fourth test run, *neither* record is present in the database.

In all test runs, it is expected that the report or enquiry produces the correct display or printout.

These tests can be extended, if it is considered sufficiently important, to the situation where a large number of records are created for a given report or enquiry, such that there are more records than can fit on one page of printout or on one screen-full of results. The test checks that the application can handle multi-page and multi-screen outputs.

As for all presentations of information, these are the main criteria for good reports and enquiries:

- Clear, informative titles.
- Clear date (and perhaps time) stamping.
- Clear, useful, and relevant supporting text and/or pictures.
- Clear, informative field, column, or row labels.
- Clear, useful error messages.
- Abort facilities.
- Consistency of layout, use of colour, font, and emphasis.
- An ordering of data fields that reflects the 'normal' or 'natural' order in which the data is to be used, or that reflects the priority or importance of the data, such that the most important information occurs first.
- A carefully chosen value for a data field which is empty, blank, or non-existent, such that it can be readily distinguished from an actual data value of zero or its equivalent in date, time, or text.

The results of whatever tests are carried out must be recorded.

Finally – thoughts on Unit 6 as a whole

We have seen as a theme running through this unit on database design the continuous pressure exerted by users for more and more data to be stored. The volumes of data already stored on ICT systems are immense; and the demands for future storage keep accelerating. The designers of storage equipment and of database management software have to keep innovating, and releasing new products to the market, in their struggle to keep their heads above water.

Just one example will highlight the tempo of the growth we shall be seeing. A recent study predicted that by the year 2006 there would be 1 500 000 000 mobile phones in use in the world. Apart from the data needed for managing all the networks of telephones, the users will be expecting to be able to transmit substantial files of data.

As specialists in the field of ICT we have to keep in mind this thought: there is no point in storing the huge quantities of data demanded by users unless they can select what they want and have it presented in convenient ways. We can add that they want to have exactly what they call for, and neither more nor less; and they want it provided accurately, attractively, and immediately.

This sounds like a reasonable set of goals, but it can only be achieved by competent design of the structure of the data, appropriate selection methods, well-chosen report formats, and thorough testing. As databases become bigger, and data warehouses become more usual, the work of the ICT professional will become ever more crucial to the meeting of users' needs, whether those users be companies, government bodies, or any other kind of organisation.

Unit 6 Assessment

This assignment is based on the Festivities Unlimited, or FUN, case study described in the general Introduction on pages xiii and xiv at the front of the book.

Scenario

The directors of the newly enlarged FUN business want to get a good understanding of the way the SAD shops operate: in particular, they want to be able to assess the efficiency of their purchasing activities.

Although SAD buy much of their stock through the YARD wholesale suppliers, they use 20 other suppliers for newspapers and a range of items some of which are not carried by YARD. SAD buy some of their fast-moving lines from more than one supplier.

Although all orders are placed centrally, on behalf of the SAD chain, deliveries are made to the individual SAD shops that had asked for the items.

The FUN directors believe that they need a database relating product lines, suppliers, and each of the four SAD shops.

Your tasks

You are required to create a database, using Microsoft Access, to meet the wishes of the FUN directors. You must use your imagination to allot attributes to the entities you identify. For example, product lines are available in various sizes, packed in various quantities, each combination available at a published price. To keep the scale of this assignment within bounds, you should assume that there are 40 distinct product lines purchased by the SAD shops.

The major use of the database will be to supply answers to queries and to provide reports.

The kinds of queries that it must be able to answer include:

- Which of the SAD shops ordered product 'xxx' last month? And what quantity did each order? Which supplier was, or suppliers were, used?

- Which supplier or suppliers did SAD use last year for the supply of product 'yyy'? What was the aggregate value of the orders placed with each supplier? And what was the total order value for 'yyy' overall?

- List the suppliers in descending order of total order value placed in the last six months.

You must design, and sketch, an order form that FUN would want to use for the SAD orders. It will need to be able to include the address of each individual shop, supplier details, product quantities, a reference number, and the date.

As a preliminary to designing your database, you will have to think about the logical data modelling necessary, about normalisation, and about the selection of keys.

Finally, you must produce documentation telling users how to load data into the database, and how to modify and delete items; and you must indicate how users will need to set about obtaining the answers they want. You are not expected to program the SQL code that would be necessary.

Appendix A: Key skills opportunities

The assignments, which follow each unit in the book, provide opportunities for the collection of evidence of the achievement of the key skills units at level 3 in Communication and Application of number.

These opportunities are set out below, arranged by vocational unit and by key skills unit.

Fig A.1   Vocational units giving opportunities for key skills

Vocational unit	Communication	Application of number
1	3.1 b 3.2	
2	3.2 3.3	
3	3.3	3.1 3.2 3.3
4	3.1a 3.2 3.3	
5	3.3	
6	3.3	

Fig A.2   Key skills – and where you can find them

Communication	Vocational unit
3.1a	4
3.1b	1
3.2	1, 2, 4
3.3	3, 4, 5, 6
Application of number	
3.1	3
3.2	3
3.3	3

Appendix B: Cost-benefit analysis

This appendix contains a discussion on cost-benefit analysis. The topic arose in Chapter 5.1, Investigation and feasibility study.

A **cost-benefit analysis (CBA)** comprises three main parts: an estimate of *costs*, an estimate of *benefits*, and a comparison of the two to yield some *'figure of merit'*. A CBA usually considers the effective life of the system. In the case of a computer system, this would be somewhere between three and five years. Allocating a longer period is likely to make a development project look financially more attractive, but it is unwise because of the uncertainties of trying to see far into the future – in particular, gauging the costs and benefits many years ahead for the application of continuously advancing technology is too risky.

In carrying out a feasibility study, and in drafting its conclusions, you must remember all the time that you are dealing with predictions. You must be prepared to say what level of confidence you have in your figures.

The following discussion will illustrate a CBA using examples from the FUN case study.

Cost estimates

Costs may be conveniently considered under five headings:

- hardware
- packaged software
- bespoke software development
- installation and training
- maintenance and enhancement.

It is usually possible to obtain quite reasonable estimates of costs in four of these five areas.

Hardware For example, we might decide to run the FUN bookings system on a new, stand-alone PC which had its own printer. Hardware costs would then be, say, £1500 for the PC and £500 for the printer.

Packaged software Packaged software costs would be, say, £100 for the operating system, and £200 for the office software for word-processing and spreadsheets. Any other program products needed would add to these costs.

Installation and training Installation might take half a day at £150 per day for an installation engineer, and training might take two days at £150 per day for a trainer. We might budget £2000 for enhancement of the system in the second year of operation – perhaps 10 days work by an analyst-programmer at a cost of £200 per day.

Maintenance and enhancement We might budget £200 per year for maintenance.

The **implementation of bespoke software** presents the planner with a totally different kind of forecasting problem. It is notoriously difficult to estimate the timescale and costs of a systems development project that involves the analysis, design, programming, and testing of bespoke software. Even a fixed-price development contract, entered into with an outside firm, carries numerous risks.

Function point analysis (or FPA), a technique devoted entirely to trying to improve the accuracy of forecasting, and thereby limit the risks, of bespoke software development, is discussed in Appendix C (see page 319). The results of function point analysis applied within a given feasibility study form part of the cost-benefit analysis: specifically the part that is most vulnerable to uncertainty.

If the project involves the provision of bespoke software the FPA would address that aspect of the costs which may be the largest and would certainly be the least certain.

Costs layout

Let us assume that a decision has been taken to assess the financial attractiveness of the proposed system implementation over a period of five years for the FUN case study. We first state the expected costs year by year.

We show the cost amounts as negative numbers, to emphasise the fact that they are business outgoings. The bespoke software cost comes from the FPA carried out for this project.

In this project there is a need for both bespoke and package software. That situation arises fairly often.

Next we review the expected benefits.

Benefits

The second part of the CBA is an estimate of the benefits of the proposed system. We are concerned here with benefits that can be valued and expressed in financial terms. While it is common to discuss and compare tangible benefits and intangible benefits, it is our view that there are very few truly 'intangible' benefits in business. We feel that, with some imagination and thought, every intended benefit of an information system can be valued in quantifiable financial terms.

The benefits that can flow from the introduction of an information system can be divided into four areas:

- cost savings

- productivity improvements

		Year 1 £	Year 2 £	Year 3 £	Year 4 £	Year 5 £
Hardware	PC	−1 500	0	0	0	0
	Printer	−500	0	0	0	0
Packaged software	Operating system	−100	0	0	0	0
	Office software	−200	0	0	0	0
Bespoke software development		−16 300	0	0	0	0
Installation	Engineer	−75	0	0	0	0
	Trainer	−150	0	0	0	0
Maintenance and enhancement		0	−2 200	−200	−200	−200
Totals(£)		−18 825	−2 200	−200	−200	−200

- better information quality

- organisational enhancement.

Of course, a particular information system can have benefits in more than one of these areas.

Cost savings

It is now unusual to find major cost savings put forward as a justification for installing new technology, though there are exceptions, as in the example described below. The subject is politically charged since the costs saved usually consist of the salaries and other costs of part of the workforce. For these and other reasons, intended costs savings from the introduction of new technology are most often presented as claims of productivity gains.

By the term *cost savings* we mean reduction in the unit cost of manufacture or service provision without any increase in overall capacity or throughput.

We achieve 'cost savings' when, without increasing production quantity or quality, we reduce the costs or the resources needed for such production or service. For example, the automated teller machine (ATM), the 'hole in the wall' in most high streets, does little that a human teller inside a bank or building society cannot do. It has not brought about an increase in the volume of money that the retail side of a bank handles. However, it has served to reduce the number of bank and building society tellers in the UK by about 75 per cent, and the true justification for ATMs is one based on very significant cost savings. Interestingly, the reasons put forward for installing them included greater convenience for customers and improved security.

Cost savings in the introduction of new technology almost always involve a reduction in other resources, whether human, space and buildings, machines, or material.

Improved productivity

While it is usual to be able to find some productivity improvements from the introduction of new technology, such improvements are not now likely to be the major justification for bringing in new technology.

Improved productivity means keeping the unit cost of manufacture or service provision almost unchanged while increasing overall capacity or throughput.

For example, the automation of the supermarket checkout has led to a doubling or even a tripling of throughput using the same number of checkout aisles and checkout staff. Improved productivity often involves the metaphor of 'leverage' – we talk about getting more out of a resource by improving its leverage.

Improved productivity by the introduction of new technology usually does not involve any reduction in resources. More often than not, there are modest increases in resource requirements, such as having to provide help desk staff as a result of employing new technology.

Better information quality

Most new technologies are currently introduced because of the benefits involved in having better information.

Better information quality means information that is available sooner than would otherwise have been possible, that is more accurate, and presented more pleasingly. It could also include information that would otherwise have been very difficult or even impossible to obtain in time to have had any use. Here are four examples.

- Early computers, electronic processing machines controlled by stored programs, were developed and used in the United States and elsewhere in the design of the hydrogen bomb, and in the simulation of its use. The need to be able to design, simulate, and develop this weapon provided a stimulus for the provision of faster computing.

- Weather service is a business that justifies its very substantial investment in super-computers on the basis of increased accuracy of forecasting. Airlines and agricultural businesses rely heavily on the accuracy of weather forecasting.

- The use of image processing in the visual media, particularly TV, has given us visually appealing, well-presented information in news and sports reports; and it allows clarity to be increased in many forms of presentation.

- The FUN booking system has, as its primary justification, the fact that management will receive reports on capacity and utilisation that previously were difficult to obtain.

Organisational enhancement

In some sense, of course, all these aspects enhance the organisation. We mean something different here – something captured by this type of benefit that is not captured by any other.

Organisational enhancement means, in this context, the ability of an organisation to pursue new business ventures and enter new markets that would previously have been out of reach.

In the first three areas of benefit discussed above, the organisation is doing what it did before, only more cheaply, or more productively, or with higher information quality. In this area of organisational enhancement, however, the introduction of new technology enables the organisation to do something it could not do before, or to do it in a completely new way not previously possible. Increasingly, we expect investment decisions in new technology to be justified by the prospect of realising benefits of this kind. The technique of searching for such benefits is known as *business process re-engineering* or *BPR*. BPR is concerned with identifying prospective benefits and bringing them into being for businesses.

A very common example of what we are calling organisational enhancement is of a business computerising its customer information, and in doing so developing a comprehensive database that it can turn into a new revenue source. It can sell all or part of its customer database to other, non-competing, businesses: this is something it could never have done with data held on filing cards or in filing cabinets.

For most businesses, this particular benefit is not very substantial or very lucrative, and therefore it would not be used in a cost-benefit analysis. There are, however, some businesses, such as those offering financial services, in which firms have invested in computer systems in order to develop opportunities of this kind, especially where large volumes of data are central to the operations of the businesses. Examples of this total reliance on computer-held data are direct telephone banking and direct telephone insurance, neither of which could have been started without investment in information technology.

Benefit valuation

Having articulated a benefit for an investment in new technology, it is necessary to value that benefit. We now look at examples of the valuation of the four kinds of benefit. In each case we show that benefits that at first sight seem to be intangible can be satisfactorily quantified.

Cost savings valuation

We earlier used ATMs as an example of cost savings. Let us imagine we are working for Bank X, employing 20 000 tellers, and we wish to value the cost savings of needing to employ only 5000 tellers after the installation of 2000 ATMs.

Apart from the savings in salary costs, Bank X would also save in direct employment costs such as National Insurance contributions and pension contributions, as well as in indirect costs such building rental, heating, electricity, and other costs. For clerical staff, employment costs could be estimated as about 50 per cent of salary costs, so if an average teller earns £12 000 per year, Bank X would save £18 000 in total costs per teller. Multiply this by the 15 000 tellers that Bank X would no longer require, and the total annual cost savings can be estimated as £270 000 000.

Notice that the cost of employing staff is always substantially higher than their actual salaries.

Productivity improvement valuation

Earlier, we used the automated supermarket checkout as an example of productivity

benefits. Let us imagine that Super Y, a small independent supermarket that uses old-fashioned cash registers, has annual sales of £10 million. We can assume the cost of acquiring stock for a year is £8 million and that £1 million a year is the cost of running the business. The total costs are thus £9 million, giving a profit of £1 million equal to 10 per cent of the sales income.

Now suppose that the introduction of automation at the checkout allowed sales to double without any other costs (other than stock) rising. We then have annual sales of £20 million for an annual cost of stock of £16 million with other running costs, as before, of £1 million. This new situation leads to a profit of £3 million or 15 per cent on sales. Thus, assuming that there is sufficient demand to take up the extra sales, the store has managed to add 50 per cent to its profitability (as expressed as a percentage of turnover) and raised the *actual* profit from £1 million to £3 million.

There may be no point in increasing sales if increased profit does not result.

Better information quality valuation

What is the value of a better weather forecast? Much of a government's income derives from its tax on business profits. If a better weather forecast enables businesses to make better profits, the government – the provider of weather services – benefits.

Suppose that a proposed supercomputer will allow the prediction accuracy of highly damaging storms to improve by 10 per cent, such that trade lost as a result of such storms is reduced by a matching 10 per cent. Under existing forecasting, let us say that the total business lost as a result of storms is, say, £1 billion a year: and if the organisations suffering those losses achieve on average profits before tax of 4 per cent, then about £40 million in net profit is lost. Assuming that the government applies a tax rate of 40 per cent to profits made by businesses, it loses £16 million per year.

Now, if the supercomputer reduces those losses by 10 per cent, the losses due to storms would fall to £36 million. The tax revenue lost to the Government, previously £16 million, would diminish by 10 per cent, that is by £1.6 million, to £14.4 million. An effect of transferring the weather forecasting work to the supercomputer would therefore be to increase the financial benefit to the Government of £1.6 million per year.

What is the value of a news report on TV that is presented in a better way? A commercial TV station charges for advertisements on the basis of the number of viewers who are likely to see each advertisement. The station TVZ charges £50 000 per 30-second advertisement at news time, based on an audited audience of 2 000 000 in your reception area. The competition is TV1 which also manages to attract an audience of 2 000 000. With better presentation of news reports, you estimate that you will be able to attract 15 per cent of TV1's audience, boosting your own rating to some 2 300 000. You then estimate that you will be able to increase your advertising charges by 2 per cent to £51 000 for each 30-second slot. There are 30 slots a day at news time, so for the 365 days of the year you estimate increased advertising revenue of £1000 x 30 x 365 – that is almost £11 million!

The FUN booking system is intended to give information to management that previously it could not obtain. Suppose that, as a result of knowing the current and future event bookings capacity, the sales staff are able to offer discounts and deals to prospective customers such that they can increase event bookings and hence turnover by 5 per cent. If turnover is currently £2 million, and the gross margin is 20 per cent, an increase of 5 per cent on that £400 000 (the annual gross profit) represents a gain of £20 000. You might, however, want to be cautious about this benefit and consider that the full benefit value of £20 000 will only be reached after 5 years. These are figures that you could use in your planning.

Organisational enhancement valuation

Let us take the common example of an organisation being able to enter a market that was previously closed to it: namely, selling its customer database. Suppose that Festivities Unlimited were to consider selling its customer database to a business that specialised in mail order gifts such as flowers, chocolates, and wine. What is the value of the list of their customer names and addresses to such a business?

We must begin by noting that the 'value' of something is defined to be the sum of money that a willing buyer would offer and a willing seller would find acceptable. FUN, the willing seller, doesn't really know what would be acceptable, so we need to establish what a willing buyer would pay for such a database.

A mail order business would use a list of names and addresses to send a mail shot which would include their catalogue. From the mail shot, they would hope to make some sales. Let us suppose that the average mail shot results in a 1 per cent response (probably a bit high for a 'cold' mail shot), and that the average resulting sale is for £25. FUN is able to offer 2000 names and addresses, so a 1 per cent response would be 20 sales. If the gross margin of a sale were 40%, then the 20 sales would yield £200 in profit. The mail order business would probably want to offer FUN no more than about £50 for their customer database, which is what they might be willing to pay for the chance of making £200 profit.

From FUN's point of view, they might be able to sell their customer database to five mail order companies each year, generating £250 a year. If they were able to convince prospective buyers that the names in the database represented mail shot targets with a better than average likelihood of placing orders they might be able to charge more than £50 a year.

Benefits layout

We now show the benefit valuations, year by year, for the two sources of financial benefit to FUN, arranged in a way similar to the costs layout.

Similar profiles of the value of expected benefit can be calculated for all quantifiable benefits.

Figures of merit

The third and final step of the CBA is to calculate some **figures of merit**. These are the financial figures formed by combining expected costs with expected benefits. Together they help an organisation decide whether the benefits sufficiently outweigh the costs for the project to go ahead.

We now review three ways of looking at the financial assessment of potential project. They are:

- **payback** which forecasts the length of time that will elapse before the project moves into cumulative profit

- **net present value (NPV)** which gives the value today, in current money, of the project's expected costs and future benefits

	Year 1 £	Year 2 £	Year 3 £	Year 4 £	Year 5 £
Better information (resulting in increased turnover and profit)	4 000	8 000	12 000	16 000	20 000
Sales of customer database	250	250	250	250	250
Totals	*4 250*	*8 250*	*12 250*	*16 250*	*20 250*

- **internal rate of return (IRR)** which shows the rate of return given on the sum invested in the project by its future benefits.

The choice of which measure or combination of measures an organisation decides to use in a given instance depends upon how badly the money is needed for other purposes, experience with the forecasting for earlier projects, current levels of interest available commercially, and perhaps other factors.

The estimated costs of the proposed development are placed against the expected benefits to yield the **cash flow** of the project. It is the cash flow that is then evaluated using one or more figures of merit. The following figure, Figure B.1, illustrates the FUN bookings system cash flow.

For simplicity the cost of borrowing the money needed to finance the project whilst it is in deficit is omitted.

Payback period

The **payback period** is a figure of merit that measures how quickly the costs of an investment are recovered. If the cumulative cash flow is plotted on a graph, the point at which the cumulative cash position crosses from a negative value to a positive value defines the end of the payback period. For the FUN booking system, this is after about 2.7 years. This is probably regarded as being acceptable for capital investment in FUN's circumstances, though it is not impressive. Many businesses consider their investments in new development projects should pay back within one year to be attractive.

There are two points to be made about the payback graph in Figure B.2, opposite:

- no cost has been included for the interest charged on any money that had to be borrowed in order to invest in the project. Had it been included, the effect would have been to have delayed the moment when the project moved into cumulative profit

- the points on the graph show the cumulative position at the end of each full year from the start of the project. The straight lines joining those points are drawn to illustrate the progression towards payback and then towards increasing profitability. The lines are there to make the predicted cumulative cash flow clear and easy to understand. They do not have any accounting significance, and would probably be deplored by an accountant.

	A	B	C	D	E	F	G
5	COSTS						
6	Hardware	PC	-£1,500	£0	£0	£0	£0
7		Printer	-£500	£0	£0	£0	£0
8	Package Software	Operating	-£100	£0	£0	£0	£0
9		Office	-£200	£0	£0	£0	£0
10	Bespoke dev't		-£16,300	£0	£0	£0	£0
11	Installation	Engineer	-£75	£0	£0	£0	£0
12		Trainer	-£150	£0	£0	£0	£0
13	Maint. & enhan.		£0	-£2,200	-£200	-£200	-£200
14	Total costs		-£18,825	-£2,200	-£200	-£200	-£200
15							
16	BENEFITS						
17	Better information		£4,000	£8,000	£12,000	£16,000	£20,000
18	Sales of customer database		£250	£250	£250	£250	£250
19	Total benefits		£4,250	£8,250	£12,250	£16,250	£20,250
20							
21	CASH FLOW		-£14,575	£6,050	£12,050	£16,050	£20,050
22	Cumulative		-£14,575	-£8,525	£3,525	£19,575	£39,625
23							
24	Payback		2.71 years				
25	NPV		£14,827	20% discount value			
26	IRR		64%				
27							

Figure B.1 Cost-benefit cash flow layout

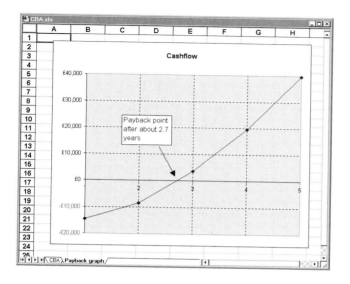

Figure B.2   Payback point

Net present value

The **net present value (NPV)** is a figure of merit that measures the net value of an investment in today's money, after discounting the projected future cash flows by some figure that represents inflation and risk.

Given the total cash flow over the five-year period, it would seem that the FUN booking system yields £39 625. However, the £20 050 projected in Year 5 alone, for example, even if correct will have been eroded by inflation for five years. And, of course, the further away this income amount is, the less predictable it is that this money will be made. It would therefore seem prudent to discount all future cash flows in an attempt to gain a more plausible and less risky view of the whole project.

The accepted practice is to reduce the figures by a **discounting factor** which represents the extent by which an amount of money some way ahead is worth less to us now than it would be if it were immediately available. There is a (rather complicated) formula which calculates the decreased value of money for different assumptions of discounting factor and different periods in the future. Using this formula, which is known as **discounted cash flow (DCF)** analysis, to the predicted cash flows of a project provides a final net value for the end of the period in question. The formula is provided in the Excel spreadsheet as the NPV() function.

If we decided to discount future cash flow by a cumulative 20 per cent each year, representing our view of the level of risk of our projections, the NPV is then £14 827, as calculated using the NPV() function in Excel. This is in contrast to the £39 625 when future cash flow is taken at face value - that is at a discount of 0 per cent. While the NPV in this case is a positive value which is good (a negative value would imply the project would lose money, not make it), by comparison against the necessary investment in Year 1 alone of £18 825 it doesn't represent outstanding value.

Internal rate of return

The **internal rate of return (IRR)** is a figure of merit that measures the effective interest rate earned by an investment. The internal rate of return of the FUN bookings system projected cash flow is about 64 per cent, as calculated using the IRR() function in Excel. This is a very high figure which, if you were in charge, you might wish to challenge. For example you might decide to look and see what the figure would be for a notional project of four years rather than five. If it were markedly less you might conclude that the five-year life was dangerously long, bearing in mind that uncertainties accumulate as the commercial behaviour of the project becomes more remote.

If FUN had the necessary money available (about £20 000) and was looking for an investment, the booking system evaluated over five years would seem to offer a rate of return much better than any which could be secured by investing the sum in a savings account, for example. However, this would be at a much higher risk.

Appendix C: Function point analysis

One method of estimating the budget and schedule of a bespoke programming development project is known as *function point analysis* or *FPA*. The output from FPA is fed into the overall calculations of the cost-benefit analysis (CBA) for a feasibility study.

There are two versions of FPA. The first version is commonly used in America, while it is FPA Mk2 that is used in the UK. FPA Mk2 has been adopted as a British Government standard. We will examine in this appendix, Appendix C, a simplified version of FPA Mk2 that can be applied to a context diagram.

The simplified FPA Mk2 procedure that we shall develop involves three steps.

- Firstly, we count the number of 'function points' in a context diagram by listing and then scoring the transactions represented in that diagram.

- Secondly, we adjust the function points according to the technical complexity of the project.

- Finally, we estimate the number of work-hours needed to complete the work, based upon the adjusted function points count.

Step 1: Score transactions

To start our simplified and approximate FPA from the context diagram, we examine the data flows shown and identify the events or *transactions* that take place in the system. We score each transaction according to whether it involves the creation or update of data records, the deletion of data records or the reading of data records for a report or an *ad hoc* enquiry. We consider that, on average, a transaction involving the creation or update of a data record scores 14 function points; the deletion of a data record scores 8 function points; and a report or enquiry scores 11 function points. A *function point* is simply a relative measure of the amount of effort that creating that transaction probably involves. The values given for these function points were arrived at after considerable research by the originators of FPA Mk2.

Transaction type	Function points
Creation	14
Report or enquiry	11
Update or amend	14
Deletion	8

From the context diagram for the FUN booking system, we can see that there is a transaction involving the creation of an event record, another involving the updating of an event record, and so on. These transactions are listed below, and their function point scores allocated and totalled.

Transaction	Function points
Create event record	14
Update event record	14
Delete event record	8
Update calendar	14
Update resource levels	14
Report on capacity	11
Total	75

The simple FUN booking system seems to

involve about 75 *unadjusted* function points. They are unadjusted because in Step 2 we consider some technical complexities that lead systems to be somewhat larger or smaller than we might at first think.

Step 2: Adjust the function points for technical complexity

FPA Mk2 considers 19 factors of technical complexity that may make a bespoke

	Factor	Description	Typical rating for small business application (eg FUN)
1	Data communications	For terminals connected remotely or locally	0
2	Distributed data processing	Distributed data or processing incorporated in applications	0
3	Performance	Throughput, response times	1
4	Heavily used configuration	Development takes place on a system that is in 'live' use	0
5	Transaction rates	Ability to cope with high rate of usage	0
6	On-line data entry	Interactive data entry	5
7	End-user efficiency	Users require on-line functions to help in the use of the system, eg on-line help, automated cursor movement, function keys, mouse, windows, multilingual	2
8	On-line update	Data is updated in real time, i.e. the system reflects the real world	1
9	Complex processing	Special mathematical, logical, device, or error processing	0
10	Reusable code	The code is designed to be shared with or used by other applications. (Do not confuse with factor 13)	0
11	Installation ease	Special conversion and installation considerations required	0
12	Operations ease	Special operation considerations required (eg backup and recovery processes)	0
13	Multiple sites	Requirement to consider the needs of more than one user site	0
14	Facilitate change	Application must be specifically developed to facilitate future change to user requirements	2
15	Requirements of other applications	System interfaces to and must synchronise with other applications	0
16	Security, privacy, auditability	Special legal or security requirements	0
17	User training needs	Special user training material or courses	1
18	Direct use by third parties	Third party connection to the system	0
19	Documentation	Eg user requirements, technical design, user manual, test data	1

Total 13

development project larger or smaller than 'normal'. Each factor is rated according to an influence score between 0 and 5, where a rating of '0' indicates that the factor has no influence on the project, and a score of '5' indicates the factor has a dominating influence.

We may consider the FUN booking system to be a typical small business application, for which the total complexity rating would be 13. The complexity rating is used in the following formula to calculate the estimated system size in adjusted function points. The values used in the formula – 0.65 and 0.005 – were arrived at after research by the originators of FPA Mk 2.

$$\text{Size} = \text{Unadjusted function points} \times [0.65 + (0.005 \times \text{complexity rating})]$$

For the FUN booking system,

$$
\begin{aligned}
\text{Size} &= 75 \times [0.65 + (0.005 \times 13)] \\
&= 75 \times [0.65 + 0.065] \\
&= 75 \times 0.715 \\
&= 53.6 \text{ adjusted function points.}
\end{aligned}
$$

This figure is to be used in the calculation for arriving at the estimate of duration and team size needed for implementing the system.

Step 3: Estimate work-hours and schedule

The productivity of a development team, that is the number of function points it can develop in an hour or a day, depends upon three major factors related directly to the characteristics of the project and the programming method chosen for it.

- The first productivity factor is whether the system is a batch system, or an on-line system. Batch systems are much easier to develop. We can consider that, on average, a batch system can be developed 50 per cent faster than an on-line system. In a small office environment, is it likely that all the systems would be on-line systems.

- The second productivity factor is whether the system is developed using third generation programming languages (3GL), or fourth generation environments (4GL). 3GLs include Pascal and Basic; 4GLs include Delphi and Visual Basic. We can consider that, on average, using a fourth generation type of environment, productivity would increase 60 per cent. In a small office environment it is likely that most systems would be developed in a fourth generation environment.

- Finally, productivity is related to the size of the system being developed. Small systems can be developed more efficiently than larger systems. This is largely because the needs of consistency and control are less complicated in a small project. As a very rough rule of thumb, we can consider that small on-line, third generation systems can be developed at the rate of about 0.10 function points per work-hour, while large systems can be developed at the rate of about 0.05 function points per work-hour.

The following table summarises these rough rules of thumb, derived from the research of the originators of FPA Mk 2.

Productivity in function points per work-hour

		3GL	4GL
On-line	Small	0.100	0.16
	Large	0.050	0.08
Batch	Small	0.150	0.24
	Large	0.075	0.12

Other factors affecting the productivity of the development team are the quality of the management of the team, the stability of the composition of the team, and the ability and experience of team members.

There is another variable to be taken into account, namely the size of the team. There will usually be a trade-off to be resolved because small teams, providing that they contain all the skills needed, are generally more productive than large teams.

We shall not present all the calculations, but they lead to a requirement for the development of the FUN bookings system of a single person to be devoted to it for about 16 weeks, or, for example, for a team of four to do the work in four weeks. For the FUN booking system, we may take it that it is a small, online system that will be developed using a 4GL. The table on page 321 suggests that 0.16 function points would be built per work-hour. There are an estimated 53.6 function points to be built, and so our analysis calculates this will need approximately $53.6/0.16 = 335$ work-hours. If we consider that, realistically, software development staff can manage 20.5 hours per week on task, this suggests that 16.3 work-weeks are needed for the project.

Bespoke software development costs

The simplified FPA Mk2 thus gives us an estimate of the amount of time or effort we would need to develop the project. The actual period of elapsed time depends upon the chosen team size. For example, we might employ one person for 16.3 weeks, or two persons for 8.15 weeks, or perhaps three people for 5.4 weeks. On that basis, knowing the amount of time needed, we can estimate the bespoke software development costs to be entered into the CBA.

FPA calculated that the FUN bookings system would need one person for 16.3 weeks. Suppose we budgeted to employ a reasonably experienced analyst-programmer for the project, and we decided to use an outside contractor who charges £200 per day. Without allowing for any risk factors which are considered in the chapter covering management assessment, Chapter 5.3, our costs for bespoke development would be £200 × 5 × 16.3, or £16 300. That is the figure used in the CBA table of costs, Figure B.1, in Appendix B (page 316).

FPA for database systems development

The discussion of FPA, above, derived the unadjusted function points from the context diagram. This is the method of choice for ICT systems which are mainly concerned with the processing of information and with the processes of storing and reporting the information.

Where a database system is to be developed, it is likely that there will not be a context diagram, and instead there will be an *entity relationship diagram* (ERD). If there is an ERD, a revised 'Step 1' is needed for the FPA. This revised 'Step 1' is shown here.

'Revised' step 1: Score ERD

We examine the ERD and the associated data dictionary and count three things:

- the number of data entities shown on the ERD (Ne)

- the number of relationship lines shown on the ERD (Nr)

- the total number of distinct data attributes listed in the data dictionary for all the data entities (Na)

We then calculate three measures of the size of the ERD:

- $Tif = 2Na(1 + Nr/Ne) + 2Ne$

- $Tea = 4Ne + 8Nr$

- $Tof = Na(1 + Nr/Ne) + 3Ne$

Finally, the number of unadjusted function points is given by the formula

$$UFP = 0.58Tif + 1.66\ Tea + 0.26Tof$$

The values given in these formulas were arrived at, as before, after research by the originators of FPA Mk2.

Let us take as an example an ERD that has 4 entities and 3 relationship lines, and an associated data dictionary that has 30 total attributes. Then $Ne = 4$, $Nr = 3$, and $Na = 30$. This gives $Tif = 113$, $Tea = 40$, and $Tof = 64.5$. Finally, $UFP = 65.54 + 66.4 + 16.77 = 148.71$. Such an ERD suggests the system involves about 149 unadjusted function points.

Appendix D: Assessment of risk

This appendix discusses the assessment of the risks facing ICT development projects in general. It then provides a simple example of the assessment method. In the sample assignment you will be able to apply the same principles to the development of the FUN booking system.

In Chapter 1.2 we looked at some of the risks threatening the operations of established ICT installations. These risks fell into the categories of deliberate, malicious acts causing loss or damage, and accidents.

Although these risks do exist for systems under development as well as for established systems that are in use, they are usually small compared with the risks that threaten development projects. Further, they are risks to which the whole ICT department of an organisation is exposed, and so deciding on the steps to be taken to combat them would fall outside the evaluation of the business case for any one project.

We are concerned here with those types of risk that relate to project development. These are the risks that need to be weighed up in deciding whether or not a proposed project should go forward.

Sources of risk

You should note that any unplanned change that affects the development activity is almost sure to lead to delay or increased expenditure, either of which would make the project commercially less attractive. Costs would rise and payback would be deferred.

Here is a list of typical risks that could affect the outcome of the system development:

- expenditure budget too low

- development timetable too optimistic

- insufficiently skilled team management

- insufficient team experience of similar development tasks

- insufficiently trained team members

- over-reliance placed on the skills of one person

- unsuitable development methodologies chosen

- inappropriate hardware and software for development

- inadequate quantities of hardware for development

- incomplete understanding of the system specification

- distracting or unsuitable working conditions

- problems with any contractors employed on the project.

This list, long though it is, may well not be complete for a specific development project – but it does indicate what great scope there is for things to go wrong!

Consequences of risk

Some or all of these risks may apply to the development of a particular new system, but usually the consequences cannot be directly linked to the individual risks themselves. We can, though, usefully list the consequences in a general way. The list shows the problems that most commonly affect the conduct, and therefore the financial characteristics, of an ICT development project. They are:

- completion takes longer than planned
- completion costs more than planned
- the resulting system fails to fulfil its specification fully
- conversion from the predecessor system is awkward
- the system runs too slowly
- the system can be made to fail: it is not robust
- the system's interfaces with other systems are inadequate
- training for the users is slower or more expensive than expected
- users find the system tiresome to use
- the system is difficult to update and maintain.

The combined effects of whatever problems arise may be so severe that the whole development process has to be abandoned.

Making proper allowance for the risks

In order to gauge the allowance that should be made in the project justification for the effects of the risks the study team must:

- estimate what likelihood there is of each risk that they have identified affecting the development project

- attribute a cost to the harm that each risk could bring about
- for each separate risk, multiply these amounts together, giving the best forecast of the unplanned cost penalty
- add the resulting figures, providing a total *exposure* of the project to the risks
- consider what *avoidance strategy* could be adopted to reduce the exposure, and estimate the cost of adopting the strategy
- compare the costs of adopting the avoidance strategy with the costs that the risks would be expected to run up without the strategy
- determine how far it would be cost-effective to adopt some or all of the avoidance strategy, so as to minimise the net exposure
- express that net exposure figure as a percentage of the planned development cost, and add it to the planned cost to arrive at a modified cost that should be fed into the cost-benefit analysis before making a final recommendation.

An example of risk assessment

Let us see how this process of making allowance for the effect of risks would work in practice by considering an example based on just one single risk.

- Suppose we assume that the development team might have less experience of working on similar projects than had been expected when the budget was drawn up. We estimate that an inexperienced team might need a further three work-weeks to complete the project, leading to the risk of an increase in the implementation cost of £3000 if we assume each work-week costs £1000. Let us say that the chance that the development team need more time is 30 per cent.

- Next, multiplying these figures together, we arrive at a forecast of £900 net exposure (£3000 × 30%) for this one risk.

- An avoidance strategy we might consider is hiring a consultant with specialised experience of our type of project, at a cost of £500.

- We might now estimate that the risk of the project needing extra time would drop to, say, needing no more than an extra one work-week with a lower probability of 10%. The forecast risk exposure, as a result of our avoidance strategy, would now be estimated at £100 (£1000 × 10%).

- We have reduced our risk exposure by £800 (£900 − £100) by our avoidance strategy.

- The question of whether it is worth following the avoidance strategy is answered by comparing the cost of the strategy, £500, with the reduction in risk exposure, £800. We compute what is called the 'leverage' of the avoidance strategy, by dividing the risk reduction by the cost: £800/£500 = 1.6. The leverage of hiring the consultant is 1.6.

- In general, any risk avoidance strategy with a leverage above 1.0 means that the benefit of the strategy outweighs its cost, but only leverages above 10.0 are worth serious consideration. A leverage below 1.0 indicates that the avoidance strategy costs more than the risk it is supposed to avoid, and so clearly makes no business sense.

- Suppose now that the estimated development cost of the whole project were to have been £18 000. The net exposure of £900 is 5 per cent of this sum, and the revised development cost of £18 900 should be fed into the CBA, and financial characteristics worked out afresh.

- There is advantage in expressing the net exposure figures in percentages as well as in absolute amounts, especially if the figures are less easy to calculate than those in our example.

This assessment process would have to be carried out for all the relevant risks, and the combined effects calculated, care being taken not to double count the effects on the behaviour on the project of any related pairs of risks. The resulting effect on the financial profile of the project might mean that the systems analysis team would want to modify their earlier tentative recommendations.

1NF	First normal form
2NF	Second normal form
3D	Three-dimensional
3NF	Third normal form
FS1 (etc)	Absolute cell referencing (etc)
AGP	Accelerated graphics port
API	Applications program interface
ASCII	American Standard Code for Information Interchange
AVCE	Advanced Vocational Certificate of Education
b, bit	Binary digit
B2B	Business-to-Business
BIOS	Basic input-output system
bps	Bits per second
CAD	Computer-aided design
CAV	Constant angular velocity
CBA	Cost-benefit analysis
CBI	Confederation of British Industry
CD-R	Compact disk recordable
CD-ROM	Compact disk-ROM
CD-RW	Compact disk rewritable
CEO	Chief Executive Officer
CIO	Chief Information Officer
CLI	Command line interface
CLV	Constant linear velocity
CMOS	Complementary metal oxide semiconductor
CMYK	Cyan, magenta, yellow and black
CPU	Central processing unit
CRC	cyclic redundancy check
CRT	Cathode ray tube
CRUD	Create, read, update, delete
CV	Curriculum vitae
DAC	Digital-to-analogue converter
DBMS	Data base management system
DD	Data dictionary
Del (key)	Delete (key)
DFD	Data flow diagram
DIN	Deutsche industrie norm
DIP	Dual in-line package
DOS	Disk Operating System
dpi	dots per inch
DRAM	Dynamic RAM
DSS	Decision support system
DVD	Digital versatile disk
ECP	Enhanced capabilities port
EDO	Extended data out (DRAM)
EFT	Electronic funds transfer
EIS	Executive information system
EISA	Expanded ISA
EPP	Enhanced parallel port
EPROM	Erasable PROM
ERD	Entity relationship diagram
FPA	Function-point analysis
FPM	Fast page mode
FUN	Festivities Unlimited
GB	Gigabyte
GIF	Graphics interchange format
GUI	Graphical user interface
HSE	Health and Safety Executive
ICT	Information and Communication Technology
ID	Identifier or identification
INT	Integer
IPX/SPX	Internet packet exchange/server packet exchange
ISA	Industry standard architecture
ISP	Internet Service Provider
JPEG (or JPG)	Joint Photographic Experts Group
kB	Kilobyte
LAN	Local-area network
LCD	Liquid crystal display
LDM	Logical data model
MB	Megabyte
MCA	Micro-channel architecture
MHz	Megahertz
MIDI	Musical instrument digital interface

MIS	Management information system	SDLC	Systems development life cycle
MPEG	Motion Picture Experts Group	SEC	Single-edge contact
MSD	Microsoft diagnostics	SEP	Single-edge processor
NATO	North Atlantic Treaty Organisation	SIMM	Single in-line memory module
NHS	National Health Service	SOHO	Small office and home office
NIC	Network interface card	SPGA	Staggered pin grid array
PC	Personal computer	SQL	Structured query language
PCI	Peripheral component interconnect	SQRT	Square root function
PGA	Pin grid array	SRAM	Static RAM
PnP	Plug and play	SSADM	Systems analysis and design methodology
POST	Power-on self-test	TB	Terabyte
ppm	pages per minute	TCP/IP	Transmission control protocol/Internet protocol
PROM	Programmable ROM	UNF	Un-normalised form
R1C1 (etc)	Row 1, Column 1 (etc)	UPS	Uninterruptable power supply
RAM	Random access memory	URL	Uniform (or Universal) resource locator
RAND	Random number function	USB	Universal serial bus
RDA	Relational data analysis	VAT	Value-added tax
RDBMS	Relational DBMS	VDU	Visual display unit
ROM	Read-only memory	VL-bus	Local video bus
SCSI	Small computer system interface	WAN	Wide-area network
		WAP	Wireless Application Protocol

Index